BOAT RACE

The Oxford Revival

BOAT RACE
The Oxford Revival

DANIEL TOPOLSKI

WILLOW BOOKS
Collins
8 Grafton Street, London
1985

Photographic acknowledgements

For permission to use photographs reproduced in this book, the author would like to thank: Gerry Cranham; *The Guardian*; Tom Hustler; Keystone; *The Observer*; Tim Page; John H. Shore; Sport and General; The *Star*; Syndication International. At the time of going to press, it proved difficult to determine the copyright holders of a number of the photographs – interested parties should contact the publishers.

Willow Books
William Collins Sons & Co. Ltd
London · Glasgow · Sydney
Auckland · Toronto · Johannesburg
First published in Great Britain 1985
© Daniel Topolski 1985

Topolski, Daniel
Boat Race – Oxford's Revival
I. Oxford & Cambridge Boat Race – History
I. Title
797.1′4′09421 GV799

ISBN 0 00 218117 7

Filmset in Ehrhardt by Wyvern Typesetting Ltd, Bristol
Printed in Great Britain by William Collins Sons & Co.
Ltd., Glasgow

Contents

THIS BOOK IS DEDICATED TO:

BLUES

1973
Dick Westlake o
James Ollivant o
Mike Magarey oo
Phil Angier o
Steve Irving xxo
Andy Hall oooo
Paddy Payne oo√
Dave Sawyier o√
Ed Yalouris oo

1974
Nick Tee oo√o
Graham Innes √o√
Dave Rendall x√
Sam Nevin ox√
Gavin Stoddart √
Paul Marsden xx√
Gareth Morris x√

1975
Mark Harris xxo
Dave Beak o√

Bob Mason o√√
Cris Money-Coutts o√
John Hutchings xo
Andy Baird xo√
John Calvert xo√

1976
Dave Edwards x√
Steve Plunkett xx√
Ken Brown √
John Wiggins √√√

1977
Paul Wright xx√
Gyles Vardey x√
Mike Moran √√
Al Shealy √√
Ag Michelmore √√
Colin Moynihan x√

1978
Russell Crockford x√√√
Julian Crawford x√√

Tristram Sutton xx√
Jim Wood √
Boris Rankov xx√√√√√√
John Fail x√

1979
Phil Head x√√
Rob Moore xx√
Chris Mahoney √√√
Mike Diserens √√
Pete Berners Lee x√

1980
Steve Francis √x
Nick Conington √√√
John Bland x√√√
Mark Andrews √√
Tom Barry xx√
Jerry Mead x√

1981
Richard Yonge x√√√
Richard Emerton x√

Sue Brown √√

1982
Alan Kirkpatrick √
Nick Holland x√
Steve Foster x√
Hugh Clay x√√
Rob Clay x√√

1983
Bill Lang √√
Mike Evans √√
Mark Evans √√
Graham Jones √√
Steve Higgins x√

1984
Jim Stewart xx√
Chris Long xx√
Dave Rose x√
Seth Lesser √

ISIS

John Colton 2
Rod Collin
Derek Richardson
Mike Dudley
Ian James

Olly Moore 2

Dave Newman 2
Hugh Craig
Jamie Pike

Nigel Burgess 2
Mark Alloway
Julian Winter
Dug Imeson
Sam Majd

Bill Baker
Ges Atherton 2
David Fitzherbert
Andrew Hudson

Mark Gleave 2
Jamie Robertson 2
Simon Shepherd

David Sears
Nick Jordan
Dan Lips
Rob Schmidt
Mark Baring
Tim Carpenter

Mathew Rutherford

Dave Todd
Fergus Murison
Steve Walter
Nick Harding
Simon Orme

Steve Potts
Ian Callender
John Graham 2
Justin Jenk
Mike Chapman

Tony Mitchell
Mike Stewart
Simon Oldfield
Mark Bloomfield
Pete Buchanan 2

John Healey

Ed Martin 2
Phil Hare 2
John Yeatman
Kathy Talbot
Linton Richmond 2

Jack Richards
Lisa Armstrong
Gavin Cartledge
Matt Thomas
Mark Dunstan
Chris Bourne

KEY
√ Won Boat Race   o Lost Boat Race   x Rowed Isis

and to:

George Harris; Chris Blackwall; Steve Royle; Hugh Matheson; Michael Barry; 'Jumbo' Edwards; Mike Edwards; Ted Phelps; Mike Spracklen; Keith Mason; Gully Nickalls; Seb Earl; Dick Fishlock; John Pilgrim-Morris; Mark Jabalé; Peter Politzer; Derek Thurgood; Jock Mullard; Ronnie Howard; Peter Tuke; Chris Drury; Duncan Clegg; Charly Wiggin; David Tanner; George Cox; Richard Hooper; Jeff Jacobs; Richard Stanhope; Andrew Justice; Jeff Easton; Mike Rosewall; Chris George; Paul Stuart Bennett; Mike Baines; John Dart; Peter Prichard; Bert Green; Albert Andrews; Mike Thorne; Piers Gough; Orlando Gough; Celia Keyworth; Ian Elliott; Desmond Hill; Richard Burnell; Harry Freeman; Jim Railton; John Garnett and Marion Everall.

SINCE 1973

67 Blues in 12 races
6 Blues with 3 or more Boat Race wins
35 Blues rowed one or more times in Isis
11 Blues rowed twice in Isis
90 Isis caps
11 Isis men rowed twice in Isis

Introduction

The Oxford and Cambridge Boat Race, labelled by detractors an anachronism, has nevertheless caught the national imagination like few other annual events over the past 150 years. Although it is just a private match between students it has become as much a British institution as it is a sporting event. Over ten million viewers in Britain and over 100 million around the world watch it on television every year, and on a good sunny day many thousands line the river banks. And though the fortunes of the two warring sides wax and wane periodically, each often enjoying extended runs of success (a factor usually conveniently forgotten by pundits and the unfortunate losing side when cries of 'unfair' and 'change the rules' are voiced), the character of the event itself has changed little over the years.

The Boat Race is a typically 'Bulldog' madcap venture. It is run at one of the most inhospitable times of the year – at the end of March when Britain is cold, wet and windy (when is it not so?) – during the off-season period at the end of winter training; it is held on an unsuitably devious course – the Tideway stretch of the Thames between Putney and Mortlake – with rough, heaving water and a fast-running stream, winding and arguably unfair at times, over the curious distance of $4\frac{1}{4}$ miles (the internationally recognised distance is 2000 metres), and it is often as much an endurance test of the 'mad dogs and Englishmen' variety as it is a race. These eccentric features and the fact that it is done for no financial reward have over the years fired the enthusiasm of the British public to the extent that on the day the nation divides itself arbitrarily, yet often with deep-rooted loyalties, between Dark and Light Blue. 'I've always been an Oxford supporter' says the London East Ender, the Brighton landlady and the stockbroker, 'ever since I was a kid. Dunno why. Suppose it's because they always lost.' That in truth is why I started supporting Oxford way back in the early 'fifties – sympathy for the underdog.

However, the preceding list of the odd features of the race, which so often lead Boat Race critics to discount its significance, can be unfairly misleading. Most of the nation's successful oarsmen train on the Tideway between Putney and Chiswick. The British team members train regularly right through the winter on its uncharitable waters (while the Oxbridge crews opt for calmer, more suitable non-tidal stretches) and follow pretty well the same training programmes as the Oxbridge crews. Their springtime goal is an identical long distance race, the Head of the River Race, over the same course as the Boat Race in reverse, facing the same bends and often sinking conditions at the same time of year. The only difference is that the 'Varsity crews are aiming for a definite March peak and tailor the final few weeks accordingly, sharpening their racing ability for their major test of the year. The other British crews, with the summer World Championships as their target, do not yet reach for such a finely-honed pitch; but the differences in their conditioning are minimal. Indeed a winter's training for the Boat Race is the ideal preparation for an aspiring international oarsman, and this is reflected in the fact that usually about a third of the British team at the World Championships or the Olympics is Oxbridge spawned.

That there are not more of them in the national team each year can be put down to the fact that a student usually wins his Blue in his final academic year and, with just six weeks left to exams, he has to return directly to his studies instead of joining the national squad. But in the last ten years Oxbridge oarsmen have come through exceedingly well to race for, and some to win, gold, silver and bronze medals at Olympic and world level for Britain: Baillieu, Matheson, Hart, Mahoney, Bland, Clay, Maxwell, Sturge, Delafield, Andrews, Christie, Macleod, Moynihan, Tee, Hall, Garrett, Lang, Harris, Pritchard. World level performers from abroad who have rowed in the Boat Race have been Cadwalader, Shealy, Cashin, Sawyier, Tourek, Waters, Brown, Michelmore, Evans, Jones. At world junior level the list is longer. It is vital that the two Universities should continue to produce the highest quality crews, as they have always done over the years, not only for their own self-respect and that of their *alma maters*, but also because the declared intention of both Universities has always been the pursuit of excellence. Furthermore the continued good health of the sport in Britain as a whole needs their high-level contribution. There will be exceptional, good and sometimes not so good Oxford and Cambridge crews, but they will always be placed among the top two or three crews in the country.

Until ten years ago it was fashionable to hear how the Boat Race had lost its appeal. 'Cambridge always win . . . it's so boring' was the complaint; and indeed with a run of 13 Light Blue wins between the wars, a sequence of six victories by large margins in the late 'sixties and early 'seventies and a paltry 12 Oxford victories since the First World War compared to Cambridge's 36, it was hard not to see their point. Well in 1974 Cambridge suddenly stopped winning and a series of spectacular races full of incident followed which brought back the crowds. Dramatic events have coloured the past decade: Cambridge sank in 1978; an Oxford man collapsed in 1980 with only two thirds of the race completed resulting in a miniscule six-foot verdict; there were three record-breaking races; sponsorship deals; drug charges; death threats; accusations of cheating; world champions in both camps; collisions; the unique and controversial achievement of Boris Rankov; the heaviest-ever crew; the heaviest-ever Boat Race oarsman, the gentle giant from Belfast, Steve Plunkett; the first-ever Boat Race twins, Hugh and Rob Clay, followed the next year by the Evans twins from Canada; Sue Brown, the first woman to cox in the Boat Race, and twice a winner; Cambridge writing off their boat minutes before the start of the race: all these factors helped to keep the Boat Race in the limelight.

Oxford have won all but two of these contests since 1973, and all of them since 1976, but they were not all easy victories, the final result often concealing heroic and tightly fought struggles. With Cambridge winning the races from 1968 to 1973, what happened to turn the tide for Oxford? How did they recover in 1974 from that series of increasingly heavy defeats – the last by 13 lengths – at the hands of the old Light Blue enemy? This book is the 'inside' story of that revival written by one closely involved with the preparation of Oxford crews since 1972. As such it is a highly personalised account of one rowing man's love affair (or irrational obsession if you prefer) with the Boat Race. I hope you will forgive the indulgence and also any inevitable Dark Blue flavour you may detect, although I shall endeavour to be fair. Let me start by briefly telling from whence I, and the obsession, come.

I
Early Stirrings:
How the Passion was Born

It is hard to justify the wanton dissipation of countless hours spent pulling an oar on the river Thames. The pleasure derived from it can hardly explain away the huge incursion into a person's life. For the past 25 years I have rowed and/or coached, and continue to do so, for Westminster School, Oxford, London Rowing Club, Leander, the Tideway Scullers, Great Britain and myself, spending at times up to six or seven hours a day on water, running track and in gymnasium in the pursuit of victory. Yet at the same time I have continually fought against being tied exclusively to the sport, against complete identification with it, against the narrow horizons such an obsession would necessarily bring. I always dreaded the label 'rower' (as in 'may I introduce Daniel, he's a rower') and in my early years at Oxford and in London I tried to conceal my consuming hobby. (My family were very encouraging – until I won my first Boat Race; then despairing as I continued to be involved long after they would have wished me to move on to other things. Now they are resigned.) I was ashamed to admit to sophisticated friends that I spent four hours a day training. Was I being an intellectual snob pretending to align myself with those who peer loftily down their noses at the sweating, toiling athlete? Or was I just a little embarrassed by the amount of time that had to be spent doing it?

By the time I left Oxford and was rowing internationally, I was also becoming known as the Oxford coach, so any further subterfuge was hopeless. I could no longer hide my awful secret. More disturbing though was that I could no longer pretend to myself that I did not find it hugely absorbing and satisfying, that in a life-style such as mine unrestrained by routine work or domesticity it provided a strong thread or theme through my life and gave a sense of self discipline and control. Without it, I suspect, I would have quickly gone to the dogs. Or perhaps on the other hand, I might have directed my energies more lucratively. Some find inner calm and peace with yoga, poetry or painting; I find it through spending a couple of hours daily sculling alone out on the river. Only an afternoon of love-making can equal the delicious well-being and contentment it brings. Physical and mental concentration, time to contemplate, time to stretch and refresh body and mind.

Time consuming though it undoubtedly is, I have still managed to fulfil other needs and to follow other passions which have perhaps helped to alleviate the feelings of guilt that rowing has caused me. I have travelled extensively, through China, India, South America, the Middle East, Africa, East and Western Europe and North America. I worked for four years at the BBC, for ten years as a freelance photo-journalist and wrote books on two six-month journeys in Africa and South America. There were TV documentaries too, on phobias, on sport and travel, for children's programmes and on South America. But through it all was the lure of the Tideway, and the simple physical need, strong as a drug habit, to get back into a sculling boat. Even in the heart of Africa I made a detour of 500 miles when I heard of a boat club on Zambia's northern Copper Belt after three months alone on the road. I took a week off from my travelling to scull round the little 'dambo' twice a day to my heart's content.

Part of the attraction is a raw deep-rooted competitive urge; part of it is the delight in doing something at which one knows one is good and successful; part of it is the sublimely satisfying feeling of overall high-level fitness and strength derived from a supremely demanding sport; and part of it is the sweet sensation of the movement of the boat across the water, the sweep of the sculls, the hiss of the shell, the surge of the bows. Poetry and power, sweat and harmony, precision timing, tactics and the individual lust to overcome self and adversary. The urge to be a winner. Then there is the added dimension of a crew—an eight or a four or a double scull or pair—the comradeship of teamwork, the joint effort producing an almost mystical intimacy when everything is clicking together perfectly. That unity is almost sexual in its intensity, and one forgives one's crewmates everything, all their annoying little quirks and habits, for those moments of bliss. There is in short nothing quite like it and those who have not been through it have missed a life-enhancing experience. That is why those old rowing types in their funny schoolboy caps turn up at Henley and on the Boat Race launch year after year. They simply want to soak up again the smell and the feel that once gave them such intense pleasure, such dignity and at times such heartache.

I first became aware of the Boat Race when as a youngster my parents took me to a Boat Race party at the painter Trevelyan's studio hard by Chiswick Eyot. It was a gathering of the most unlikely sporting enthusiasts: architects, actors, writers like A. P. Herbert, the Empsons, the Redgraves, Stanley Spencer, Hugh Casson, Maurice Collis, Elizabeth Frink and other old Fabians—a wonderfully eccentric typi-cally British affair. The crews swept by and were gone in a moment and we all cheered and rushed back inside to see them finish on telly, and I decided to support Oxford because they always seemed to lose.

14

Holding my hand on one of these slightly bemusing occasions, my mother confided to me *à propos* nothing in particular: 'one day, you'll do that'. She could hardly have known then that I would grow up to be painfully undersized for such an endeavour, or that her words might be prophetic, for ours was not a rowing family, there was no history of the cursed disease among our forbears. Besides I wanted to play football, even though my father, who claimed to have occasionally rowed and punted fishermen's boats on the river Vistula in Warsaw, took me to the boating lake in Regent's Park opposite our house and taught me the rudiments. Frank and George who managed the boats there taught me more and the Colonel who cleared the leaves around the Park and was an avid rower himself encouraged me relentlessly. He had his own clinker skiff on the Thames to which he would inveigle the young boating assistants – Little Jim, Big Jim, Ian and Johnny Green – to join him on his fortnight's leave rowing his boat down from Reading to Tower Bridge. I began as an 11-year-old to work there on the boating lake in the school holidays, earning seven pounds for a 91-hour week. I was thrilled to be friends with the older tough young men, pushing the boats out and pulling them in, baling and varnishing, and above all being entrusted with the task of rounding up the stragglers late in the evening, sculling in the battered, patched and ancient 'shell' which gave me my first real rowing 'fix'. How I loved that boat, the solitariness and the speed of it and the superior feelings it gave me.

Yet, when I left the French *Lycée* aged 12 and began at Westminster School I still wanted to play football. But somehow (I think my father played a behind-the-scenes role) I was diverted to the river and the boathouse at Putney by the rowing master Ian Ross, an ex-Isis oarsman, and I never really escaped. Although I was, in rowing terms, pint-sized, those years in the battered old shell on the lake in Regent's Park paid dividends and I pushed the sons of traditional rowing families unexpectedly off their pedestals. Quickly I developed a real thirst for it. 'The bigger they are the harder they fall' became my maxim. The more they said 'you're too small, find another sport', the greater became the challenge, right through to captain of the first eight at school (we paced both Oxford and Cambridge on the Tideway – a great morale booster), Henley, and the club level sculling regattas like Weybridge, where winning events like the Junior Silver Sculls and breaking the record by 57 seconds acted as an additional spur and gave me a belief in myself. And then on to Oxford where, despite a modest reputation as a sculler, I found myself once more at the bottom of the pile. But the rowing bug had bitten hard and I was irrevocably hooked.

Being comparatively small I suppose I developed a tenacious, 'never say die' and deeply competitive instinct which helped later on both in my own rowing career and in the attitude I brought to Oxford as a coach. In that first year rowing at Oxford my application to join the Boat Race trials was considered a bit of a joke. The Dark Blues were enjoying a bumper period of success. I sat proudly and as tall as I could at bow in the senior 'A' trial crew in the first days of selection, until chief coach Ronnie Howard put me firmly in my place: 'For God's sake bow, stop trying to look so big'. Next day I was dropped. Glandular fever later in the term ruled out a place in even the junior trial crews, but in the summer term four of us rejects from the Oxford squad, Dozy Driscoll, Geoff Hand, Nick Bevan and myself, formed on our own initiative a crew that raced to the semi-finals at Henley as an Isis four in the Wyfold Cup in July. Other Oxford crews were at the same time winning the Prince Philip (the American stern four from that year's Oxford crew), the Thames Cup (Isis), the Ladies' and the Visitors' (St Edmund Hall), and reaching the Goblets semi-final (Freeman brothers) in what was one of the best ever years for Dark Blue rowing. In my second year in 1966 I squeezed into the bow seat of a very strong Isis crew (the Oxford reserves) which turned out to be a thorn in the side of President Duncan Clegg's Blue Boat. On Boat Race day we were reckoned to be faster than Cambridge when we trounced the Light Blue reserves, Goldie, in the curtain raiser race half an hour before the main event. Our Blue Boat won that race too. Oxford was in the ascendancy and enjoying a brief renaissance.

Although still an 11-stone, five-foot ten-inch weakling in the company of 14-stone 6-foot 3-inch giants, I came under the influence – and probably the protection – of Group Captain 'Jumbo' Edwards, the Oxford head coach and guru to a large chunk of the British rowing fraternity. Those who did not look to 'Jumbo' took their lead from London-based Lou Barry of the Tideway Scullers or Colin Porter and the Barn Cottage breakaways. 'Jumbo' was an experimenter, an innovator who too often used his Oxford crews as guinea pigs in his pursuit of success and suffered the consequences. He won but five of the 18 races he coached, yet he remains one of the sport's great legendary figures. 'Jumbo' was also an Old Westminster and had coached me briefly at school when he was asked to take on the first eight for a month. We boys stood in awe of him, hanging on every slow, deliberate utterance of the great man. His cohort during those all-important final Tideway periods (usually three weeks in those days) with Oxford was Ted Phelps, a Tideway expert and a former professional sculling champion. Ted was also a paid adviser to the Westminster School Boat Club, and he was probably my most influential coach during those formative years. He had also taught the student 'Jumbo' in 1927 and 1928 and during my five years at school, Ted instilled in me, and in my close colleague Brent Tanner, the finer points of the sport. He would follow us in a launch for miles, just the pair of us paddling at half pressure in sculling boats, coaxing us towards his ideal. Sometimes instead he would sit on Putney Pier where he worked as a pilot, his legs dangling over the edge, getting us to scull back and forth past him, identifying a point of technique and then sending us off to Kew to practise it. 'Don't come back until you've mastered that', he would say. We were enslaved by his charm and his confidence in us, because he made us feel so special.

At half term, while others took off for home and holidays, Brent and I would pack our lunch behind our foot stretchers and head off in sculling boats up to Twickenham and beyond, 25 or 30 miles, lunching on Eel Pie Island, trying to catch the tide both ways, crawling home late in the evening hands and arses sore as hell but delighted with our marathon mileages. We became good scullers, putting in the sort of mileage that makes champions as the saying went–the type of 'steady state' training programme followed by the East Germans and later by most other national teams, although we didn't know it then. We were just pleasing ourselves.

Ted Phelps was an excellent technician and a master of the vagaries of the Tideway, and he moulded my technical style and racing canniness in much the same way that he had influenced 'Jumbo'. Another of his 'pupils' was Bert Green, boatman of the National Westminster Bank Boat Club where Oxford always stay for their final fortnight before the race. He learned Ted's lessons well and when 'Jumbo' and Ted moved on, Bert and I took over their double-act. Lou Barry, coach of the Tideway Scullers, the country's top club, performed the same role for Cambridge during their triumphant years between 1968 and 1975 when he won seven races for them. Now Cambridge have Graeme Hall and Alan Inns, two more Tideway-wise men.

Back in 1967, after gruelling trials, 'Jumbo' declared his faith in the lightweight rower from Westminster and stuck me in the seven seat of the Oxford crew. 'Get your hair cut,' he ordered, 'or you'll slow the boat down.' It was never short enough for him, and my off-duty dress sense appalled him. As for his crew selection, press cuttings at the time suggested that his choice for 'seven' was a bad mistake: 'Topolski is good value for his 12 stone, but lacks the natural physique of a seven' (Burnell, *The Times*); 'The two number sevens could hardly be more different–Earl is big and imperturbable, if a trifle stolid, while the mercurial Topolski has vast experience but no weight. I just give this to Cambridge on points' (Hill, The *Daily Telegraph*). When they asked 'Why is Topolski in the crew?' 'Jumbo' replied: 'It's simple. When he's in, the boat goes faster.'

My selection not only surprised the rowing *cognoscenti*, it also came as a bit of a shock to my colleagues. Three of us in particular that winter spent time together travelling to and from the river, dining in the evenings and discussing our progress within the squad, the likely final line-up and our own chances. Josh 'Pud' Jensen was a 16-stone, six-foot six-inch dry-humoured American mountain of muscle, though still a relative novice as an oarsman. 'Humph' Nicholls was a more experienced South African with whom I had rowed in Isis the previous year. We three argued our various merits and concluded to each other that there was no way any of us could possibly be excluded from the crew. Each of us presented our own version of the 1967 crew, carefully including the other two. It was only during the summer, after the race, that we admitted that in those endless chats each man had secretly believed only he stood any real chance of winning a place, while the other two had no hope. As it turned out 'Pud' and I made it, and 'Humph' dropped out altogether.

My year in the boat still remains a vivid experience and that coupled with all my subsequent racing affords me extra insight into what the boys are going through as they approach the race. The days before the race are agonising. Every waking moment is spent talking tactics, thinking about the trial ahead and imagining the race again and again, how it will feel, trying somehow to exude confidence while feeling only an empty sickening hole deep down in the pit of the stomach. Race day draws inexorably closer and it is not anticipation or even elation that is the key sensation for the first-timer. It is fear—not of the impending battle, but fear of losing face, fear of a personal failure to function properly under stress, despite the endless months of practice; fear of letting down crewmates, friends, family and the whole damned tradition of the century and a half old Oxford and Cambridge Boat Race. And it's all over so quickly. Twenty minutes of life and no second chance. It is such a public affair too, and it's always the losing crew that features in all those distressing television close-ups.

At first of course, it was to win the Blue, to take part. But that initial pride in wearing the colours, sporting the Blue, evaporated very quickly once the final selection was made. Then only one thing mattered—to win. Yet if the torture of the last few weeks had been known in advance many might never have started the long haul way back in October in the first place. But, needless to say, it all started long before that. As a six-year-old rowing on the Serpentine or in a dinghy at the seaside; and then at school and beginning to row competitively: the Boat Race was always there, a unique pinnacle of achievement . . . an impossible dream. Rowing fathers and uncles, traditional Boat Race families (from which I was not) all pushing and encouraging their sons and nephews towards the ultimate goal. Not the Olympics, not the career in the City, but the Race. Things would take care of themselves after that.

It was hard enough just getting into Oxford or Cambridge in the first place. Then there were the trials, before Christmas, for which one sometimes had to risk the ire of tutors or even expulsion by entering at all; only the best schoolboy internationals made the last 16 along with the Blues and the Isis and Goldie reserve crewmen left over from the year before. They all seemed so sure of their places, that élite group. And when you made that top 16, probably not until your second year, the competition to get into 'the' crew became unbearably intense; it lasted for months. The training was brutal—five hours a day—endurance rowing, interval sprinting, circuits and weight-training. Christmas slipped by unnoticed. And then the final selection process at the end of January which set friend against friend, brother against brother. Once 'in' there was little time to celebrate. The exhilaration of those first few days as a crew when the names were announced soon wore off as the long hard grind—the meat of Boat Race training—took over. Early morning run, lectures and work until lunch; meeting up at a quarter past one to catch the van to Radley, ten minutes outside Oxford, where the river Thames was less congested and where we spent two hours or more training at full stretch. Sometimes we went to Reading or Henley or Wallingford or Pangbourne or Marlow—all a good 40 minutes away—where the river was more suitable or convenient for the coach. And then, as darkness fell, we headed back to the gym in Oxford for concentrated endurance work. Academic work after all this was hard to do—mental and physical tiredness left little energy for evening studies. Evening meals were taken as a crew at one college or another, where our double helping high protein platefuls would be ogled jealously by the other diners. February was a long and monotonous month, a hard routine during which we all got to know each other well. A fixture or two—a rare excitement when I rowed under 'Jumbo'—helped to sharpen us and reassure us that we were still on target despite the isolation in the depths of the countryside.

Even during that time we did not dare relax, for any sign of weakness or loss of form would result in relegation to the second crew where each reserve man was striving to prove himself better. Changes in the top boat were known to have been made as late as the last week. The training got tougher and at times, when nothing seemed to go right as we pounded up and down the river, a dark cloud would settle over us. For days on end there would be despondency and anxiety but then a good outing would transform the mood, a piece of work in which the boat sang along, everyone moving in perfect unison with the water hissing beneath the shell. Moments of supreme pleasure like those made the toil and agonising strain worthwhile – spirit and life would surge back into the crew.

Soon the Press attention began to intensify and suddenly we were on the Tideway and into the last two weeks. The first sight of the opposition is always a shock. They look so slick, threatening and so confident. That final fortnight is the acid test. Psychology plays a vital part and spirits have to be maintained. It's a time for tuning up; there are two outings a day often against carefully selected pacing crews. Every outing is closely scrutinised by the Press and potential speed assessed. Confidence is fragile now and the slightest set-back brings despair and becomes magnified as an indicator of possible failure. If we get a bad press we scoff at their lack of insight; but we gloat over any misfortune on the other side. A mixture of bravado and inward turmoil colours the atmosphere at the crews' respective hotels. Everyone reacts differently to the mounting pressure. Excited and keen to talk tactics, I could never fathom those loners who went off to their rooms to ruminate in solitary anxiety. Why couldn't they join in the endless discussions so that we all knew what was in our collective mind all the time? Besides, it was such a special time that I wished to share it with my team-mates. The calm confidence of the more experienced members is immensely comforting for the first-timers.

I remember very little of the coach's detailed analysis in the pre-race briefing, and I was only vaguely aware of the police escort and the crowds yelling support as we drove down to the river. One could have enjoyed it all if one had not been so bloody scared. The booing from rival supporters came as a surprise. Mind racing yet unable to grasp a single thought. Familiar faces smiling 'good luck': was that a mother or a girlfriend? Mechanical responses. The tension in the changing-room is oppressive while we begin to warm up. Crewmates' faces are drawn and grim while we wait to hear the result of the toss. Coach and President rush in with the news. Last minute advice as we prepare to go afloat. The reserve crews race past outside – trail-blazers, sparring partners cast in a supporting role.

Now everything is moving fast. Only 20 minutes to the off and it is all reflex action. Damn the cross wind, the water looks rough. Getting into the boat and setting off for the start. Body feeling drained of power, a by-product of all that swirling adrenalin. The 'needle' is so severe, the feeling of nausea so overpowering, you wonder how on earth you're going to find the strength to pull a single stroke . . . wish we had raced more in training. Mind on the job. Remember what the coach said: 'Stay cool and relax'. After a few minutes paddling the strength comes flooding back into the muscles. Curious items catch the attention. A girl in a pink frock waving from a launch, a dog squatting by the water's edge. The river is bouncy and difficult but the last 30 strokes of the warm-up feel powerful. Drift down on to the stakeboat. Wish the man in front 'good luck'. A quick handshake behind and a tap on the shoulder in front. Contact helps. Force the mind to concentrate. The umpire is on his feet. No more rehearsals: this time it's for real although it seems like a dream. 'Mustn't panic, daren't catch a crab, must sit back and draw the first stroke. Deep breathing. Why am I here?' 'Are you ready, Go!'

The sickening hollow feeling leaves the stomach in a rush. 'One stroke at a time, don't hurry the recovery. Dare I sneak a look at them? No it'll break the rhythm.' Then the crew settles into its racing stride. You can sense the other crew there alongside, hear their cox urging them on. A sudden attack of anxiety: 'God, we can't lose; please don't let us lose'. It's terribly hard in mid-race, when the pressure is on, to keep your head; so easy to stampede. Oarsmen dread the really close race, yet they look back at it with pride and say: 'Yes that was the best race I ever rowed'. The last mile out in front is pure elation. It feels so easy, so magical. You cross the line, hardly out of breath it seems, and cheer the dispirited losers.

For the trailing crew the last half mile is purgatory. Desperation and utter exhaustion. It's hard to believe that you've lost the Boat Race. All the fantasies and daydreams, the coaching talks, the crew spirit, never covered the possibility of losing. It just was not a part of the overall scheme. But after a few minutes, when the boat is back on the rack and you see the winners toasted and cheered the full realisation begins to dawn. Some men break down, some slink away, but both vanquished and victors have to continue the show. Interviews, families, the formal dinner as guests of their respective Old Blues to tell all who will listen just how they did it, or failed to do it. Then on to the Ball. And of course, in the end, the feeling of anti-climax steals over you. Is that all? Is that it? And all that is left is a gentle secret smiling glow deep inside for the victors.

Oxford beat Cambridge by three and a half lengths in 1967, and in the summer we raced well at Henley but lost to the redoubtable East Germans by one and a half lengths in the Grand. Later we failed to win the nomination for the European Championships but went instead to the North American Championships in Canada where we finished fifth.

The struggle against prejudice towards the slight in build—which, sad to say, is often justified, since, all things being equal, the basic punch of a 14-stoner carries far more weight than that of a lightweight 11-stoner—continued for me and for others in like predicament until lightweight rowing for 11-stone crews was introduced at World Championship level in 1974. But until then the pleasure of unseating the big boys was an endless sport in itself, and was I'm glad to say fruitful. They fell like flies.

In rowing there is for oarsmen nothing quite like the attraction of competing in the Boat Race whether they be schoolboys or hardened internationals, and they come from all over to try for a Blue. World champions come, American college graduates and Youth internationals too, and some go on to row internationally afterwards. But the Boat Race holds a special place in each man's list of rowing achievements. That is why John Pritchard, already a World and Olympic silver medallist in eights, and a member of the Cambridge coaching team of 1982 and 1983, decided at the age of 28 to go to Cambridge to take a degree in law. In fact he wanted to row in the Boat Race. In 1968, for the same reason, I decided to stay on at Oxford to do a course in Social Anthropology and to row in my second Boat Race, and took part in the first Oxford defeat in four years which began a disastrous run of failures. That probably is why I am coaching them now, for in the dark recesses of my mind I am atoning for the guilt I felt in contributing to that defeat.

I learned a lot from that defeat and many of those lessons I used in my later rowing career and also in the preparation of Oxford crews these past 12 years. In 1968 we made the elementary mistake of thinking beyond the Boat Race to the Mexico Olympics. We regarded Cambridge as a mere stepping-stone towards that goal, and lost our edge. My own complacency resulted in my removal from seven to bow and even an extended period out of the first boat altogether, rowing in Isis while I was recovering from a dose of 'flu, which shocked me back to reality. During my first year I had given up drinking three months before the race, at Christmas, and had forced myself to bed at half past ten every night. In 1968 I was nowhere near as disciplined. The race was, after all, pretty well in the bag. In addition, we—the coach, the crew—made a number of mistakes each one not crucial in itself, but in their sum enough to turn a sure-fire winning line-up into a loser on the day. Defeat by one second at the hands of the University of London at the Reading Head two weeks before the Boat Race sent 'Jumbo' into a panic and he re-organised the crew order into an unusual Italian frig-rig seating arrangement. He dropped our excellent 1967 cox Peter Miller because there was a lighter though less experienced cox available in Isis. That the London University crew's performance was a reflection of their speed rather than our sluggishness was never considered. They went on to represent the country in the Olympics while we slumped into oblivion.

Cambridge beat us from Hammersmith Bridge home and ended both our winning streak and our ambitions to represent Britain in Mexico. Two of us were dropped from the summer Olympic challenge crew and in a fury we formed a club four at London Rowing Club, bent on revenge and in an attempt to win selection for Mexico that way, but in the end none of us were selected, although I made my own way out to Mexico to watch the Games anyway.

I had had the experience of being on the outside at Oxford, a reject from the squad, and I didn't like it one bit. For the only time in my life I wished them ill fortune. But it did fuel that competitive urge, that ruthless edge which you need if you are to race in winning crews. I knew what it felt like to be axed, and later as coach I knew what the candidates I turned down were feeling. It seemed important that they should know precisely why they were not being chosen and exhaustive selection tests with publicised results seemed the only answer. Team spirit is important of course, but not if it means carrying passengers on board. The club crew of good mates, good team lads, could not be the team for me if we were out to win races. I chose to row with proven winners, otherwise I preferred to scull on my own. And in the selection of Oxford crews today the same holds true. No one gets into the crew because he's a good chap or because he went to the right school. He's there because his results demand that he be there; they show him to be one of the eight best men and the rest of the crew know it. And so does he. A strange and perhaps obvious point to make, but in the past (and even now) coaches liked to think that they could select by instinct, feel and experience. Furthermore there are still oarsmen who like to row with their friends in 'happy' crews, believing that they will be more successful. They exclude the temperamentally difficult man in the interests of harmony. Good! That makes them easier to beat. All you need is one weak link in a crew; for when the pressure really comes on he breaks. For months in training he may get away with it, and the coach may well not notice (or he may know but will hope for the best), but come the big race, if it's a close one, that suspect link gives way. I may nowadays rely on friends to include a less than fully fit me in their crews, but if I wanted to win top class races I would not put me in a crew any more unless I had proved my worth in selection tests. Past reputation counts for nothing. If it does it's just jolly boating for fun, good chaps and all that, but not a basis for the best crews.

After Oxford came a personal road back. I needed to restore my own confidence in my ability to win races. At this stage though I had no thoughts of coaching. I was asked to finish Isis, to take the last fortnight, because I knew the Tideway well, but I didn't consider this to be a serious step. In 1969 I teamed up with Chris Blackwall to row in a four at London Rowing Club. He had rowed six behind me in the 1967 crew but we had failed ever to see eye to eye while at Oxford. He considered me a scruffy hippy with highly dubious friends, while to me he was a prissy prude. But two years on we sank our differences in the interests of forming a fast four, and soon became the closest of allies and eventually friends first as fellow crew members and later as partners in the revival of Oxford's fortunes between 1973 and 1977, when together we joined their coaching team. Also in our four were ex-international Nick Cooper, dragged happily out of premature retirement, and a new sculling hope, Peter Harrison.

We won the Henley Wyfolds at a trot and went on to the national trials where in three scorching races we twice beat the budding young Thames Tradesmen four who were later to become the backbone of Britain's resurgence at world level. During the 'seventies, under Bob Janousek, Fred Smallbone, Jim Clark, Lennie Robertson and Bill Mason won nine silver medals between them. We were the last British crew to beat them, but we went on to race disastrously at the European Championships in Klagenfurt. Thereafter followed a rowing career for me which involved 22 Henley appearances including 16 semi-final or final races between 1962 and 1984 and three more Henley wins, a cupboard full of domestic and international cups and medals, and silver and gold lightweight medals in four and eight at the 1975 and 1977 World Championships.

All this rowing was interspersed with journeys to many different parts of the world in a continuing effort to avoid a life completely dominated by rowing. It was during one of these journeys, in India, that I received a letter from the newly-elected Oxford President, Andy Hall, asking me to coach the 1972–3 Oxford crew. I had coached two final fortnight stints for losing Isis crews and a winning 1971 senior trial eight since leaving Oxford, but that hardly, in my opinion, qualified me to take on the mantle shed by 'Jumbo'. Besides I was still happily competing. I had only been helping out because of my experience on the Tideway. And frankly I was thinking more of trying to extricate myself from the sport altogether. It was, I felt, time to do something a little more serious career-wise. I have been trying to wriggle free of the sport ever since, but the harder I squirm the more deeply embedded I seem to become. In the long term and financially I want out; physically and emotionally I am helplessly trapped.

For the next 12 years, I combined my own rowing with coaching, surmising that since I was still racing and training myself I might as well go on taking care of Oxford, and then later the national women's Olympic squad in 1979 and 1980. All the while I was attempting to make a living as a freelance writer/photo-journalist. Now that I have finished racing internationally I no longer have that excuse – yet I'm still coaching Oxford. So why do I do it? What is the appeal? After all I'm certainly no traditionalist. All I can say in my defence is that I cannot resist a good fight, the lure of the river and the sport itself, the intensity of that growing emotional link with Oxford's Boat Race fortunes, the rivalry with Cambridge, the pleasure in helping to weld together a finely-honed fighting machine and the undoubted attraction of trying to maintain a winning streak, the equal longest ever for Oxford (but still lagging a long way behind Cambridge's 13-win sequence between the wars and their overall lead of seven in the series). If this sounds like an apology, that is precisely what it is.

Enough then of me. Let the rest of this story be that of the men who have rowed Oxford to the most successful period of her Boat Race history. Let it be an intimate look, not a public record or a dry history of races, but a behind-the-scenes view of how it all happened. Allow me to put flesh and blood to the names of those unsung Boat Race heroes, my family of 67 Blues and 55 Isis men, who have given so much of their lives and character to the event. For make no mistake, they are a very extraordinary breed of men.

2

Reconstruction

Three and a half lengths, four lengths, three and a half, ten, nine and a half–thirty and a half lengths behind Cambridge between 1968 and 1972 and five defeats in a row. What a mess. To be fair though, Cambridge were boating some outstanding crews during that period. Delafield, Baillieu, Maxwell, Sturge, Hart and Cadwalader were all Olympic class men. Oxford were in complete disarray and the Boat Race was the subject of agonised letters to *The Times*, some of which even called for a relaxation of the stringent academic requirements for admission. A University education was about more than just academic excellence they argued. Others were more impassioned: 'Cambridge has quite plainly been bent on dominating the event', wrote Alexander Walker of Maida Vale on 7 April 1972, 'Such an attitude is intolerable today'. Hardly! The Oxford crew, or any sportsman for that matter, would be likewise motivated to win and win again. One could not really expect one side to enter a sporting contest not wanting to win!

The plain truth was that Boat Race success runs in phases, each successive win building confidence in the squad and coaches, leading them to international experience and to contact with new ideas which in turn adds to the development of the blossoming squad. New recruits faced with a choice of rowing for a thriving squad or an ailing one naturally go for the winners. The ailing squad meanwhile struggles to regroup, to regain a successful formula and this is bound to take time. And ultimately, as they begin to find that formula, as they redouble their efforts and intensify their training they force the standard of their event higher still–which in turn keeps it in line with developments on a national and international level. It may well frustrate the supporters of the losing side to watch their men thrashing about trying to get back into the fight, but the nature of the event is such that all winning streaks come to an end and all losing streaks likewise. But that knowledge gives little comfort to those in the throes of reconstruction, when there seems to be no way out of the morass.

In 1972 Oxford were in such a position. Nothing they tried seemed to go right. There were new coaches each year, tried and discarded by increasingly desperate Presidents who were and still are young students unused to such responsibility. Oxford's teetering bandwagon retreated further and further up river to nurse their wounds away from the hurly-burly of domestic competition, afraid to test themselves in advance lest they be found wanting, only to emerge each year to ever heavier defeats. Yet they were not boating bad oarsmen by any means – Matheson, Tee, Dale, Hawksley, Fink, Saltmarsh, Dart, Nevin, Payne, Hall, Willis – they had all achieved considerable distinction before coming to Oxford and many went on afterwards to win top awards. And it wasn't really the fault of the coaches – Peak, Reynolds, Fink, Fishlock, Howard, Langfield and 'Jumbo'. The problems were the mix, the loss of motivation, the difficulty of who held ultimate responsibility, the very talented opposition and the ever-changing set-up which gave no possibility of continuity in the system. There were oarsmen at Oxford who were becoming satisfied with winning the Blue, just taking part in the race, rather than beating Cambridge.

'I had to fight against the most terrible apathy', recalls Andy Hall, President in 1972 and now an oil company executive. 'It was hard to raise even the 18 men necessary for the two crews and I spent depressing, humiliating hours touring the colleges knocking on people's doors literally begging them to turn up for trials. London was just an hour down the motorway from Oxford and it was the age of sex and drugs and rock and roll. No one wanted to know about sport and the Boat Race. It was just too uncool.' Andy had had a battle for the Presidential nomination against Adrian Burns who although not a Blue was nevertheless the college captains' choice. Andy was keen to move Oxford University rowing towards more of a squad system while the captains feared a subsequent drop in college crew standards. A strong University crew could only grow from a strong college base, they believed. The voting was close. The following year Hall's re-election for a second term, a rare occurrence, was even closer and was only decided by the casting vote of the Boat Club Treasurer, Michael Barry, one of the Oxford coaches and a firm supporter of Hall's policy views. 'He gave the appearance of being very establishment,' remembers Hall, 'but in fact he was quite radical in his views on the OUBC.' The Blue Keith Bolshaw had opposed Hall, again with the backing of the college captains.

The survival of serious rowing at Oxford was Andy Hall's primary concern, and although he never enjoyed success in the race itself, his devotion and efforts as President in 1972 and 1973 played a crucial part in laying the foundations for future years. 'It was a battle to get the trialists to train at all', says Andy. 'A mark of that lack of interest is the fact that the President's Boat Race ledger had no entries to cover the previous five years. I sat down during the vac. and wrote up six years of notes for future generations of Presidents.' He is sceptical now of the way in which his crews prepared for their races. 'In 1972 the crew was treated with kid gloves and we never knew how slow we were until the day. If anyone complained of tiredness we cut the outing. "Jumbo" was great to start off with and we all believed in him implicitly, but it didn't last.'

Andy was facing his second year as President and his fourth Boat Race when he wrote to me Poste Restante in India. Rowing trips at the time to Spain and Egypt had brought the current Blues into contact with us recent Old Blues—the last Oxford winners—who were still rowing, and he was prompted to enlist our help. He and his squad also liked the way I had coached their 1971 pre-Christmas trial crew. He came to see me in the Hospital for Tropical Diseases to which place I had returned from my Africa–India odyssey, heavy with hepatitis, to discuss his plans. He complained then that too many good schoolboy oarsmen were opting out 'to write poetry, organise exhibitions and generally party', once they arrived at Oxford. Admissions policy had changed too, he said, from the more tolerant years of the 'sixties and before. Academic requirements were getting much tougher. He was however desperate to end his Oxford career on a winning note, yet here he was putting his trust in a completely new and untried coaching team whose main feature was its lack of Boat Race coaching experience. It may well be that he saw potential in me because I was a little more extrovert than some, and perhaps gave the impression of having a lot to offer because I tended to speak my mind. He did not want to appoint a head coach for fear of offending the others but, as finishing coach I quickly found myself taking on a central role partly because as a freelance writer with haphazard working hours I had more time to devote and partly because I am impatient by nature and like to get things done quickly. There were seven other coaches on the Oxford team with me, four of whom concentrated on Isis.

Derek Thurgood had coached Andy's Keble College summer eight. While I was still recovering in hospital he went early in November with Andy to West Germany to consult Karl Adam, architect of the highly successful Ratzeburg eights and a rival/partner to 'Jumbo' in innovation. They returned with a bulging folder of notes on training methods and advice which Derek set out as a training schedule to suit our Boat Race requirements. Some of Adam's suggestions were beyond the capabilities of a University crew—both in time and the amount of work required—but his advice was invaluable and still formed the basis of our programme in 1984.

Dr Michael Barry, the Oxford University Boat Club Treasurer and a fellow at St John's College was the only coach amongst us who had actually been in charge of an Oxford crew before – namely the winning 1966 crew. However his style was to leave overall training programme decisions to the other coaches, preferring to offer the benefit of his experience and advice quietly in discussion and take the crew for a two week stint. George Harris, boatbuilder, Christ Church boatman since 1926 and ex-professional sculler was probably the most able and experienced coach amongst us, and was certainly the best technique man. This was his first Boat Race coaching job despite his long and successful association with Christ Church. Although he was shy and unassuming he commanded the greatest respect from oarsmen and fellow coaches alike. He had the keenest eye for a good crew and a sharp sense of humour too. When I commented once as we sat in the launch about how well the crew was coming on under his tutelage, he retorted: 'Distance lends enchantment to the view, Dan', and continued his coaching.

Chris Blackwall was in charge of Isis. He was tall and blond, and in his other life worked as a photographer and male model. We had rowed together in the 1967 Boat Race and the British 1969 European Championship four. He had further represented the country in the 1971 coxed pairs. Throughout the next five years of reconstruction Chris played a vital role as we planned our strategy, bouncing ideas off each other, adopting the newest training methods used by the national team both on land and on water. Although he took overall responsibility for Isis and was their finishing coach on the Tideway, we worked closely together on all aspects of the Oxford recovery. Chris says now that during that time he bridled at playing the subordinate role in which he found himself cast, but thankfully he chose to put the Oxford cause above pride, since neither of us could have managed those early trying steps alone. He recognised that his abrasive quick temper and lack of ease and cunning with people hindered his coaching abilities while I, and indeed all of us, relied heavily upon his technical skills, his precise planning and his meticulous attention to detail. He kept himself abreast of the latest developments in the sport and attended all the coaching courses. The experience he gained coaching with Oxford later helped him to become Britain's chief national coach in 1977 and 1978. 'My inability to take people into my confidence and my insistence on doing everything myself meant that I made a lot of enemies', he says. 'So I didn't last long out there on the front line. But as a duo we complemented each other well as Oxford coaches even though perhaps I didn't realise it at the time.' He left Britain in 1980 to take up an administrative job in the United States where he now organises rowing for the American National Federation.

Chris was always fascinated by how successfully the group of coaches method worked. He felt that one of the main contributions we both made to the Oxford effort was that of motivating not only the oarsmen but also the other coaches and blending all the individuals into one cohesively working unit. One of our more successful achievements he believes, was that we managed not to select any duds, not as simple a task as one might suppose. That was the measure of the success of our stringent testing procedure. Once the crew was selected, though, the coaches were allowed their head within the overall framework of the plan since it was important that they should not go off at a tangent, even though there was a natural element of rivalry between coaches. We had to control and subdue that competitiveness to the common goal. Chris remembers how he found it difficult to take what he felt were arrogant young Presidents. At one stage he planned to resign from the coaching team because of one President's disinterest and later uninformed interference in the selection of the Isis crew and the lack of respect and support that loyal squad men in the reserve crew received. 'But I reckoned if I backed out I'd be letting down Nigel Burgess and the others, so I stuck it out.' Chris's philosophy was that if only one Isis man won his Blue the following year then all the effort he took with Isis was worthwhile. He and I believed strongly in the principle of objectivity in selection and were angered if a President rode roughshod over that strategy. 'Although Sawyier was a bear,' says Chris, 'he always saw sense in the end. But one or two Presidents were just pig ignorant.'

'Nick Tee was the best President', says Chris, 'even though he lost. He recognised the importance of Isis and he left the best legacy of all. Michelmore, although he did not know the ropes so well, did a good job too.' He remembers in 1973, while we were training the squad in pairs and singles on the Isis, the Oriel College boatman Len Andrews cycling by with a disparaging look. Chris commented: 'We're going to do something this year, Len. What do you think?' Len shook his head. 'You can't make meat pies out of shit, sir' he replied and cycled on. 'Well I think we did', says Chris in retrospect. 'Just look at some of them now.' Whether we made meat pies or not, we certainly caused the transformation to happen, and laid the foundation for the change to take place. We made mistakes of course, but overall the strategy was sound.

A very vital element to the development of that strategy was George Harris, a steadying hand and a wise sage while Chris, Hugh Matheson and I were headstrong young bucks. Hugh's contribution, though limited by his national squad duties in the British eight, was important as a galvaniser. He was the only Oxford success story to emerge from those lean losing years and as such his presence in the squad inspired the Oxford boys and gave them a morale-boosting smell of achievement. Hugh's enthusiasm and competitiveness coupled with his experience at the top end of international rowing gave the lads a model. His reporting of the intimate details and workings of that squad's training programme, devised by the national coach Bob Janousek, taught Chris, me and the Oxford oarsmen a lot in those early days. Hugh's intelligent interpretation of the programme and his constant questioning of Janousek's theories earned his seat in the eight the nickname 'Speakers' Corner' amongst his colleagues in the national crew.

All the coaches on the Oxford team were carefully chosen for what they had to offer, for what they each did best. We culled our techniques and physiological training methods from the best coaches—Janousek and his national squad programme, Karl Adam, Phelps, Barry, Spracklen, Neilson, 'Jumbo', even the Cambridge training programme, bits of anything and everything that made sense—and added our own thoughts. Then we adapted it all to our specific needs, the needs of that strangest of animals the Boat Race. All the time we picked up new ideas and re-organised the programme. We never stood still. And still, of course, each year it changes in small but significant ways and intensifies as we try to keep abreast of current developments.

The strategy we devised over the months in 1972 and streamlined in the following years followed a number of different lines. The essential ingredients we had to develop were skill, endurance, strength, motivation and relaxation. First we drew up an integrated programme of land work and water-based training which radically increased the amount of work done by previous Oxford crews. In October and early November it consisted of long distance running and body circuits in the gym using some light weights to build up muscle endurance, improve the cardio-vascular system of the body, train the men aerobically and prepare the muscles for the heavy weight work that would follow. On the water the emphasis was on technique training and long distance steady state work at low ratings for 50, 60 and 70 minutes at a time. In November a programme of heavy weights was introduced to follow the fast high repetition body circuits and the running. This land work the men did three times a week in addition to their daily water work. Extra attention was paid to developing the quadrucep muscles of the thighs by way of a high number of repetitions of an exercise designed to reproduce the rowing action on land. In the boat we added 'over distance' training: more intensive stretches of work at higher ratings for periods of seven to 12 minutes repeated a number of times during the outing. We also introduced occasional high-speed sessions of short 20-stroke bursts to maintain the feeling of race pace.

Because we were dealing with such a disparate spread of men showing a great variety of strength, weight and age we needed a very widely based programme. On the whole, though, they all needed the heavy weight work which we maintained into February before changing the emphasis to medium weights and a higher number of repetitions, while still continuing with the circuits. The running changed in character too as we brought in a thrice-weekly series of sprints over different distances to improve the crew's explosive anaerobic capacity. On the water too the work intensified over shorter distances with the rating coming up and the quickness of the stroke through the water at a premium. But we did not abandon the steady state and alternate work; we simply changed the emphasis of the work pattern as we moved through the winter and as the men developed the sort of fitness that would enable them to cope with the new type of work. Quantity changed to quality and throughout the year the importance of good technique under pressure was reinforced. Other finer adjustments were constantly being made to this overall pattern.

Rowing is arguably after the marathon the most demanding sport there is, the training more arduous and more comprehensive than any other. Few athletes, swimmers or footballers would put themselves through the punishing regime that oarsmen are subjected to daily throughout their careers and that goes for the women rowers too. 'Before 1960 we were never really flogged in training', recalls Dr Michael Barry. 'In the 'forties when I rowed we did long low rating paddles to Abingdon and back on the river, concentrating on technique, and supplemented that with some mild runs which were never timed or competitive. We did no weight training or gym circuits and we never raced other crews before the Boat Race. That sort of thing is all new. The Boat Race was the hardest anyone would ever have to row and some men cracked themselves for life. Now the crews do harder work in training than they do in the race and no one blinks if they row two full courses in an afternoon. The fear that we had for the race is not so fierce now; but on the other hand technique and timing is not as good as it was in our day.'

We decided early on that selection would be entirely on merit, and seen to be so, and that no seat would be considered safe including that of the President. Andy agreed to just about everything we put forward because he clearly saw that far-reaching and perhaps painful changes had to be made. We devised a series of gruelling physical tests in sculling boats, in the gym (with weights and as body circuits), on the running track, on the ergometer machine and in seat racing, the results of which would be published for all the squad members to see and which would determine the composition of the eventual crew. The accent was on competition within the squad in everything they did— man against man and man against his own previous performance. It was necessary that every squad member should be able to see where he stood in the group and that there was no underhand horse-dealing or subjective selection going on. They were a pretty intelligent lot these University boys and they could be very argumentative. They needed proof. There could be no doubts about the fairness of the final selection. Most squad members usually made up their own lists of the likely Blue Boat and Isis crews which they amended from time to time through the winter as various squad men's stars rose or fell. Most lists would agree on four or five seats but the numbers five to 11 were always the crucial ones. Every word and action of the coaches was construed to mean something significant. A crew order change or a word would send a frisson running through the squad. Was it a sign that someone was out? Or in? The tension was enormous; but then it had to be to get the best out of them all and ultimately to isolate the toughest men for the crew.

We proposed too that there should be much closer monitoring of performance not only during testing but throughout training in the gym and on the water, and that all the coaches should agree to attend together a selected session on the water every two or three weeks so that they could liaise more closely with each other and keep track of progress through the year. Too often in the past coaches had taken over for their stint with little background knowledge of what had gone before, and, equally important, had had little chance to brief the person to whom they were handing over. We had to detail a full year's programme in advance with overall control and supervision resting in the hands of the finishing coach so that every coach knew what he was specifically expected to achieve in his fortnight. We transferred the week-long January pre-term training camp from the Leander Club at Henley—which had an unprofessional ivory tower feeling about it—to the harsher atmosphere of Putney and extended it to two weeks, beginning the day after New Year. We camped out in private homes since funds were always low. It seemed an obvious advantage to spend that period on the Boat Race course so that everyone became fully conversant with the wicked vagaries of the Tideway. By facing the four and a quarter-mile stretch of winding river day after day in all its various moods; flood and ebb, angry or gentle, swirling or sluggish, in eights, pairs, or sculling boats the squad members learned how to cope with it on their own, how to make their own decisions in the heat of a race and ultimately to lose their fear both of the distance and of the course itself.

One major task was to rekindle in the crew a belief in themselves as individuals – to instil a killer instinct and to rebuild a squad confidence badly dented by five years of failure. You can snarl and look tough and tell yourself and each other how mean you are until you're blue in the face, but it's entirely another thing to believe it deep down. We had to tackle that thorny psychological barrier faced by all athletes when confronting a major test – fight or flight. Some lads would never admit or even realise that they lacked the courage for a tussle; others would never be able to cultivate the hunger to win however hard they tried. It was down to us, Chris and me really, to select the fighters. With this in mind we determined to take on in training contests every important club crew in the country – the national team too – throughout the six-month period leading up to the race at the end of March. In such a make-or-break initial year we were possibly over-zealous in seeking out combat situations, and in training, in purely physiological terms, we probably raced in top gear too much. But in 1972 over-training was not our problem. We had to leap a psychological chasm and these contests could do wonders for morale. It paid off beautifully. By carefully choosing the type of work, the distances raced, where they were raced, the order in which we met the opposition and by preparing the crew properly for each fixture, we were able to give them the best chance to learn from the encounters, even if they got beaten, which as it turned out they did not.

Fear of failure is a terrible hindrance to any athlete's development and it inhibits him from taking the chances he must take with himself if he is to succeed at the highest level. When he realises that to lose a race in training does not necessarily have any bearing on the result in the main event two months later, and more importantly that his coaches are not going to castigate him or write him off for losing (unless he deserves it) but are eager to help him learn from his mistakes, then he begins to relax and to anticipate each new bout with relish. Different stages of training and fatigue are all factors in the relative performances of crews in mid-preparation and have to be taken into account. How much more useful to race the University of London, and if it so happens lose one day but analyse the encounter and use the experience to beat them the next day, than to avoid the chance of racing them altogether. Of course a series of beatings with no sign of improvement which simply demonstrates to a crew that they are patently too slow is hopelessly demoralising. A coach must decide the pros and cons and exercise his judgement. Obviously a sound crew is a prerequisite and the coach must really know his crew and their capabilities well. He should never set them unachievable targets.

The Oxford squad had to discover the art of constructive analysis where their own efforts and results were concerned. Simply throwing themselves wholeheartedly into the fray and hoping they would emerge the victors was too hit-and-miss, too naive and unprofessional. We wanted them to take on responsibility for their own performances rather than looking constantly for some outside magic hand to push them in front. Chris spent a lot of time on the weight training programme and we tried to supervise the work in the gym as much as possible to ensure that it was done correctly and efficiently and that injuries were kept to a minimum. Too often in the past such vital elements of training had been left to the squad members to organise for themselves, since the coaches, mostly working family men unpaid save for travelling expenses, could hardly be expected to cover every aspect of a comprehensive programme all the time. (This is still a problem and even now the squad is regrettably sometimes left to fend for itself.)

The coaching system which has evolved over the years both at Oxford and at Cambridge depends upon the coaches taking leave from their jobs for fortnightly stints with the crews. Occasionally a retired 'Jumbo' figure might take responsibility for the whole year as sole coach, but such a situation is the exception rather than the rule. Normally the President, who is overall chief, appoints his head coach who then takes on the job of co-ordinator and coach, produces a training programme for the year, supervises selection, oversees the whole project and takes the crew for the last fortnight. He hopes to be able to attend as many sessions as possible, and maintains a close liaison with the President who, as an oarsman in the crew, is more in touch with the day-to-day running of the squad.

Presidents obviously vary from year to year in character, efficiency, motivation and approach. Some are excellent administrators but poor public relations officers. Others are great in-crew motivators and fine leaders but hopeless organisers. Some leave a healthy optimistic University Boat Club behind them when they hand over office, while others leave chaos and a disgruntled residual squad of oarsmen and coaches. Some Presidents are assertive and opinionated with strong personalities and ideas while a few have been shy and have preferred to hand over the whole job to the coaches. But on the whole they are young working students, trying to gain degrees and row in the Boat Race at the same time and are, in the nature of University life, basically in transit. So their experience is limited and depending on their age, character and confidence they delegate responsibility to a lesser or greater extent to the coaches for the selection, training schedule and crew preparation, while retaining overall responsibility for the end product themselves. So the President's choice of head coach is quite an act of faith. Many coaches however, particularly those outside Britain, would and do refuse to work under such inhibiting conditions since they would insist on retaining full responsibility and control. But that is one of the eccentricities of the unpaid Oxbridge system, and although less than perfect it just about works. But as academic pressures on student Presidents continue to grow, the position may well change so that some time in the future a full time professional coach will have to take charge.

Since my freelance writing work afforded me a certain flexibility, I was able to devote more time than some to the task and consequently was able to identify and iron out problems as they arose, keep in closer touch with day-to-day events and establish that vital constant thread from year to year, learning from the mistakes of previous Boat Race build-ups. That consistency was something that had been lacking in recent years as each new President and each new coach repeated old well-worn mistakes. During the 'seventies and early 'eighties the hard core of coaches has remained the same, although some have retired and new ones have gradually been introduced into the system, learning the method so to speak. But let us be clear that there was and is no magic formula. Just a solid reliable basis, willing hard graft and attention to detail.

As we planned our strategy and chose our coaching team we agreed that there must be far more consultation and agreement between us all, rather than leaving things to chance. Simply booking five good coaches was not enough. They had to co-ordinate their efforts. Each would inevitably be keen to produce as fast a crew as possible in his particular fortnight, but that might not be the best thing to do in terms of the overall scheme. Furthermore not all coaches agree on technique and it became essential to clear up differences early on, so as not to confuse the oarsmen. 'But that's the opposite of what I was told to do last week' is one of the rowers' most common frustrations. We spent considerable time discussing the speed of the hands around the turn and away from the finish with Derek taking one view and I another. We had to agree on what we were looking for, and we had to bury our own egos for the overall good of the crew. To turn out an Oxford crew at the end of January racing along at 38 strokes a minute with no run, even if it was beating an embryo national team working at a low rating of 32, was of little benefit in terms of the long range build-up to a race over four and a quarter miles at the end of March.

In an attempt to cut costs, but also to stimulate a more professional, more relaxed and less formal approach to the race, we decided to cancel our booking at the Star and Garter Hotel in Richmond, the traditional Oxford resting place for the last phase leading up to the race. I remembered from 1967 and 1968 the stiff black-tie dinners every night, the polite conversation with endless guests smoking cigars and the excruciating monologues from ancient Old Blues on the subject of the Boat Races between 1905 and 1909. The delightful Eugene Millington Drake, well into his eighties, would have fascinated us with his tales and reminiscences on any other occasion, but not a few days before the biggest event in our lives at ten o'clock at night after an exhausting day on the river and a long dinner. 'Jumbo' used to enjoy those evenings enormously; he would get a bit drunk and seemed unaware of our suffering. I was determined not to put our crews through such torture. So we reduced the formalities to a minimum. One formal dinner for Old Blues early on in the fortnight was enough with another informal one for the rowing journalists and a third for young Old Blues from the previous couple of Boat Races who were still friends of the current crew. Smokers were refused permission to light up and were sent out of the room to do so if they wished. Although we were loth to break with tradition in most ways we were keen not to let archaic uncomfortable habits stand in our way.

So for £150 a week I rented a house in Hammersmith along Castelnau within easy reach of the boathouse at Putney which cut out the twice daily 20-minute hired bus ride back and forth to Richmond. It meant losing the company of Uncle Den, our supportive and outspoken bus driver for 30-odd years, but it was cheaper and more convenient to use our own Land Rover. But Den still came for the last couple of days to drive us elegantly to the river in his huge de luxe Isleworth coach. We did not want to lose entirely the effect of the grand entry. I then recruited Piers Gough, a large, enthusiastic, multi-talented architectural student with a headful of wild curly hair, who had a penchant for silver lamé jackets and blue horn-rimmed glasses, to cook three meals a day for a pittance. Once we had established that good, basic, high-calorie fare – and a lot of it – was required rather than anything exotic, Piers' fine cuisine, served up with great panache, his extrovert no-nonsense character and his tolerance of undergraduate humour and horseplay helped to produce the perfect atmosphere of domestic ease away from prying eyes and formality. The Press liked our eccentric genius cook too and they did photo features on him three years running. 'Nothing tinned, nothing frozen, no instant coffee and nothing for cox' said Piers. 'That's how to make 'em go fast.'

In any year attacks of self-doubt and indecision are normal but in this first year, 1973, with nothing to work with save enthusiasm, energy and a gut feeling for what we believed was the right course, the anxieties were magnified a hundredfold. It took a certain *chutzpah* to create an impression that one knew what one was doing, that we coaches were on top of the situation, for any sign of indecision would have been pounced on, and the ensuing loss of confidence, particularly with a group of young men whose belief in themselves was already so delicately balanced, could have spelled disaster. Andy Hall in his second year as President was a big six-foot four-inch 15-stoner rowing his fourth Boat Race; chipper, sharp but nursing a deepening insecurity about his own ability which caused him to adopt a faintly cynical air. As a junior at Hampton school in Molesey he had rowed internationally in the British youth team in 1968, winning the small final (seventh overall) in the coxless pairs; he had come to Oxford with a big reputation and high hopes.

It is unusual and unwise to put a freshman straight into a 'Varsity crew. The step up from school rowing is deceptively large and the pressures of the heavy increase in training and responsibility are hard for 18- to 19-year-olds. The better bet is a year in the reserve crew Isis, where they can get a full 'dress rehearsal' year for the big event. But sometimes lack of good material at the top requires their early promotion and Andy's size and talent were sorely needed for the 1970 Boat Race. But three defeats in a row had dented his confidence. Just before the third one, in his first year as President, he took his crew out for a traditional dust-up with an eight of Oxford Old Blues a few days before the race. The Old Blues were young, unfit but spry, and in a few short sprints (a gift for the untrained but canny Old Blues) the Blue Boat was beaten and Andy and his crew broke down. Coach Dick Fishlock tried to put them back together again, but they took a hammering from Cambridge, all confidence blown. Yet realistically what could they have done against a Light Blue crew containing five Olympic trialists? Rational reasoning of this nature, however, can play no part in the Boat Race. There are no excuses.

In the 1973 Oxford squad with Andy was a Youth international from Radley, Dave Willis, who had finished fifth in the 1967 coxless fours and fifth in the 1969 eights. He was another young giant with two soul-destroying Boat Race defeats behind him. Paddy Payne, a second Hampton Youth international (ninth in the 1970 eights), with bags of talent and the Australian mature student Mike Magarey had, as freshmen the year before, also shared in the 1972 nine and a half-length humiliation. The American cox, Fred Yalouris from Harvard, steersman that year, was back for a second try too. At Henley Royal Regatta after that 1972 Boat Race, Andy, Dave, Mike and Sam Nevin, a Blue from the 1971 Oxford crew who had rowed in the losing 1972 Isis crew, formed a four to race in the premier coxed event, the Prince Philip Cup. They reached the final and then lost to the visiting Canadians, but here at least was evidence that they did not lack talent or racing spirit. However the Boat Race is not the same thing, and at the start of the 1973 trail, the ingredients that had lost the previous Boat Race were almost the same—but not quite.

What was different that year was not just that there was a new coaching set-up and a new strategy; not just that their anger and frustration was being channelled and used to fuel the new approach; but that a brooding manic power-house in the shape of a large American had arrived from Harvard by way of the stroke seat of the US fifth-placed Olympic coxed four a few months earlier. Dave Sawyier was aggressive, intensely, deeply competitive and a workaholic *par excellence*. His sudden presence in the midst of the homely despondency of the Oxford squad was explosive and positive although he often proved to be disruptive with his relentless, uncompromising approach. The young Englishmen, losing Old Blues, Isis men and freshers alike, were taken aback at first but soon began to respond to his bludgeoning knife-edge attitude. No friendly rivalry with Cambridge here—his view of the opposition reflected mine perfectly and a deep-rooted hatred of the enemy and hunger for battle began to develop within the squad. In many ways as coaches we could not have asked for a better instrument with which to effect our Oxford revival. He played back everything we threw at him, in terms of work, with interest and pretty soon the rest of the crew were emulating him. Inter-squad competition took on a new dimension, and the intensity of it has not really diminished since then. And if some of the lads found it difficult to keep up the pace they did their best not to show it. But it could be seen in their faces and in the increasing sluggishness of their movements in the boat and in the gym and ultimately in their test results. They were stretching themselves beyond their limits.

Clearly, the danger was that Dave would kill off his own team as well as the opposition, especially if he was in the stroke seat—his favourite driving position—with his insatiable hunger for more and more work. But what in fact happened was that the whole crew, so recently humiliated as a squad, went with him and as a unit they became barely controllable. I found myself in the unfamiliar position of having to hold them back, of trying to explain to Dave that some of the others couldn't take the unremitting pressure. They all had to understand the need for rest periods and recovery, that muscles cannot operate as efficiently as the brain always tells them to without rejuvenation. 'They're not letting you coach, Dan', said Chris at one point, when the crew had asked for an extra session. 'You're letting them get away with too much.' But what a crew spirit they were developing and how invigorating it was to be in charge of such a highly strung, unpredictable machine. 'We're being chicken!' cried Dave if ever we cut something from the day's workout. 'We can't go in yet. We're just not getting enough done.' And the crew took up the chorus. 'More work!' they demanded, and it took all the coaches' combined patience and cunning to keep the thing on an even keel.

When I called for rhythm or pace, or if I scheduled a technical outing or a day off, Sawyier would growl his disapproval. No amount of explaining could get the point across, and it was not until the following year as President that he finally got the message and calmed down. 'Less haste more speed', advised the coaches. But to everything he tried, Sawyier had to devote all his energy and attention. He carried things to the extreme; if he didn't, in his book, they weren't worth doing. A hard man to deal with, but rewarding if you found a way through. He was Oxford's greatest asset in 1973 but he created as many problems as he solved and in the end partly contributed to disaster. The coaches also came in for the occasional barbed comment from Sawyier, and he seemed bent on testing, nay unnerving, each new coach early on in their fortnight stint, to establish a sort of ascendancy. He created a tautly-stretched relationship of constant anxiety. 'He was so damned rude', recalls coach George Harris, the most mild mannered of men. 'He would sit reading a book while the coach gave the crew its pre-outing talk. It really was very hard.' George was quite astonished that anyone could behave in such a way. Endlessly questioning, challenging, Dave had no sense of diplomacy or any idea of when to keep quiet. The thing that gave me comfort, though, was that I knew the Harvard coach Harry Parker, one of the world's best, had experienced the same trouble. Freddie Yalouris, our cox, an ex-Harvard man himself, was a valuable source of information on Dave's past record, and the various methods that had been employed to control him.

Intimidating, dedicated, and rude, Sawyier was a confusing contradiction. The coaches found it hard to concentrate on the usual crew briefing while Dave began to carry out a noisy land warm-up; should he be stopped (he was, after all, performing the essential warm-up exercises we required everyone to do before each outing), or should we assume he was listening while he exercised? Always testing like a troublesome child. So sometimes he would be called to attention, while at other times we would let it ride; but the sparring was constantly there – probing for weakness, provoking an outburst of anger. He played on the fact that he was such a powerful weapon in the Oxford armoury and the coaches bit back their irritation and restrained themselves with remarkable patience because everyone recognised that the Oxford revival had to take precedence over personalities. And out on the water, in the boat, David Sawyier was arguably the most powerful human machine the Boat Race had ever seen. Perhaps not the most fluid – or even the most effective – but probably the strongest. On one occasion after a Tideway Scullers fixture in which we were well beaten Sawyier was beside himself with rage. He blamed me for the defeat: 'You've not coached anything before' he ranted, 'and you've only rowed in dog shit crews. You don't know anything.' The crew were very embarrassed and quietly melted away. 'Instead of losing your cool, let's analyse what went wrong' I countered, but he was in full flood and quite irrational. It was some time before he calmed down. Yet despite Dave's belligerent manner Andy Hall never felt threatened by him and the two of them, with Paddy and Fred Yalouris, whose contribution to the squad was very important as a sensible Harvard counterweight, formed a tight-knit, stern clique. It was bracing stuff, and hot to handle, but better that, sparks and all, than a crew of stuffed dummies.

An interesting insight into this complex character who, in common with so many of his stateside compatriots, possessed an urge to explore almost to *extremis* the many facets of his own personality and the possibilities that life has to offer, was his reason for abandoning a promising future as a tennis player. As one of the three best junior players in America he had the ruthless single-minded approach that was guaranteed to take him to the top. But overnight he gave it all up and turned to rowing. Why? Because he hated the one-to-one element of tennis which required you to look your opponent in the eye while you destroyed him. He preferred the team effort of rowing, which did not personalise the competition to the same degree.

For the previous five years, Cambridge had been under the canny tutelage of Lou Barry, the wise Tideway expert with the rumbling gravel voice, a dispenser of well tried wisdom and spiky subjective anecdotes. He was also one of the country's leading coaches and creator of the hugely successful Tideway Scullers school, that loose fraternity of top British scullers which dominated the national rowing scene and represented Great Britain throughout the 'sixties and early

41

'seventies. I rowed on and off for Lou's crews through the 'seventies and I knew his style. He knew mine too, but if you compared the two Boat Race finishing coaches of 1973 you would have had to conclude that it was the story of the cheeky upstart daring to challenge the wily old fox on his own home water. 'Your crew looks very good, Dan', he would tell me with a hint of a smile, and I knew he was sussing out our weaknesses and trying me for any chance slips of the tongue. 'Never misses a trick, that Lou Barry' said the Tideway pundits. 'Lou used to call you a cunning little bastard', Chris Blackwall tells me now. 'But you know the reason you did even better with Cambridge than he did was because Lou was not a Tab. Cambridge never took Lou to their hearts and he was hurt–Janousek too. There was an arrogance there which we also have at Oxford, but which we manage to curb better. At least, we try not to let it spill over into our contact with outside opponents. But Cambridge have upset a lot of people over the years, at home and abroad.'

This year Lou had a strong and heavy Cambridge crew to finish and he knew it: Olympians Mike Hart and David Sturge (a member of my own Henley regatta four in 1970), Chris Baillieu, Steve Tourek and talented college oarsman Mike Webber, plus three men from the winning 1972 reserve crew, Goldie–a tough act to match. How we thought we had a chance, how we managed to persuade ourselves that we could pull it off and how we actually came to the post as real contenders against such a superlative line-up says a lot for our cheek, but a lot more for the massive input of effort, daring and dedication of that 1973 Oxford squad. At Oxford we had the five remaining losing Blues–Hall, Willis, Payne, Magarey, and cox Freddie Yalouris–plus Sawyier. Also there was losing Isis man Steve Irving, and from Westminster school Phil Angier, who had rowed successfully for Leander for three years, although a student at Oxford, and had shunned the Oxford trials. He had tried unsuccessfully for a place in the national Olympic team in 1972. Now in his third year he was ready to try his luck with Oxford. James Ollivant was an Eton Youth international in his first year at University and Dick Westlake was an Oxford college-taught oarsman in his last year. They were the successful eight candidates out of a squad of 40 which in October 1972 set about its training with a will led by a very determined Andy Hall.

The weight training started on the first day for the probables, and the best of the new hopefuls were added as they came to our notice through the University fours and pairs races that took place in the first month of term. We decided to give the squad some early competition and entered them in the long distance single sculling 'Head of the River' races which take place every weekend in and around the Thames Valley, just to gain a little competitive urgency. They didn't shine on the whole, but then it was their first foray into the wider world of national level racing, and true to our new policy we wanted them to bite the bullet–win or lose. We wanted to see them under pressure individually, to see how they reacted weekend after weekend, and to let them gauge their improvement from race to race in these processional timed competitions where they met the same people again and again.

Although the Oxford boys were obviously not fully prepared for them, and sometimes complained like hell, it was still useful for them. In fact very few of the other competitors they faced got in much sculling during the week either, but these races served to maintain competitive interest in an otherwise dull training term, and most importantly, made them think for themselves and taught them better watermanship. Some squad members, particularly the strong ones who were not good scullers, were reluctant to expose themselves in small boats and tried all manner of tricks to avoid participating in these events. But the value derived from the experience, and the fact that they did improve enormously throughout the period paid off in the end. We took them to the national trials at Nottingham as well, throwing them in at the deep end in pairs and fours against Britain's aspiring internationals; and they came out of it well. By the time we were ready to boat two senior trial eights in November it was clear that we had a competent if rough squad.

Press coverage concentrated on Sawyier, but to start with discounted Dark Blue chances until David Maxwell and Richard Clarke pulled out of trials at Cambridge. Yet another new coaching team for Oxford did not inspire confidence amongst the *cognoscenti* of the rowing world. But our good showing at the national squad trials in pairs raised a couple of eyebrows, and a hard fought trials race at Henley at the end of term produced a few guarded words of admiration. Three aggressive trial crews went on show. The senior crews, 'Faith' and 'Hope', were stroked by Phil Angier and the freshman James Ollivant and they raced at 34 over the Henley course and more on a fast stream. The third junior trial, 'Charity', joined in at halfway and promptly caused a clash with the leading crew.

Dave Sawyier was yearning to stroke but he settled in at six behind Angier and Paddy Payne and they won the trial by a length after grabbing an early half-length advantage off the start. Six is possibly where Sawyier should have rowed in the Boat Race itself, where his power would have locked the middle of the boat beautifully and from where he could have galvanised the crew most effectively. But such was his driving ambition and aggression that he intimidated any other stroke and would have done the job of stroking from whichever seat he occupied. In the end it became clear that he would have to lead the crew. He was clearly phenomenal, but rough too, in the way his blade flew about, skying into the air just before the catch and then crashing down and in and through the water in a flash; ugly to watch for purists perhaps, with his rounded back and hint of a bum shove. But if you watched the power of the blade through the water rather than the man himself his effectiveness was obvious. Yet with Olympic trialist Angier and the Blues Payne and Willis with Sawyier in the stern, plus talented newcomers James and Westlake in the bows, the crew could still take only a length from 'Hope'. There had to be some pretty effective pullers in that other boat with the young Ollivant backed by two Isis men, Marsden and Irving, and the two Blues Hall and Magarey. Rendall and Blackett for 'Faith', and Collin, Harris and Dudley for 'Hope' made up the 16 seniors.

Overall there was a marvellous atmosphere of determination and enthusiasm at Henley that day and for the first time it began to look as if we might be able to produce a crew to match the Tabs. Isis, the Oxford reserves, were also facing up to a run of six defeats in a row in the mini-Boat Race against the Cambridge second crew Goldie and the importance of their performance and preparation was stressed in our efforts to build up a strong base to provide a grounding for subsequent years. Chris Blackwall took Isis on as his own personal crusade and in 1975 he produced a superb crew which finally ended Goldie's dominance and set the stage for the run of Oxford successes through the late 'seventies and early 'eighties.

'Jumbo' Edwards came up to those trials and shared in the sense of optimism. But he never got to see the resurgence of the Oxford he so loved and to which he had devoted so much of his life and effort. He died a few days later at the age of 66. Almost all of his rowing had been directed at Oxford, all his experimenting aimed at improving their results, using the crew he was coaching as guinea pigs although not always with success. But there is no doubt that most new developments and innovations in the sport in Britain during the 'fifties and 'sixties emanated from his shed workshop behind the windmill at East Ilsley, not only in terms of training methods but also the technical and mechanical aspects of rowing. His long-suffering but devoted wife Mike endured his passion with great spirit, cooking massive meals for all the crews he trained for so many years. As an oarsman he rowed for Westminster, Christ Church, Oxford, London Rowing Club and Great Britain. In the 1926 Boat Race he passed out during the race but fought his way back into favour during a two-year break from Oxford, winning the Grand and Stewards' for London Rowing Club in 1930 and 1931, and taking gold medals in eights and coxless fours in the 1930 Empire Games. He lost a second Boat Race in 1930, during the depressing years of Cambridge's 13 successive wins, but in 1931 added the Henley Goblets to his other two triumphs (three Henley medals in one day–a unique achievement), and then repeated the feat in 1932. That year he capped his previous successes with gold medals in the Olympic Games in Los Angeles in the pairs and also in the fours where he came in as a last-minute substitute.

'Jumbo' retired from rowing to join the RAF where this eccentric genius distinguished himself in a variety of ways. It was not until well after the war that he was tempted back to the towpath as Oxford's coach in 1949, but again it was an Oxford defeat. He had to wait until 1952 for his first win and thereafter he guided Oxford's fortunes until 1972; coaching 18 Boat Race crews, taking Oxford to the 1960 Olympics, and introducing spade oars, interval training and the doomed 13-foot oars to Britain's backward rowing fraternity. He devised a variety of technical aids to measure boat speed and an oarsman's effectiveness and pioneered the use in this country of the continental rig, Donoratico boats, aerofoil riggers and a host of other innovations, some successful and some not, which kept Britain from falling too far behind the rest of the world in rowing. He wrote a delightful book of memoirs, *The Way of a Man with a Blade* which captured perfectly the essence of the man. If any criticism could be levelled against 'Jumbo' it would be that, from an Oxford point of view, he used the Boat Race crews along with all their hopes and aspirations for his experiments, taking risks with them when caution and a well-tried programme and equipment would have been preferable. A number of good and potentially winning Boat Race crews were sacrificed on the altar of the East Ilsley workbench. Chris Blackwall also wondered whether his deep-rooted Tab fixation might sometimes have had the opposite effect to the one he intended, intimidating his men and causing some of his Oxford crews to fear the Light Blues. However, there is no doubt that 'Jumbo' will be affectionately remembered as one of the great names in British rowing. Without him as an adviser in 1973, we felt a definite vacuum as we continued our build-up to the race.

We disbanded the group for the Christmas break, a month during which it was all too easy to lose the valuable conditioning gained in gym and boat during the term. We issued strict and detailed instructions for a daily vacation training programme which required the men to seek out their nearest gym and boat club, to take a sculling boat from the

Oxford fleet away with them, and to work diligently until we reconvened at Putney a fortnight before the beginning of the following term, a day into the New Year. Everyone was given advance warning that we were going to regard those first two weeks as a make-or-break period, that their selection would depend entirely on how they performed in the various tests we would apply at that training camp, and that they had better turn up on the first day, fit, ready and raring to go because it was going to be the toughest fortnight of their lives. In short, we wanted to drive them into the ground and would select the Oxford eight from the men still standing at the end. Not very scientific perhaps, but we wanted no *poseurs*, only winners. We tried to keep track of their movements during the break, and we also tried to instil in them the idea that no one, Blues included, could expect to coast into the 1973 Blue Boat. The policy was no late arrivals, everyone treated equally and judged purely on merit, no semi-reserved seats for Blues or friends of the President. Blues back for their second or third Boat Race were and still can be notoriously difficult to manage. They had often been disruptive and arrogant in the past, challenging the authority of the President, their peer, at every turn, convinced of their own talent and not prepared to work as hard as they had done in the year when they were first fighting for a seat. Often this was not overt but there was still a subconscious slackening of effort–'I've done this before so I'm halfway there'–which was just as dangerous in the final analysis as the more obvious 'throw me out if you dare' approach.

Happily this attitude has pretty well disappeared in recent years, because every crew member now knows he has to fight for his place every time, but it always threatens to re-emerge. Of course there have at times been genuine anxieties about work, and pressure from tutors, which have resulted in a rower deciding initially not to put himself forward for trials but then subsequently changing his mind. Other experienced men have been dragged out of early retirement dangerously late in the day to bring desperately needed strength to a crucial seat in the boat. These are difficult decisions to make, not only because the latecomer will certainly be behind in his training, but also because they can undermine the confidence of the rest of the squad in the system, all of whom have trained diligently only to see that final seat taken–no, stolen–by someone who was not initially in the running. These decisions are not taken lightly but they can mean the difference between winning and losing. Such situations happen rarely, but if they do it is essential to establish beyond doubt the sincerity of the man who is returning late. There is no room for the loafer who reckons to sit it out for the first term, and maybe even that gruelling January fortnight, without training, knowing that the squad is struggling to find men of the necessary calibre, and then to pitch up at the last possible moment.

In retrospect I think that I was probably guilty of that subconscious easing back during training for my second Boat Race in 1968 when we lost. I vowed never to let that attitude creep back in again while I was coaching. It meant close monitoring throughout the year, and it meant keeping a still closer watch on those returning Blues who tried to trade on their acknowledged abilities by horse-bargaining their commitment: 'I've got so much work; my tutors don't want me to row this term.' 'I reckon I could swing it with work for the beginning of next term if I keep myself fit.' We knew all the excuses. In 1973 there was none of that. No one had any reason to be complacent.

However a month on their own over Christmas could do untold damage to our preparations if they failed to follow the vacation programme of work. It would be plain to see who had skived by the way they performed during those first couple of days back in training at the beginning of January, and they would ultimately jeopardise their chance of selection for the final Blue Boat; and of course that would hardly help us to win the Boat Race. We could not afford to lose a single one of our trialists and we reiterated our call for unstinting application. The first two weeks of January became for Oxford the crucial and decisive period of training. We eschewed our carefully learned knowledge of modern principles in physiological training methods for a more basic blood-and-guts approach. It was an unprecedented workload – four sessions a day, two on water in sculling boats and eights plus a morning run and evening gym session – all with the emphasis on inter-squad cut-throat rivalry. Forget the niceties of technique – the raw battle was on for a seat in the Blue Boat, no holds barred. We wanted to throw that do-or-die element into the ring – no softening, no compromise. We let it be known that we would be watching their every move. It was an endurance test *par excellence*.

Within a few days, President Andy Hall and engine-room certainty Dave Willis, with two and three Boat Races behind them, were dropped down into the 'B' crew for the afternoon trial eights outing. Their results in individual tests during those first couple of days just did not measure up and we felt obliged to stick to the principles we had so recently tried to establish and on which we were basing the new approach. But at the same time it was a tough decision to take, not just because we risked rebellion – and the ire of our employer, the dropped President, Andy – and the sack but because we also risked the loss of Andy's confidence in us as coaches and ultimately, and more importantly, the loss of the squad's confidence in their President and chief coach. It was a risk, though, that had to be taken if we hoped to break out of the losing mould and fan the flames of the Oxford revival. Here was the key: fight or flight – how would they react? They both rowed in the second eight that afternoon burning with shame and resentment, their efforts and commitment rudely questioned and exposed. Both heads spun with speeding and conflicting thoughts, self-justification, their egos rejecting the slur on their reputations, yet analysing too their recent performances, planning their responses. Their lacklustre work in the gym, in the running races and most pertinently in the inter-squad sculling Head race earlier in the day had dumped them out of the top eight. Swapping them over with Ian James (an Oxford-taught oarsman) and Richard Westlake resulted in the 'B' crew going four lengths slower over seven minutes than the day before, when the two crews had raced level. The evidence was cruelly apparent.

Four 400-metre running races were scheduled for the evening land session after the outing on the water. The squad was grouped into waves of six, with Chris starting them outside the London Rowing Club, our training base for the fortnight, while I took the finishing times and order at Beverley Brook, a quarter of a mile along the towpath. Andy Hall, not normally known for his running ability, won each of his races in convincing style, spurred beyond fatigue by his anger. As he finished each one he spat out a curse at me – 'you fucking bastard', 'I'll show you, you shit-face'; but Dave just went through the motions, trotting disdainfully a long way behind the pack of racing colleagues, already decided in his own mind that he was not going to tolerate such treatment. Within a couple of days Andy had battled his way back to his rightful position near the top of the squad and never looked back, while Dave resigned and returned to Oxford to concentrate on his degree. He was sadly missed, but it was a test that all of us had to face. Dick Westlake won his place while Ian James came very close to unseating Andy Hall. But experience finally told, and the rejuvenated President improved so convincingly that he soon took over the all-important six seat. Ian James stroked Isis but his disappointment at not making the Blue Boat unfortunately kept him out of rowing thereafter.

They were difficult days, but the self-confidence and stature of the group grew markedly, and when the two crews were finalised a few weeks later, there were no arguments, no surprises. Everyone could see where they stood. The seat racing, the sculling races and the dreaded ergometer had seen to that. It is only by looking back over the 12 years of records of those January fortnights that the sheer blood, sweat and tears emerge, and no one fortnight more so than that first one because it was so much more brutal than anything that had gone before. Seeing those test results, the xeroxed notes of exhortation that we passed round to the squad in that first year reminds me of how desperate and intense it was for all of us, and how nerve-racking too, because it was all untried and could so easily have gone wrong. Later it became easier because we and the squad men knew that it did work. And possibly, because we were on a winning streak, the pressure might indeed have eased a little too—a dangerous development. But the pain and effort of those early days leap out from the cold lists of statistics fleshed out by pencilled notes and asterisks which tell the fuller story.

The simple notes that 'Innes sank', 'Plunkett boat broke in half' or 'Evans hit police buoy' conceal tales of dangerous icy moments in a mid-winter Thames, the sudden initial shock of submerging followed by a desperate hanging on to a broken or swamped boat waiting for help; or struggling frozen for the shore caught in the grip of a fast moving tide. An arrow on a rough sheet of results directing my name above Sawyier's into second place in one domestic sculling Head recalls an intense rivalry between us as Sawyier's sculling improved by leaps and bounds through those early months from complete novice to very good senior class. A mistake in the timing calculations had put him three seconds ahead for a while; then it was corrected. In recent squads such a small change—especially since I was not even in the team—would mean nothing, but in those highly-charged days it resulted in demands for a recount, arguments and calls for a re-row.

In recent years experienced men have wheedled out of some tests like the running and the sculling, which has undermined overall attitudes a little. But again different squads need different stimuli and members change. Sawyier had by sheer force of character and tenacity overtaken the whole squad bar Sam Nevin with just a couple of months sculling experience. His presence was continuous proof of what could be done with the right mental application. The endless lists of weight lifting maximums, ergometer results, running, sculling and seat racing results and gym tests detail statistically the huge amount of work the squad did, and still does, and the amount of trouble we went to to make sure they knew that the work was being noticed, logged and analysed and that ultimately it was going to win them the Boat Race. To record too closely now those work programmes might give the game away a little, although I doubt that the Cambridge schedules are much different. But there are special quirks and extras, and the mix of them, which seem to work well for us.

During my endless drives along the motorway to Oxford from London to coach the squad I invariably work on these results and scores, precariously balancing notepad and calculator against the steering wheel, which I hold steady with my knee when I need two hands to make notes. On one or two occasions I have built up a strong head of steam when I have been worried that dangerous complacency might be creeping into the squad or that we might be falling behind in our training. I have prepared the warning words I intend to say when I arrive, getting more and more het up in the isolation of the car, driving more and more erratically as I scribble furiously. Luckily the narrower winding roads after the motorway prove distracting enough to force me to slow down and concentrate more on the driving than on the squad, who are usually spared the full flood of ire when we finally gather for the pre-outing chat.

The tension generated by Sawyier was never more oppressive than in the ergometer room at the Amateur Rowing Association head-quarters in Hammersmith. One after the other the Oxford squaddies clambered aboard the intimidating contraption, a sweep oar rowing machine which measures total work output, the consistency of that work, the weak points of each man during the whole workout and within each stroke, the length of each stroke and *it's* consistency over a seven-minute test against a predetermined resistance. All the ingredients are there to minutely observe the flagging oarsman's performance, nerve-rackingly exposed for all to see—his coach, his colleagues, himself. The oarsmen feared the ergometer; the burning muscles, the throbbing pain in the chest. The very way one performed on the ergo, regardless of the result, was revealing. How one kept one's form, how much under strain one looked, how strong. There was even a mirror there in front of you so you could monitor how you appeared during each stroke. 'Do my crewmates feel confident in me as they watch me now?' 'Does it show how godawful I'm feeling?—and I'm only halfway there.' I've seen rowers collapse on the machine, fall off it, act out exhaustion, exaggerating the effects to impress, call out 'No, I can't', turn blue in the lips, stop short of the finish and burst into tears. It is such an uncompromising machine and ultimately you have only yourself to beat. Paddy Payne was one man psyched out by the 'erg'. He was due to go on last and had watched all the others hard at work. He panicked. Halfway through he cried out to stop, his rating dropped, and he struggled to pull the infernal handle through. He was roused by encouraging yells, regained his stroke and in fact his score was not too bad, but the sight of one of the top men in the squad in such a state of stress had quite a sobering effect on the rest of the squad. Fortunately, Paddy was able to recover his confidence, but it was a shock to him.

The ergometer may be a test dreaded by some oarsmen (although as they become more acquainted with it and use it for training purposes without the pressure of test conditions, they lose their fear) but it does provide for the coaches, in addition to valuable detailed scientific readings of their strengths, a fine close-up view of how the men react and perform under pressure in comparison with each other, alone and uncushioned by the protective shroud of seven crewmates in a boat. Rowing an eight may be the ultimate in team sports but you have to be sure, too, that the individual parts excel on their own. Only then can they inspire confidence in each other to produce what will in the end be a far more effective and co-ordinated machine.

To Sawyier, the ergo was like a red rag to a bull. This was for him the ultimate macho test to find the strong man of rowing. He wanted it so badly. Top man on the ergometer in the British national team was the 1969 Oxford Blue and new member of the Oxford coaching team, Hugh Matheson, and Sawyier rose to the challenge. Matheson's score was as alive to Sawyier as if the man himself had been lining up alongside him to race. He sat in a corner of the dilapidated changing-room in which the testing was to take place, rocking back and forth, a menacing frame of coiled, taut muscle. No one dared approach him, no one chanced to speak to him to break his concentration. The others tiptoed around and spoke in whispers as they prepared themselves for their own tests. At the other end of the long changing-room, Chris Blackwall and I called encouragement and information to the oarsmen on the machine, one after the other, providing each one with ratings, stroke lengths, elapsed time and snap evaluations of their progress as they worked. They pushed along hard and well, but no one was in any doubt that we were all in for something outstanding. Dave was next on, and he was warming up, a model of the single-minded athlete preparing himself for a supreme effort and a vivid lesson to the younger oarsmen gathered round trying to look nonchalant and busy with other things while covertly awaiting the moment. Without a word he got on the machine, made himself comfortable and asked for a rating as he rowed an easy warm-up minute. Then he was ready. 'Okay, let's go.'

He was quite electrifying. The machine jerked and shuddered as Sawyier went off at a suicidal rate of 43 strokes a minute before settling to 39, five pips above the usual and recommended pace. His extraordinary power had never been more in evidence than now in close-up as he drove on, never straying from his metronomic beat. It really was quite a performance. The boys could no longer conceal their awe. He never flagged, never dropped his rate. His stroke length and his power output showed scant fall off, and he became the top performer in Britain for 1973. There was no masking his pleasure and pride when his fellow squad men broke into spontaneous applause. They were glad Dave Sawyier was in their camp.

However, they still found his unrelenting manner quite trying at times. Often during a break in practice he would turn round in the stroke seat to face the crew sitting behind him and berate them unmercifully about everything ranging from laziness through lack of commitment to incompetence. On one outing at Henley against a talented Eton crew, the schoolboys had managed to hold Oxford off by sneaking close to the bank out of a very strong head stream while the 'Varsity crew struggled in the thick of the flow. Almost as if it were calculated to fuel their frustration, I was subbing in the Eton crew for their sick seven man. 'Gosh, thank you, Sir!' said their delighted captain when we had finished. Afterwards Sawyier was furious and ranted at his crewmates for what he saw as their lack of guts. 'This crew is pussy; you guys just don't know how to work. We're not fit.' Then he turned on his heel and headed towards the hillside at the back of the Leander Club where he proceeded to run up and down it over and over, a lone distant figure pounding up a 45-degree slope, watched from the Leander garden by his confused and hurt crew. They gazed in despair at their incensed guru for a while and then made their way disconsolately to the showers, for once refusing in silent agreement to be goaded into trying to match his crazed obsessiveness. They were dressed and ready to leave when he finally returned panting and sweating, and they waited patiently while he showered in silence. Fortunately he had worked off his ire, but it was a warning light; he was like a wild animal that demanded careful handling. He had somehow to be brought under control. For six months crew and coaches lived on a tightrope.

Each year a Boat Race crew, and perhaps even the whole initial squad as well, would develop its own distinctive style and character, different from year to year, sometimes as a group, sometimes dominated by the presence of one or two strong personalities, not always necessarily the President. Within the crew, too, definite roles existed into which members would fall or be cast, sometimes consciously sometimes not, but often complementing each other within the crew line-up; the leader, the joker, the scapegoat, the whiner, the fall guy, the thicko, the rock. Nicknames took root quickly—the Filth (Cambridge), Lard, Noddy, Ron the Projectionist, Normie, the 'Stick With Yer Mates' crew, Jacker, P.G., Worm, the Substitute Filth (Goldie), Squeaky, Musclemouth, Moron, Woodpecker, Bazza, Stig, Scrot, Top Pork, Lumpy, Marmite, Half-wit, Jobber, E. Lime, Shaky, Rosie, Angle Dangle, Mean Man, Barryphone, Bonbons, BBK. In 1973 the dominant character was Sawyier. As coaches both Chris Blackwall and I respected the man's potent power and determination, and we recognised in him the bloody-minded self-centred personality that creates winners. But we felt like sacking him or walking out at times, and Chris more than once threatened to resign. There we were, trying to feel our way gently into the job in our first year out of school so to speak, and we had to be dealt the Sawyier card straight off. Hackles rose often as we stood on dignity, feathers ruffled, while trying to establish ourselves in the roles of guiding lights instilling confidence and attempting all the time to control his more excessive outbursts. It was a baptism of fire, but subsequently over the years we have been confronted with equally taxing problems of different complexion, since no Boat Race preparation has ever gone smoothly.

The transatlantic influence was always an interesting addition to an Oxbridge crew. As post-graduates usually, they were a little older than the just-out-of-school undergraduates who populated most of the crews on the reaches of the Cam and Isis, and they startled the youngsters with their unrestrained pushiness and confidence. Some had rowed at American, Australian or Canadian colleges before coming to Britain, and one or two had even represented their respective countries, but more importantly they brought an extra maturity to the crews they rowed in. They also introduced a far more basic and outrageous lavatorial student humour which quite horrified the post-pubescent English boys. 'Mooning' or 'bare-assing' and 'grossing' crossed the Atlantic too and became part of the 'Varsity rowers' vocabulary. However, Sawyier entered into none of that. His influence was of an entirely different nature but no less effective. One of the new regime innovations inspired by him was seat racing, which we only toyed with in 1973. But in 1974 and thereafter it became integral to our selection process.

Seat racing, which we do at Henley in two coxed fours, involves a series of precisely monitored three-minute races over the Royal Regatta course exchanging rivals for a seat back and forth to see who makes the boat go faster. It is a gruelling affair and there is something very final about it; an oarsman feels desperately exposed and isolated as he is plucked from one boat and swapped with his opposite number in the rival boat. His team-mates can do nothing to help him since they too could be called upon to seat race at any moment. So everyone is pulling at maximum strength. Too much seat racing can set antagonisms alight within the squad as tensions grow, but there is no doubt that it sorts out the boat movers from the pretenders, the efficient operators from the boat stoppers, the strong from the weak. After surviving all the

January fortnight tests, those four daily sessions of work, and the three months before Christmas, failure at this last but crucial hurdle is a cruel blow.

The seat racing adheres to the following formula: two coxed fours are boated, stroked by two already selected men who are charged with the task of maintaining a set rating and pattern over a three-minute race to allow the men who are being seat raced behind them to function at their best and to cut out as many variables as possible. Thus the coxwains, too, are told to follow exactly the same course for each race. The three oarsmen behind each stroke are not told which pair or pairs are being tested thus ensuring maximum effort from all of them throughout the session. They are then set to race downstream and back, the starting and finishing distances between the two boats being precisely measured, after which two men are asked to swap seats in mid-stream, and the process is repeated, swapping other pairs, but establishing after each group of races how much each oarsman improves or impedes the pace of the boats. Heads are on the block and any failings are brutally shown up. Sometimes there is little to choose between two men and in 1976 freshman John Wiggins and Isis man Paul Wright endured 32 seat races with just a few feet gained either way each time. In the end the choice between them had to be based on instinct and coaching 'nous'–but not before all possible means of separating them had been exhausted.

A couple of years later, Ges Atherton, a big strong likeable man, who had rowed two years in Isis, looked to be certain of a place in the Blue Boat. No one expected little Phil Head, a lightweight from Hampton school with one leg shorter than the other, to offer a serious challenge. Yet Phil twice took one and a half lengths off Ges. His chance of winning a Blue gone forever, Ges dropped out of the squad, not prepared to row in what looked likely to be a weak Isis crew for a third year.

Besides determining the best men, seat racing is also an excellent form of training–the races so absorbing, the quality of work so good that a tremendous amount of good intensive rowing is achieved without the rowers themselves being quite aware of how much they are doing. Their concentration is high, far higher than for a normal training session. It also forces them to adapt quickly to new seat orders and it does wonders for crew cohesiveness at short notice. All in all a fine exercise; but the oarsmen involved hate it because it is so intense and so much depends on the results. The seats on trial in 1974 were as usual in the bows. Steve Irving, who had twice rowed for Isis, had provided sufficient proof of his worth in earlier tests, as had Sawyier, Andy Hall

54

and Paddy Payne. So too had the Blue Mike Magarey, a hard-nosed Australian who, though rough, was very effective and Phil Angier, the quiet, intelligent, single-minded man who had preferred to row at Leander during his first two years at Oxford, winning the Thames Cup at Henley. Angier's excellent showing in the 1972 scullers Head of the River race (fifth out of 325) proved that he was good value for his 12 stone and he consequently won a place at four in the crew. A sound and determined man to have in any crew who thrived on hard work. James Ollivant and Dick Westlake had to fight off challenges for the two bow seats from Ian James, Paul Marsden and Dave Rendel. Westlake, James and Rendel had all learned to row at Oxford during the previous two years, while Ollivant's experience with Eton gave him the edge. Freddie Yalouris was facing his second Boat Race as cox, and knowing Dave Sawyier, the likely strokeman, from their Harvard days gave him a big advantage since they would be working closely together.

Painstaking selection by merit and obvious commitment to the cause by coaches and crew inspired the new-look Oxford. We began to seek out good opposition against whom we could test ourselves. We drew up a series of fixtures against the best crews in the country. Wily Lou Barry, who was in charge of Cambridge for the sixth time, had again closeted the Light Blues with the star British crew, his own Tideway Scullers. It was on a diet of regular tussles with them throughout their five-year winning streak that Cambridge had cut their teeth and developed their racing edge. However in 1973 the Scullers were facing a challenge to their supremacy from the fledgling British national squad trained by Bohumil (Bob) Janousek, a top international coach recently recruited from Czechoslovakia. Bob's Munich Olympic team had clawed British rowing back into international reckoning by dint of a complete and ambitious overhaul of our domestic rowing scene. First he had to learn English, during which time he also found out a bit about the British character and our supremely amateur approach to sport. Then he turned the whole system on its head, shook it about (upsetting top coaches Lou Barry, Alan Watson of London University, and the rest of the establishment in the process) and continued during the next five years to prod Britain back to the top of the international scene with silver, bronze and gold medals in eights, fours, pairs and double sculls in World and Olympic Championships. Between 1974 and 1981, although Janousek retired from the forefront in 1976, Britain held third or fourth position in the world rankings and was widely acknowledged as the best in the West. Bob was aided and abetted in this resurgence by the ex-Cambridge Blue Mike Sweeney who, incensed at the unfair selection procedures which left him out of the 1968 Olympic team, got himself elected as Chairman of Selectors and ensured that all deserving oarsmen would in future be justly served. We, the competitors, responded eagerly.

As a result of the success of the national squad, the Scullers had lost a couple of their best men to Janousek, but more important Lou's boys were now being faced by a united national team training to a tougher and more scientific regime. At Oxford we were picking up the theme tune laid down by Janousek and adapting his methods to our needs. If I could not have the Scullers for friendly matches then I wanted Leander, the University of London and the national team so I set up fixtures with them in order of increasing severity. We had to learn what we were up against. The fact that we were training for a side-by-side race gave us a slight advantage against most other crews who were preparing for a processional timed race also in March – the Tideway Head of the River Race – over the same Boat Race course in reverse. They were often a little less advanced in their preparations since they were geared more to a summer season of competition. But the training that they were doing was essentially the same as ours, derived as it was from the Janousek master-plan. And of course they were all experienced racers. We were novices by comparison. Oxford, however, came out fighting, and surprised everyone when they acquitted themselves well.

Before Christmas the letter pages of *The Times* had been sprinkled with frustrated Oxford supporters bemoaning the demise of their University's rowing prowess, offering all sorts of reasons and cures. 'Wake up Oxford' ran one headline in *Rowing* magazine. The apparent growing lack of interest in the Boat Race perceived as a result of Cambridge's continued dominance was worrying both journalists and *aficionados* of the sport. But by February it was quietly being noticed that Oxford had rowed against more real talent in two months than all their recent predecessors put together, and what is more they were winning.

Our first major test was against the highly fancied University of London whose trials before Christmas had been reckoned a definite cut above the Oxbridge ones. We had planned a series of short pieces on the Saturday and a couple of seven-minute races on the Sunday morning. Paddling up to meet the opposition, Oxford looked anxious and rough, finding difficulty in the rolling water of the Tideway. UL by comparison looked spot-on and ready to go. But Oxford narrowly won the first encounter and then all the subsequent ones by ever-increasing margins. As their confidence grew, so their rowing improved and by the end of the weekend we knew we were a crew to be reckoned with. To press home the point we beat UL in a three-mile running race as well when fog delayed the Sunday morning encounter on the water. Two weeks later we returned to the Tideway for a full course trial into a headwind and on a barely moving tide recorded a respectable time of 19 minutes 2 seconds, despite an exhausting series of 2000-metre rows two days earlier. It was a good fighting row at 34 with better technique too. Kingston came with us for the first seven minutes, starting on the inside of the first bend, but were three lengths behind at the mile and five down when Molesey took over at Harrods for the next seven-minute leg. They dropped out at the Bandstand four lengths in arrears and Kingston's second crew took us home with Sawyier driving past at 36 to the line one and a half lengths up. They showed great spirit throughout, particularly in the last mile where a crew three-quarters into a full course is usually easy game for any club or school crew. That the Oxford crew charged by the Kingston boys told reams about their fitness and wonderfully aggressive panache.

Cambridge nervously reshuffled their crew, and in a calculated piece of brinkmanship I challenged Lou to put his Tideway Scullers crew against us for a full course. A week earlier against Cambridge, they had rowed two six-minute races, winning the first but losing the second by one and a half lengths. I suppose it was the sheer cheek that made Lou accept the challenge, allied to the desire to unseat our threat to his Cambridge crew as early as possible. And of course the smell of a battle appealed to his competitive instincts. Whatever his reasons, ours were clear; we needed more proof, more ego-boosting competition. When the day arrived we were hampered by illness and were rowing a substitute. But then the Scullers had their problems too since they were rowing in a borrowed boat. Within seconds of the start, Sawyier's seat jammed and immediately Oxford trailed by a length. A violent tug released the seat and, undaunted, they set off in pursuit. Rowing with tremendous power, it took them three minutes to draw level. By four minutes they were past and away, stretching out more with every stroke, striding and running with the exhilaration of knowing they were taking the crew that had matched Cambridge only a week before. How their rowing improved stroke by stroke, and how their confidence and crew maturity blossomed in those 19 minutes. They were within three seconds of the course record at the Mile Post, and as they raced on into the headwind to Mortlake they left the Scullers 23 seconds or seven lengths behind.

However not everyone was impressed with Oxford's new look. Ted Phelps, my old coach, and the man who had for years guided 'Jumbo' Edwards and other coaches along the Tideway as Oxford's professional adviser, was very dismissive about the current crews in general and Oxford – 'a crew in a hurry' – in particular. Ted had been professional sculling champion of the world in 1930 and had coached the Uruguayan national team while they were under the influence of British Government representative Eugene Millington-Drake, an Oxford Blue and hero of the River Plate. Later Ted coached the sculler Bob Pearce to Diamond and Olympic wins, and after the war he joined the Oxford coaching team as an employed adviser. Since Ted had taught me all I knew about sculling while I was a boy at Westminster, I had asked him to help with Oxford's technique during the January fortnight but he had declined, although he was seldom short of biting criticism. He was scathing about the standard of modern rowing, and blamed it on the new amateur coaches, me included, although he was too polite to say so to my face. Every time I asked him what he thought he started with the same thing: 'You've got to get back to basics' and after a while it got depressing. He never seemed to have a good word to say, but even so much of his advice did rub off on me.

On many occasions, I had to defend the new aggressive Oxford approach in long arguments with him over several pints at the London Rowing Club bar. The crew lacked poise, he said, it lacked rhythm, it lacked run, it lacked timing. 'They've got no finishes, no beginnings, no length', he went on as my heart sank. 'Their slide control is awful.' He told me that in his opinion they were chasing ratings for ratings' sake instead of learning to row properly. 'Throw away your stopwatch and teach them to row' he counselled; 'forget about ratings and get them on the tank.' 'I'm taking them on the tank, Ted,' I protested, 'but they also have to learn to be much tougher racers.'

Ted was not alone in thinking that we were working them too hard. The Press expressed their doubts as well. But that particular crew thrived on the tough diet and if their technique looked a bit rough round the edges, it was a sacrifice we were prepared to make if it meant that we had a more mentally hardened team to work with. But still Ted wanted us to concentrate on the basics. 'Teach them to relax on the way forward. They're wasting too much energy. They're short in and out of the water, and they're not pulling their weight.' And having torn my crew to shreds he left me with the words that were to echo in my ears after the race: 'Rough conditions are no excuse. You've got to teach them to be better watermen.' It was their fear, or more to the point Sawyier's dislike, of rough water that was to prove a major factor in the iminent race.

But with three weeks to go to the Boat Race Oxford's tails were up and they were flying. The Reading Head of the River always provides us with a good test under racing conditions against some good opposition just before we move to the Tideway, and this year Leander were defending the title with a crew full of current internationals. They were the top crew of the moment, the embryo national eight, and were tipped to take the Tideway Head title the following week from Lou Barry's Scullers, who had enjoyed a nine-year reign. At Reading we failed to catch them by six seconds – less than two lengths over the 13-minute course – but we were well on target, and left Goldie, the Cambridge second crew, 20 seconds back and London University with their crew of internationals 17 seconds behind. If there had been any sign of arrogance or dangerous complacency creeping into the Oxford camp before Reading, their defeat by Leander knocked it on the head. They, I, all of us wanted to be the best in the country; second was last in our book and we did not wear defeat graciously. We wanted a return match. Oxford were straining at the leash and it was my job to hold them back, a task I did not enjoy, since I too was anxious to prove to ourselves and to the world how good we were, what winners we were after so many years as also-rans. We wanted to grab every possible opportunity to show what we were made of. But we also had to consider their overall preparation for the Boat Race. The dangers of staleness and over-conditioning had to be taken into account. After much negotiating, Leander agreed to race us twice over six minutes on the Tideway on the Tuesday evening, ten days before the Boat Race. It was very late for us, but we had to accommodate their office-hour commitments. Luckily they were as eager as we were for a side-by-side test. It would also be a good sharpener for them before the big weekend Tideway Head of the River Race where they hoped to depose the Scullers. The rivalry was intense between the hardened professional squad men and the upstart students. Oxford needed to be put in their place.

As night began to fall the crews lined up, their bows running level for the 'go'. It was a titanic struggle, every inch desperately fought for. Oxford's racing spirit was tested to the full and was not found wanting. Both times the more experienced and talented crew from Leander stole a three-quarter length lead off the start and each time Oxford held them and then proceeded to pull them back, stroke by heart-bending stroke, inch by inch. And on both occasions Sawyier edged the Dark Blue nose in front at the line. The crew just would not give in, and Andy Hall, Mike, Paddy, all of them, brought everything they had to offer to bear on that contest. Their pride, their hopes against Cambridge, their very lives depended on it. And they did not fail. 'After five years in the wilderness', wrote Desmond Hill in the *Telegraph* next morning, 'Oxford must, if only temporarily, be favourites for the Boat Race . . .'. 'The three Blues in the boat were unrecognisable from the year before', wrote another correspondent. 'How they fight, those Oxford boys!' added a third. The mutual respect between the two crews hung over the black water as they thanked each other for the fight. 'Good luck in the Boat Race', called one of the squad men as Oxford turned and paddled off into the darkness towards Putney, heads held high, the boat running beautifully between the strokes. They had arrived.

We were now tempted to take on the rest of the country in the Tideway Head of the River Race at the weekend. It was a timed processional race, the country's biggest sporting event until the introduction of the city marathons, with nearly 4000 competitors. Crews started at ten-second intervals, and we reckoned the race could replace our full-course trial which we had pencilled in for Thursday; here we would have every crew in the country as our pacemakers. What better final test? The idea appealed to our collective extrovert nature not least because no other Boat Race crew had ever competed in this race before the 'Varsity match. Now here was a chance of winning it–or at least of coming very close–and at the same time putting paid to all those uninformed critics who sought so often to denigrate the standard of the Boat Race crews. The crew wanted to do it, I wanted to do it, but was it the wisest strategy in the light of our highest priority–to beat Cambridge? There were many disadvantages as well. It was after all only a week before the Boat Race and a poor showing could do untold damage to morale with little time left to restore confidence. On top of that there were so many things that could go wrong. With over 400 crews jostling for position at the start, a clash and an accident was a very real possibility. There was the danger, too, of racing the crew too much, taking the edge off them. They had to be hungry for Cambridge, and a race such as this could distract them from their main purpose.

Outsiders were advising us to take the pressure off, not to work the crew too hard in the final build-up, to concentrate instead on the fine tuning. But we in the Oxford camp in that year of 1973 could not turn down a scrap and the Tideway Head, with all the top British crews represented, beckoned invitingly. Besides Oxford had a good starting position of ninth where Isis had finished the year before and it placed them well to challenge for the Headship. Indeed, to add extra incentive, if such a thing be needed, I myself would be starting one place ahead of Oxford in the Tideway Scullers third crew, coached of course by Lou Barry, and rowing with Chris Rodrigues, one of the Cambridge coaches, and Lou's two sons, Pat and Bill, both experienced internationals. Starting in front of Scullers III would be Goldie. It was a gamble but how could we resist? Although we decided early in the week that Oxford would take part we kept the news to ourselves to keep the opposition guessing. We did not want unforseen reactions to our decision to undermine our plans. The newspapers got wind of the possibility early on but we managed to keep Dark Blue intentions secret until the moment the crew went afloat on the Saturday with their starting number displayed on the bows. All week the rowing correspondents had pleaded for a decision so that they could write up their predictions, but they finally had to go to press with stories full of ifs and buts, provisos and let-out clauses.

I was rowing at seven in Scullers III behind Pat Barry, the stroke, with Bill Barry behind me at six when Oxford came steaming up behind us at the halfway point, inexorably eating away the ten-second starting interval. We were going well and had also closed on the crews in front, and our cox, Tony Wisdom, the frizzy-haired little venereologist to whom the rowing world took all their problems when not afloat, was determined not to lose any ground. 'Move over Tony, let them through!' I shouted as the Oxford bow ball came sneaking up looking for a way past. 'Stay where you are', growled Bill threateningly from behind me. I was desperate for the Oxford boys to have a clear run even if it meant losing a little ground for my own crew, but the Barrys were having none of it. A comic battle broke out between us as we rowed along at full pressure, with Pat and Bill cursing me as I tried to get Tony to move over a bit, out of the best stream, worth a couple of seconds at the most, to let the Oxford cox, Fred Yalouris, steer through on the fastest water. Poor Tony, he was damned if he did and damned if he didn't. Yalouris went tight on the corner under Hammersmith Bridge, forced us out a bit and in a few strokes they were gone. I yelled a few fruity expletives as they passed to send them on their way. As my Scullers crew neared the finish, catching up Goldie and Leander's second crew along the Putney Boathouses, Oxford were nowhere to be seen. In fact after taking us they had stormed past Goldie, who had been pressing Cambridge in practice only days before, Leander II and Thames Tradesmen to finish second, just five seconds or one and a half lengths adrift of Leander I, who had deposed the Tideway Scullers first crew from their perch at last.

Oxford had proved themselves a quality crew, however, and thank God they did, because without that fine result we would have had little evidence to show the world that we had indeed achieved much of what we had set out to do back in October. It was a strong performance and proved our staying power over the second half of the course. If

Cambridge had been banking on rowing us down after halfway with their half-a-stone a man weight advantage, our Tideway Head result would make them think again. In fact I don't think the Tabs were thinking all that much about us during those few days. They had had more than their fair share of problems since arriving on the Tideway. Illness and injury had struck the crew with Steve Tourek, their number seven, out for a number of days and President Chris Baillieu damaging his back in one of the few hard pieces of work they managed to do during their fortnight. They had to forego a full-course trial and most competitive tuning-up work and it was not until the Wednesday night before the race, with Baillieu declared fit, that they took on a makeshift Tideway Scullers crew rowing three Cambridge Old Blue substitutes for a bridger – Hammersmith to Putney – and took four lengths off them. It was an excellent row and must have restored their confidence after a very harrowing week. But then confidence was not the same problem with them that it had been for us. We had needed to prove ourselves over and over to wipe out the awful spectre of those preceding five sad years. By the middle of the week, the stage was set at last for an absorbing and evenly matched Boat Race.

We had had a little injury problem ourselves. Steve Irving had hurt his back and as fate would have it I took him to the same specialist that Chris Baillieu was to visit a day later. We had hoped not to reveal our difficulties, and with treatment, Steve had not had to miss any outings although the journalists did notice that he was rowing awkwardly. 'It must be the new rigger we put on yesterday' we suggested when *The Times'* correspondent asked about it. 'The pitch can't be quite right.' All was revealed however when Baillieu returned from the doctor to announce that his back was getting better and was certainly no worse than that of the Oxford oarsman who had been treated the day before.

Apart from that our Tideway fortnight went by without a hitch. Two Old Blue Presidents, Duncan Clegg and Miles Morland, who were contemporaries of mine, invited the crew for a sumptuous dinner in a leading club soon after our arrival in London. It was a welcome gesture of support. Our rented house in Barnes was ideal; it was light and airy, with a garden, a dining-room, a sitting-room and enough bedrooms to sleep two men to a room. With his girlfriend Rosie and Paddy's sister Rosemarie to help, architect Piers, our spectacular chef, produced huge, colourful meals three times a day for a ravenous crew. We had a couple of semi-formal dinners early in the fortnight, one for a small gathering of venerable old Old Blues like the adored Gully Nickalls, the Bishop of London Gerald Ellison, and the huge Seb Earl along with some younger Old Blues including Ronnie Howard, Dick Fishlock and Ian Elliot, who had coached Oxford crews in the past. Also a regular visitor was Harry Freeman, our team doctor, a garrulous, heavy-smoking, pink-cheeked story-teller held in great affection by many generations of Oxford crews, all with tales to tell of Harry's outrageous outpourings and some of his more dubious ministrations. The journalists came on another night, which provided the crew with a chance to get their own back for the reports they considered deeply wounding to their collective pride. Every day the crew and indeed Boat Race crews every year would avidly read the morning reports by the late Desmond Hill, Jim Railton, Richard Burnell, Chris Dodds, Roy Moore and Geoffrey Page on the crews' activities of the previous day, and were always disappointed with the newsmen's interpretation which was invariably at variance with their own. Or maybe the report did not do them full justice, did not extoll at great enough length their exceptional performances, or did not pick out individuals for special praise. 'Oh Jesus, can't you write about anyone other than Dave Sawyier?' they groaned in mock despair. 'There are seven more of us you know – and a cox.'

Of course if they performed poorly they preferred to forget the whole incident and did not thank the journalists for reminding them of it the next day. Some years there was easy banter, but occasionally the oarsmen were really offended by a piece and relations were a little strained, with the errant journalist being given the cold shoulder. But it was important for the crew to see themselves as others saw them, and to get an unbiased and realistic report of their water work, so I did not, as some coaches had done in the past, ban the papers from the breakfast table for the duration of the fortnight. If the reports were bad then it was no use pretending that things were fine if they were not. 'That's all very well if your crew is in contention', the sorely pressed coach with a sure-fire losing crew on his hands will say. 'But how can I keep up morale if the papers are telling them they haven't a hope in hell?' Difficult certainly, but in the end you cannot afford to kid yourself or your crew or you lose credibility. Besides, my crews always know what I'm thinking anyway because they can read it in my face. I am not the impassive inscrutable type. My face shows happy when we're going well and it shows gloomy black when we're not – there is no false bounce. I am considered a hard coach to please, never satisfied, always looking for more, for better. So it was nice to see a few years ago one of the Oxford crews which we took on to Henley in the summer racing by on their first training row all wearing vests with a message printed on the back: 'I've satisfied Dan Topolski'.

In 1973 when the journalists came to dinner, the crew were buoyant, but not overconfident. They were spoiling for a fight and the Press had given them good coverage. Andy, Paddy and Mike, though, held grudges from the years before and found it hard to see the journalists as human beings. But I wanted Oxford to co-operate with the Press, not to react sullenly and rudely the way students, with their youthfully exaggerated cynicism, can so often do. More than anything it's usually just a self-conscious reaction to so much sudden public attention. Although we do not court the Press or instigate publicity stunts in the way our rivals would have it, we recognise that we need to take account of the fact that the Press have a job to do and we try not to obstruct them unnecessarily. As long as their demands do not inconvenience us too much, then more coverage is good for Oxford, good for the Boat Race and ultimately good for rowing which tends to get badly dealt with on the nation's sports pages. The Boat Race does, after all, get more attention than Henley, the World and the National Championships put together. Besides the media coverage gives the crews a sense of importance and the event significance. Of course when a crew is down and morale is low, negative coverage does little to help; but if they cannot take criticism and bad write-ups how can they be expected to take the tensions of the Boat Race itself? In the end it is all useful for hardening a crew to outside pressures and helps to galvanise it and weld it into a closer unit; us against the world.

Other more informal dinner guests have been the Isis crew, our boatmen – Albert, Bert, Mike and Ernie, some younger Old Blues from the most recent Oxford crews and, later on, our Ladbroke sponsors. Sometimes there was a 'girlfriends' evening (although not in 1973), and a lunch invitation for the umpire, the London representative of the Boat Race and Cecil Foster Kemp, who faithfully and for many years arranged for us to have feature films and a projector for our spare-time viewing. We have even invited Cambridge for lunch during the past 11 years and on one occasion they actually accepted and turned up hungry and expectant!

Another visitor to the Oxford camp in those early days was Pat Sweeney, cox of the British national squad. Through his period with Bob Janousek's silver medal-winning eight he liked to come out on the launch during the last fortnight to watch the crew training. Not only was he one of the world's best coxwains, but he was also a very good coach and his comments were always useful. He would come back for breakfast with us and chat to the crew and especially the cox, giving them just that little extra taste of the big professional world on the international circuit. They relished that contact and it gave them an added boost to have such interest shown in them. They also enjoyed meeting the young Old Blues from recent years whose names were almost legendary in the world of rowing and who had inspired them when they were hopeful boys rowing for their school eights. On the other hand they were glad to give time to the youngsters to whom they were now the heroes. Old Blue Dick Fishlock's children came loyally every year to watch the crew rowing their final practice on the Saturday morning before the race. These were the Oxford Blues of the future and the crewmen were keen to encourage them.

For the rest of the time, and particularly in the last few days before the race, the Hammersmith house was a haven, a quiet informal retreat where the crew could do what they wanted. Generally that consisted of watching films, dozens of them, violent and stimulating for the most part. There was music too and of course conversation; how often the talk would turn from whatever subject back to the Tabs and yesterday's outing, and the prospects for the race and today's work and what's for lunch. The jokes came fast and furious, the teasing never stopped and the fellowship bloomed. Discipline on the river was tight but at the house there were few restrictions. There did not have to be. The Boat Race engenders such a mood of professional dedication, particularly in those last weeks, that rule-breaking is rarely a problem, not that there are any rules as such. The single-mindedness of the crew creates its own discipline. Contrary to popular myth that last fortnight in training retreat hardly ever creates a need or a desire to break out. They know that cinemas, pubs and crowded environments are the likeliest places from which to pick up 'flu, and that as super-fit athletes they are particularly vulnerable. Any rules are determined by common sense and consensus since no one wants to jeopardise his chance to race Cambridge. They don't smoke, they don't drink much apart from the odd beer, and all that keeps them up after ten-thirty or so is the last reel of a feature film or a discussion about race tactics. With two training sessions a day and an early morning run on the programme, they are pretty tired out by the end of the day.

On the other hand if an athlete is used to regular love-making with his girlfriend, it is probably less conducive to a peak performance for him to abstain for 14 days than that he meet up with her two or three times during the final fortnight for a couple of hours after dinner. It's far better for peace of mind and a good night's sleep. What wears a fellow out is the late night cut and thrust of the chase and the frustration of possible failure, not the loss of a teaspoonful of bodily fluid. But then again few crewmen in the last ten years have had such a craving. It is astonishing how an imminent Boat Race concentrates the mind and diverts attention from almost everything else. Nothing really matters outside the race. All aspirations and all dreams circle around it and practically no life beyond it is seriously planned or considered. For most of the contestants it is a once in a lifetime chance and although some return the following year, none of them want anything extraneous to interfere with the uniqueness of their shared experience. Cup Finals come round once a year, Wimbledon, the Derby, Henley too for that matter, and the World Championships in any sport can be attempted for several consecutive years. But to win a Boat Race is a lifelong thrill, a supreme life-enhancing satisfaction; to take part in it is a milestone in a life; to lose it one of the most lingering and painful of disappointments.

In the week that led up to the race, the 1973 crew went from strength to strength and as the day approached they found themselves running neck-and-neck in the betting stakes with a very classy Cambridge crew. All hung on their racing ability on the day. Hopes were high; the first Oxford win in six years was on the cards despite the fact that they weighed nine pounds a man less than the Light Blues. However the weather was turning mean. By Thursday the wind had blown up and the Putney reach was taking on a nasty aspect when the tide turned at mid-day and began to flow in against a strong north-westerly breeze. The first three minutes of the course looked distinctly unfriendly. The morning outings on the ebb were fast with the wind strong behind the crews going down the Putney reach, and on one occasion Dave hit a phenomenal starting rate of 47 off a stakeboat start, leaving the rowing press in their launch reaching for hyperboles and their coach checking and re-checking his stopwatch. They looked formidable.

Back at the start of training we had decided to stick with our Swiss-made Stampfli shell of the previous year, because it was a good boat and rode the rough Tideway well. But the coaches were less happy about the five-stay riggers which came with the boat and we wanted to replace them with 'Jumbo' designed two-stay aerofoil ones which had been devised by our innovative mentor specifically for the Boat Race and the turbulent Tideway conditions usually found in March. The aerofoils cut efficiently through the crashing waves, and did not scoop water into the boat like other riggers. In most situations the Stampfli riggers would have been fine, particularly on the normally calm waters of an international 2000-metre course or lake in mid-summer. But the Boat Race was a very peculiar race on very inhospitable water and special tactics had to be adopted to deal with it. However, when we had discussed the problem back in November the President had been critical of the 'Jumbo' riggers. They flexed during high pressure rowing, he said, and he and the crew preferred the greater rigidity of the five-stay riggers. We had decided then on a rough water test, but ironically at that unsettled time of year the waters remained calm and unruffled. So instead we drove the launch ahead of the crew to disturb the water and they sailed through the wash without difficulty. It was a singularly inadequate test in the light of the conditions we were to encounter on Boat Race day but for the sake of peace and quiet we made a decision which proved to be our one major mistake. The coaches gave in and the experience 'Jumbo' had gained over many years of Boat Race training was set aside by less wily coaches and crew. We thought no more about it until that Thursday when the wind blew up, so absorbed were we by the hundred and one other details of training and so swept along by the fact that we were developing into a very fast crew. Cambridge on the other hand had adopted the 'Jumbo' aerofoil riggers designed specifically for Oxford and wore them happily on the day.

Anticipating the impending north-west sinker, we spent frantic hours stretching heavy duty tape along the tops of the riggers to act as splashboards in an effort to keep the water out of the shell as an extra precaution, although we still believed that the five-stay riggers would not let us down. I was more concerned with calming the crew for the big day. I knew that Sawyier felt particularly uneasy in bouncy water, and had spent a lot of time trying to get him and the whole crew to relax through the rough. Whenever we encountered turbulence though Dave tightened up and the tension showed in his face and shoulders as he held the oar handle far too tightly. Every time his excessively-gripped oar hit a wave the shock reverberated through the boat, upsetting the balance. It was essential to get the crew to ease their grip, to allow their hands, arms and bodies to act as shock absorbers, so that the blade when hit by a wave would bounce harmlessly without affecting the sit of the boat. It was a lesson they had found hard to take on board all year, and Dave in his two years with Oxford never really managed to come to terms with the Tideway. Yet the Tideway and its many moods was part and parcel of the whole eccentric event, and good watermanship was an integral element of a Boat Race Blue's makeup. On flat calm water Oxford were unbeatable, but when the waves blew up, they became vulnerable, their fast edge blunted by the turbulence, especially off the start.

In our final pre-race talk on the evening before the race I concentrated as much on the minutiae of tactics in all situations, on a race plan in normal conditions, as on the special actions to be adopted in sinking weather. We covered that necessary ground too in the talk, but I failed to stress strongly enough the need to pick carefully through the roughest water, the need for Dave, should the conditions dictate, to forego our superb fast start and settle instead for a safer lower starting rate. Even if we had concentrated on that rating factor alone in our briefing it is doubtful whether the crew, hyped up as they were, could have held themselves back in the heat of the start. It was the do-or-die moment they had been waiting for all year and passion ruled over cool analysis. Besides, the chances were that the wind would abate by the morning. From experience I knew that the last couple of days before the race were inclined to slip by in a blur, especially for those facing their first Boat Race. I remembered going on to automatic pilot, relieved that I was well enough prepared to go through the necessary actions without thinking. Luckily in my first year nothing had gone wrong, but I knew that given an unexpected set of circumstances it was difficult to readjust in the flurry of the moment. These were not experienced athletes on the whole, not seasoned performers. They were young undergraduates or graduates facing their biggest event, under the eyes of millions of people around the world for the first time. In the all important pre-race briefing I needed to prepare them for that feeling of vagueness and unreality. They had to concentrate on the task at hand, keep their eyes in their own boat, listen to the cox's instructions, not be distracted by the shouting from the shore and remember the most crucial elements of the race plan.

The cox has such a vital role to play at this time. It is he who must stay the most alert, thinking fast, anticipating, keeping the crew on their toes. His eyes must be everywhere, for the eyes of his crew are blinkered within the boat. Rehearsing and preparing the crew for these moments over the last few days helps them to deal with the real thing more easily, otherwise even the most simple of actions could all of a sudden become an insurmountable problem. We discussed all the accidents that could possibly happen, how they would deal with them in the boat in mid-race, and we ran through different sets of circumstances. And of course it was impossible to account for everything that could go wrong, since that is the nature of athletics, of rowing generally, and the Boat Race in particular. The one thing you just did not think of happens.

The crew in 1973 had over the months found that they took quite a while to warm up before a race, and we planned a slightly longer series of warm-up bursts on the water than the usual 22 minutes that were allowed for in the Boat Race programme plan. There was nothing odd about this. Different crews have different ways, and when I had timed our warm-up earlier in the week, it was apparent that we would need some 30 to 35 minutes. Also the crew preferred to do the warm-up over the first half-mile of the course in the manner of a normal international 2000-metre race warm-up. But this was unusual in the Boat Race. The warm-up was normally done below the start, beyond Putney Bridge alongside Hurlingham Club down to Wandsworth. The day dawned windy but our early morning outing, wind with stream, was relaxed and sharp on comfortable water. The crew looked in superb condition, tense naturally, tight-lipped but level-tempered and building up an awesome head of steam. While they went back to the house, I busied myself around the boat, checking nuts and pitches, bolts and riggers and rudder, making sure the makeshift splashboards were tight and secure. They were untried – a dangerous experiment to be forced to make on Boat Race day.

Bert Green, our Tideway launch driver, confidante and course coach for the cox, drove Fred Yalouris, Chris Blackwall and myself over the first two miles of the course soon after the tide had turned and we made last-minute decisions on how Fred should steer the race in the light of the increasingly rough conditions. He needed to know how much he should sacrifice the fastest centrestream for the protected calmer waters closer inshore, and which bank to make for should the water become too rough, so that he would not be left isolated on the outside of an important bend with the enforced choice of either a turbulent crossing later on or an extra long route to the finishing line. But it should be understood that these were drastic measures we were discussing, survival tactics in possibly horrendous conditions rather than the neck-and-neck and inch-by-inch cut and thrust of two crews fighting for a few feet either side of a racing stream. We had to cover all eventualities on this ugly stormy day.

The crew arrived in Uncle Den's huge red and blue coach, looking smart in their special kit, and went directly up to the changing-room. A few minutes later the toss of the gold sovereign gave Andy Hall the choice of station and we opted for the Surrey side and possibly the less good conditions, but hoped that once through the worst of the rough in the first mile we would get the advantage of the longer Hammersmith bend where the four-stone heavier Cambridge crew would be planning to kill us off. We had confidence in our strength over the first half of the course and our ability to hold Cambridge round the outside of the first bend at Fulham. After all we had beaten the fastest crew in the country twice over six minutes, and besides the water still looked manageable at the time of the toss three-quarters of an hour before the race. The die was cast. Last-minute instructions in the tense atmosphere of the changing-room and then they were 'hands on' the boat and carrying it out to the cheers of their supporters and the boos of the Cambridge camp from the Light Blue Barclays Bank boathouse two doors down. The boat was on the water and one by one they stepped off the launching stool and into their places. They looked powerful as they pulled away from the hard and coped well with the waves as they made a pass along the boathouses over the first stretch of the course. The Isis/Goldie race went by as they turned back to the start.

It was quite rough already but not impossibly so, although they got a little splashed with spray. Contrary to some Press reports they did not take on a significant amount of water before the race otherwise they would have come ashore to empty out. Instead they absorbed what water there was in the boat with their sweaters which, when they were attached to the stakeboat at the start, they passed down to the stakeboat man who was holding on to the stern of their boat.

As they waited for the 'go' we in the launch behind could see the river ahead. The first half-mile of the course had become a turbulent sea in the space of 20 minutes. But there was no time to think. The race was on. After a few strokes they lurched to one side as they carried out their fast rating start and took on water in a cloud of spray; but then they led briefly as Dave forced them through. After three-quarters of a minute, Mike Williams, the Cambridge cox, began to coax his crew over to the relatively calm water under the lee of the Middlesex shore and at a lower rating the Tabs picked their way into the lead, their aerofoils slicing through the waves. Freddie Yalouris kept Oxford on centre course as Sawyier drove his men on, never dropping below 35 strokes a minute to Cambridge's 32. The more water they took on board, their five-stay riggers scooping the Thames over the side and into the boat, the lower it sat and the less was the clearance of the riggers above the river thus, sickeningly, making it all the more easy for more water to flow in. The tape splashboards flopped uselessly in the water providing little resistance to the relentless flood. A wall of water surged up and down the boat at every stroke.

Although all was lost, the crew bravely rallied behind their stroke, the boat barely an inch from submerging entirely. As they came into the calmer waters round the Fulham bend and beyond, the danger of a sinking disappeared almost as if to mock their efforts in front of an audience of millions who did not know and merely thought that here was another pathetic Oxford crew coming second in a procession and yet another dull Boat Race. How could we let them know that really, honestly we were a good crew, a brave crew, a crew that had boldly pulled itself out of the doldrums with an unconscionable amount of dedication and hard work? How could I have done that to them, betrayed them like that, humiliated them so publicly? Why should

Andy Hall have to say self-mockingly in future years: 'Yes I'm the guy who lost four Boat Races in a row', when in all honesty I believe he should have won the last one? At Mortlake barely a trickle fell from the Cambridge boat as they took it out of the water and threw it up into the air and on to their shoulders – the Oxford boys had to summon the Isis crew to help haul their craft to waist-height and then to tip out a torrent of the Thames water they had carried with them for four and a half miles to the finish. It was a heartbreaking disaster. But that was the Boat Race. Over the years almost as many crews from both Universities (although Oxford probably score higher in this department) have contrived to lose the race when in an unassailable position by messing things up as have won it on merit. I keep a colour photograph of that half-submerged Oxford crew in mid-race on my mantelpiece to remind me never again to go out without aerofoils.

For Dick, Mike, Phil, Andy and Steve, 1973 had been the last chance. The others could try again next year. But would they want to? Sawyier for one was adamant that he would never row again in a race which could be decided on weather conditions rather than the speed and power of the competitors. It was not boat racing, it was a lottery, he complained bitterly. When would Oxford ever have such a good chance of beating Cambridge again? This had been their best crew for six years. Although it was another victory for Cambridge it was a frustratingly hollow one since they were denied a proper race. They were not allowed to show fully what they were capable of and how well they had coped with their problems during a build-up in which they had had little chance for competitive work and had come to the line with what was undoubtedly a fine and powerful crew. Whether Oxford could have matched them will never be known. We at Oxford could only apologise to them for our pathetic showing. That Cambridge contained some excellent oarsmen was demonstrated by the performance of Chris Baillieu, with four Boat Race wins in his pocket, and Mike Hart racing double sculls later in the year at Henley and the World Championships where they won the first medals of their highly successful partnership. David Sturge made the final of the Henley Diamond Sculls, while John Lever and Steve Tourek won the Visitors'. The Press were disappointed and disparaging. 'Instead of yawning indifference from the public, intolerance is abroad' wrote the correspondent of the *Field*. 'Reasons are required.'

In retrospect, I know that Lou Barry briefed his crew according to the conditions, while we at Oxford, desperate to break the Light Blue stranglehold, gambled too much on our speed off the mark. But in 1973 a fast start was suicide. As the Oxford boys rounded the Fulham bend, chasing vainly after Cambridge dragging their waterlogged shell with them, the water slopping over their feet, they were praying that perhaps Cambridge too had suffered the same flooding. Had Oxford sunk before the end of the Fulham wall – two minutes from the start – the race would have been declared null and void, and a re-row announced. 'Someone in the boat should have kicked his foot through the bottom and sunk her to get the re-row', suggested one bankside observer, wise after the event, when all had become known. 'No need' said another. 'They could have tilted her hard over to one side to take on enough water to swamp her.' Not very sporting perhaps; yet I suppose possible tactics within the context of the harsh realities of the competitive outside world. But in the heat of the moment all thoughts were directed at staying afloat and beating Cambridge. How could they have known so quickly that they faced a hopeless task?

Cambridge won as they pleased by a massive 13 lengths and we were left to pick up the pieces after one of the most humiliating defeats on record. To make matters worse Isis had lost by five lengths to Goldie in the mini-race. So much for the new approach, so much for the new coaching team and their revised training programme. It was back to the drawing board. Yet, the disaster apart, it had all gone so right up until the day. In the face of all the turmoil and depression would a new President recognise that, and keep faith with those elements that had worked well, rather than throwing the whole lot out of the window and starting again? And anyway who would the next President be?

In his anger and frustration Sawyier had vowed to the Press that he would never again take part in such a farcical event even though he had another year at Oxford. Yet if Oxford were to have any chance in 1974 his presence in the boat would be essential. The Blues' dinner that night at Simpson's in the Strand was a sombre affair. The Old Blues traditionally invite the crew to dinner and a bottle of Champagne is provided for each crew member which he is supposed to drink on his own. As the Oxford slump had continued over the years, attendance had dwindled and support for the cause had gradually turned to dismay and then to irritation. This year the Old Blues had come back in force expecting a victory. But though they were disappointed they were supportive and there was a lot of behind-the-scenes arm-twisting and ear-bending as Blues old and new discussed what had gone wrong and how to put it right.

A month later, burning now for revenge, Sawyier accepted the post of President, unable to face life with such a defeat on his conscience. Because make no mistake; for those who aspire to a Blue and take part in the Boat Race, it is not just a race. It is The Race, and it represents to the contestants far more than anything else that they have done in the past or will do in the future. It is a very personal thing and each man defeated carries the burden of that defeat with an irrational sense of guilt. He has failed those who went before, those who built the event into what it is; and furthermore he has failed them, himself and his University in such a painfully public way. Defeat in a closely contested race is easier to bear – not much easier, but a little – while a defeat such as ours in 1973 called out to be avenged, especially if one had the good fortune still to be there and able to take part. Bob Mason, after rowing in the losing crew of 1975 remarked that there were precious few things quite as terrible in life as losing a Boat Race. To eradicate, to exorcise that feeling is one of the many things that drive a Boat Race oarsman to try again. 'Why did I change my mind and decide to row again?' said Sawyier in one interview. 'Because it is a unique event. I had let the Boat Race down once by losing – not to compete a second time would have been to let it down again.'

Bravely, perhaps foolhardily, Sawyier invited the same coaches and the same finishing coach to come back for another try. Hell, the poor fellow didn't know any other coaches in Britain, so he had little choice. Besides he appreciated the freakishness of the conditions that day and recognised the value in keeping faith with a coaching team beyond a one-year trial. Too often coaches had been sacked and replaced without ever having had the chance to get to know the job properly or to learn from their mistakes. This time it would be different.

Despite the shock of losing when all seemed to be going so well, it was not hard to revitalise the squad and to restore confidence. They knew they had been fast, they knew full well what had happened and they believed in the new regime, the new training methods and the selection process. But it was a sceptical group of coaches who gathered at Leander during the summer at the invitation of the new President to discuss plans for the 1974 Boat Race. Sawyier was late arriving and as we waited, we all agreed that his obnoxious behaviour during the year had been unacceptable. Some of the group were considering turning down his invitation to coach – yet there we all were, gathered and waiting. Chris Blackwall had been particularly affronted and I would have been very uneasy about carrying on without him if he had decided to walk out. At the very least we were determined to tell Sawyier what we thought of him and to demand guarantees and assurances that he would control his temper and leave the coaching to the coaches. In he walked, profusely regretting his tardiness. 'Before we discuss any-thing,' he began, 'I would like, here and now, to apologise for my behaviour throughout the year. It was unforgivable, I know, and I can only assure you that it will never happen again.' Completely disarmed by his candour and contrition, we settled without further ado to plan our strategy for winning the next Boat Race.

3

Second Chance:
The Long Road Back

The lean Boat Race years had been glaringly reflected in the results at
Henley Royal Regatta where the last Oxford win had been that of
Cherwell in the Ladies' Plate in 1968. Sawyier set about redressing the
balance. He formed an Isis coxed four with Paddy Payne, Paul
Marsden, an Isis oarsman and a strong contender for the 1974 crew,
and Dick Westlake. (Andy Hall put in a couple of guest appearances
during the season as substitute, but he was now concentrating on his
degree.) They enjoyed a successful season visiting small and large up-
river regattas around the country on the summer circuit, learning the
pleasures of winning again. At Henley they won the Britannia Cup in
record time. This was good confidence-building stuff for all of them
and it provided a solid basis on which to build the 1974 crew. The stern
three of the four went on to fill the stern three seats of the next Boat
Race crew. For good measure Dave and Paddy doubled up to row a
pair in the Goblets and raced remarkably well, beating national team
men Robertson and Yallop (world silver medallists in eights the
following year) before losing to the eventual winners from America,
Borchelt and Adams, who broke the record to halfway in the process,
and finished seventh in the world a couple of months later.

An Isis eight with Westlake and Marsden doubling up also raced
well at Henley but went out to University College Dublin by a canvas,
with the Irishmen having to break the existing course record for the
event to beat them. There were also Oxford entries from a junior Isis
eight and a Cherwell four. There was in these performances some
cause for cautious optimism, and with the return of another hard
operator in place of Phil Angier, Sam Nevin from Westminster school,
who had been a Blue in 1971 and had rowed for Isis in 1972, and the
1969 and 1970 Blue Nick Tee, a talented lightweight, the 1973–74
Boat Race winter programme began well. Newcomers to the Oxford
squad were Gavin Stoddart, Andy Baird, Paul Wright and Graham
Innes, who together with the Isis oarsman Mark Harris were all good
ex-schoolboy oarsmen, but all unnervingly light. There were two large
freshmen as well, unfit, clumsy and unathletic but showing promise on
the water if not on land. They were John Hutchings from Canada and
Boris Rankov from Bradford.

James Ollivant and John Dart, another Old Blue from 1970, were both up at Oxford but unfortunately were not prepared to row. We seemed to be in reasonable shape nevertheless until Paddy dropped his bombshell: he was pulling out, just a week or two into training, through pressure from his tutors. It was a serious blow but no amount of argument would persuade him to return. Although training for the Boat Race took up a lot of time, pretty well the whole afternoon six days a week, a well-organised oarsman could usually handle his studies and his rowing well enough. Indeed more often than not when an oarsman was pressed into leaving the squad, he found paradoxically that he was not doing significantly more work than before. Oxford has a remarkable knack of absorbing a student's hours without his noticing, and time-wasting is the undergraduate disease. Sports activity tends to sharpen the mind, and a fit alert body is a far more efficient working machine, both mentally and physically. But not all the Oxford tutors saw things that way. So a running struggle of compromise was endured year after year to enable the oarsmen to study and row effectively.

Land training started on the first day of term for the known candidates and college fours were boated for the inter-college fours event in the third week as usual. George Harris and irregularly Chris and I began immediately to peruse, coach and select trialists from amongst other squad candidates not taking part in fours. From these contenders a junior trial crew would be formed and usually two or three oarsmen would progress quickly into the top group. As a rule we would choose four or five members of the junior trial crew in December to join the January fortnight squad of 16 senior trialists at Putney and as often as not a couple of the junior men would succeed in pushing their way into the finally selected Isis crew at the expense of a couple of less competitive senior trialists. That this was possible was well known and indeed publicised within the Oxford set-up and it reinforced our stated policy that seats in the first and second boats would be allocated on merit only. Only Sawyier, Tee and Nevin were Blues. All the rest were either Isis, freshmen or college oarsmen. In the Autumn sculling heads Mark Harris, Sam Nevin, Paul Marsden and Paul Wright performed quite well while in the Open Fours Head of the River Race on the Tideway Christ Church with Sawyier at stroke finished seventh. In the December national trials our coxed pairs finished second and fourth and our coxless pair was fifth.

As President, Sawyier was intent on one thing only – and that was to win the Boat Race. He was less concerned about efficiency and planning, and in laying the groundwork via Isis for the future. As a result he often came into conflict with Chris Blackwall who, as the Isis finishing coach, took it upon himself to represent the interests of the reserve crews and to champion the cause of developing a more productive structure within Oxford for the oarsmen immediately below the top group. I sympathised with and supported his stand but left him to it because like Dave I was primarily occupied with getting the first boat to the line ahead of Cambridge. A full-time salaried coach could have organised the whole squad far more efficiently, but since we were amateurs, our time was limited and we had to be sparing in the way we apportioned our coaching hours. Luckily, whether by design or good fortune, Chris and I were able to work complementarily, covering all these important facets reasonably well. Although most Presidents tended to short-change Isis in their efforts to win, Sawyier was perhaps one of the most blinkered in his search for success. That ruthless American streak – the 'taking care of number one' syndrome – perhaps made for unpopularity in some quarters, but it certainly helped to concentrate squad members' minds on the task in hand.

Peter Politzer, head coach at Pangbourne College, was recruited on to the coaching team and he worked long and hard with the trial crews during the first term. As we have regularly tended to do during the last ten years, we produced two very even trial eights for the end of term test race over the course at Putney. It seemed a logical move to transfer our major trial from Henley to the stretch of Tideway water on which we were to meet Cambridge. Sawyier relinquished his favourite stroke seat for a change and rowed six behind the lightweight freshman Paul Wright. They drew the outside of the first bend at Mortlake racing the reverse course towards Putney, but still managed to steal a quarter of a length from the less experienced crew stroked by Isis stalwart John Colton. Yet by halfway the positions were reversed. Poor steering by the Blue Fred Yalouris allowed Wright, steered by the Isis cox Gareth Morris, to steal back into the lead and they went on to win by three lengths. The American had clearly been outmanoeuvred by Morris.

With another aggressive Oxford squad showing promise in December, short perhaps on outstanding talent and finesse, but eager for the fray, the unexpected announcement from the double Blue Nick Tee that he was joining Paddy Payne on the sidelines made for a glum Christmas. This brought the freshers Baird, Wright and Hutchings to the fore, with the prospect of Blues at their first attempt which made us uncomfortably reliant on inexperienced youngsters with little pedigree and not a lot of hard-trained weight. The January fortnight would have to be particularly gruelling to toughen up these rookies. Simply learning how hard they could push themselves in training was going to be the principal lesson, a difficult one to learn in the space of a few weeks. George took them early on and tried to get the point across.

'You have to produce even more effort in training than you may need in the actual race. I want that extra bit. I want you utterly spent, so that you're really hurting. Forget about rhythm and being clever; I want you falling out of the boat with exhaustion. Piston-like legs, horizontal drive – sit back and let her fly.'

It is easy to think that you are giving your all because you are feeling pressured and tired, but Boat Race endurance conditioning only begins to take effect if the oarsman can redouble his effort when he is in a highly stressed state. To turn on the power and the pressure when your muscles and lungs are already aching and crying out to stop is the mark of the competitive athlete; and to be able to do that in competition, you must first do it again and again in training. It is hard for the coach to spot how hard a man is working, and ultimately he has to go by results. He cannot rely wholly on impressions and instinct or the technical style and ability of the oarsman under scrutiny. He can of course spot when an oarsman cracks completely or begins suddenly to move less and less water, but that does not always happen in an obvious way. Sometimes the athlete simply cannot cope physically, sometimes he does not have the heart for so much effort, sometimes he tries to cheat it. And sometimes he is willing and aggressive but needs time to catch up physically. It's the coach's job to spot which is the case. There is nothing necessarily underhand in an oarsman's reluctance to produce the work levels required. It is often simply his inability to absorb mentally and understand what is being asked of him. Both Chris Blackwall and I were loth to take freshmen into a Blue Boat, because we believed they would always benefit from a good year's grounding in Isis where they would go through the same training programme and the race itself without the pressure of the Boat Race proper. Isis was the perfect dress rehearsal. However we could only play the hand we had been dealt and this one looked weaker than the year before. But then Cambridge too seemed to be in a vulnerable position. The Blues Tourek and Sturge had decided to take a ringside view of the 1974 Boat Race and two talented ex-Goldie men, Christie and Macleod, who were disdainful of the proposed programme, had also opted out. But the Light Blues did have the services of Tom Yuncken, a good 26-year-old graduate from Australia, the Blues Jacobs and Duncan, winning Goldie men Langridge, Sprague and McGarel-Groves and junior world silver medallist freshman Henry Clay.

Like the previous year we were determined to run our pre-term January fortnight at Putney, boating from my own club London, and living in the homes of those squad members who lived in the city. That meant that Chris and I took most of the squad to our respective homes and landed our mothers and sisters with housefuls of large oarsmen with even larger appetites for two weeks. They laboured uncomplainingly for the Oxford cause. Harry Freeman, our doctor, took a couple of squaddies too, and somehow everyone was housed, on floors, mattresses or two to a bed. It meant that they were all able to get a sustained taste of the Tideway in eights, fours and on their own in sculling boats. It meant too that I could bully Dave Sawyier into coming to terms with rough water and learning how to relax into the teeth of a storm. On Boat Race day he was the model of disdain and sailed through the turbulence opposite the Mile Post as though butter wouldn't melt in his mouth.

One of our first tasks was to get the Stampfli fitted up with aerofoil riggers. The boat itself sat well in all types of swell and rough, and she was comfortable to row. Besides we could ill afford a new boat, or oars for that matter, and the newspapers made great play of our poverty and the fact that Oxford were a cut-price crew compared to the Light Blues, who were lodged in a luxury hotel. Cambridge also had the benefit of a wisely-invested capital donation from an Old Blue to finance their programme while their new boat had been bought for them by another Old Blue. Our Oxford forebears had not seen fit to provide for us so generously, or perhaps they just had less business acumen. Once again we embarked on a punishing six-hours-a-day routine with all thoughts and effort devoted to that one race. Even Dave reckoned he trained harder in that winter of 1973–74 than he had ever trained in America – or for the 1973 Boat Race.

Conditions in the January fortnight were hardly bearable, but this was not unusual. We have over the years suffered blizzards and gales when sculling boats, inadequately secured on London Rowing Club's outside racks have been hurled to the ground and badly damaged; there have been floods when an inclement high tide has intruded into the boathouses and carried away oars and sculls and all manner of floatable essentials; and there has been fast-forming black ice, deposited by a retreating tide along the towpath which serves as our running track to trip up the less fleet of foot. Only fog prevented the oarsman from carrying out his daily training. All other obstacles were masochistically tackled in what must be the most spartan of sports. My open-sided Mini Moke came in for a lot of flak at times like this. 'God, Topolski, what the hell are we *doing* here', sobbed a frozen Dave Sawyier from the seatless back as we sat in a traffic jam engulfed by a snowstorm following a particularly vile afternoon on the river. He was one of the three men staying with me that year for the fortnight and had to suffer the icy, windblown half-hour journey between my house and

Putney twice a day. Yes, we were tough in those days! Now I drive a saloon car but I still have the Moke for those occasions when the boys get out of hand. In retrospect I suppose I did submit them to more than their fair share of hardship, but at least the 1974 crew did not have to spend a Sunday after one of their more gruelling Tideway visits carrying some 200 cement bags full of rubble from my new, half-converted third-floor flat down to street level. That little surprise I reserved for the 1978 squad.

Apart from a number of long haul outings up beyond Richmond and back or down below Westminster, covering 18, 20 or 24 miles in an outing, the squad was also working very hard in the gym. They were developing too an excellent competitiveness. At the end of the January fortnight the crews were set to row a side-by-side piece at a controlled rate of 28 from Kew to Putney. It was more of an exercise than a race, over a distance some six minutes longer than the Boat Race. But the two strokes Innes and Sawyier saw things differently. They shot off the mark, each looking for an early lead, and despite my angry instructions to control the rating they battled neck and neck at 30 then 32 then 34 all the way to Putney. 'It's not a race!' I yelled in vain as the coxwains clashed and separated again at Barnes. There was still only a canvas between them as they pushed into the headwind at Harrods. Innes went up to 35, then Sawyier did too, and finally the President scraped home first by a few feet. It was stirring stuff and a fine way to end the fortnight; and Graham Innes had certainly shown what a fighting stroke he was.

On the whole Presidents usually found themselves weighed down by responsibilities during their year of office and their training would suffer accordingly. They were often forced in the individual tests to lead their squads from behind, or at least from halfway down the field. Not Dave Sawyier. He led from the front and set the standard. Furthermore, although the coaches felt that, because of Presidential cares and the resultant loss of top form, it was normally unwise to allow a President to take on the crucial role of stroke, it would have been perverse to keep Sawyier out of that seat. At one time at the end of January we were boating a crew with him at six behind Graham Innes and Gavin Stoddart at stroke and seven. But a session at Henley with the embryo national eight which was to win a silver medal at the World Championships later in the year soon put paid to that idea. They beat us comfortably in a series of two and a half-minute races. We were patently not as strong as we wanted to be. We tried a number of different orders, swapping men from stroke side to bow side since we had a couple of ambidextrous oarsmen.

Oxford crew, 1973 *(left to right):*
Sawyier; Payne; Hall; Irving;
Angier; Magarey; Ollivant;
Westlake; Yalouris (cox)

Oxford crew, 1974 *(left to right):*
Sawyier; Payne; Marsden;
Stoddart; Nevin; Rendel; Innes;
Tee; Morris (cox)

Oxford crew, 1975 *(left to right):*
Innes; Tee; Mason; Hutchings;
Money-Coutts; Beak; Harris; Baird;
Calvert (cox)

Oxford, Cambridge, Harvard and
Yale leave the Temple of Luxor for
the 1971 Nile Boat Race

1975: Oxford's Hardy Amies fashion show

BELOW

Left: Jumbo Edwards, Oxford's postwar coach
Middle: Lou Barry *(standing),* Cambridge finishing coach 1968-73 and 1975, with Donald Leggett *(far left),* Cambridge Blue and coaching team member since the late 1960s

Right: George Harris, Oxford coach

ABOVE

Left: Mike Spracklen

Right: A constant reminder of the 1973 débâcle

Oxford crew, 1967: future fellow coach Chris Blackwall is behind me at six

Oxford crew, 1976 *(left to right):*
Baird; Wiggins; Brown; Plunkett;
Mason; Edwards; Innes; Beak;
Calvert (cox)

Oxford crew, 1977 *(left to right):*
Michelmore; Wiggins; Shealy;
Money-Coutts; Mason; Moran;
Vardey; Wright; Moynihan (cox)

BELOW

Oxford crew, 1978 *(left to right):*
Michelmore; Wood; Shealy;
Moran; Rankov; Crawford;
Crockford; Sutton; Fail (cox)

Above: Boris Rankov

Dave Sawyier

Steve Plunkett, the heaviest man ever
to row in the Boat Race, behind
American World Champion Ken
Brown in 1976

Above left: The 'official' challenge in 1977 with Presidents David Searle and Bob Mason

Above right: Cesar's Palace Charity Show. HRH the Princess Margaret with the Oxford crew

Upper middle: Cambridge sinking in 1978

Middle: Oxford's six-foot victory in 1980

Lower middle: Oxford crew, 1979 *(left to right):* Diserens; Wiggins; Mahoney; Crawford; Rankov; Moore; Crockford; Head; Berners-Lee (cox)

BELOW

Oxford crew, 1980 *(left to right):* Francis; Conington; Andrews; Bland; Rankov; Mahoney; Barry; Diserens; Mead (cox)

So a crew of Sawyier at stroke, Marsden, Nevin, Stoddart, Innes, Rendel, Wright and Jones gave way to one with Innes stroking, Stoddart, Sawyier, Marsden, Nevin, Rendel, Baird and Harris. At one point we even had Sawyier at four. By the beginning of February Cambridge had announced their crew and we were boating yet another combination: Sawyier, Stoddart, Nevin, Marsden, Baird, Rendel, Innes and Wright with Yalouris coxing. We decided to announce the last-named crew, confident of the eight men although we were still not sure how they would sit. Before seat racing Stoddart, Marsden, Nevin and Sawyier had established themselves unquestionably so they were not tested further. The seat racing however produced a surprise front-runner in David Rendel, certainly no prize-winner for style, but a very determined and hard operator. Innes too staked his claim, but there was little to choose between the candidates for the last two seats. Sawyier revelled in the cruel sport of seat racing which was his favourite elimination process. Finally Harris, Jones, Colton, Hutchings and Moore were edged out by Wright and Baird. A weekend outing against the Wallingford eight showed good form and we settled down to weld the combination into a winning crew. I handed over to Derek Thurgood for his fortnight and returned to London.

Three days later I had a call from Derek to say that Sawyier had made one last attempt to win back Tee and Payne without telling anyone on the coaching team, and had persuaded them to sign up. They had been out with the crew already and looked good although they were clearly lacking in fitness. Chris and I were pretty irate about these new developments. The trials to test the suitability of the two newcomers had certainly been less than exhaustive and with less than a month and a half left to the race it was a tremendous gamble. Besides a decision like that undermined all the confidence-boosting and selection procedures we had fought so hard to establish. Furthermore it was a decision taken without consultation, probably because of the anticipated opposition that the coaches would have put up against such a move. I was furious and Chris was all set to resign, but we were persuaded to wait until the weekend when the crew would be tested to the full by the University of London in a prolonged two-day fixture. There would be no allowances made for the two men and if they were found to be wanting they would be replaced immediately.

In retrospect it was clearly an experiment that we dared not ignore. If we had the talent at Oxford and they were prepared to commit themselves wholeheartedly, then it was worth a try even at such a late stage. It would have been sheer obstinacy and narrow-mindedness to turn the offer down. But Chris and I certainly did not see it that way to begin with. We resented the fact that the decision had been taken behind our backs and we were worried about the effect it would have on the rest of the squad, and on the credibility of the coaching team and their policies in subsequent years. Initially, these things concerned us more than whether the two newcomers would make it or not. The principle was very important. It was unfair to those who had worked hard all winter in good faith, and it encouraged laziness amongst the more talented Old Blues who would feel that they could delay their return to training in the expectation of being selected anyway. It was not a healthy way to operate. But then again we were all working in a difficult situation and the demands of academic responsibilities weighed heavily on squad members. Sometimes we all had to compromise. I was always dead against adopting rigid postures, against backing into a corner out of which I could not extricate myself. I preferred to stay flexible so we could always retain the freedom to adapt if circumstances required it. Chris was more for setting down the policy and sticking to it. However, as long as there was no doubt about the integrity of the men involved then I was prepared in the event of dire necessity to try them out. If we had not been flexible then, and later, Oxford would certainly have had a far harder time maintaining their sequence of wins over these past nine years.

As far as the men themselves were concerned, they were certainly high-calibre performers. The lightweight Nick Tee had rowed with the magnificent Emanuel school eight of 1966 which won the Princess Elizabeth Cup and narrowly failed to take the Ladies' Plate for Colleges the following year when they crabbed and ground to a halt along the enclosures in the final. Tee was a Youth international that year too, in the double sculls, and he won again at Henley rowing with Leander in the Thames Cup. He lost the Boat Race with Oxford in 1969 and 1970 and had returned this year as a postgraduate. Paddy Payne's record as a Youth international in 1970 and a Blue for the two preceding years also spoke for itself. Neither were backsliders and neither had gambled on being taken in at the last moment. They were both honest workers, talented oarsmen with considerable experience who knew the score and were quite capable of assessing their ability to get fit and effective in the short time remaining. A lot also depended on the flexibility of the crew to absorb such a major reshuffle which required Paul Marsden to change sides—no mean feat with so little time left, especially since he would be rowing in the all-important six seat. Crew cohesion had to be re-forged.

The coxswains Fred Yalouris and Gareth Morris were also on trial that weekend when we gathered at the University of London boathouse for the decider. Our opponents UL were in fighting mood and caused a series of clashes throughout the encounter, almost pushing the Dark Blues into the bank on one occasion; but both Oxford coxes emerged well with Morris just winning his private battle for selection against Yalouris. In the two main contests over seven minutes Oxford won by two thirds of a length and a quarter of a length against a strong London crew and Nick Tee and Paddy Payne came through it well, although the crew as a whole looked rushed and a little desperate. The boat was not really running and the timing was a bit ragged.

Paul Wright and Andy Baird felt pretty hard done by, and justifiably so, while the rest of the squad were more than a little disgruntled by the turn of events. John Colton, although he realised he would not have made it anyway, resented the decision on grounds of principle. Nick Jones, who had tried hard for a Blue boat seat, was in his last year and withdrew from the squad. Geoff Howles, whose father had stroked Oxford in 1953, was edged out of Isis and was probably the most unfortunate casualty that year. But the decision to take our chance with the two latecomers firmly restored the balance to level pegging with Cambridge. Thankfully Isis settled down again with Paul going to stroke, and Andy sitting in at six, but Fred Yalouris decided not to carry on coxing leaving the way clear for John Calvert to take over the Isis rudder strings. From that Isis crew six oarsmen and Calvert would win their Blues in subsequent Boat Races, while Ollie Moore and John Colton would go down as two of the most loyal and hard-working non-Blue Oxford oarsmen. These Isis stalwarts were the very backbone of the whole Oxford effort and rowed in a series of gritty reserve crews.

While Oxford were agonising over their final selection against the University of London at Kew, Cambridge were downstream at Putney testing themselves against the national eight. They rowed four six-minute pieces, losing by two lengths in the first three and four lengths in the last, but they were rowing a substitute for their President Ben Duncan. Goldie too gave us more than a little hope by giving their seniors quite a race in practice during the early part of March. This Cambridge crew was certainly weaker than its predecessors. However we were more than a little in the dark about our own likely form. All depended on whether, and how quickly, Nick and Paddy could return to fitness for a four and a quarter-mile race. We embarked once again on a brutal diet of hard work. We had three weeks in which we were able to lay on a massive amount of endurance training before easing off for the final tuning on the Tideway. We could afford not to wind down (and so pick up speed in the short term) for the Reading Head or for any of the other fixtures we had planned. The crew would be tired for these test pieces, but it was a race against time.

Initially the crew looked more cohesive following the change. They now had better rhythm and run and they looked less hurried. George Harris worked miracles to give them pace and by the Reading Head of the River Race they were going fast enough to take the title from Leander by three seconds, knocking 28 seconds off the course record in the process. It was the first Oxford win there since 1967. Despite winning the race we were only seven seconds ahead of Goldie, the Cambridge second crew, so we still had a lot of speed to make up. We had heard, but did not know for certain, that Goldie had on occasion been able to beat their first crew. It was not a piece of gossip we could rely on, and in fact it could easily have been a Light Blue rumour spread deliberately to lull us into a false sense of security. At Reading Goldie beat our Isis crew by a full 24 seconds or eight lengths in a race five minutes shorter than the Boat Race. (Though their task a month later on Boat Race day was hopeless Isis raced with great courage, pulling back more than half the Reading deficit in the curtain-raiser event.) With just 18 days to go to the Boat Race and only three weeks together as a crew, morale was high. We were moving our training camp to Henley since it was the end of term and we planned two outings a day there before going to Putney for the final fortnight.

As we were loading the boats on to the trailer after the Reading race for the journey back to Oxford, Paddy drew me aside for a private word. 'Dan, I don't know how to tell you this, but I think I'm going to have to pull out of the crew again.' I could not believe what I was hearing. 'Paddy we're on our way, we're going to win; you can't do this now, not after all the trouble we've been through.' 'It's very personal', he said, trying to give me some sort of explanation, but it all sounded so half-baked. 'We can't talk properly now', I said. 'Let's get together tomorrow and try and sort something out.' We agreed that he would come for breakfast with me in the morning in London. He was obviously very upset. 'I can't cope with Dave any longer', he told me as I cooked bacon and eggs for us both. 'His intensity is driving me mad; I can't take any more of it. We've been close friends now for a couple of years and I know he'll want to share a room with me during the last fortnight, but I really can't go on. I'm at breaking point.' I knew it had to be serious for Paddy to throw our whole two-year effort into jeopardy in this way and we talked it through all morning. Finally he agreed to stay on if I could ensure that he shared a room with someone else and if I would handle any problems if they arose. Thankfully, none did, because everyone's full attention was geared to beating the hell out of Cambridge. 'Please don't mention any of this to Dave will you', he said as he left. 'There was an emotionally highly-charged stern group in that crew' remembers Gareth the cox. 'I think there were many undercurrents that were not appreciated by others in the boat and it produced a bit of a clique in the squad, although not a divisive one.'

True to policy we took on Bob Janousek's national squad crew within a couple of days of arriving on the Tideway. Again it was a gamble so close to the race with little time to pick up the pieces should anything go wrong. We could so easily have blown the psychological boost that we had got from our Reading result. But the crew needed the side-by-side pressure of a top class eight in order to prove to themselves that they would get more basic boat speed by relaxing and allowing the boat to run, than if they chased and hurried each stroke. To relax and stay loose in the throes of the battle makes the difference between winning and losing. A crew that begins to tighten and tense will lose rhythm and fall behind and it becomes a case of them losing the race rather than the other crew winning it. So the key is to make no mistakes, to just stay there alongside the opposition and force them into committing the errors. That needs confidence – more confidence than a coach can instil just by telling his crew that it will be so. They need clear evidence. So we took Oxford out on to the Tideway to find that evidence. They raced neck and neck for two seven-minute pieces with the British eight designate – those silver medal heroes at the World Championships four months later. Oxford held their own and learned the lesson well. It was stirring stuff and earned them considerable respect. When we heard that the Tideway Scullers had soundly beaten Cambridge in a similar series of rows, we knew we were in the hunt with a chance.

Lou Barry had decided not to coach Cambridge this time round after his six consecutive victories, and they were missing his cunning ways. Dr David Jennens, an ex-Light Blue stroke and long-serving coach based at Cambridge who usually took them earlier in the year, had been asked to take on the job of finishing coach on the Tideway. He was a good coach and a very nice man but he did not know the Tideway as intimately as Lou or I did. In any event I felt at that moment ten days before the race that we had the upper hand. But we had to be careful. Cambridge had a reputation for coming on fast in the last fortnight, while Oxford had at times over the years appeared to be ready too early. This year, it was us who still had improvements to make in those last days, bearing in mind our recent crew changes, and it was Cambridge who seemed not to be getting it quite right. A couple of days after their length-a-minute drubbing by Scullers they arranged for Goldie to take them over the first part of their full course, and I sensed they could be in trouble. A crew going for six minutes against one facing an 18-minute full-course trial would always have the edge if the crews were evenly matched, and by all accounts Goldie were not much slower than their seniors. Unless the Tab reserves were very carefully briefed to do a pacing job only, their natural rivalry and their desire to prove themselves could cause no end of difficulty. Sure enough, the Cambridge full course did not work out well at all. They looked ragged and insecure and Goldie took six seconds off them to the Mile Post. Worse followed. Lady Margaret, a college crew with future Blues Macleod and Christie on board, picked them up there and dealt even more severely with them. The rest of their trial must have been a numbing experience. They were having trouble keeping their rate up and they looked sluggish.

Now we had to be sure not to repeat any of the mistakes of the year before. At last we were equipped with the right aerofoil riggers and splashboards and we took all other conceivable precautions to prevent a repeat of the 1973 debacle. We decided to play safe and pulled out of the Tideway Head of the River Race even though the crew were eager to take part. We stood a fine chance of winning it outright since the national squad were having to start at the back of the field on a slower tide as a new entry. From the second starting slot we would have been beautifully poised to take the title from the Scullers who eventually won the event. But this year we wanted no distractions. Another indicator of the relative speeds of the two 'Varsity crews came a few days later when they both rowed against the Imperial College Lubrication Laboratory. The Lube Lab was a curious crew of current internationals put together by their rowing-obsessed Professor Cameron for what seemed to be the sole purpose of pacing the Boat Race crews. Professor Cameron also liked to experiment with the design of racing boats and would recruit his graduate students from the ranks of the élite of the rowing fraternity, charging them to pursue experiments in racing shell design, and to appear occasionally under the Lube Lab flag. It was unusual in Boat Race preparations for the two crews to take on the same opposition so close to the race and in such swift succession because they preferred on the whole to keep their comparative speeds relatively secret. But good testing opposition was hard to come by and in these highly competitive times the Boat Race crews need the pressure to sharpen their act. However, in order to cloud the issue we tended when working with the same pacemakers to undertake different length workouts on different stretches of the course so that direct comparisons were less easy to make. But these were pretty flimsy smokescreens and the Press took great pleasure in building their 'prospects' cases on the evidence they were able to glean from all these various encounters. We coaches were no less thorough in our analyses. The Lab agreed to come with us for the first seven minutes of our full-course trial. We knew they were fast and we planned to race them as if in a direct bridge to bridge confrontation rather than to settle to a four and a quarter-mile Boat Race pace. We would have to take the rest of the row as it came and trust Isis to carry out a pacing rather than a racing job from Hammersmith on to the finish at Chiswick.

The speedy scientists from Imperial College flew off the start and Oxford scrambled in their anxiety to establish an early lead. They seemed to have forgotten everything they had learned against the national team a few days earlier. The Lab led by a length at the Mile and two at Hammersmith where, exultant, they dropped out. With the pressure gone Oxford relaxed and began to stretch out, and by the time Isis picked them up they were looking much better, but the Lab had startled them more than a little. If I had planned to slap the crew down for possible complacency after their successful encounter with the national eight I could not have stage-managed it better, but that had certainly not been my intention. The lesson there was clear: less haste more speed. They were learning that they were vulnerable the moment they forgot the value of relaxation and good technique. Pure bulldozing muscle was not enough. Even the most experienced oarsmen were liable to forget this under pressure. When the Lube Lab dropped out at Hammersmith Bridge, Isis took over the pacing, starting on the outside of the bend. They were under strict instructions to pace rather than race. It was easy for a fresh crew to tear off from a tired crew in mid-course and so they had been carefully briefed. They were told they could have their head after four or five minutes, but initially they had to stay alongside if they were to be of any use as pacemakers. By the time they had been rowing for five minutes their fresh edge would be blunted and the more powerful stride of the Blue Boat could be tested to the full.

Isis performed their task admirably, well-managed as they were by Chris. They dropped out once we had gone by and Westminster school joined in for the last three minutes from Barnes Bridge in. It was always a tough test for Boat Race crews facing a series of fresh competitors like this, but it certainly gave us the information we required about their form under pressure. They had looked a little ragged in the middle of their row, and we decided to ease their gearing a notch on the button, to allow them a little more ease around the turn at the end of the stroke. It would give them a fraction more flexibility. Such a move ran contrary to Sawyier's psyche. It was 'pussy' to ease the gearing. The crew should just row harder. I had had this trouble with him the year before when I had wanted to ease the buttons into a headwind. The crew, led by Dave, had resisted the move. But it really wasn't a matter of showing weakness; it was sound tactics. Easing the gearing was a sensible adjustment for the headwind, the conditions and the psychology of the crew in question. The 1973 crew had been so adamant in their resistance to such a change it would probably have upset them more to have made it. Some coaches might make such changes without telling their crews but I reckoned that that was bad strategy akin to the old habit of secretly shaving down the strokeman's blade. With most crews they would probably have recognised the rationale behind the gearing change, but in 1973 they traded on their 'macho' reputation. Half that crew wore stylish headbands and they revelled in their tough-guy workaholic race-hungry image.

Each crew was so different: a law unto itself. There was no rule by which we as coaches could work. Every year we were dealing with a new band of men. They thought differently, they had different styles and approaches and the crew spirit they developed varied enormously from year to year. In 1974 Dave Sawyier was a changed man–the height of consideration–and the crew had no qualms about small gearing changes.

Cambridge must have believed that over a short distance they could match the speed of the Lube Lab for they challenged them to a series of three two-minute rows at the beginning of the last week. Again the scientists leaped away at the start and left the Light Blues a length behind each time. What emerged from these encounters was that neither of the Boat Race crews were particularly fast away and that the crucial stage of the race would come further down the course, around the three-minute mark. Lube Lab a length on Cambridge in two minutes; Lube Lab two lengths on Oxford in seven minutes. All this showed that the crews were quite evenly matched and the Press were delighted. A tight race at last; something to dispel the depressing ten-, nine and a half- and 13-length processions of the previous three years. In just six years Oxford had conceded 43 and a half lengths in the heaviest series of defeats for over 100 years.

But besides being pleased at the prospect of a close race the Press were pretty disparaging about both crews. Mediocre, humdrum, second-rate, below the standard of their predecessors–were their more polite utterings. 'Topolski and Jennens have been left with a lot of problems to solve' wrote Jim Railton in *The Times*. The breakfast-time reading could well have dampened the spirits of both crews but the reports simply served to raise their ire and their 'needle' all the more and they turned the poor notices to useful effect. 'We'll show the bastards' they said, glowering at the Press launch. The last reports in the days preceding the race began to favour Oxford, albeit grudgingly in view of their poor record since 1967. But the odds strengthened when Cambridge decided to have a last thrash with Goldie despite having been beaten the previous week to the Mile Post. They seemed to be setting themselves up for a morale-damaging tussle. There were men in that Goldie crew who thought they should have been in the Blue Boat and they were not about to let this chance of proving the point pass them by. At a lower rating they took a length off their first crew in a three-minute race three days before the Boat Race. Cambridge seemed to be compounding their selection mistakes.

On the same day Oxford took on the Tideway Scullers for a final bridge to bridge race from Hammersmith as their last major piece of work and beat them by five lengths. It was a weaker Scullers crew than the one which had just won the Head but the row itself was one of the best Oxford had done. There was rhythm and run and the lessons were beginning to show results – and not a moment too soon. The main work was now completed. All that remained was to quicken the starts, add the polish and rest up for the last few days. In all the 12 years that I have been Oxford's finishing coach, there has not been a single final fortnight that was not utterly engrossing, full of incident, with problems and crises perhaps, but never one which I or the crews involved did not look back on without contentment and pleasure. At the house in Barnes we made sure there were as few tensions as possible because the crew had to be able to unwind. In deference to each other more than by ruling they preferred not to have friends calling round to visit, although of course some did turn up every now and then; but they were gently discouraged. Family too could be very demanding, with their queries about tickets for the steamer, and where they should go to watch the race from, and their problems with meeting up for the Ball after the race. Such little details could occupy an excessive amount of an athlete's time and energy, worrying about parents' and girlfriends' logistical problems. I tried to keep all that distracting trivia out of the way. Piers meanwhile provided a constant flow of wholesome plain food and dealt diplomatically with individual dietary eccentricities. But he did try to draw the line at custard which offended his expert palate. He finally relented in the face of persistent whining from custard devotees, and provided the sickly substance for one meal in spite of his culinary conceits. He did, however, remain mindful that he had to switch the emphasis in their diet from protein to carbohydrate as race day approached.

Although Chris Blackwall was closeted with Isis, who were lodged around London in the homes of various loyal Dark Blue supporters like Dr Harry Freeman, he did pass by the house often and we plotted together daily at the National Westminster Bank boathouse–Oxford's riverside berth during the final fortnight. Every day there were new problems to solve, new tactics to adopt in the light of a change in Tab activity, details to attend to, boat rigging to check or adjust, crew members in both Isis and the Blue Boat to pacify or gee up. We shared the load as much as possible, encouraging each other, giving moral support. One year the crew dubbed us the 'odd couple', because we often bickered at each other as we busied about and sometimes huffed and puffed if we didn't get our own way.

Through all the comings and goings, the uncertainties, the grumbles, and the succession of oarsmen are the boatmen–Albert Andrews, Bert Green and Mike Thorn. They represent a rare element of constancy in the whole transient affair. Large (though smaller of late), genial Albert has been with Oxford since 1952 and attends to the maintenance of the boats, the boathouse on the Isis, the summer bumping races in Oxford, the launches and provides a consistent link from year to year as the man who has seen 33 Boat Race crews, at the last count, and a wide assortment of coaches, styles, new looks and crises over the decades. He is a shrewd judge when it comes to assessing the year's intake of talent and their progress through training and a cheery 'They don't look at all bad, sir' is enough to tell an uncertain coach that he's on the right track. It's good whoever you are to have that sort of support. But when Albert has difficulty finding the words, you know you've got trouble on your hands. His opposite number at Cambridge is Alf Twinn, boatman there since 1934, and a more forceful, opinionated character than Albert. He plays an important role in the coaching scene on the Cam and has considerable say in what equipment is used each year. Some reckon he can be a bit of a liability, intimidating coaches he does not like and pressing the claims of his particular protegés in the squad. His prime object though, which he states firmly every year, is to 'break Oxford hearts'. He likes to have the last word and right at the beginning, when I was first rowing for Oxford in the 'sixties he nicknamed me 'golliwog', and has greeted me thus ever since. 'Hello golly' he will yell from the Barclays boathouse, 'so they've dragged you in again have they? They must be hard up for coaches.' 'Oh no, Alf, not you again; I can't believe they haven't found a decent boatman yet.' He's a good boatman and a definite Light Blue asset, but illness in 1983 and 1984 relegated him to a less dominant role, although he still rides in the launch on the day.

Another major Cambridge asset is the good Doctor Bevan, an Old Blue, once and for long their doctor, and a true gentleman of exceptional charm and good sportsmanship. Every year we have won I have received from him a letter of warm greetings and congratulations tinged with a hint of old sporting rivalry. He has supported the Light Blues through thick and thin. Indeed the Old Blue backing enjoyed by Cambridge is far more constant and fullsome than that enjoyed by the Oxford crews. The Tab launch during practice is always filled to overflowing with large red-cheeked men in the Cambridge greenish-blue coloured schoolboy caps, huge wraparound scarves and fawn greatcoats. No one else can ever find room aboard except coach Graeme Hall's young son Mark and their boatman Alf. The Oxford training launch by contrast carries a bevy of girlfriends, college colleagues, hopeful school oarsmen picking up tips and begging a ride, mothers, sisters and fathers. Only when the race is a day or two off do the Oxford Old Blues begin to appear, seeking prime seats on one of our two launches for the big day. It is, I suppose, the way of things. At first we thought the lack of interest was due to our dismal record, but then when we began to win and still they stayed away, we realised that there was indeed a more fundamental difference between the Dark and Light Blue camps. In saying this I trust those ardent Old Blue supporters who do come regularly will not be offended, but then they too remark how often they seem to be alone with the coach in the launch on cold, blustery February afternoons. Gully Nickalls was one Old Blue who loved Oxford and never failed to attend a Boat Race. One of Britain's greatest-ever oarsmen, he was a well-loved character at Henley where he reigned as senior Steward throughout my early rowing career. He had been an exceptional athlete, winning Henley and Olympic medals galore. His fine biography *A Rainbow in the Sky* showed him to be a man of wit and charm, an artist of no mean talent and a poet. His contribution to British as well as Oxford rowing was enormous and we were glad to have him by our side in the sharp bow end of *Bosporos*, Oxford's elegant Victorian coaching launch, on race day.

In 1974, we coaches huddled there alongside Gully, shamelessly nervous but pretending confidence as we moored up alongside the Cambridge launch *Amaryllis* to await the arrival of the crews on the stakeboats. It was exciting but horrendous sitting there for those few minutes before the race, the tension all the greater since our jobs were over. There was nothing more we could do but sit in silence and watch as the race unfolded. We were forbidden to shout support or advice to our crews. They were out there on their own. Gully was not well and his

91

doctors had tried to prevent him from coming to watch the race. 'Dear boy,' he said as he climbed into *Bosporos*, 'my wife told me I should stay at home and watch the race in colour on the telly. But I said sorry, I'd much rather go down and see the thing live in black and white thank you very much', and he burst out laughing in his gruff, boisterous way and jammed his cigar back between his teeth. He had suffered with Oxford through six defeats in a row. Would this year see the turning of the tide?

Sitting at the driving wheel of *Bosporos* is Bert Green, coach and boatman to the National Westminster Bank crews who are Oxford's Tideway hosts. Albert defers to Bert when we arrive on the Tideway, remaining ashore to take care of things while we are afloat. Bert took over this role when Ted Phelps went abroad to work in the Middle East. He knows the Tideway well and learned many of the same tricks from Ted that I learned while I was at Westminster. Ted had been right hand man, launch driver and confidant to 'Jumbo' through the 'fifties and 'sixties, and now Bert had assumed the same role for me. Each year we have come to understand one another better until now we hardly have to exchange words when watching the crew training because we find we are thinking along the same lines much of the time. I tended to work most closely with Chris in the first years but quickly Bert's contributions became more and more important to our race strategy and when Chris left to take on the job of national coach and then moved to America Bert and I found ourselves conferring about practically all of the important day-to-day decisions on rigging, changes in crew, course problems and choice of station. It is Bert who takes charge of the daily run over the track with the Oxford and Isis coxes, coaching them on the trickeries of the shifting Tideway current and guiding them to the best possible course. We chew over the plans for the day, for the week, analyse progress, sort out technical problems and make provisions for unforeseen difficulties. The experience gained from a growing succession of years prepares us all the better for such imponderables. 'The wind's turning north a bit' says Bert, sniffing the air and checking the flags fluttering above the Putney boathouses; and we both know we may have to consider different race tactics. 'What do you reckon on five's blade; he's scooping up a bit of water at the finish?' 'Let's check his outward pitch after the outing', I answer. 'I'll put a bit of tape round it for now and see if it helps.'

We always seem to have to re-rig the boat when we arrive on the Tideway. Pitches and heights, nuts and bolts and even spans can slip with continuous use or when the boats are being transported and the bouncy Putney waters often require certain fine adjustments to be made to oar, rigger and boat. 'I couldn't hold them on that start', says Bert, gunning the throttle from the launch driver's seat—and we know the crew is travelling very fast. He can set the throttle at a certain number of revs as the crew gets into their stride and we can judge their speed and whether they fade at any point quite accurately when the eye would be hard pressed to notice a difference. 'Not so good that piece', I tell the crew. 'But Dan, it felt great!' comes a protest from the men in the boat. 'Maybe it felt good, but it wasn't as fast as the one before. Give it a fraction more time on the slide. Let the boat run more between the strokes. Sit back a touch.' Now they look better and Bert confirms their extra speed as he juggles with the controls. The crew concurs and report that they can feel the difference, even though to the outside observer there is no perceivable change from the previous piece of work. The wider gap between bow's puddle and seven's catch underlines the improvement. 'That's it, let's push those puddles down to the stern post. When I say "row" I mean row harder in the water, not faster. Forget the ratings.' To the coach's eye there is a fraction more smoothness and run about the boat, a touch more relaxation—the key to a fast moving boat and the equivalent of an inch or two per stroke translating to maybe a length over the 18-minute, four and a quarter-mile Boat Race course. The difference between winning and losing, perhaps.

Ah the joys of that final fortnight and those barely imperceptible improvements which derive from changing to twice-daily outings and concentrated high quality work. The heavy quantity stuff, those grinding miles of soul-destroying (or character-building depending on whether you are rower or coach) steady state and alternate long distance stretches of work are at last behind them. Now it's quality. To watch the crew growing in stature and confidence, striding out as they feel their strength flowing back more and more each day after months of continuous energy-sapping training, as their timing improves markedly and as they relax and go with the flow—that is the pleasure of a Boat Race crew reaching its peak. Although problems always abound in those final two weeks—illness, injury, damage to equipment, unexpected and unwelcome defeats in important fixtures, poor unsettled outings, rough conditions, all of which can cast a gloomy pall over the household—there are still those moments of true contentment when the crew does it all right, just when you were beginning to despair (do they ever bloody well listen?) and all of a sudden everyone can feel and see it and there is a group sigh of satisfaction, and let it be admitted, relief too: That's it, that's what we've been looking for. At least now we know how it should feel.

In his year as President Dave Sawyier became quite the traditional-ist, the classic yank at Oxford. There were few ruffles apart from the late Payne/Tee introduction and we had an excellent run-up to the race. On the whole Dave and I saw eye to eye that second year and we presented perhaps a less flamboyant front than the image of the year before. We knew too that we were probably not as strong as the 1973 crew and that the spirit and unity was not as great but the way he bustled them along at 35 gave the impression of a crew with something urgent to take care of although they sometimes looked a little short on finesse. They were also apt on occasion to make mistakes. We could never be sure that each outing would show that all-important small improvement on the preceding one or even match it for quality. But if we were a little inconsistent, we were consoled by the fact that Cambridge were even more so. Their defeat by the Lube Lab, Goldie and the Scullers, their proneness to crabs—they were even forced by a crab to stop rowing altogether when racing their far from speedy host crew, Barclays Bank—and their inability to hold a hard racing rate for more than a minute or two resulted in them presenting a somewhat dispirited and ill-assorted front. Somehow their selection process had gone wrong and they did not quite measure up to their fine predecessors.

In the last few days the wind began to pick up as it had done the year before and I made a point of rowing the crew through rough water, practising starts and hard rating work in order to overcome the residual fears that Dave and some of the others still had from the previous Boat Race. It still looked tense but with aerofoil riggers the boat was subject to less buffeting and the relaxation began to come. On Boat Race day, the wind was still up, but not uncomfortably so, along the first reach at Putney. Checking round the corner with Bert and the cox in the launch a couple of hours before the race, we found that the crews would encounter rough water along by the Mile Post, and we planned our final tactics accordingly. After three minutes of the race both crews would be stressed and vulnerable and the sudden headwind and rough conditions could do severe damage to an ill-prepared crew. We knew that it was at this very point that Oxford would have to show particular character. They would have to maintain their racing rate of 34/35 through the rough water. But it would have to be done with confidence and looseness just when the natural inclination would be for the rate to sag, and consequently the work output too, as they turned into the teeth of the wind and popple. If Oxford could be hard at the moment when most crews would go soft then they could take the race.

Our pre-race talk concentrated very much on our strengths and the

Light Blue weaknesses, the points which we could score. I also stressed the need to stay loose in the rough water and the crucial strategic moments along the track where the race could be won or lost, and where their opponents would be at their most vulnerable. Oxford went to the line determined not to make any mistakes this time round and to heed the advice. The burden of avenging six successive defeats weighed heavily on each man. Dave lost the toss, but Cambridge decided to take the Middlesex station even though the conditions at Putney were not that unfriendly. Clearly they were banking on holding our start and going for the advantage of the first bend. In the popply water beyond that first corner by the Fulham football ground they would be in trouble unless they had stolen a substantial enough lead to move over on to our Surrey station for the inside of the Hammersmith bend and the calmer water beyond.

It was a well disciplined no-nonsense Oxford crew that went straight into the lead from the 'go', settling after 90 seconds to a punchy 35 strokes a minute while Cambridge sagged first to 33 and then lower as they hit the headwind round the Fulham bend. With Oxford in the lead by one third of a length on the outside of the bend, it was obvious that the Light Blue gamble was failing and Sawyier quickly realised this. He relaxed, the crew settled behind him and they sailed confidently through the choppy waters, turning the screw just as we had planned. They kept pushing on at 35 in the knowledge that if they could find the extra effort now when the wind was at its worst, they would gain an advantage great enough to take them safely and joyously home, running before a tailwind and a fast tide from Hammersmith to Mortlake.

As Cambridge faltered at the Mile Post and dropped to 31, Oxford stretched their lead in the next two minutes from one third of a length to over two lengths by Hammersmith. Although they did not know it then they were on target for a very fast second-half row; fast enough in fact to break the race record by 15 seconds and the course record set up by the fine 1965 Oxford crew in practice against the Tideway Scullers by two seconds. In the launch I was still holding my breath. While others were smiling and congratulating each other with the race only half completed, my innate pessimism held me back. 'Not yet', I begged, 'something could still go wrong. Let's wait until they cross the line.' But nothing was going to stop them now and they raced on to a famous victory, five and a half lengths in front of Cambridge in a time of 17 minutes 35 seconds. 'Oxford has today restored its self-respect most emphatically' said Dave in his speech that night, and all those Old Dark Blues who had waited so long for such a moment sat a little taller in their seats. Gully was overjoyed. Sadly, he died three weeks later, but at least he had seen them that last time, victorious in black and white. The Press reports next day seemed on the whole remarkably reluctant to give credit to this Oxford performance, this so painfully won revival. Only Ray Moore in the *Daily Mail* and *Rowing* magazine were really impressed while poor Harry Carpenter in his BBC commentary tried vainly to excite his unenthusiastic fellow commentators: 'But this is magnificent!' he cried. And so it was.

Isis's performance was promising too although they were beaten by four lengths by a far superior crew. They never dropped below 36 and lost only nine seconds after Goldie's initial length off the start over the main body of the course. This was the mark of the new attacking Oxford mood, and provided a first flush of Boat Race fever for seven future Blues. Paul Wright had to wait for three more years while the unathletic first year student Boris Rankov, later to become the most successful Boat Race oarsman of all time, would not row in his first race until 1978.

Soon after that victorious moment bowman Nick Tee confided that a few days before the race he had complained to our doctor Harry of a sore throat and had been given some antibiotics. 'They gave me the shits' he said ruefully, 'but I didn't dare say anything. I lost over ten pounds in a week. I rowed the race well under 11 stone.' Gareth Morris remembers that his bow oarsman had worked like fury in the first half of the race, but after that his puddle left a lot to be desired. Tee's dilemma was one that is faced by many top athletes – to compete or not to compete because of illness or injury; to admit to illness or to keep quiet. It is a dilemma made all the more critical in a team effort as tightly knit as a rowing eight. That he did not say anything was irresponsible since he was jeopardising the outcome of the race without the benefit of sound medical advice to help decide whether he should row or be replaced. Yet it was an understandable deception if he believed himself strong enough to race but was worried that the decision if discussed more widely might rule him out. His unexpected loss of weight turned out to be quite useful later in the year when he rowed as a lightweight in the World Rowing Championships.

After the Boat Race, Gavin Stoddart and Paul Marsden were selected to row in a pair as part of the British team effort at a number of international regattas. Nick Tee and I joined future Cambridge finishing coach Graeme Hall and Chris Drury, a Dogget's Coat and Badge winner and ex-Youth international, to form the first lightweight crew selected by Britain for the inaugural lightweight World Rowing Championships in Lucerne later in the year. This was an event for crews averaging 11 stone (70 kg) and we won at Mannheim, our first international regatta abroad. We found that while in Britain lightweight rowing was a totally new discipline, in Europe, Australia and America it was already well advanced and of a very high standard. In August we won the small finals in Lucerne by finishing seventh overall, having failed to make the final by 7/100ths of a second. We stayed together for a second attempt the following year and in a dramatic world final rowed from last to second to take the silver medal.

Nick Tee was elected President for the 1975 Boat Race and since we were rowing together all summer we had the opportunity to lay plans for the following year. Although we were losing a number of good men, we were determined not to let our new and hard won initiative founder. Nick was a methodical well-organised man, the complete opposite in temperament to Sawyier, but no less single-minded. His would be a well-run Presidential term, efficient if perhaps lacking a little in drama. He decided against nominating a head coach, loth to allocate what he considered was too much formal authority to one coach amongst equals, which might have rankled with the others. Instead he asked all the coaches to do a specific two-week stint, taking a lot of extra and unnecessary planning work on to his own shoulders. Nevertheless, Chris and I were both delegated to continue in our roles as overall organisers of the land training and water programmes, taking on the all-important January period of selection and with me doing the final Tideway fortnight at Putney. Titles were not important; Oxford winning was what mattered, and 1975 promised to be a hard race to win.

Oxford's Henley Regatta efforts in the summer showed a poor return with Sawyier's Christ Church four of last year men (of no practical use to us) reaching the final of the Visitors' Cup, the leading college crews Oriel and Christ Church failing in the Ladies' and only Tee in our lightweight four managing a semi-final slot in the Wyfolds. Although it would seem logical to have sent an Oxford/Isis eight to Henley as a training crew made up of oarsmen hoping to try for a Blue the following year it was not always possible to do so. Coaches had other commitments and it was hard for us part-time amateurs to tag on a further four months' involvement after a six-month winter. Yet although it was obviously difficult to keep the continuity right through the year we tried to do so since it was vital to our continued success. Furthermore colleges had first call on their top oarsmen once the Boat Race was over, and college loyalties as well as the desire to take part in the bumping races in the fifth week usually held sway during the summer. Also the better college crews wanted to carry on to Henley where in the past they had raced so gloriously and with such success.

But the days of a University college crew mustering enough talent to take on all comers for the Ladies' Plate are gone. Nowadays the composite college and university second crews at home and from abroad are far too strong. We have tried at Oxford to find a compromise, releasing the best oarsmen for their colleges until the end of Eights week but maintaining an extra outing or two each week in their prospective Henley-bound composite Oxford squad crew. When the bumping races are over they are free once again to train full-time for the last month before Henley. Sometimes the system has worked, most notably in 1981 when Oxford took the Grand from the British national eight; but more often we have fallen just short.

Some colleges still send crews to compete for the Ladies' Plate but until the Regatta alters its rules to provide a specially restricted event for colleges, they will have to be satisfied with limited success in the opening rounds at Henley. The Universities meanwhile will have to look to composite crews if they wish to achieve any success beyond the occasional win at provincial regattas. Of course that is not to denigrate the pleasure to be derived from rowing at that less exalted standard. Non-élite rowing need not be in any way less satisfying or enjoyable. But my own interest as a coach and competitor in the sport has always been at the top end – winning at the highest level.

4
Set-back

Until term begins in October there is little way of knowing what sort of material we are going to be working with for the forthcoming year. As we have seen, some old faces – namely the returning Old Blues and those Isis men who had hoped to make their play for the top boat – find that academic pressures catch up with them and they have to withdraw. The freshman intake varies unnervingly from year to year. Sometimes there may be some talented but lightweight just-out-of-school boys, sometimes some large, clumsy overseas graduates, sometimes some hardened Youth internationals who have survived the tough world of international school rowing often in composite crews. And occasionally we get a senior international who can bring real class to a 'Varsity crew.

In October 1974 a young crop of Youth internationals turned up to join the remaining Blues, Nick Tee (Emanuel) and Graham Innes (Pangbourne), and our Isis oarsmen, Andy Baird (Radley), Paul Wright (Hampton), Mark Harris (St Edwards), Boris Rankov (Bradford), Ollie Moore (Eton), Steve Plunkett (Belfast) and John Hutchings from Canada. Two giant Etonians, Bob Mason and Crispin Money-Coutts, were the products of a successful school eight, which came seventh in the Nottingham World Youth Championships in 1973; Money-Coutts had doubled up in the coxless pair event with Henry Clay (who had already spent a first year rowing for Cambridge) to win a silver medal as well. In that same British Youth team of 1973 was a third Oxford fresher, the Radleian David Beak, who had won the *petite finale* in coxed pairs with his schoolmate Robin Waterer who subsequently went on to Cambridge. As if to demonstrate what a small, interconnecting fraternity the rowing world can be, Graham Innes had also been there at Nottingham for his third World Championships at this level before coming to row for Oxford in 1973–4. Another man from the successful 1973 British team was John Wiggins, rowing in the bronze medal Wallingford coxed four, who was himself due to come to Oxford in 1975–6. With John in that very talented Wallingford crew was Bill Lang, who quit rowing a year later after winning a second coxed four bronze medal to become a doctor. He re-emerged eight years later as a graduate at Oxford where he fought back to form and fitness to row bow in the 1983 Boat Race and seven in 1984. He, like so many of us, is an active example of how irresistible a draw rowing is, and how difficult it can be for oarsmen to turn their backs on the river completely. Another talented but unpredictable rowing fresher was Andrew Hudson from Westminster, who sculled twice for Britain in the Junior Championships before coming to Oxford. He finished 12th in 1973 and sixth in Ratzeburg the following year, but other involvements at Oxford diverted him from realising his potential and sadly he failed to make a mark. The foregoing list highlights an intricate family tree of rowers with the best men concentrated very early on in national composites and all rowing together during their careers at both junior and senior level.

So there we had it, a crop of talented new youngsters but with only the two remaining Blues Tee and Innes possessing any real experience at senior level. However there were a number of college-trained oarsmen and some average schoolboy first and second eighters appearing on the scene as well; big and strong but rough. These presented quite a challenge, for if they could be brought on effectively they would form the basis of a useful pool of oarsmen on which to draw in subsequent years. Dave Edwards, Jamie Pike, Steve Plunkett, Ollie Moore, Boris Rankov, Gyles Vardey, Dave Newman and 'Hugh' Craig were all put through the mill and emerged later with great credit rowing in a superlative Isis crew coxed by the mercurial Colin Moynihan.

Cambridge on the other hand looked to be an entirely different proposition to their 1974 crew. Their winning Lady Margaret four in the Prince Philip Cup at Henley, which had chosen not to enter the Light Blue trials in 1974, were back for 1975. Three of the four, the 1973 Goldie men Neil Christie and Jamie Macleod and the Blue David Sturge, also represented Britain in the Senior World Championships later that year, finishing ninth, their fourth man, the new Cambridge President American Steve Tourek, being ineligible to row for Britain. I knew David Sturge well. In 1970 at Cambridge he had failed even to make Goldie, but had joined me in a London coxed four, with Nick Cooper once again seduced from retirement and John Dart, a 1970 Oxford Blue, to race at Henley. David had been making quite a name for himself as a sculler but we were quite unfancied as a crew initially and were made to race in the pre-Regatta qualifying races. Indeed a week before the Regatta we had considered calling the whole thing off because it felt so uncomfortable. But we qualified easily and then went from strength to strength through the heats each day winning our last two races by a quarter and two-thirds of a length to take the Britannia Cup. David Sturge went back to Cambridge where he gained a Blue in 1973 and was now returning for the 1975 race, nine years after matriculating, on a post-graduate course as a twice-capped senior international, a two-times winner of the Wingfield sculls (the British Amateur Sculling Championships) a double Henley winner, and a Diamond sculls finalist. The Light Blue line-up, then, presented an awesome array of talent.

To enable Sturge and Nick Tee to row in the Boat Race, the rules governing eligibility had to be amended to incorporate graduates of their particular standing and the Presidents Steve Tourek and Tee (both married men incidentally) agreed the amendment at a joint meeting of the two University Blues Committees, also writing in the controversial clause '*in statu pupulari*' which was to allow Boris Rankov eight years later to race for his record sixth win in the Boat Race.

Besides this formidable quartet of internationals Cambridge were also able to call upon the world Youth silver medallist and Blue Henry Clay, Money-Coutts' pairs partner at Eton, and a number of good Goldie men. But undaunted by Cambridge's high-class pedigree Oxford set about their task with enthusiasm entering the usual autumn sculling heads, pairs and fours races. What we lacked in experience and maturity we made up for in hard work and aggression. Inevitably, but with misgivings, we were forced to put a lot of responsibility on to the shoulders of our young freshmen. They may well have stood at over six foot five and weighed over 14 stone, those two Etonians, but their hugeness belied their strength for such a gruelling task as the engine room of a Boat Race crew. They were after all spring chickens, and not used to the workloads that we foisted upon them particularly in the weight-training room.

David Beak, though smaller, was more used to heavy weight-training which he had done at Radley and his exceptional talent as a sculler brought him quickly into the running. He was however a little unorthodox in his movements and throughout his period at Oxford was always marginally out of time with the crews he rowed in although he was undoubtedly an effective oarsman. He became quite a handful in his third year and demonstrated perfectly how unsatisfactory it is to promote freshmen directly to the Blue Boat. A year or two in Isis is always preferable if it can be afforded, because as often as not, Old Blues, unless they are particularly mature, develop the 'old lag' syndrome and become cantankerous and obstructive. The problem is that they know their worth. Their experience, especially if they are winners, counts for a lot, but occasionally one of them will push his luck too far until we find that in the final analysis he is dispensable. A first year in Isis gives them perspective, experience and hunger.

During this period with Oxford I was in the throes of competition myself, racing with a fair measure of success in all the sculling Heads, fours races and eights with London Rowing Club. Using my own rowing activity as an example for the Oxford squad was useful. All the things the coaches were trying to get them to do they could see being put into practice and more importantly achieving results. I could set myself up as a target for them in running and open sculling races around the country. I was also free to go to the Head of the Cam, into the enemy camp, to scull against the Cambridge squad who regularly took part in that open event. From my result there I could gauge their strength and compare their results against my performance with those of the Oxford squad, giving me good early indicators of the standard of the crew we were likely to face in the spring. Sculling and competing with the Oxford boys gave me a vital extra insight into the way they performed, since I could judge precisely how I was feeling at any given stage in a race and could assess their comparative individual efforts accordingly. In our January four and a quarter-mile sculling heads on the Tideway, in which the slowest scullers started first to be chased by the faster men, I could tell as I came up to overtake each man how hard he was working, how successfully and for how long he could hold me off, or whether having closed fast on him, I then had to struggle to get by. This suggested that he was producing an extra effort just to impress but was taking an easy ride during the main body of the race. If a man went sick in the eight I would take his place eagerly rather than call up a substitute from Isis. It gave me a chance to get a feel of the crew from the inside and to sense how well the boat was running, how well together the crew were rowing. From outside it was often hard to spot differences when blades and bodies appeared to be moving together. All these factors helped me to get to know my squad better, to learn their quirks and weaknesses. Constant surveillance meant that weaknesses would show as the pressure increased even if at first they were being well concealed. The programme was designed to winkle out the flaws.

Some men professed to being unable to run. 'I've never been a runner', complained the flat-footed Rankov when he first arrived at Oxford. And sure enough he was horrible, and finished five minutes behind the rest in a four-mile race. If we had accepted that Boris could not run, we would have given him tacit encouragement not to try harder. 'Why do I need to run if I'm going to row?' he wailed. Chris Blackwall joined Boris in the second four-mile race on the third lap behind the runners exhorting the poor man, whipping him along with cutting words, driving him beyond himself. 'Come on, Boris!' he yelled. 'I can't' cried Boris. 'Faster Boris!' 'I'm trying' he groaned. 'Push yourself!' screamed Chris into the struggling athlete's left ear as

they tottered in tandem along the embankment. It was a comic sight—
the tall, aristocratic, slim blond and the cowering, overweight, swarthy
'serf' plodding along under the whiplash tongue of his master. But it
worked, and although Boris never became what you would call a
runner, he did learn how to work himself much harder and derived
tremendous conditioning value from it. He improved his times again
and again by sheer grit and forced himself into the reckoning by pure
strength of character. From the most inauspicious start, Boris Rankov
became the most successful Boat Race oarsman in history, with six
wins to his credit and only one Isis defeat out of two in all his years on
the Tideway.

Other perhaps more talented men arriving at Oxford with high
hopes but lacking his sort of commitment dropped out of the picture
quite quickly. They lacked the courage and the motivation, the hunger
that makes a Boat Race winner and whatever their excuses for pulling
out—work, pleasure, pressures from girlfriends or boyfriends—in the
end they simply lacked the heart for the battle. So they fell by the
wayside. Yet even the most unlikely candidate, if he has the will and
character, can make it or at least come close, simply by being there day
after day and doing the training. He gets carried along with the others,
not necessarily excelling at any one thing, but just putting in the time,
learning the tricks of the trade, learning about himself and how much
further away are his limits than he at first thought. So in the end the
coach's task is to help his athlete discover unexplored levels of mental
and physical effort, to go beyond the point where the brain and body are
saying 'no more'. For beyond that point there is a special kind of
ecstasy.

I have always been a little ambivalent about my coaching role. I
would always prefer to be in the boat myself than in the launch, and
often a crew could sense that, especially on the occasions when I got
into the boat to substitute. The squad seemed to respond well to the
active coach who consequently could identify that much more closely
with their own individual problems. It was easier for me to tear a man
off a strip for lack of commitment in a piece of work when I was
obviously training at the same level. It is possible that a coach's
credibility weakens the longer he has been out of competitive rowing.
The respect you gain from beating the hell out of your charges in actual
competition is invaluable. It also makes you more accessible, easier to
talk to. It is important to assess the mood of your crew carefully, not to
be too aloof yet not to be too much one of the boys. The degree of each
depends on the crew each year since no two crews are the same. As a
coach you have to judge the temperaments of all nine individuals in the

boat, yet not ruled by their prejudices and anxieties. On the other hand, it is counterproductive to ride roughshod over deeply felt worries, particularly those concerning equipment or a colleague in the crew. A coach can do as much good just by listening to his athletes as he can by yelling at them 24 hours a day. Feedback from everyone is important and here again, some members may be inclined to talk openly in front of the whole crew, while others may out of shyness or deference to a crewmate prefer the quiet word. Whatever it is a coach in a team effort needs to monitor the thoughts of his men as thoroughly as he does their physical performances.

Coaches obviously vary in temperament. Some are men of few words and their crews hang on every syllable. 'Jumbo' was such a man. Others talk constantly and some crews feel reassured by such attention while some get irritated. Some coach for crew discipline and overall improvement, while others concentrate on the individuals in the boat, picking on them mercilessly until they get it right or scream out under the strain. Most coaches though would feel awkward about calling attention to a man's faults too often, fearing he might lose confidence in himself. There are training rather than technique orientated coaches, and there are those who excel at organisation. I tend to be a little unorthodox in my approach with Boat Race crews (if not with national squad crews), and I think they quite like that, although they are a little startled at times by some of the things I say. Giving the final pre-race talk one year, I wanted to give them a sense of turning the screw on Cambridge at a critical moment and I suggested that each man imagine he was holding the balls of his opposite number in his hand and that he was squeezing them tighter and tighter as the race progressed. The trouble was we were being filmed for a BBC documentary at the time, and their faces showed a lovely array of reactions. But the words tend to tumble out the way they do because they seem to express the mood of the moment most usefully.

Sometimes it is difficult to judge that mood, but it is a coach's job to get it right. There is nothing better geared to losing the confidence of your men than to fail to identify what they are thinking and feeling. The worst time for this is when they have just suffered a defeat in a training race or in a minor fixture, always an unexpected shock for a top athlete no matter how realistically he reckons his chances before the event. Whether to talk immediately, or to wait; whether to harangue or to sympathise; whether to analyse (hard if they were performing well and you could spot few faults) or to concentrate on the good aspects of the performance. A crew is extremely vulnerable at that point and they are praying for you to voice something convincing enough to give them hope for the future. If however it was the final race, their pinnacle event, then words are of little consequence and a mournful look is about all anyone, coach or athlete, can muster in their joint disappointment. There is always for the coach a fear of losing touch with the squad, of losing contact with their thoughts and with their efforts. Because I find it hard to conceal my feelings and I have no deadpan expression on which to fall back at difficult moments they can read my reactions to their performances all too easily. A bad training row, slow times, poor cover, means a glum-looking me. As a result there have been some in the various crews who have watched my face for a reaction, hoping that they might detect signs that they were not rowing as badly as they knew they were. It is in the last few days before the race that the strain begins to show, although perversely I tend to feel more anxious with a crew I know to be very good than I do with a crew that is facing a tough race. When the odds are even the adrenalin really flows and that is when I reckon I'm at my best, with a lot going on to keep me busy. Probably the humiliation of defeat at the hands of a supposedly inferior opponent is harder to bear—the prospect of ridicule too great to risk.

With some crews there are strong-willed, experienced men in the boat who may feel a need to assert themselves or challenge a coach's authority and his technique and judgement, and this can undermine the confidence of the less experienced men in the crew let alone that of the coach. The mature athlete chooses to air his deeply felt grievances privately man to man, while the insecure one who wants to show off, or who is intent on a power struggle, will argue loudly and publicly. The coach has to operate accordingly, knowing when to take a tough line, and when to sit back and let the boys blow off steam. If he can adapt year by year to the different characters in his successive crews, he will find that with one lot he may play a leading role with paternalistic firmness while with another he may prefer a quieter guiding role, allowing them their heads more, trusting in their instincts as much as in his own. He needs guile, stamina and tact. He must know which men to tease, which to insult, which to lay off, which to harass and goad, which to encourage, to confide in, to trust and distrust.

While coaching the women's squad for the 1980 Moscow Olympics, I experienced at one point some difficulty with a couple of girls in the crew. In conversation with one of the young coxes, I found out that she had been told never to trust the coach, never to tell him what the crew was thinking, that the overriding relationship was one of crew versus coach, a battle of wits. Any significant dialogue between one squad member and the coach would be considered tantamount to a breach of faith by her fellow rowers. 'We would never trust you again', the two experienced girls told her, 'if we found you'd been talking to the coach.' Yet a cox was one person who, if sensible and mature, could provide a constant stream of vital information about how the squad were feeling; whether they were confident, hopeful, depressed, unhappy about any of their colleagues. He or she could relay the information not as a spy, not as a gossip with illicit news, but as the provider of an extra dimension on which the coach could operate in getting the best out of his crew. It was a sad reflection on the past arrangement of women's rowing and the buffeting and betrayals they must surely have suffered at the hands of their administrators to make them adopt such a siege mentality, and it could hardly have been less conducive to producing the fastest crews. Top performance can only come from a joint effort between mutually trusting partners – coach and crew.

A coach, like any teacher, is sometimes tempted to tell his charges things they want to hear. But he is treading on dangerous ground if he knowingly tells them things that are incorrect even if he thinks it might help them in the long run. To give them targets they cannot realistically achieve is to leave them dissatisfied and distrustful at the end of the season; so achievable aims, a series of targets they can reach for and manage week by week will build confidence far more effectively than ambitious words can ever do. If anything, I err on the side of being downright pessimistic and shy away from raising hopes particularly before I have solid evidence to back up my claims. So much of the approach to a race like the Boat Race involves the psychological massaging of confidence especially when the crew is young and relatively inexperienced.

Clear cut evidence of a crew's superiority is a help of course, but too much of it can have the opposite effect, that of instilling complacency, dangerous because it undermines their resolve. Disdain or a lack of respect for your enemy, however much you may tell yourself you are still alert, can do untold damage to your chances. You have to believe completely that you are facing the toughest test of your career, whatever the predictions, whatever the evidence. A momentary loss of concentration, of sympathy or pity for the opposition, and you will be undone. Complacency is insidious and hard to detect, and even harder to eradicate. A stage-managed or unplanned defeat from an unexpected quarter can concentrate the mind of the self-satisfied oarsman or crew wonderfully and restore their hunger immediately. If it happens quite close to the race it gets the adrenalin flowing and reintroduces a level of immediacy and tension that may have deserted, however momentarily, a good but arrogant crew. With an experienced or mature

106

crew, men who have faced a lot of tough races before, the likelihood that they have been beaten in the past when they least expected it is greater and they are less prone to let their guard down. They know not to underestimate opponents, however bad they look, however poor their reputation and past record. No crew, whoever they are, are beaten until the finishing line has been crossed.

So the balance between building the confidence of a crew, even the creation of a quiet arrogance which dictates that no one on the river had better dare challenge your superiority or they will suffer the consequences (backed up of course by the will and power to make good the threat), and guarding against complacency is an all-important equation which can have a huge bearing on the eventual outcome of the race.

In 1977, I rowed in an unbeaten lightweight eight throughout the year, and we approached the World Championships in Holland as favourites for Britain's first rowing gold medal in 25 years. Praise was heaped upon us. A few weeks before the Championships we went to Copenhagen Regatta and lost by a good length to the Spanish lightweight eight. We were stunned. All comfortable expectations were dashed and suddenly we could see that gold medal turning to silver or worse. We trained like slaves for the next month. The Spaniards' time in the opening round of the World Championships was again two and a half seconds faster as we both finished first in our respective heats. But alerted to the fact that they were very fast, we prepared ourselves for a supreme effort. We won the final and the gold medal in a desperate race by 3/100ths of a second or seven inches. There is no doubt that we would have been less mentally aggressive if we had not suffered that Copenhagen defeat and had those early warning signals. Without them we would surely have finished as runners-up in Amsterdam.

Any athlete can nowadays prepare himself or herself physiologically to the necessary peak of condition in which to compete barring the use of drugs. Given that the athletes or the crews are evenly matched physically in weight and strength then a large element in the mix which decides the eventual winner must be their psychological approach to the race. Over and over again the top lightweights are proving that will and spirit can overcome size. A good little 'un will always beat a so-so big 'un. Belief in himself and his ability to succeed is the athlete's greatest asset. My job, particularly in those last weeks, is to give the crew the opportunity to reinforce that belief, to show the squad how best they can put their fitness and abilities to the most effective use, and above all, reach the finishing line at Mortlake ahead of their arch rivals Cambridge.

It was clear that we had a very competitive and talented young group when we gathered in 1974 at the end of term for the trials race at Putney. The two crews under Peter Politzer and the 1967 President Jock Mullard spent three days on the Tideway acclimatising. Then they mounted a fine race to halfway after which the lighter crew stroked by a fluid Andy Baird went away from Nick Tee's crew, who were not helped by their own cox Moynihan's over-aggressive steering tactics, to win by five lengths. The squad were in good spirits as they disbanded for Christmas. We did not in those days run a two-week camp before Christmas like we have done since 1978, and they went off for their month long vacation with a detailed daily programme of work tucked under their arms.

I joined Dave Sawyier, now a Chicago lawyer, and an assortment of other Old Blues for the annual Boat Race on the Nile. Our Egyptian hosts, the Ministry of Tourism, did us proud for the fifth year running but this time they had only invited Oxford and Harvard having become exasperated with the nonchalance of Yale and Cambridge during the first four years of the fixture. We preferred to send past Boat Race oarsmen abroad for Oxford and Cambridge events because we were loth to prejudge the race itself and we did not want to risk the health of our trialists. Indeed it was a nice perk for past Boat Race Blues.

It was only when we went abroad that we realised how far the tentacles of our famous event spread worldwide. 'Jumbo' was fond of telling us how he had travelled through the African bush and had stumbled upon a remote village. 'They asked where I was from and I said "England", and they all shook their heads blankly. So I mentioned the Queen of England and Great Britain and the Commonwealth and still they made no connection. So I said "the Oxford and Cambridge Boat Race" and immediately their faces lit up with delight and recognition.' It was even reported once that Indira Gandhi changed a Cabinet meeting so that she and India could listen in to the race commentary. The Boat Race was considered abroad to be one of the most prestigious of traditional British institutions and our hosts in Asia, Europe, Africa and the Americas treated us like heroes.

Apart from our rewarding series of trips to the Nile we were fêted on the Seine and on the Danube, in Spain against the Basques of Orio, in Seattle, Miami, New York and St Catherines, in Yugoslavia, in Japan and in Nantes, Cannes and Bordeaux, and in Rome competing against local competition and usually against similarly representative crews from Cambridge. It was startling on such trips to discover that the Light Blue lads were quite human away from the hot house atmosphere of the Tideway and we all got on well. I am currently opening negotiations to take the travelling Oxbridge Boat Race circus to Brazil to race on the Amazon, to India for a Ganges regatta and to China to compete on the Yangtse. Who knows; it may be an idea that could catch on!

The January fortnight saw 17 hopefuls fighting for places. We covered the course again and again in sculling boats and eights and made one 30-mile trip up to Molesey and back in one session. It was another bitter January. The icy weather always tended to fray tempers and heighten anxieties. It also nearly cost lives on more than one occasion. Steve Plunkett, huge as he was, contrived to break a sculling boat clean in half by the sheer force of his weight as he was passing under Hammersmith Bridge in mid-race. A comic incident on a summer's day at an up-river regatta perhaps, but in sub-zero conditions on a speeding tide it was a frightening experience. Steve clung to the wreckage and propelled himself shorewards to safety. Later in the week I asked Gyles Vardey and Colin Moynihan to fetch the coaching launch *Nicea* which was moored to a buoy in mid-river in front of the Putney boathouses. This was usually a task I undertook but on this occasion I was busy. So this Oxford cox and his prospective Blue Boat oarsman colleague took the little dinghy and proceeded to capsize the thing. The swift running tide whisked them away before they could catch hold of the boat and they were swept off downstream towards Putney Bridge. Fortunately we were able to catch them as they passed the Pier, but after six or seven minutes in that freezing water they were in poor shape. Colin particularly was barely conscious for he was in the process of trying to lose weight and there was not a lot of meat on the poor man. Lewisham East nearly lost their future Member of Parliament that day but luckily he revived with the help of a few brandies. 'The worst thing about it', says Colin now, 'was that you wouldn't let me cox that afternoon in case I caught pneumonia. I was furious because I wanted to go against John Calvert in the trials race.'

When we moved to Henley for seat racing, we still had 12 people for the last eight seats and there were difficult decisions to make. In the midst of it all we took two fours to the national trials where we met Cambridge, also in two fours, who were in the throes of seat racing themselves under their President Tourek's Dartmouth coach Peter Gardiner. At the end of the first day, the results of the private Oxbridge duel read: Cambridge first and fourth, Oxford second and third. But what really shook the Light Blue camp was the next day's effort when, after a little reshuffling, both Oxford fours finished just behind the fastest squad four but just ahead of both Cambridge crews. Cambridge it appeared had judged the 1974 race result to be a flash in the pan, an aberration, and that basically their well-tried system was still sound.

But that weekend in January gave them a severe jolt. In retrospect it is probably a pity that we alerted them to the danger of our challenge so early, but by the same token the result was a welcome boost to Oxford's morale, and we returned to our training with renewed will.

Cambridge almost immediately settled their crew, while we still had a few selection problems and crew order difficulties to sort out. At first Andy Baird was entrusted with the stroking while the Etonians rowed at five and six, but in the end we felt that Graham Innes's experience was needed in the stern with Nick Tee behind him. We were also not altogether happy with the two young monsters holding down such vital places in the middle of the boat. Within days of announcing their crew, Cambridge lost David Sturge with glandular fever, and although their President Steve Tourek remained confident that they would still be fast enough to beat us, we felt encouraged as we embarked on a series of demanding fixtures. While we went looking everywhere for a fight, Cambridge, who were once again in the hands of Lou Barry, kept a relatively low profile. We took on the embryo national team and hung doggedly to their coat-tails in a series of two- and three-minute rows in which the world silver medallists could never get more than half a length. Cambridge, closeted once more with Lou's Tideway Scullers, gave their hosts short shrift during a weekend of 'friendly' training. In one visit to the Tideway Oxford paddled over the course unpaced with bursts and recorded the fourth fastest time ever by a Boat Race crew.

With three and a half weeks to go to the race, and a few days before the Reading Head of the River Race, disaster struck the Dark Blue camp. We had just rearranged the crew yet again, beefing up the engine room by splitting the two young Etonians and putting the powerful, more mature Canadian John Hutchings at five in a tandem with Money-Coutts on the same side behind him. Transporting the boats by trailer after a bruising weekend on the Tideway where we lost by a length to London University, a strong gust of wind lifted one section of the eight up into the air and brought it crashing down on to the road. We had remained faithful to our three-year-old Stampfli and now three weeks before the race she lay in pieces at our feet. A change of boat at such a late stage would be difficult, and all the more so because the feel of the Swiss-built eight was so different to any British made craft. It would take valuable time to get used to a different style of boat. And then while we despaired it was suggested that the American national team, which kept their own Stampfli eight in winter storage at Nottingham for their European rowing tours, might be prepared to lend it to us for the Boat Race. A series of long distance phone calls secured the loan of the American eight which thankfully was identical to our own.

We defended our Reading title in a new boat, a new order – because stroke man Andy Baird was taking exams and Innes had to move to stroke – a new continental rig arrangement and rowing Ollie Moore as substitute, and lost to Leander by a bare second. But we reversed our result against London University who were eight seconds behind us while Goldie finished a further 21 seconds behind them. Against the odds we had managed to finish a traumatic week with our tails up. A week later, Isis went to the Kingston Head and won it outright defeating the same University of London crew by six seconds and establishing themselves as firm favourites for the Isis/Goldie race a fortnight later. Their result showed that they were not much slower than the Oxford Blue Boat. This all augured well for the future, since we were boating young crews with time on their side while Cambridge were relying on final year men. More important, they had less good material coming up behind. However there was little respite for us to consider such theoretical possibilities. We were underdogs in an imminent Boat Race, but the crew were showing terrific fire and resolve and were certainly making the running. We challenged our Reading conquerors Leander to a duel on the Tideway where they were training in preparation for the Open Head. We planned a couple of short races and came out just on top in both, the crew racing with considerable maturity and dash.

At this stage, I was again rowing in the Tideway Scullers second eight for Lou Barry and I managed to arrange a fixture for us with Oxford despite Lou's Light Blue affiliations. He tended to enjoy these games, as I did, jockeying for the ascendancy, pressing for a phsycho-logical booster. Oxford whopped us, and while I did not like being beaten, I could not help but enjoy the manner of their performance. At least I did not call out to them the way Cambridge coach Mike Muir-Smith had done from his seat in a losing Scullers eight a few years earlier: 'Go on Cambridge beat the hell out of us!' much to the disgust of his own crew. A few days later the national team won the Head, my own Scullers crew came third, Leander fourth, UL were fifth and Goldie 11th. From our fifth starting position I could see, with a brief turn of the head, our first crew up ahead on the bend being overtaken by the squad. We finished less than a length down on them. These results showed that both 'Varsity crews were well up with the best in the country. Oxford also took on the internationals from the Imperial College Lubrication Laboratory and avenged the previous year's defeat, beating them by three lengths between the Bridges.

This flurry of competitive fixtures reflected my own avowed love of competition and my belief that the best training for racing was racing. I had always thrived on such a diet and Oxford did too. Lou, in his wisdom, knowing he had a strong experienced eight, did not feel the same need to race them, and he kept them hungry, holding them back from discovering their true speed. We finished the week with a record-breaking row between Hammersmith and the Mile, not madly significant since records depend as much on the wind and a fast tide as they do on the speed of a crew, but good to get under your belt anyway. A short one but a nice one with which to go away for the weekend. Briefly, the newspapers generously made us evens with a week to go, but they had little evidence from Cambridge on which to assess their predictions. Hearts were with the keen young Oxford boys, charging about and making a splash, but hard heads could hardly fail to recognise Cambridge's impressive pedigree, with such telling advantages in weight, height and age. We watched them from the boathouse just before the weekend as they powered downstream from the Steps to Putney and were suitably impressed.

Almost as a tradition in the last week before the race we took on a pacing crew of young Old Blues, a fixture I preferred to get out of the way on the Monday, bearing in mind the morale-damaging defeat Andy Hall's crew had suffered three years earlier at the hands of their irreverent and happy-go-lucky seniors. We also had outings with Isis, but sometimes these needed to be carefully orchestrated so as not to sap the confidence of either crew so near the race. Short pieces, starts, an outing in consort was the line rather than a last minute chance for the two crews to do humiliating damage to each other. Isis this year were after all a classy crew, winners at Kingston and due to show Goldie a clean pair of heels for the first time in nearly a decade. The wealth of talent in that crew heralded a new era for Oxford's Boat Race fortunes. But for the moment we needed to harness their enthusiasm just a trifle to prevent the possibility of them undermining the confidence-building work we had been doing with the first crew. Cambridge's experiences with Goldie the year before were a lesson in squad mismanagement, and this Oxford crew was still a little wet behind the ears. They could have been caught off their guard despite the warnings, but I need not have worried. The crews worked together with maturity and good sense, Isis ably marshalled by Chris Blackwall who was sensitive to the dangers.

In our full-course trial on a cold and windy day Isis had done a fine pacing job, taking us over the middle part of the 19-minute course. It was always easier for a crew going only a part of the way to produce an extra turn of speed against one rowing nearly three times as far. The idea was to sit level or a few feet down, to test the senior boat and extend the crew fully, and this they did superbly. On the same day Cambridge did what they called a 'phantom' full course, paddling over an hour later with a series of pressure bursts. The differences in speed of tide and work pressure made precise time comparisons meaningless, but their quick progress at a paddle gave us serious food for thought.

Mindful that our winning margin over UL at Reading had been eight seconds, while Isis's had been six seconds, we chose to do a couple of three-minute pieces in mid-week together and while the first boat was charged up for the first encounter and won well by nearly two lengths, they were less explosive in the second, scrambling to a half-length win and perfectly demonstrating to themselves how easily a momentary complacency could blunt their edge. They had to beware the second row of a series, and know that a crew beaten in the first row would be a far tougher proposition in the second; usually a first effort was just to blow away the cobwebs with the two crews sizing each other up. The unwary crew will, if they beat a crew in the first of a series of rows, relax, subconsciously believing the job to be more or less done, and that the other crew now knows its place. Wrong and bad strategy. The true competitor never knows when he's beaten, and if he has any instinct for racing, he will know that most crews will be that bit softer next time around. Only by demonstrating it can the point be properly learned. Ultimately, unless one crew is patently quicker, it will be the final row that will be the toughest, and therefore the most telling. That is the one to win – that's the one that really counts. So the lesson learned during that session with Isis was that even though they thought they were alert, they were still capable of losing their sharpness as a crew, and that tiny alteration in approach could mean the difference between winning and losing. They all had to be 100 per cent on the ball, all the time.

We were trying to establish a mood within the Oxford rowing set-up of hard no-nonsense professionalism. We wanted the rowing world to think of Oxford as a serious squad, one that could not be under-estimated. Aside from the tougher, more aggressive style of racing that we were developing, we were also being careful not to lose friends by boorish behaviour. We tried to keep calm under race pressure, eschewing the usual abusing and shouting that can happen when crews are locked in mid-struggle on the river. We wanted to be sure that we always started a piece of work level or competitively a man up, but never down as so often happens with inexperienced crews, and we prepared the men constantly to expect little mercy from the pacing crews they met. Everyone wanted to beat the Boat Race crews, and the wily Tideway-reared oarsmen were masters at stealing every little advantage. The Oxbridge students were naïve – they were polite and gentlemanly. So we had to educate them in the ways of the world, and prepare them to be firm and ruthless but fair, not to cheat – that had to be absolutely clear – but to recognise and learn the tricks of the trade. For rowing, like any sport, is not just a matter of blokes rowing together in a boat. It involves a tremendous array of clever moves and sleights of hand, of intuitive knowledge of an opponent's weak moments, of the signs that indicate his lessening resolve – when to stick in a few hard ones, of the twists and turns of the river and the ever changing direction of the wind. How important it is to drill into a crew the tactics of the cut-and-thrust sparring that you really only learn from racing, like the trick of hardening your stroke into a wash when the natural reaction is to go soft for a couple; against most crews you can take a seat or two just like that which at a crucial moment in a race, approaching a bend for instance, could mean successfully defending your water or breaking right away a minute or two later on in the contest. And of course it is no use one, two or even six men doing it. It has to be a subconscious crew reaction. Too late to say afterwards that you didn't hear the cox.

How vital it is, too, to know that athletes go through a soft spot between three-quarters of a minute and a minute and a half as they move from anaerobic to aerobic work; if you can train yourself to be hard at that moment in a side-by-side race you can gain enormous advantage later further down the course. Under pressure many less wily oarsmen really don't want to have to think too much about tactics and what is going on around them. They are at the edge of their effort and they would prefer someone else to do the thinking for them – the cox, stroke, the engine room – anyone. And so they hope. But the winners are not these mindless performers hoping for a miracle; the winners are the intelligent ones, those who can go on reading the race under fire, go on stealing the advantages, stay alert however tired their muscles, however numb their brains. And to get a crew to think like that collectively so that they react as one man is the magic of crew boat racing. There is after all no substitute for experience unless an oarsman really is in a class of his own in terms of strength and natural ability. Only then can he sit there and simply pull according to race plan, so long as he reacts fast to cox's instructions. But I know from years of competing how a little 'nous' can go a long way. Rowing in a crew with other likeminded oarsmen who react instinctively in the same way not only produces the results, but it brings a pleasure that far exceeds just the simple joy of winning. There is a sublime contentment at the cleverness of it, at the unity and the complete harmony with one's crewmates.

Oxford's Boat Race oarsmen responded well to these lessons. They looked far more workmanlike just walking about, loading and unloading the boats, rigging up and getting ready for outings. Sure they fooled around on the bank sometimes like all crews do. They sent Cambridge a shoe box containing a piece of driftwood with 'Stride' written on it, following news reports in 1975 which opined that the search for a good stride was reckoned to be coach Lou Barry's main task; they posed for Press photographers in their smart Hardy Amies-designed outfits. But they also began to realise that the fooling could all too easily carry on into the boat and spoil the outing. So they learned to switch on as soon as the cox called 'hands on the boat'. They learned not to collapse over the oars at the end of training races and fixtures with other crews however depleted they felt. It was bad form to show vulnerability, and so they took to paddling on at the end of a piece of work, breathing hard to be sure, but upright and in control. You never knew when you might race these people again, and anyway word would undoubtedly get back to the Tabs.

Discipline in the boat is important, because ultimately it commands the respect of one's competitors. All this probably sounds a bit sergeant-majorish—like those military style letters to the *Telegraph* about bringing back conscription—but it does build up a crew's self-respect and pride and although we don't necessarily harp on about little things like wearing the same kit, the point still gets across and the crews begin to feel the benefit. After a while it becomes second nature and they wonder why they used to go through all the histrionics of falling over backwards in the boat at the end of every single race.

This superficial but important display of discipline and control applies in public training and in minor races and competitions, but of course it does not necessarily hold true at the finish of *the* race. The big one, the one for which all the training is for, will probably require a supreme effort especially if it is closely fought, and a World Championship final, a Henley last race or a half length Boat Race finish would without doubt reduce the participants to jelly. In private training too the coach may well ask for maximum effort and on occasion might reduce his men to a state of collapse, but the point is that the suffering and the display of obvious physical distress is kept within the group and should not be witnessed by rivals who will log it in their computers for future reference when it comes to psyching themselves up for another race against you. It gives them just another weapon, however small, to use on you even if all it does is simply bolster their resolve by the merest fraction. Athletes are great self deceivers. 'I rowed the bloke into the ground last time; he may have beaten me but he was lucky. Another ten

115

strokes . . . I'll have him this time.' That's the sort of attitude you can well do without, and if you can keep him that little bit softer and demoralised just by sitting up at the end of a race and looking nonchalant, then why pass up the chance? Confidence: such a tenuous ingredient, but so crucial.

During our Tideway visits and before outings, the squad looked somehow forlorn and lost if they stood about doing nothing. It made them seem wet and unprepared. If the boat was rigged and they had made all the last-minute adjustments they should have been warming up in readiness for the session or they should have been inside and off their feet, resting. 'Even if you've got nothing to do,' I would say 'for Christ's sake at least pretend you're doing something.' 'But Dan, we don't know what we're supposed to be doing now. No one's told us.' Pathetic! 'Well look as if you know. Look purposeful.' So brows would furrow and serious attention would suddenly be paid to the unnecess- ary turning of a gate or the sliding of a seat. In time it got to be: 'Oh-oh chaps here's Dan. Look like you're busy.' But the point got through, and they developed a much more professional, alert air. Eventually they began to take secret pleasure, when our Tideway visits clashed, in watching Cambridge wandering about, hands in pockets, seemingly at a loss. 'You're beginning to look a little Cambridge-like today' would usually snap everyone to attention if they were being slowed by bad weather or if they were on to their third session of the day and wingeing about aches and pains. Little things, hardly worth thinking about, yet important in giving a crew a sense of identity and purpose. Fast movement just getting into the boat was preferable to slow ponderous preparations or the distraction of desultory chatting or forgetting something in the boathouse, all of which suggested a reluctance to get on with the outing. Such procrastination would often herald a poor session.

However it could also be a sign that the crew was tired and would alert the coach to the possibility of overwork or creeping staleness. It is hard to distinguish between the crew that appears less than eager for another gruelling round of work, but is nevertheless physiologically quite capable of usefully doing it and one which is comprehensively exhausted. With all the will in the world such a crew will simply be unable to find the strength to do the work effectively. A sudden change of programme – 'We'll do some starts this afternoon and a couple of fast two-minutes pieces instead of the 48 minutes alternate' – can lighten their day immeasurably and produce a scintillating outing which would otherwise have been dire and unproductive. But the crew would genuinely have to be pretty down to need that, and too many changes to the programme, especially if the workload is being lightened, can produce unease in a crew and a feeling that their coach doesn't think they're up to it. That can have the opposite effect and undermine their confidence. It's always nice to hear a crew (not just one man expressing bravado) say 'no, we'd rather not cut the work—we'll pick up once we're on the water'. You know then that you're dealing with a crew that is thinking for itself. It is a sure sign of maturity. Chris Blackwall recalls that at one time Cambridge thought that we were getting too professional. 'But it wasn't that really', he says, 'we were just better organised than they were in those days.' However, the Light Blues have caught up since then and there is little that is 'amateur' about them now.

As race day approached, we practised our starts again and again, at first using a length of rope over the side of the launch with the cox hanging on. Bert backed up to hold them against the stream, and just as John Calvert was about to be hauled out of the boat, I'd say 'go' and the crew would leap away like a greyhound from a trap. They learned to hold the boat level with blades buried in the flowing water, but not allowing themselves to be pulled out by the stream. They coped well in the swirling water of those first few strokes of the start when the boat is in danger of swinging and tilting, and when we progressed to the stakeboats later in the week, they were taking off cleanly and fast at 39 to 40 strokes in the first minute. The pundits, though making Cambridge the marginal favourites in the last remaining days, had developed a sneaking respect for the energetic young Dark Blues and some even tipped them to take the race. We believed we had an outside chance and our strategy had to be geared to placing ourselves in a position to seize upon any mistakes that Cambridge might make during the race. We had to put them under pressure for that is when errors are most likely to happen. The crew that makes the least mistakes, that keeps out of trouble, is usually the one which comes through at the line. Doug Melvin, a successful sculler and coach to his son John, a lightweight gold medal oarsman and silver medal sculler, used to coach me at London Rowing Club. One of his key lines was 'No mistakes, no mistakes off the start', and he would purse his lips, and go through the hand motions at the finish of the stroke with fingertip delicacy as if on a tightrope.

Coaches are like that. It is often not so much what they say as how they say it, and the funny accompanying sounds and movements they make as they speak: 'Doooway' and 'Whoosh' and 'Wheeeee' and 'quick quick' and 'sshhhhh'. The scene outside the boat tents at Henley is always a comedy of gestures and balletic steps as dozens of coaches brief their young crews before they race. Some balance precariously on one leg as they illustrate the Moriarty theory of the 'whoosh' through the finish and the recovery while others sit on the ground, legs bunched up demonstrating another detail of the rowing stroke. Others circle the air with their hands imitating the approach of the blade to the water. They look like an early morning Tai Chi session in a Peking park.

We went through the whole spectrum preparing the 1975 Oxford crew for the race, rehearsing in our minds the unexpected accidents that could occur and how to react, anticipating the likely development of the race, debating our best line of attack. Our fitness was not in doubt, but we were, compared to them, underweight, less experienced and less powerful. To compensate we had to work more intensively, we had to draw upon all the racing 'nous' we had so recently acquired. We had to put in more strokes a minute but not just any old how. Each stroke had to be spot on, fully effective. The power had to be built immediately from each catch rather than increasing it gradually through the stroke. And we had to relax, let the boat run, rest between strokes.

Cambridge had raced Goldie on the Tuesday and had managed to gain less than half a length in two one-minute rows. Later in the day they had taken only one length in the first half of a six-minute row. So we knew they were not impossibly fast off the start. We plotted on. And after we had talked ourselves to a standstill and the oarsmen had gone to bed to lie awake imagining the possible scenarios they might encounter the next day, I sat down with the cox John Calvert and ran over everything again. He was a dour, rather shy northerner, and we had spent a lot of time trying to bring him out, make him more assertive and pushy. We found after the first year that it paid to take a lot more time with the coxswains and that on the whole coaches tended to leave them to sort themselves out too much. Then everyone blamed the coxes if they made a mistake. John became a very good cox in time but at this moment we were both pretty tense. There were things that he had to know that his crew did not need to be aware of, even some tactics that he should adopt in certain cases which could unsettle the crew unnecessarily if they were asked to think about them. So we discussed clashes and evading tactics and washing off a crew or being washed off, shouting misleading instructions so that the opposition would pick up the wrong signals, and what to do if he found himself on the outside of a big bend and down, and how to react if faced with very rough water, or a weakening stream, or a breakage or a man collapsing in mid-race. Poor John went to bed, his mind buzzing with tactical manoeuvres. In one sense I was unloading all my own anxieties on to him, but then again he was the only one who could do anything practical in mid-race.

Race day. A quick run for the crew, breakfast, a look at the papers for the race predictions and then down for a short loosening outing with a couple of extended bursts to raise a sweat and ease the tensions a little. Back to Piers for a light lunch, nothing stodgy, and a short briefing about any new developments. Then a rest until it's time to get ready for the race. I go down to the river with the cox a couple of hours before the 'off' to run over the first half of the course with Bert in the launch. We discuss our last-minute plans in the light of the weather conditions and which station we will choose if we win the toss. The BBC camera towers and trucks are all in place along the embankment, and Harry Carpenter's camera stage is being erected between the two boathouses. There is a variety of crews boating from the clubs lining the shore but the river will be clear well before we are ready to go. If I have time, a quick outing in my sculling boat helps to settle the nerves. All the 'heavies' are gathering outside the clubhouses of their respective crews, and I hand out the 24 launch tickets, priceless possessions for a Boat Race lover, to the chosen Oxford camp devotees as they arrive. The crew meanwhile have boarded Den's big luxury bus and with a police escort they drive down to the river, the growing partisan crowds cheering or booing their progress to the embankment at Putney. They disembark and thread their way through gathered supporters, oblivious to the familiar faces, the whole thing passing as if in a dream. They've been prepared for this feeling of being outside themselves, but it is still unnerving to find how difficult it is to stay alert.

Into the National Westminster Bank Boat Club changing-room and away from the crush and noise of their friendly fans and the television set on which Harry Carpenter is discussing the crews' attributes with Jim Railton or Penny Chuter. Go through the routine of changing, each man lost in his own thoughts, faces tense, some trying a couple of jokes, others putting on the lucky socks or shorts they wore when last they won a race. How superstitious some sportsmen are. Put the kit on in the right order, never race wearing new, untried clothing. One rower used to take a teddy bear mascot with him everywhere, while in 1979 the crew adopted a 'Dennis the Menace' cut-out as a mascot which rode the bows. In 1974 Gareth's sister made a huge, fluffy, dark blue duck called Puddles but we were wary of getting too dependent on one mascot (think what would happen if we lost it on the day), so Paddy's sister made another one for us the following year. I've still got them both, but subsequent crews have known nothing of these lucky fellows who keep benevolent watch over our fortunes, and so have no superstitious worries about them. For the same reasons I never lay bets on the outcome of the race nor do I dare advise anyone to back us when asked for a tip. It seems to be tempting fate unnecessarily as is writing this book about a period of Boat Race history while it is still going on.

While his crew remain nervously warming up in the changing-room the President goes out for the televised toss and Harry Carpenter introduces the two protagonists and the Umpire to the audience. The gold coin is tossed, the call made and the stations chosen. A few more televised words, numbingly forgettable for the young Presidents, and it's back to the crew. Now come the last-minute instructions, reminding the men how precisely they must tackle the race in the light of the station they have drawn; what it means, what its advantages and its drawbacks are. They know already of course, but the strategy is now hardened up and underlined. A few more minutes stretching and warming up and then it's time to go. Isis and Goldie are on the stakeboats which means we have half an hour to the 'off'. As the mini-Boat Race passes the Putney boathouses the crew give a cheer, especially loud to give vent to their own nervousness. Then they lay hands on the boat and walk her down to the river to the applause and 'good lucks' of the Dark Blue contingent.

The Thames was rough again that day, but the hot favourites Isis on the Surrey side were already a length up by the Black Buoy. Then their cox Colin Moynihan performed what seemed to us on the shore to be a worrying move. Warned by Chris Baillieu the Umpire not to cross further in front of Goldie towards the shelter of the Middlesex bank, and as Dave Edwards at seven had to shorten the finish of his stroke to avoid hitting the Goldie bows, he turned hard to his left and was caught by the wind which forced him round almost at right angles to the shore. Suddenly he was heading for the Surrey bank, out of the worst water but way out of the stream and far off to the outside of the bend. This eccentric manoeuvre cost his crew dear and approaching the Mile Isis were two lengths down. But such was their power and class that they took five lengths in the next three minutes, came sharply out for the centre arch at Hammersmith and went away to win by 33 seconds or nearly ten lengths for the first time in nine years. Isis had lost 50 lengths to Goldie since 1966 and revenge was sweet. They were the one and only Isis crew ever to be awarded their oars.

'That Isis crew was a very happy one', recalls Colin Moynihan, the cox. 'We had a lot of laughs. On the day of the race, Chris Blackwall, our coach, took us for a final crew lunch at Hurlingham. The boys should have been eating sparingly but one man couldn't resist the food. We watched in amazement as our five man Steve Plunkett consumed five huge courses just a few hours before the race. We pitied poor Olly Moore the man sitting in front of him in the boat who was bound to be the unlucky recipient of the meal when it all came back halfway over the course. But somehow Steve managed to keep it down.' Chris Blackwall had lent his beloved Isis cap to Moynihan for the race and after the first half mile through bouncing waves the boat had taken on quite a bit of water so he used the cap to bale out. 'For over 60 strokes the crew raced without me steering', says Colin, 'because I had to let go of the rudder lines to scoop the water over the side. But I lost the cap overboard and for a split second I wondered whether I should stop the crew to pick it up!' Boris Rankov, rowing in the four seat, remembers being tucked well under the Surrey bank out of the rough water as they passed Goldie before Harrods, and as they approached Hammersmith Bridge he heard Colin's voice, relaxed and calm, wafting over the internal speaker system: 'I'm not sure,' he was musing almost to himself, 'but I've got a feeling we're supposed to go through the centre arch in this race. Does anybody know?' 'Christ yes!' screamed Boris when the words had sunk in. Moynihan yanked hard on the right rudder line and the boat lurched sideways and careered towards the Middlesex side, missing the buttress of the bridge by inches. There are very few rules in the Boat Race but breaking the one about the centre arch demands disqualification. Had they held their course and taken the inside arch, they would have had to stop, jam the blades in hard and back the boat down against a fast-moving stream to retake the bridge correctly. Colin was a very spontaneous coxswain.

Isis's victory was heartening news to the Oxford crew as the result was called across to them while they removed their sweaters on the stakeboat. We believed that we were quick off the mark and were prepared should we win the toss to risk taking the Surrey station and the outside of the first slight bend in order to have the advantage of the big Hammersmith bend later on when Cambridge's power was more likely to help them. One or two critics felt this to be a questionable choice in view of the windy conditions but stroke Graham Innes and the boys recognised the logic of it. As luck would have it we won the toss, the water flattened out a little and our specially-fitted splash-boards became unnecessary although we kept them on just in case.

Oxford showed great courage in the race. They led briefly to the Black Buoy, but Cambridge took over the lead as they got the benefit of the inside at Fulham, and although Graham at stroke pushed to stay level, John steered Oxford a little wide and for a moment they lost the scent of the Light Blue crew. In that moment at the Mile, Neil Christie, the experienced Cambridge stroke, grabbed his chance and forced his men from their cruising rate of 33 up to 37 with a sustained burst which opened up a few feet of clear water beyond Crabtree, just enough for David Kitchen, his cox, to move over for the best of the tide. Fighting to defend his water, Graham went again to 36 trying to push his bows up for an overlap, and although the umpire Christopher Davidge warned Cambridge to move out, it was just a moment too late and Kitchen was able to ignore the instruction without causing a clash. Cambridge steered over into Oxford's water and shot Hammersmith Bridge half a length ahead, washing their rivals down. It was still critical, and Graham attacked yet again; miraculously Oxford began to creep back. They strained and reached out for something more and at that moment Andy Baird at bow fell back in the boat, the pressure suddenly gone from the end of his oar and it now lay uselessly across his lap. The gate holding his oar in place had sprung open. Crispin shouted 'throw it away' as he realised what had happened. Mark Harris, sitting at two in front of him, added 'and throw yourself after it!'.

But Andy quickly assessed the situation and then, cool as an ice cube, leaned out over his rigger, plopped the oar back into the gate and screwed it tight. He had lost maybe 14 strokes, and the crew had fallen back by nearly a length, but it is unlikely that Cambridge or indeed most of Andy's own crew had noticed anything amiss. However their chance was gone and though they fought bravely all the way and were rarely below 35 they finished three and three-quarter lengths behind. 'They just wouldn't give up', said one Cambridge crewman later, 'they kept coming at us again and again.'

It is probably unlikely that they would have caught this very powerful Cambridge crew, but if they had been able to hold on to their station at Hammersmith, which they so nearly did, who knows what might have happened; Cambridge would have been forced to go round the outside of the bend and that could have left the crews level at the Eyot with an absorbing race from halfway home. But all that is conjecture and could be no consolation for big Hutch and Dave Beak who slumped miserably in the changing-room at Quintin after the race, tears streaming down their faces. 'God,' groaned Bob Mason 'I never dreamed losing could be so unbelievably awful.' Their belief had been so great, they had done all that had been asked of them, and yet they had still failed. No amount of rationalising could comfort them. A couple of the Cambridge boys came round to thank them for the race and left again. And then with the tears still running, Beaky said: 'All right. Next year we're going to annihilate them', and they began to plot there and then. For John Hutchings it was the end of the road, but the rest were young and resilient and the future was there if they wanted it.

And clearly this lot were hooked.

In the inaugural lightweight race between the Universities at Henley, Cambridge took the honours by 12 seconds, and their women likewise in what was for them their 11th straight win in 11 encounters. Nick Tee and I rejoined our lightweight four, Mark Harris went into the lightweight eight and we went on to win silver and bronze medals at the World Rowing Championships in August. Nick's Presidential tenure had been excellent for Oxford; he laid sound foundations for the future with painstaking and time-consuming thoroughness. The only thing he failed to do, though, was to win the race. Graham Innes, with one win and one defeat in the Boat Race behind him, was elected to succeed Nick, and he asked the same coaching team back for another try. We put together a summer crew after eights week, but despite breaking the Ladies' Plate record to the Barrier at Henley, Isis lost the final by one and a third lengths to the strong University of London eight which was selected (with the inclusion of Macleod of Cambridge) to represent Britain in the World Championships a month later, finishing third in the *petite finale*. At least though, the Oxford youngsters were getting good racing experience and the occasional taste of victory.

Morale back at Oxford amongst the colleges was surging too and there was much river activity during the summer. We had a second go against Cambridge a few weeks after the Boat Race when both crews were invited to Paris to re-run the event as part of the May Day celebrations and the Head of the Seine Regatta through the centre of the city. A quarter of a million people turned out to watch and Cambridge won again, this time by just over a length. Princess Grace of Monaco presented the prizes with her daughter Caroline. Her brother Jack Kelly and her father, too, had been US Olympic scullers, and her association with the sport as a youngster in support of her menfolk made her quite an *aficionado*. Six years later she came to Henley to present the prizes with her husband, Prince Rainier, and watched the final of the Grand from the umpire's launch as Oxford took the coveted prize for the first time in over 100 years. Apart from Nick Tee and Mark Harris joining the lightweight team for the World Champion-ships, a couple of the others tried for selection to the national heavyweight squad but were not considered strong enough and soon rejoined the Isis crew. For Cambridge, David Sturge, finally cured of his glandular fever teamed up with Henry Clay in a coxless pair, won selection but failed to make the last 12 at the World's while Jamie Macleod rowed in the composite eight. Of the 39 British competitors in a large national team, 13 were ex-Oxbridge, again giving the lie to the suggestion that the Boat Race has no relevance to top class rowing.

That year, 1975, was also the turning point in Oxford's Boat Race fortunes. After only one victory in the previous eight years and only ten since 1946 we were about to shed the mantle of underdog and embark on the most successful period of Dark Blue Boat Race history this century. Yet although Oxford mostly took the honours, Cambridge were producing fine crews and made sure that the races provided all manner of excitement, controversy, records, drama and close verdicts. And the vigour with which the two Universities fought each of the contests has forced the standard of the race higher and higher, keeping it well abreast of the international field.

5
Finding the Winning Way

In 1976 we consolidated the system we had established over the previous three years. The groundwork was beginning to pay off although we lost the services of three men. Crispin dropped out to pursue the undeniable delights of Oxford's social life and his elusive girlfriend Lucy, Isis man Boris Rankov reckoned he was unlikely to win a Blue the following year and left to row with Leander while Colin Moynihan decided to pursue a boxing Blue and the Presidency of the Union. However, we still had a wealth of talent to work with, which meant that even the returning Blues had to fight for their places. Back for a third year was Graham Innes the President, his fellow Blues Bob Mason, Andy Baird, David Beak and cox John Calvert and the three Isis heavyweights Steve Plunkett, Dave Edwards and Jamie Pike plus the talented but lighter Paul Wright and Dave Newman. In addition two exceptional freshmen arrived in October to boost our rich crop still further. Ken Brown had won a gold medal in the American national eight in 1974 in front of our own British silver medallists in Lucerne; and John Wiggins was probably Britain's most successful junior oarsman ever, winning, as a member of Bruce Grainger's formidable Wallingford school group, two bronze and a silver medal at three successive junior World Championships.

Sensing that there was a good crew in the making and possibly a good story to go with it, BBC television in the shape of Jonathan Crane and the *Inside Story* team, asked if they could do a documentary about us, following the squad's preparations through the year right up to the race. After some deliberation we agreed, realising that the film unit would probably be quite intrusive, though not to the extent that it finally was. We made it clear at the start that we could not interrupt outings for filming, that we were not prepared to repeat things for the cameras, and that they would have to get what footage they required as we worked. But we did co-operate on interviews and filming away from the training environment and for most of the time it all worked well.

Newly arrived at Cambridge was Ken Brown's crewmate from the US World Championship boat, Dick Cashin. But apart from their President, the 1974 and 1975 Blue Henry Clay, the Light Blue line-up looked less formidable than their 1975 squad. David Searle, a Youth international, Mike Wells, Kim Swithinbank and American John Hale had rowed for Goldie the year before, Robert Breare was a 1973 Goldie cap and Mark Gritten was a Sandhurst trained oarsman. They also had some useful freshmen as well as Cashin–Charlie Arbuthnot and Mark Horton from Eton, Will Dawkins and cox Jo Manser from Westminster–and Peter Davies and Richard Harpum, who had both learned to row while at Cambridge. This year the pre-race roles looked like being reversed. It was Cambridge's turn to work with a new, less experienced group. But as we began training in October such thoughts were far from our minds. Each year, each new crew was a different proposition, presenting different problems–as many of them specific to each boat as they were common to them all. One of the mystiques of the Boat Race was that very factor–that no two years were alike and that each time we were faced with a new set of circumstances although from the outside, to the casual observer on the day, the line-ups and race pattern were not noticeably different. The Presidents, obviously, were very different from year to year, and Graham Innes was a less assertive, shyer individual than the three previous men we had worked with. But he knew what he wanted and he had the experience of two Boat Race appearances, one of them a winning one, to back up his role as leader. That counted a lot with the men in his squad and they recognised that although he was a quiet man he was if anything more determined than most. He also preferred to pass a larger chunk of the responsibility on to the coaching team than his predecessor, con-centrating on managing the squad's daily organisation at Oxford and leaving the programme, selection and overall planning to us. It meant that we had the wholehearted co-operation of a squad that had, apart from Brown and Wiggins, rowed their hardest and best years under the prevailing Oxford system.

The first term then was spent concentrating on technique on the water under the supervision of Ronnie Howard and Jock Mullard, the Radley coaches (both past Oxford Presidents), George Harris, the Christ Church boatman and boatbuilder–a Grand Master of tech-nique–and Peter Politzer, the head coach at Pangbourne College. After the fours races in third week the senior group usually moved into eights covering many miles at low ratings for the all-important muscle endurance and cardio-vascular work. They did most of their con-centrated specific training on land, in the gym with weights and on the running track. These early coaches, with the help of the President, secretary, Chris and myself, also sorted through the junior trial candidates looking for new talent which could be developed for Isis, and by the sixth week–mid-November–we were down to 32 men and four coxswains for our trials race at the beginning of December.

We were in need of a new boat since all we had been able to salvage from our old Stampfli were the shoes, and we placed an order with the local boatbuilders, Salters. We had a number of old fours (one an Italian Donoratico), a whole fleet of ancient sculling boats, a few pairs and a couple of ageing Donoratico eights. But we were in no position to replenish our stocks. These were the OUBC's only assets, for it was a club in name only with no premises, the barest facilities, and the nine men of the Oxford crew each year its only members. We even had to train on stretches of river far from our own short, congested Isis. Money was low and whereas loyal Cambridge Old Blues were apt to donate a new eight every so often and leave the occasional £100,000 to the CUBC, Oxford had no such benefactors, nor were we so well-organised. We lived hand to mouth while Cambridge drew interest from a tidy capital sum wisely invested. The costs of running a squad were soaring. Ten years earlier, as Captain of the New College Boat Club, I purchased a new eight for £400. Now we had to lay out £3,500 and by 1984 our new Empacher was to set us back £6,000 without riggers.

So when impresario Lew Sherman approached me with a proposition to raise money for the Boat Race we were ready for anything. Lew, also the manager of a pop group and a past band leader, had read a news item about the dire financial problems of the Boat Race which threatened to sink it as a major sporting event. Since we could not charge gate money on this major sporting spectacle our sources of cash were limited. It would, ran the story, be reduced to a humdrum race between two mediocre crews turning up on the day. Lew, like the good traditionalist he was, was horrified and suggested a charity show to raise money and bring publicity at the same time. There might be £4,000 or £5,000 in it, he hinted optimistically, to be shared between the two Universities. His friend was the manager at Cesar's Palace in Luton, a Ladbroke Group enterprise, and he was willing to lay on a special evening in aid of the Boat Race if both crews would appear.

Alan Mays Smith, the London representative of the Boat Race and Dick Fishlock, ex-Oxford Blue, past coach and organiser of the post Race Blues dinner, had both been investigating the possibility of sponsorship for the race for some time, more out of concern for Oxford's financial predicament than for the better off Cambridge club. A charity show, although not quite what they had had in mind, seemed a feasible interim solution and they agreed to go along with the idea. Cambridge were reluctant to play ball at first because they thought the idea a bit down market and embarrassing. Besides they didn't need the money. I went to a meeting at Cesar's to discuss the idea. It all appeared

very straightforward and they guaranteed us a minimum of £3,000 –
'We can seat 1500 and we'll have Jack Jones appearing that week.' But
they felt something was missing. 'Royalty, Daniel; we need Royalty'
they said firmly. 'Well,' I ventured, 'Lord Snowdon coxed Cambridge
back in 1950 when he was plain Tony Armstrong-Jones. What about
asking him?' 'If you can get Snowdon', said the committee, 'We'll
guarantee you £5,000. How does that sound?' 'I'll try' I said reluctantly,
knowing that Cambridge were not too keen on the idea of the soirée
anyway and that any approach to Snowdon would have to be made
through them. But Cesar's were already thinking further ahead. 'Tell
you what,' they said, 'if you can get him to come with his wife we'll make
it £10,000. In fact forget Tony. If you can get Margaret to come we'll
still make it £10,000.'

The problem was how to approach Princess Margaret. Hopeless to
do it through her rowing connection with Snowdon. So I sought advice
through friends who by good fortune understood the Royal ways and
within a couple of weeks I had word that an invitation might be
favourably considered. And so it proved. Princess Margaret agreed to
come, Cambridge were persuaded and the show was planned for the
Sunday before the beginning of the final Tideway fortnight. The
Cesar's committee were delighted for it meant that they would be
playing host to all the top Ladbroke executives as well. The evening
was a success; Jack Jones led the performers, Lew's own band got a
hearing, Cesar's Palace the kudos and the Boat Race a welcome
cheque. At the height of the celebrations, our Royal guest asked why
the Boat Race was in such financial straits and I mentioned the
problems we were encountering in the search for a sponsor. She leaned
across me to ask Ladbroke's chief Cyril Stein whether that was not
something on which he could offer advice, and before I knew it a lunch
meeting was arranged for the following week and the Boat Race had
found a most generous sponsor and benefactor. In 1981 Ladbrokes
renewed our agreement for a second five-year term guaranteeing
upward of £10,000 a year to each of the two Boat clubs. The event was
secure and over the next couple of years we were able to overhaul our
fleet of boats; buy a van, a rubber coaching launch and an outboard
engine. We were relieved to know that we could buy a new eight every
year if we needed it. We were not exactly flush with money but it was a
lifeline that came in the nick of time. With costs rising so fast Oxford's
representative crews for the Boat Race still live on an uncomfortably
tight budget, but the immediate dangers are past.

In the Open Tideway Fours Head of the River in early November
ten Oxford colleges competed, with Oriel and Christ Church finishing

well up the list; but no Cambridge colleges had entered which gave an early indication that they might be short of talent. In the domestic races on the Isis, Oriel College heralded their arrival as a rowing force beating Christ Church in the autumn fours event by three-quarters of a second with a strong crew composed of President Graham Innes, David Beak, Paul Wright and freshman Nigel Burgess. Paul also won the pairs event a week later with Andy Baird, impressively beating crews composed of the Blues Innes and Mason, David Beak, and the freshman John Wiggins, the huge Belfast man Steve Plunkett, and the world champion Ken Brown in the process. All of these other men made the 1976 crew but Isis oarsman Dave Edwards got the last seat while Paul narrowly lost a long drawn out selection battle with John Wiggins. The pairs event was usually well attended and provided a good form line for later selection, but in the years that followed the event fell by the wayside, like the double sculls and the Silver Sculls before it, through neglect and laziness on the part of less attentive subsequent officers of the University Boat Club. Yet there was such an upsurge of enthusiasm within Oxford's rowing fraternity that these events should have been buzzing with activity. But because it is hard for students, stretched as they are between the library and the demanding Boat Race training programme, to turn their attention to the details of OUBC organisation outside the daily running of the squad, some important future-building decisions are not taken, or at any rate not followed through.

We chose our trial crews for the end of term contest which was now held over the Tideway track as a matter of course and moved to Putney two days before the race. Perhaps because we seem to assess the form of oarsmen better or at least earlier than Cambridge, we generally manage to select pretty well-matched crews and our trials races are always exciting, often more so than the Boat Race itself. They are closely fought affairs while more often than not Cambridge trials-winners walk away from their rivals early on in the race, giving little opportunity for coaches to see their candidates under real race pressure.

In one of the best races seen in the series, the trialists rowed stroke for stroke beyond halfway, with the college taught Jamie Pike at stroke holding his crew brilliantly round the outside of the big Hammersmith bend and proving that it was possible to contain that disadvantage and still come out on top. From a few feet down as they came off the corner Jamie pushed up the pressure along Chiswick Eyot and forced his bows in front in a classic Middlesex tactic, taking a third of a length lead at the Steps. The experienced Blues in the other boat, having failed to take advantage of their bend, could not respond and began to falter and with the bend turning to favour him Jamie began to edge away. By Barnes Bridge he had two lengths and made it three by the finish, just failing to catch the junior eight which had joined in at halfway. With only two years of rowing behind him, Jamie Pike had turned into a first-class oarsman, but he still had a hard fight ahead of him for a seat in the Blue Boat in this his final year. The individual tests in January would sort them out. But overall the standard was very high, despite the fact that Crispin and Boris Rankov were on the bank.

It is hard to drop a man who has tried his best, given everything and more to win a seat. The coaches know full well how much it means to an oarsman who has sacrificed maybe the highest academic qualifications, social life and sometimes career prospects for the chance to earn his Blue. For some who fail there is a second chance or a third in subsequent years, but for the final year man his sacrifice is if anything all the greater, because with exams approaching his academic work is so important. But we dare not take such considerations into account when we make our decisions. Why should Jamie not have secured his seat beyond doubt after that trial race? John Wiggins was after all a freshman. He had two more years at Oxford, and Paul Wright had one more year. They were so evenly-matched these three, all with their different strong and weak points. Wiggins had experience as a successful junior international and was extremely talented, but he was still a youngster, his strength not fully developed; also his individual results did not place him in the top group with the Old Blues, Ken Brown and the best Isis men. Because he initially had not intended to row in this his first year, he had also taken some time off and was not yet fully fit. But his potential was enormous.

Paul Wright was stocky, short really in the company of some very tall men, but he had stroked Isis and was a Youth international; furthermore he was very strong and had won all the domestic events on the Isis. He was a good sculler too and throughout January he and Wiggins produced near identical results in the individual tests. Jamie Pike was the biggest of the three, had the longest limbs and had stroked a very fast Isis crew and a winning trial crew. But his individual results were less good; his running, his small boat work and his gym results fell short of those of the other two. But while Wiggins and Wright fought it out on the ergometer machine, returning similar scores, Jamie left them both standing. So it all came down to the seat racing at Henley. However Jamie was a strokeside oarsman and he now looked unlikely to displace the other strokeside men Mason, Brown, Baird and President Innes. Earlier in the term we had tried rowing the President on bowside because we expected to be weaker on that side, but he had found the transition difficult so we had to abandon the idea and he returned to strokeside in mid-January. Jamie could not manage bowside either and sadly, not for the first time and certainly not for the last, a very talented oarsman failed to find a place in the crew. Now the last bowside seat was being contested by John Wiggins and Paul Wright. John was naturally a strokeside man, but he changed after the trials when it became clear that Innes was finding bowside difficult. So the ambidextrous Wright was facing a challenge from the newly converted Wallingford boy. After five days and an unprecedented number of seat races there was still nothing to choose between them and the coaches finally had to make their judgement on the basis of instinct, experience and feel. Wiggins had the pedigree despite being a freshman, his rowing stroke was longer, more fluid and well-connected and the fact that he was level pegging with Paul within a few days of changing sides suggested that he had the greater potential and flexibility. So John got the bow seat, and he fully justified our faith when three weeks later as a result of his rapid improvement we were able to move him down to seven in place of the less experienced Dave Edwards. Dave moved back to three pushing the awkwardly sliding Blue David Beak to bow.

A strange thing happens when you get dropped. Your recent crewmates seem suddenly to close ranks and you begin to feel ostracised, barely able to talk to them because the atmosphere is so uncomfortable. Maybe it is embarrassment, maybe it's a natural animal reaction based on a fear that it could happen to them. Whatever their reasons the effect can be quite devastating. The crew – the eight – have only one thing in mind and that is to win. So whatever decision is taken to achieve that end is all right by them, as long as they do not feel that it is a flagrant miscarriage of justice. Any disagreement from the crew at this level will not be along the lines of: 'poor old Jock, he's OK. It's not fair to drop him because he's worked so hard all year', but 'Jock is certainly stronger than Mike and we will go slower without him'. The law of the jungle does not side with loyalty and friendship, it sides with winners. Having been in the position myself of being dropped or not selected at all I remember how stunned I was by how easily those who were so recently my closest colleagues were suddenly no longer there. It seems at such a moment as if the others fear they might be tarred by the same brush, that they might catch the disease of failure.

Once the crew was settled, they came together very quickly and when they went afloat in their new Salters eight at Wallingford in early February they already looked promising. They had gone to the January national trials in fours and had won the coxed fours division, so by the time they made their first appearance on the Tideway to race University of London, they were being hailed as a potentially fast unit. Although Bob Mason was out of the boat with 'flu that weekend we were ready to carry on with a substitute but UL withdrew at the last minute with two of their men suffering from the oarsman's most common complaint, tinosinovitis or creaking wrist. So instead we took on the nippy University College Hospital on Saturday and Isis on Sunday, with first me and later Paul Wright substituting for the absent Mason. The work was done – a length a minute against the opposition – and the necessary acclimatisation, especially for the cox, on the less familiar water achieved; and we caught a brief sight of Cambridge (guaranteed to release a rush of adrenalin), also suffering from sickness, getting beaten by Thames Tradesmen.

Curiously Cambridge were rowing their world champion Dick Cashin at four rather than six which suggested that he was having more difficulty settling into the British style of rowing than our own very adaptable Ken Brown. The American style, developed under their national coach Al Rosenburg, emphasised a very slow recovery of the hands at the finish of the stroke ostensibly in order not to interrupt the surge of the craft at the end of each stroke. The crew would then accelerate up the slide for the next stroke in a movement that was in complete contrast to the English stroke pattern. A quick movement of the hands after the finish characterised our way of rowing with a brisk transfer of the weight sternwards with the body rocking over in pursuit of the hands and a slowing steadying approach up the last part of the slide for the beginning of the next stroke. It was difficult to change styles even if the oarsman was 100 per cent willing to do so. When he also had expectations of returning to his national team later in the year, and when all his success at the sport had stemmed from that different style of rowing, then to effect such a radical change in his rhythm and movement sometimes proved to be an uphill battle.

Ken however in that first year was an exceptionally co-operative and flexible oarsman, and his assimilation was painless. He also brought a special maturity and single-minded purposefulness to the squad which was illustrated by his adherence to the Chinese art of Tai Chi. Rosenburg taught his American crews Tai Chi to discipline their minds and improve their body control. It also strengthened their concentration and their ability to relax, excluding extraneous and distracting activities and developing in them a lightness of touch and a finer sense of timing. Ken was an excellent exponent of the art and would spend much time doing his exercises. The soothing effect on the rest of the Oxford crew as they watched Ken rolling an orange repeatedly away from him across a table and retrieving it just as it was about to roll beyond his reach was remarkable. He was a man of few words and demonstrated a commendable self-discipline.

As race day approached some members of the crew were becoming a little tetchy with the constant surveillance of the film unit, and when Jonathan Crane the director approached me to ask if I would let him film our final preparations in the house, our crew briefing, their bus ride under police escort to the river and the tensions of those last few moments in the changing-room before going afloat, I knew the crew reaction would be negative – divided perhaps but generally negative; and the last thing we wanted at such a late stage was disruption in the crew. I told him that my instinctive response was no, that I did not want to put the crew under extra pressure, but we finally agreed that he would speak to the crew, put his proposal to them and that he would abide by the majority decision. If any one of them was unhappy about it then the idea would have to be abandoned.

Six of the crew did not seem to mind when Jonathan had finished speaking, but three of them were dead against it. The intrusion was too intimate at such a critical moment, the distractions too great. They did not relish their vulnerability being so publicly exposed. But the key to *Inside Story* was just such a glimpse of those behind-the-scenes pressures and for Jonathan they represented the very essence of his documentary. Without them his film, and ultimately the representation of the boys as *the* Oxford team, would be diminished, rendered run-of-the-mill. He argued that the drama and the hugeness of the event in their lives should be made as vivid as possible. The crew debated ferociously, conscious that they held the deciding vote, and one or two of them undoubtedly enjoying the power to make or break the film. Finally, when the issue looked like resulting in a stalemate with the power of veto resting with the anxious minority, Ken, who had not yet spoken, broke in. 'Listen', he said quietly. 'If you can't take the pressure of having a film crew, and all the distraction that that entails, around you, how the hell are you going to deal with Cambridge on Saturday? Let's just use the tensions of their presence as practice for the race and learn to concentrate on our job no matter what's going on around us.' That settled the argument immediately and Jonathan was able to get all the sequences he wanted and produced what was eventually a very effective documentary.

Apart from Ken Brown, Steve Plunkett, the six-foot seven-inch Ulsterman, was also a calming influence on the crew with his soft, lyrical way of expressing himself and his 'gentle giant' image. It took quite a lot of work to get all of that 16 and a half stone Boat Race fit, but he was dedicated to his task and had set his sights early on as a schoolboy in Ireland to row for Oxford against Cambridge. His habit of removing one hand in mid-recovery to push his John Lennon specs back up his nose was unnerving, but he felt lost and disorientated without them when I suggested he leave them off altogether for an outing. Finally we sorted out a little elastic to hold them more firmly in place. Studying for a law degree, our Ulsterman had a poetic turn of phrase and was prettily quoted in the film as being determined to 'make each stroke personal, like no other; each second feels like minute, each minute an hour' when asked to describe the joys of his beloved sport.

Bob Mason, rowing in his second Boat Race at four in the boat wore dark glasses whenever the sun shone and gloves to protect his hands from blisters. He had acquired a dog since his first year and enjoyed playing the role of country squire. The dog accompanied us everywhere and became the 1976 mascot while Dave Beak's moth-eaten lucky cap, another constant companion, had finally, despite purist protests, to ride with him for the race. David's family relationship to the Vesteys and Dewhursts had resulted in the generous gift of an unlimited supply of meat throughout training, which supplemented the skimpy meals the crew ate when left to their own devices at college, so he could hardly be begrudged his display of independence. He had also made a great effort to adapt his rowing technique so that his sliding phased in with the rest of the crew. A happy Beak was an effective Beak. So he kept his lucky cap. As for the lucky ducks, the previous year's defeat had ruled them out as mascots. Only my tattered old fur-collared greatcoat has survived all 12 Boat Races, while most other items have come and gone with the passing stream of successive oarsmen.

On the weekend before we moved to the Tideway we embarked on a mammoth 18-mile outing with the Tideway Scullers, dropping down to Albert Bridge before turning to do a series of 'alternate' pieces of work up to Kew. Throughout we had the edge but the crews were closely enough matched for the exercise to be of great benefit to both eights. It was hard to get highly charged competitive crews to work side by side, sharing the stream, helping each other, because each wanted to show its superiority, and each was deeply suspicious of the other. And of course it was difficult too for a coach to do anything other than hype up his crew for the session and instil that vital ingredient, 'needle'. But on this occasion both crews felt they had gained from the outing. A week and a half later, with just ten days to the race, we revived the previously aborted fixture with the University of London. The outcome was a complete reversal of the mutually useful Scullers session. We should have known there would be trouble when we saw the UL launch arriving alongside their crew with two spare oars aboard. Within moments of the crews meeting to paddle lightly together downriver in anticipation of a series of timed pieces of work, the UL cox began pushing and shoving. I was suffering from a blinding attack of conjunctivitis and with my eyes streaming and the crews a blur before me, I found it hard to control the outing properly. The whole exercise was a nightmare. Before the work had even begun the coxes were clashing, trying to force each other off the best of the tide and in the end the last of the four contests was abandoned. UL won the first by a canvas, Oxford the second by a length and with the crews colliding and swearing, UL got away in the third leaving an angry and dispirited Oxford boat sulking in their wake. Oxford were given a bruising introduction to the ungentlemanly bustling behaviour of hardened Tideway crews. They were caught napping as UL jumped them off the start and stole their water. Cries of 'unfair' went unheeded and rightly so. These were lessons they had to learn fast.

There is little a cox can do for his crew if they are being led except to try to give them the clearest run of water and the best tide possible, but too often they try to barge and harass the other cox and crew to the extent that their own boat loses rhythm and flow and gets quickly left behind. The cox who swerves repeatedly into and away from the opposing crew not only loses pace but causes his own men to become more and more anxious about the other boat as it looms closely with oars interlocking; they soon begin to lose concentration on their own stroke pattern. Aggressive coxing means knowing your course and the stream and sticking firmly to it, taking the bends to the advantage of your own crew and protecting them from being distracted by erratic manoeuvres. Too many coxes push for pushing's sake, carrying their crew beyond the best of the tide and into the slacker water in their efforts to steal their rivals' course. They get blinded by their own bullying tactics and their eagerness to show who is the better cox and forget that they are trying to help win a contest by giving their team-mates the fastest conditions possible. The aim is not, as they sometimes appear to think, to force the other crew into the bank, even though Colin Moynihan, cox to the 1980 Olympic silver medal eight, lists aggressive shouting at the opposing crew and keeping your rivals waiting among his tactical coxing tips. Both UL and Oxford get a lot of flak from the Press whenever there are incidents of this kind, but in some ways it is a measure of the intense competitiveness that is generated by these fixtures and by the changing face of sport generally.

Bringing that extra edge to the battle on pitch, track, river or pool and the greater professionalism and thus dedication required, has meant a subsequent decline in the gentlemanly sporting attitude that used to be synonymous with athletic endeavour.

Now so much time, money and effort goes into the preparation of an athlete for top class competition that a little of the 'it is not so much whether you win or lose, but how you play the game' approach has died. Although rowing is one of the last real amateur sports left, the months spent and the sacrifice – five or six hours a day, year in year out – unpaid, are little different from the professionals, who at the top end earn big money playing their sport. It may not be right to countenance such cut-throat do-or-die rivalry at the expense of the old values, but nowadays that is where many of the winners come from. The 'John McEnroe' syndrome leaves a nasty taste in the mouth, but it is a reflection of the pressure that our expectations and demand for results has placed upon young competitive shoulders. We can and should all regret the passing of the 'good loser' but not many of today's top athletes will be content with the thought that the paramount aim is to 'take part'. The expression 'nice guys come second and second is last and nowhere' has gained common usage, although fortunately honourable competitors abound and 'nice guys' still win. However an athlete has to make serious choices. Either he must be content with the club level 'sport for fun' approach (which does not necessarily mean that it is not highly competitive) or he decides to go for the big time and all the sacrifice, pain, injury and ruthlessness that that entails. He will be pushed beyond endurance by coaches, colleagues, and family, and ultimately by the fans and supporters who want medals, records and the reflected glory of vicarious victory. Our media-gorged society is ever hungry for heroes no matter what the cost in health, integrity and lifestyle. The Boat Race has not come to that yet, because the financial stakes are still not that high, and it is after all just a private contest between amateur student sportsmen. But the pressures are there nonetheless and at both Universities the coaches have had to encourage a more professional approach to the whole affair. Without it winning nowadays would become virtually impossible.

We had planned to work hard in our penultimate week, leaving the last six days to polish and sharpen our challenge, but it was a tricky week for both 'Varsity crews. The day after our UL debacle, Cambridge lost to Goldie by over two lengths in a five-minute row, while on the Friday we went over the full track during which we suffered a whole series of mishaps. In the warm-up before the start against the ever potent Lube Lab, big 'Plunk' smashed his oar on a floating log. A

20-minute delay ensued while we replaced it. By the time we were ready the river had cut up rough. Off the start the Oxford stroke Andy Baird crabbed badly and the Lab went half a length up; but by the Black Buoy the deficit was recovered and at the Mile Oxford led by a length. As they moved out to nearly two up at Harrods a launch wash ahead caused a lurch and John Wiggins at seven jammed his seat on the slide. It took three-quarters of a minute and 20 ungainly strokes with only the bow five men rowing before he could disengage the seat with the help of 'Mr Cool' Brown and the crew could resume its pace. By this time the Lube Lab had pulled past and led by a length at Hammersmith Bridge where they dropped out. An unfortunate accident perhaps but one that could easily happen on the day. Commendably and without any prompting from me in the launch they grimly settled down again to complete their full-course trial as if they had just handed Cambridge a two length advantage. Isis picked up the pacing at the pier and took them to Barnes where an inevitable Police launch washed them all the way home to Mortlake. Despite the traumas they did at times look very good, but their vulnerability in rough water was a worry.

The troublesome week had done wonders in dampening down any possible complacency. The crew were now quite anxious and needed a morale booster. To take on the national Olympic training eight, which we had arranged to do next day, did not seem like quite such a good idea in the light of the past few days but to pull out smacked of cowardice. Besides we knew we were fast despite the disasters and a duel with the toughest in the land, a crew containing six world silver medallists (a placing they were to repeat in Montreal later in the year) could prove to be the making of the 1976 Oxford crew. It could also prove to be its undoing. We were not pleased with our showing so far on the Tideway and we geared ourselves up to high pitch for the following morning. We had planned to do three pieces, two short two-minute rows followed by a five minute one, starting from Putney. In the first two races the national eight took a quick lead off the start but after a minute Oxford were able to hold them at three-quarters of a length and then pull back each time to half a length down at the end. It was character-building stuff. But the longer last race would be the real test. We started the five-minute piece at the bottom of Chiswick Eyot, with Oxford starting on the outside of the short third of a length Surrey bend which would come into effect a minute into the row. Not only that, but the squad managed to steal an extra canvas lead on the 'go' and at the end of the first minute Fred Smallbone, the national eight's stroke had taken a three-quarters of a length lead rating 37. At this stage with the bend in their favour, the squad should have walked away from the students, but with enormous courage, Andy Baird at 35 pushed hard and held on round the outside of the corner. Then as the bend unfolded Oxford began to inch back and by the third minute they were level and moving by. Looking more and more confident with every stroke, they pushed on to a third of a length up when suddenly the opposition ground to a halt as their strokeman stopped rowing and slumped over his oar handle shaking his head. The men behind him angrily voiced their dismay. While Janousek raced his rubber coaching launch alongside their boat to calm them down Oxford drove on to complete the piece of work. Their tails were up and the traumatic week was placed firmly behind them.

Next day the crew went to Henley to watch the Oxford versus Cambridge match between the lightweights while the women's Boat Race was held on the Isis. Both Oxford crews won, the women for the first time in the 13-year history of their event. Meanwhile, on the Tideway, Cambridge succumbed to the Tideway Scullers in a seven-minute bridge to bridge by three lengths. I rowed in the bow seat of that Scullers crew and was able to observe the Light Blues at close quarters. Things looked good for Oxford and although Cambridge beat the Lube Lab a few days later in a second much improved bridge to bridge row the weight of evidence still favoured the Dark Blues. Watching both crews practising starts with the umpire off the same stakeboat moored opposite the Boat Race starting stone on Wednesday, the riverside pundits were clocking the crews for a minute as they raced up on a fast moving flood tide. 'You're OK, Dan' they confided. 'Your boys are getting a length past Thames Rowing Club in the minute while the Tabs are just reaching the flagpole.' It was encouraging news but we could not let the crew know that there was a possibility that they might lead by a length at the end of the first minute. They would surely go off half-cock and undermotivated if they really believed they had such an advantage. But of course rumour spreads and in our pre-race talk at the end of the week, we had to take great pains to divest ourselves of such dangerous thoughts. At the weigh-in, Oxford became the heaviest crew ever to row in the Boat Race, averaging 14 stone and half a pound, while Steve Plunkett at 16 stone 5 pounds broke the record as heaviest ever oarsman.

We spent the last days sharpening our edge and perfecting our take off, which by any standards was now fast. The accent was on high quality. In the last major piece of work, the crew rowed an excellent bridge to bridge alone beating the record set by my own Oxford crew in 1967 by an extraordinary 17 seconds. They were certainly fast but not that fast! Clearly conditions were perfect: no land water to hold back the flood, a good easterly breeze and a flat calm river on a high tide, the ideal platform for record-breaking. Not even the fastest crew in the world can get close to a Tideway record unless the conditions are very favourable, while a moderate crew can record exceptional times given a fast tide and following wind. In one practice start they finished just short of Barn Elms, the normal three-minute mark, in two minutes! If the wind stayed in the same quarter and the cold weather did not bring any rain we were due for a very fast race on the day.

While the 'heavy' rowing Press, *The Times*, the *Telegraph* the *Guardian* and the Sundays, covered the daily progress of the crews in a serious way, some other papers carried the usual sneer stories about 'this sporting dinosaur', 'this damp squib', 'this élitist rich man's game'. A few though like Roy Moore of the *Daily Mail* and Peter Ayling on the *Express* looked for more personal human interest stories. The *Express* picture desk brought the American world welterweight contender Hedgmon Lewis down to sit in the seven seat for a photograph. In other years Miss World, the actresses from a St Trinian's film, rowing fanatic and racing driver Graham Hill, Prince Philip and Jackie Genova have all played their parts in public relations. When an *Express* photographer called unannounced at our Putney house one day at seven in the morning to photograph Celia Keyworth, our cook in 1979, he found her in her dressing-gown and the crew just surfacing for breakfast. 'Can I have a picture of you in bed with the whole crew?' he begged. She shut the door firmly in his face. Another year the *Sun* wanted to cash in on the streaking fad and offered the crew hard currency to strip off and carry the boat naked from the river to the boathouse, with the boat strategically held to shield their embarrassment. On the same theme the *Star* got into the changing-rooms and persuaded the lads to pose topless, towels draped and muscles flexed, for a group cheesecake shot. All good publicity perhaps but in the opinion of many Old Blues not quite in character with the traditional aspect of the Boat Race. On the whole the crew members were scathing and reluctant when bombarded with these Press induced stunts but occasionally for the sake of peace and good public relations they relented. The Boat Race was, after all, a public show and the more coverage they attracted the better it was for the event.

In fact since Ladbrokes took over sponsorship of the race, not a year has gone by without some incident or other hitting the front pages. The sponsors have been blessed with high drama and farce and yet at first they were very sceptical about the publicity potential of the race for them. Even now each year they say, 'yes, but last year was special – there was Sue Brown, or there was Boris, or Cambridge sank or there was that close finish or there was a record or the cox hit a barge—but what about next year? It doesn't look as if there'll be anything to tempt the Press this time'. But curiously something always crops up.

In 1976 the knockers were out in force. David Hunn of the *Observer* even enlisted the help of national coach Bob Janousek to denigrate the significance of the event. Yet a couple of years later Janousek himself was chief coach at Cambridge. That the race distance and location is not the same as in 2000-metre six-lane international summer racing was yet again misconstrued by ill-informed journalists to suggest that the standard of the men involved was consequently low and that their training and effort could therefore be discounted. Hunn misinterpreted Janousek's comment that the Boat Race was a different sort of race as meaning that it lay outside the parameters of serious rowing. He omitted to point out that the training they did was fundamentally the same as that of the national team and that their speeds were often not greatly dissimilar. This kind of blanket misrepresentation rankled with the Oxbridge squads since it seemed to be trying to diminish their achievement and efforts.

It was the Cambridge President Henry Clay's 21st birthday when he joined Graham Innes with the umpire and Harry Carpenter on the Putney hard for the toss. He lost but got the Middlesex station, which in the circumstances was probably his best chance of minimising Oxford's fast start by placing his crew on the inside of that first Fulham bend. However it was a faint hope. Within a minute Oxford with a superb start were a length up as predicted and they were flying. By the Mile Post they were two and a half lengths ahead and at Hammersmith they were leading by three and a half. With the race firmly in their grasp they relaxed into a lazy stride, dropping their rate from a punchy 34 to a ponderous 32. Yet with the racing tide carrying them along they broke every intermediate record on their way to Mortlake, and pulverised the course record by 37 seconds breaking the 17-minute barrier by two seconds. It was Oxford's second course record in three years. 'Oxford's amazing record could stand for all time' wrote Desmond Hill in the *Telegraph*. In fact he had to wait only eight years for the record to go again. The crew were obviously delighted with their six and a half length win (a conservative estimation based on a timed calculation for a much slower tide) but though pleased with the result I was a little disappointed with the quality of their rowing after Harrods. It was perhaps a churlish reaction to such a triumph but I knew how well they could go and I had wanted a performance nothing short of magnificent.

Still the scene was set for a future run of success with Isis coming home two and a half lengths in front of a fast Goldie crew to complement the women's and lightweight successes, completing a grand slam over the arch rivals from the Fens. It was an understandably elated crew that arrived at the Ball that night. Even the normally reserved and self-controlled Ken Brown ended the evening unconscious on the floor of the gentleman's rest room at the Dorchester and had to be carried home. At Cambridge the only Blue due to return the following year was President elect David Searle. They were facing the same meagre future that Oxford had faced in 1968. The pendulum had swung and the tables were turning with a vengeance.

While I went to America on a short writing assignment, Wiggins, Baird, Mason and Edwards combined in a coxed four to challenge for Olympic selection under the guidance of Bob Janousek. We both felt that they had the potential to become a fast crew and he absorbed them into the Olympic squad in preparation for the early continental regattas on the international circuit. But somehow there was a reluctance on their part to bid for the top. While ex-Cambridge oarsmen Baillieu and Hart in the double sculls, Clay and Sturge in the coxless pair and Macleod and Christie in the coxed pair got stuck in and won selection, the Oxford four were impatient and when in their first race they were beaten (mainly because they failed to raise their racing rate sufficiently above a sedate Boat Race rhythm) they lost heart and withdrew from the selection battle. Balmy summer days in Oxford were a far more attractive proposition. John Wiggins had been determined to take a break from rowing after his junior efforts the year before and had joined even the Oxford squad reluctantly. Now he dug in. Bob and Andy also wanted a break and only Dave was keen to continue. The lure of the Olympics was not strong enough to tempt them. I was dumbfounded. I had spent the winter sculling 15 miles a day—two and a half hours per outing—under Mike Spracklen's gruelling sculling squad regime in an attempt to get into the British Olympic quadruple scull. Against all the sound advice of my lightweight colleagues, I persevered managing to match the heavyweights in single sculling trial races early on in the year. 'He'll never take you. He's only using you', they told me. 'You're far too light. You're wasting your time.' But I still reckoned I had an outside chance. What I obstinately refused to acknowledge, although deep down I knew it, was that early in training, especially over the longer distances usually covered in mid-winter for endurance, men under 11 and a half stone can race level with the big boys whether within an Oxford squad or at national level, because they work like terriers, stretching themselves to the limit in their efforts to stay in contention. The heavyweights are less motivated during the winter training months and while the lightweights are burning themselves out, their necks on the line every time there is a time trial, the heavies are biding their time, relying on their superior strength and weight to keep them in the picture. But when the real racing season starts the gap begins gradually to open as the heavyweights get themselves in gear, and most of the lightweights are left flailing a natural ten seconds or so in their wake over a 2000-metre course. A lightweight 11-stone gold medal eight could in some years make the heavyweight six-boat Olympic final but they would still end up three lengths adrift of the winners in fifth or sixth place. The same goes for the other categories too – in fours, doubles and singles, but nevertheless you find through the season that the best lightweight crews and scullers will often race in the heavyweight events to get the best competition. Some excel. In Los Angeles the Italian lightweight world champion double scullers Esposito and Verroca finished fifth in the Olympic final, eight seconds behind the American gold medallists, while the exceptional Spanish lightweight Climent won his silver medal magnificently in the coxless pairs rowing with the heavyweight Lasurtegui.

My friends proved right and I was dropped from the quad group so I turned my attention to lightweight rowing instead, only to be told I had left it too late to be considered for selection to the eight. So I joined a Tideway Scullers coxed four for Henley where we won the Britannia Cup, and spent a relaxing and very hot summer, rowing for pleasure, winning the Home Counties match in Ireland, and, in the absence of the Olympic team, the gold medal for quad sculls and the silver for fours at the National Championships. However Oxford's Henley showing was disappointing yet again. With training impaired by exams, college racing, cocktail parties and Commemoration Balls, the top oarsmen withdrew entirely leaving the Isis men and various lightweight Cherwell and college crews to represent Dark Blue hopes. Cambridge colleges abounded in all the Henley events but from our spring Boat Race crew, only Graham Innes appeared rowing for Leander in the final of the Grand. All Oxford's keen supporters and Old Blues at Henley felt badly let down by the non-appearance of their champion crew.

6
The Colonial Boys

The following year those Oxford supporters felt even more let down. Here was another fast crew at Boat Race time, and though they did stay together to contest the Grand Challenge Cup at Henley their poor performance did not do them justice. Lack of commitment, desultory training and a preference again for cocktail parties when outings were scheduled put paid to any real chance of success. Not that anyone was against parties. It was just that outings were being cancelled in favour of any little social function. It was a matter of priorities. I have always been a dedicated party-goer myself, often well into the early hours, appearing at the river heavy with hangover. But it never prevented me from making the outing more, or perhaps less, on time. My social life had to fit round the training, not the other way round, if serious races were to be won. The priorities for those winning Oxford men in 1977 were all back to front.

The prospective 1977 crew had the benefit of another American world champion from Ken Brown's 1974 gold medal eight. Al Shealy had been the stroke of both the Harvard eight and the American national eight and his reputation had preceded him. Here was another larger-than-life character; debonair, with slicked black hair, moustache, a wicked sense of the sickest humour, which, it must be said, could pall on the third or fourth hearing. Al's ambition was to be a Hollywood actor. When he held the floor there was no way that anyone else could speak, and at mealtimes his crewmates would be convulsed in either mirth or revulsion at his rancid jokes and bizarre utterings. He was not even deterred by the presence once of the Bishop of London, an Old Blue and past umpire, who writes every year to wish us God-speed and attends when Easter does not intervene. Shealy's forte was General Patton's pre-battle speech from the film *Patton* (how Al loved movies–the more violent and war-orientated the better) and he was often called upon to regale an assembled group with his vivid imitation of George C. Scott's rendering of the extravagant nationalistic mono-logue. He had, so rumour had it, beefed up the challenge of one US national team at a World Championships when, dispirited by a poor showing in the heats, the team were dining together the night before the semi-finals. Al's stirring 'blood and guts' performance sent them out the next day charged with a truly warlike determination to kill or die in the attempt and some say that their improved performances and final placings that year were partly due to his efforts in the dining hall. Al Shealy was a winner and no mistake.

With Al's arrival, Ken Brown promptly departed from the squad, explaining that he was getting married and would have no time for rowing. In fact he and Al had fallen out during the summer over selection procedures for the US Olympic team in Montreal. Andy Baird dropped out too, leaving just Bob Mason, the new President, David Beak and John Wiggins from the year before. Dave Edwards began trials and lasted until Christmas when work pressure forced him to retire as well. He had after all won his Blue and he wanted to turn his attention to other things. However Crispin Money-Coutts decided that he wanted another go. He did not like to think that his only appearance in the Boat Race would be a losing one and he rather regretted having missed out on the success of the year before. It was a tougher more motivated Crispin who turned up for trials in the autumn of 1976. There were good Isis men too. Paul Wright, the man who failed so narrowly in all those seat races the year before, was determined to make it this time around. There was also Nigel Burgess, a Youth international from Radley and a gutsy performer but a bit on the short side in a squad of very long men. So too was Mark Alloway, who dropped out altogether after trials when he saw that he was unlikely to make the first boat. Tristram Sutton was less experienced, a little ungainly perhaps but built well enough to be in contention as his strength and consistency improved. He was apt to be a little vague at times and seemed often to be pointing left when everyone else was pointing right, but he showed up well in the individual tests. In addition to the remaining men from the 1976 crews were Gyles Vardey, the unpredictable Youth sculler Andrew Hudson and some talented freshmen. Rob Moore, who had rowed for Kingston before coming to Oxford, looked technically very able, Mike Moran from Canada had won the Stewards' fours event at Henley in the summer and Ges Atherton, Russell Crockford and Julian Crawford were useful school first eight material.

Best of the newcomers though was undoubtedly Shealy; but in the same high calibre mould was a world lightweight fours champion from Australia, Ag Michelmore. He was a first-class exponent of effortless high technique rowing. No extraneous boat slowing movements marred Ag's style. He was a perfectionist and it did not take him long to establish himself in the squad. In terms of power he was average, his sculling was nothing to write home about and his running was not so great, but in a crew his fluidity, rhythm and discipline were a pleasure to behold. It took the coaches somewhat longer than it took the oarsmen in the squad to recognise openly his undoubted talent because we were keen as always to avoid prejudging issues. Past records were not supposed to count with us. It was what a man did at the time that counted and Ag's individual results in the tests were not particularly impressive to begin with. So we took our time in promoting him to the stern of the trial crews. I knew Ag's background well though. He was in the Australian lightweight four that had won the gold medal in Lucerne in 1974 when Nick Tee, Drury, Hall and I were finishing seventh. They were a fine crew then, a class above the rest of us with remarkable control in their rowing and splendid technical ability. We used to watch them performing their in-boat exercises as they warmed up and no one at Lucerne that year could have failed to be impressed by them. The next year they were not quite as good and in the World Championship final both we and the French winners rowed through them at halfway. To be fair the water was bouncy and difficult at that point on the Nottingham course and they were not able to derive the full benefit of their precision rowing while we, more thuggish, were able to drive on through the rough in the familiar windy British conditions.

In 1976–7 apart from Oxford's Boat Race cause, I was deeply committed to the national lightweight eight. All year I stretched myself uncomfortably thin between the Isis and London but it was, I suppose, good for getting down my weight. Writing assignments had to fit in with both training programmes and I missed a number of lucrative foreign trips because nothing could be allowed to jeopardise our chances at the World Championships. We hoped to become the first British crew in over 20 years to win an international rowing gold medal so everything took second place to that aim. At Oxford those early months at the beginning of training proved to be more than a little disorganised and the squad, through design or absentmindedness, failed to appear at any of the Head sculling races. Instead they worked in pairs and fours at Radley under Ronnie Howard and Jock Mullard, emerging only once from Oxford to race in the national pairs trials at Nottingham. Although Mason and Money-Coutts went reasonably well in the first race, they faded badly thereafter and overall the squad did not fare too happily, demonstrating a distinct lack of grit and fitness and an air of complacency. However, more cheerfully for me, Chris Drury and I were going particularly well in a new first production line Carbocraft pair and we emerged at the end of the weekend as overall winners of the coxless pair trials in both the heavyweight and lightweight divisions.

The infant company Carbocraft were keen to sell their first production eight to Oxford and their Managing Director and inventor of the glass and carbon fibre boat, John Vigurs, inveigled his old crewmate Dick Fishlock, stroke of the 1960 Oxford Olympic eight, to make representations to the Dark Blue coaching team on his behalf. The pair I was racing in felt fast and responsive and so we agreed to try their new eight after Christmas. I was enjoying my own rowing enormously that autumn, finishing regularly in first, second or third position in the sculling and pairs Heads. In November I teamed up with the Melvin family, 47-year-old Doug, 22-year-old John and 17-year-old Simon to race a 65-year-old quadruple sculling boat called *Chuck Chuck* in the fours Head, and we won our division. At the Head of the Cam I came up against the Cambridge squad in single sculling boats and was able to gain a measure of the Light Blue talent. Simon Clegg, a freshman from Shrewsbury, seemed to be their best man, in a sculling boat at least, and indeed he became the stroke of the Cambridge crew of 1977.

In keeping with the somewhat haphazard approach of the squad to training that year the Oxford trial eights were formed late, a few days before the race in early December and they did not arrive on the Tideway until the Saturday morning. Al Shealy and Paul Wright were the strokemen of two rather rough looking but powerful crews and they raced from Chiswick down to Putney. Shealy took a lead at the start on the outside of the first big bend but at Barnes Bridge Paul had sneaked back and led by a quarter length as they shot the bridge. Then the coxes steered into each other and a clash forced Shealy's crew back a length from which, surprisingly, they never recovered. With the Blues Wiggins and Beak and the Australian Michelmore and the Canadian Moran behind him the coaches had expected Shealy's boat to overpower the other crew over the second half but they fell further and further behind, finally losing by six lengths at Putney.

Such a reversal of fortunes – perhaps the size of the defeat more than the result itself – gives useful indications to the coaches of the failings of some oarsmen initially considered top rate; it also reinforces the dangers of prejudging selection issues and brings to notice some otherwise poorly considered candidates. For the oarsmen themselves it shatters self-satisfaction in the arrogant, forcing them to reappraise their standing and their chances within the squad while it builds the confidence of others and thus raises the level of their future performances in the individual tests. For Wright, Vardey, Sutton and Burgess the prospect of a Blue loomed closer while the confidence of Mason and Money-Coutts, the Blues in the winning crew, was reinforced. The result also suggested that although Shealy was a top class 2000-metre US stroke he might not, with his different style, be the best man to lead a Boat Race crew from Putney to Mortlake. Indeed in the two years he rowed for Oxford he sat in the number six seat, a tower of strength, supporting a lighter less powerful man at stroke but one with a better more comfortable Boat Race – that is long distance – rhythm. Added to that, Al recognised that we did not have a real six man in the squad. That Shealy never fully came to terms with what he thought deep down to be a subordinate role only emerged a few years later when I heard that back in the States he joked with self-mocking irony tinged with regret about how he had stroked Harvard and stroked the fastest crew in the world in 1974, but at Oxford was not considered the right man to stroke the Boat Race crews of 1977 and 1978. Clearly it stung long afterwards and he found it hard to reconcile his different role to his peers at home.

The old maxim 'they all rowed hard but none so hard as stroke' still carries weight and the image of the stroke as leader continues to endow the role with special heroic stature. Yet the six seat is perhaps one of the hardest ones to fill. It needs a fluid and very powerful interpreter of the strokeman's rhythm, a man who can provide the driving force for a crew. Other coaches regard the seven seat as the most important. Steve Fairbairn, one of the architects of modern rowing, wrote in his book *Rowing Notes*: 'Seven is the accelerator of the crew; he is stroke's stroke and combines the two sides and should be the best man in the crew both as an oarsman and general'. Bowmen have their champions too but in the end it must be the best and most cohesive mix of eight top class performers, all of whom have a role to play, who are all seated according to their strongest attributes.

Shealy's reactions to Oxford after his American college and national team experiences were constructive. He found our emphasis on running, weights and small boat work very useful and felt that it improved the overall conditioning of the squad considerably. At Harvard they did most of their work in the eights. He also enjoyed the concentrated technique work that we did while he gathered from Cashin that the Cambridge set-up was less integrated. However, he felt that there was a definite and very uncomfortable split between the colonials and the Etonian elements in the crew and though he liked the English boys well enough he was surprised at their nonchalant approach. At school I remember how it was always considered so uncool to be keen and show enthusiasm and the same instincts seemed to be surviving with the public schoolboys of Oxford. To be seen to be making an effort, even though one cared desperately, was out of order. 'They were always in such a hurry to get away after outings', complained one member of the crew later. 'They never seemed to want to be part of it all.' 'It was as if the Boat Race was all but won with so much talent available, and there was therefore no reason to train too hard', said another.

The coaches were not fully aware of the extent of the dissatisfaction that prevailed in the squad in the first months and it emerged that the commitment and motivation of some senior members in the group was in question. The colonials suspected that an element of nepotism existed and that the Old Blue syndrome was rearing its ugly head, but they did not report this to any of the coaching team. They were used to a strict meritocracy when it came to selection and the two-month period before Christmas in which an undergraduate President ruled proved to be a very confusing arrangement for them. It was sad for us who had worked so hard in those first four years to discover this sudden lapse of commitment. It was also not the sort of picture we wanted to present to the new members of the squad. Because I was heavily involved in my own rowing in London, I was unable to monitor as closely as usual what was happening at Oxford and I missed these early warning signals. All our efforts to eliminate the old unprofessional habits were being eroded and we did not know it. We did not realise that some squad members were regularly missing or cutting short training sessions, and that partying, drinking and even smoking were commonplace. The experienced overseas freshmen and indeed many of the home-grown men found this attitude hard to take, and not surprisingly since in any serious squad it would not have been tolerated.

While Oxford took their normal three and a half-week break over Christmas, Cambridge took the unusual step of releasing their men for a few days only, hoping that two and a half weeks of extra formal training in camp would give them added speed. They also attended the national pre-Christmas trials as an eight. When the Oxford squad reassembled for the January fortnight at Putney where Chris and I took over for the selection process, we were a little disappointed at the level of fitness and the lack of a sense of urgency displayed by one or two in the group. Even the undertrained Andy Baird, returning briefly in the hope that academic pressures would have eased, coped quite well until he had to withdraw once again. In the gym circuits which we do at the end of the day after rowing the exercise repetitions were sometimes incorrectly done either because of fatigue or out of laziness and as usual we called attention to those that were unsatisfactory in terms of range and pace. Under pressure any athlete gets exasperated at being reminded that he is not working properly, but puts the matter right anyway whether with a curt nod, a grin or a snarl. David Beak at first ignored the instructions and then as I repeated them again he lost all self-control and came bounding across the floor, fists flailing. He was restrained by startled colleagues as Chris and I stood in bemused astonishment. The fact was that his lack of conditioning was being exposed and it had upset him. He calmed down and an uneasy truce held for a few days but it was the beginning of the end. Back in Oxford he continued to disregard the basic rules that govern a man in serious training and even the protective umbrella of Old Blueship could not save him. The crew was being coached by Hugh Matheson at the time, and Beak finally overdid it. Hugh was not prepared to compromise and dropped him from the crew.

There followed a general post as crewmen were changed around and a replacement selected. Ken Brown, David Edwards or Andy Baird could all have been possibilities but it was already too late to commandeer one of them even if they had been willing. So it fell to Gyles Vardey, who had impressed in the January fortnight, to replace the errant Blue. A short while earlier, disenchanted with the way some of the men were training, he had resigned from Isis. Fortunately for him and for Oxford, he had been persuaded to return by Hugh Matheson. Instead of joining the 'Brit' faction, Vardey teamed up with the colonial group of Al, Ag and Wiggins (an honorary Colonial) while the newly engaged Paul Wright remained a little apart. Mike Moran, the Canadian, leaned a little towards the 'Brit' faction but the sad fact remained that there were two camps which clashed fundamentally. 'It was not a spiritually cohesive crew' explained Shealy; 'we could have been much faster'. 'Basically there were two different sorts of approach' says Colin Moynihan, the cox. 'Shealey, Vardey, Ag and Wiggins were hungry for success and only enjoyed the rowing if they were winning and they trained accordingly, while the others seemed to have the attitude that they were born talented, and wasn't that lucky— no need to train hard.' He struggled to keep the peace within the crew.

We took delivery of the long awaited black hull Carbocraft just in time for our trial row at the end of the Tideway fortnight. We boated an 'A' and a 'B' crew, setting the 'B' off nearly half a minute ahead into the teeth of a blizzard. The 'A' team fairly leaped over the course in pursuit, relishing the light feel of the new carbon boat and caught the second crew before halfway. They then took a further half-minute off them to the finish, covering massive amounts of water between the strokes all the way. Despite the antagonisms within the squad the Oxford crew designate looked formidable. Carbocraft were to become the dominant boatbuilding company of the late 'seventies in Britain and they recruited Bob Janousek, the retiring national coach, as a director of the company. Although there were internal fitting problems with the boats in the first year or two, which took a long time to sort out, with both shoulders and riggers being prone to weakness, the hull shapes were sound and their lightness and stiffness excellent. They were very well suited to the Tideway and we insisted that they made aerofoil riggers for us rather than their normal production model ones after we found that the originals caused us to take on water in rough conditions.

Over the next six years we stayed loyal to Carbocraft despite occasional problems with twisting or blistering boats and varying decking heights. No subsequent boat was as comfortable as the first one that they made for us, but on the whole their craftsmen were always on hand to solve our problems until they went into liquidation in 1984 and we changed to a German produced Empacher boat. Cambridge had by then been racing in Empachers for two years as had nearly everyone else on the international regatta scene, but we had always felt that the German shells were better suited to 2000-metre calm water racing than the turbulence of the four and a quarter-mile Tideway course. However both their wooden and plastic boats are more comfortable to row in than the Carbocraft ones, and oarsmen regard Empacher as the Rolls-Royce of rowing eights.

In 1977 though we were delighted with our new Carbo and the crew quickly settled into it. The selection upheavals continued a while longer and when the smoke had cleared, four very good Blues and two Isis men had left the squad leaving space for four junior eight men to move up into Isis–Julian Crawford, Russell Crockford, Rob Moore and 'always in a daze' cox David Fitzherbert. Tristram Sutton, trying for the second time to win his Blue was given the benefit of extensive trials in the first crew. He was inconsolable when the decision went against him and it took the tactful ministrations of the whole coaching team to pacify the tearful candidate in the corridors of the University of London boathouse after a heavy weekend fixture. Oxford had been taking nearly a length a minute off UL on the first day and when next day our cox Colin Moynihan fell ill the somewhat overweight UL boatman, Jim Wallis, took over our rudder strings. Even then Oxford were able to give the Londoners a length start and beat them by three over seven minutes.

Throughout training, Al Shealy was educating the English boys in the US college arts of 'grossing out' and particularly 'mooning'–the American equivalent of 'streaking'. Timing, positioning and perseverance were of the essence here and Al was a master of all three. He found a number of willing pupils amongst the young fresh faced just-out-of-school Oxford rowing lads and he impressed them early on when he responded to a challenge to 'moon' from Moynihan's open sportsmobile along the full length of the M4 motorway from London to the Henley turn off. To ensure that there were witnesses to this momentous 'moon' the rest of the squad were to drive alongside in the Oxford van. Sure enough and to the wonder of the admiring throng, the Shealy posterior remained exposed to view and air–and in mid-February this was no mean feat–from the Chiswick flyover all the way to Maidenhead. When the ice-blue cheeks were finally withdrawn, a hero of almost mythical proportions had been established.

The rest of the crew were now beholden to take the lesson on board or at least those among them feeble-minded and suggestible enough to be so persuaded. Returning from an outing at Radley, a quiet country backwater where the local school are our hosts, the crew went into action. Four pairs of bared buttocks were thrust to the windows of the speeding van as they approached two ladies astride broad-backed horses. They scattered as the van swept by but just managed to catching fleeting glimpses of the fast disappearing cheeks before their horses stampeded off across the meadows. The village was outraged of course and complaints duly arrived. Although Bob Mason summoned his men to the Blue's club Vincent's for a severe dressing-down, Oxford were banned from the reach. It was well over a year before the repentant squad, sworn to adult behaviour, were allowed to return. Undaunted the whole crew mounted a full moon for the benefit of Cambridge boatman Alf Twinn when they arrived at Putney. 'They're prettier than their faces at least' retorted the sharp-tongued Twinn.

Our sponsors Ladbrokes conceived of a publicity stunt to mark the official Boat Race challenge. Usually it is done by phone, letter or telegram in an off hand 'hope you turn up on the day' sort of way, and is issued by the President of the losing University of the year before. Cambridge's David Searle was induced to ride through the streets of Oxford in a horse-drawn dray with a town crier calling 'Oyez! Oyez!' He and his secretary, Mark Horton, dismounted outside Bob Mason's college, Keble, and then read a prepared text in 'Olde English' containing phrases like 'Nine good men and true'. The Oxford President accepted the challenge and they then rode off slightly embarrassed by the whole affair. Another year Cambridge and Goldie cycled through Oxford on a bicycle made for 16 and were pelted with eggs and firecrackers when they arrived at Corpus to deliver the challenge.

On the rowing front the squad attended the January national trials and performed much better than in November, finishing first and third on Saturday and second and fourth on Sunday in coxed fours. They then settled down to the eight. With Shealy installed at six, we experimented with both Paul Wright and Ag Michelmore at stroke. Either way the crew looked cohesive and strong; but it was the Australian who got the seat. Michelmore's maturity and fluent rhythm provided the crew with that bit more time and over the following weeks they developed a wonderful stride and run. Ag delighted in the technical exercises we did on the water and the crew's boat control was a pleasure to watch. There was no doubting their power and they won all their fixtures in February and March against UL, the national heavyweights now under Chris Blackwall's tutelage and my own lightweight eight. For that session we were set to row two three-minute pieces but we lightweights simply could not match Oxford's strength. They took nearly a length a minute in both rows as they had done against UL. A few weeks earlier Cambridge had invited the lightweight eight to spend the weekend with them training in Ely, and they too had finished in front of us, but only marginally. We had won a couple of the set pieces and enjoyed a most hospitable two days. It was also a very instructive weekend for an Oxford coach.

When we arrived at Putney for the final fortnight both 'Varsity crews set about establishing their credentials by way of testing pre-race efforts. At the end of the first week we rowed an alternative to a cancelled full-course trial (John Wiggins being ill on the scheduled day and me deputising for the outing) from Chiswick Steps to the Stone at Putney, breaking the record for the distance by 12 seconds in the process although the time was unofficial in the absence of a Press launch for the necessary corroboration. On the same day Cambridge beat the Tideway Scullers by two and a half lengths over seven minutes so we invited the Scullers for a bridge to bridge confrontation as our final set piece row on the following Tuesday. Lou Barry, their coach, always keen to be a cat amongst the pigeons, gladly accepted the challenge.

Conditions were rough and windy when we lined up with the Scullers late on Tuesday afternoon to race downriver from Hammersmith Bridge. Both Lou and I were a little anxious about the white-capped waves in the Crabtree reach but his pride in the almost legendary watermanship of his crews and my keenness to prove to my lot that they could and might need to tackle any kind of weather on the day (the Boat Race has never been postponed because of rough water) egged us both on. After two minutes it was clear that both crews were taking on a lot of water and by Crabtree Wharf the Scullers were beginning to go down. Oxford wound down the rate and began edging gingerly towards the Surrey bank where they succumbed in shallow water, disembarked and emptied out. Fortunately there was no damage and no one caught a chill, but the exercise had certainly involved a calculated risk. On the whole it is not common for crews simply training in rough conditions to sink because they usually seek the shelter of the shore well before they take on enough water to swamp them; but in races the likelihood is more acute since neither crew is willing to stop racing and concede unless the contest is officially aborted. Crews, coaches and umpires alike always believe that they can go just that little bit further, especially on the Tideway where the water conditions change as quickly as the river course changes direction. Furthermore boats do not really sink. Rather they become water-logged, unrowable to be sure with the river flowing over the riggers but still supported by the eight oars sticking out on either side. So as long as the oarsmen remain with their boat they are usually safe. Besides they are all supposed to be able to swim under the laws of the Amateur Rowing Association! But it is still no joke when you suddenly end up in a cold fast-flowing Thames. The main danger when a boat sinks stems from the fact that most rowing is done on rivers, and when heavy rains increase the speed of flow, waterlogged boats and crewmen can be swept over weirs, into bridges and under passing motor craft before they are rescued. On the Tideway the fast current presents a continual threat. But with coaching launches usually in attendance when crews are racing such risks are minimised. It is the endurance-test nature of the Boat Race that requires extra levels of masochism from the oarsmen, but we get terrible press whenever there is an incident of this kind. The Oxford boys were singing the Eton boating song as they foundered.

Barely a week before the race Cambridge changed boats. Professor Alistair Cameron, the Imperial College Lube Lab chief and ex-Cambridge Blue, had developed a lightweight monocoque shell in his workshop which he now offered to the Light Blues. Pat Delafield, their finishing coach, jumped at the chance to abandon the Cambridge boat which by all accounts was some 50 pounds heavier than Oxford's black Carbocraft. President David Searle and his crew took to the *Priory* happily and they soon picked up extra speed. There was great interest during those last weeks in the new lightweight shells of the two Boat Race crews, and almost more was written about them than about the men pulling on the oars. Much was made too of our cox Colin Moynihan. Two weeks before the Race he won another Blue against Cambridge in the ring as a bantamweight in the annual boxing match. He lost. 'That's the last thing they'll win', he growled and climbed back into the coxswain's seat. He had to build his weight up to 8 stone 7 pounds to fight and then shed 11 pounds to cox. His Presidency of the

Oxford Union also impressed the journalists and they asked: 'Could this man be a future Prime Minister?' Colin was elected to Parliament in 1983 so taking the first step towards confirming their long term predictions.

A contemporary of mine at Oxford, John Wolfenden, a coach and former Isis oarsman, offered the crew a pre-Boat Race weekend relaxing at his rambling family-run hotel in Ventnor on the Isle of Wight. In 1967 and 1968 his parents had hosted Oxford and we had enjoyed the excellent fare of Peacock Vane, welcoming the break from the tensions of that last fortnight before the race. We now accepted the invitation with alacrity. To make the weekend even more luxurious Derek Thurgood, one of Oxford's coaches from 1973 to 1975, made available a 12-seater bi-plane to fly us there and back. In the previous four years we had simply released the crew for the weekend to go home for a quiet day. Either that or they had stayed together in London reading the papers, taking a walk in Kew Gardens and enjoying Piers', and later his brother Orlando's, cooking. The idea of the 'weekend retreat' had always been traditional for both 'Varsity crews but through a scarcity of willing hosts and a lack of effort to seek them out, it had gone by the board. This had been a shame really because it was an excellent way of further knitting the crew together both spiritually and emotionally.

The Putney house always provided a delightful time and Boris looks back on those days each year with particular pleasure: 'Eat, sleep, row— what could possibly be better?' Shealy remembers enjoying his two Tideway fortnights more than any camps he had attended at home. 'I'd do it all again in a second. I could never experience the whole tradition of such an event in America; not even at Harvard. But the media here, the former Blues, the sponsorship, all the crowds and interest and attention are amazing. Back home you just never felt the same appreciation of it. It's a flavour you just don't taste. Anyone from the US who has rowed in the race would agree.'

Oxford went to the post as hot 6-1 favourites in the first year of Ladbroke's sponsorship. Experienced observers reckoned them to be the fastest Boat Race crew ever and they confirmed all expectations. Winning the toss they chose Surrey and as in 1976 they sped off the mark at 43 to lead by a length in a minute. 'After eight strokes I heard Al's voice come over the speaker system', remembers Gyles Vardey. '"All right!" he drawled and I knew we were going to win.' They were two lengths up at the Mile and, with the conditions extremely rough and unpleasant from Harrods on, Moynihan kept them out of the worst of it as they cruised on to a seven-length win, the biggest Oxford margin for 79 years. Cambridge never had a chance but their cox Jo Manser held them out in mid-stream as they battled bravely on, always a couple of strokes higher than Oxford.

Though I was paranoid about the dangers of laying bets on the outcome of the race Colin Moynihan had had no such scruples. While he was waiting to go over the course with Bert and me a couple of hours before the race, he had slipped up the road to the Ladbrokes office where they were offering eight to one on an Oxford victory by seven lengths. 'I put a fiver on', he told his crew after the race. I didn't dare tell you before in case you thought it unlucky.' 'Ah ha!' they cried, 'so that's why your bloody course was so erratic in the last mile. We were going too fast for you. You had to slow us down to make sure the margin was only seven lengths!' Cambridge did however look a good bet for the future. Their second crew Goldie, after delaying the race for 20 minutes with a broken gate, beat Isis comfortably. It had been a close race to halfway with Isis, stroked on bowside by Nigel Burgess, leading by over a length to the Mile Post. Many of the young Cambridge men, including five Blues, were due back the following year while Oxford had but three returning Blues and most of the losing Isis men.

Two weeks after the Boat Race the crew competed in the Head of the River Race against the best of the rest in the country. Without having had an outing in the preceding week, and starting as a new entry on a slack tide at the back of the field, they finished a creditable second behind the star-studded international Leander crew and one and a half seconds in front of my own lightweight eight. Isis, also starting at the back, reversed their defeat by Goldie, slipping home three seconds ahead. But although Oxford stayed together for the summer with Ken Brown coming into the boat in place of President elect Michelmore who had to return to Australia before Henley, the internal wranglings increased. Ken was not the calm, conscientious man he had been in the 1976 squad and he joined the punting, strawberries-and-cream brigade leaving his world champion team-mate Shealy on the other side of the ideological fence. Shealy was at stroke and what should have been an exceptional crew disappointed its supporters by finishing last at the Nottinghamshire International Regatta and then going out in the first round of the Grand at Henley to Chris Blackwall's national eight. The British squad were then beaten in the final by the 'Huskies' from Washington University.

The antagonisms that had been apparent all year came to a head during the summer. Neither Ag, Chris nor I were around to monitor training in anything more than a minor way, but the two factions nearly came to blows at Henley. 'It turned very ugly' recalls Moynihan. 'The "born lucky" brigade didn't want to live and train in Henley for the last week while the "winners" were convinced that to succeed they needed to knuckle down to training camp conditions. The arguments were really very unpleasant and soured the whole effort. Shealy in particular after that Grand race was in a mood to spill blood.' So yet again a successful Boat Race squad could not produce the goods at Henley. Cambridge although not winning were at least sending a mass of college crews to contest the various Royal Regatta events – 13 eights and six fours to Oxford's five eights and one four, all of which were first round losers.

However, while Oxford were failing to live up to their expectations, the national lightweights, competing as London Rowing Club, were far exceeding theirs. In a series of thrilling races, and against all the odds, we reached the semi-final of the Thames Cup, beating the Belgians and the Vesta heavyweights with some wonderfully composed precision rowing. Then we came up against the University of London, yet another heavyweight crew with an advantage of two stone a man, or a total 16 stone of muscle-power, over us. At the Nottingham International Regatta only a week earlier, they had beaten three Henley Grand contenders, Oxford, Harvard and Washington – the eventual Grand winners – and expected a clear victory in the Thames Cup. They never saw us. We had half a length at the quarter mile, a length at Fawley and then, with Royal guest Princess Anne, Chancellor of London University, watching from the launch, we cruised home one and a half lengths ahead keeping the Purples well within our sights, but conserving energy for the final later in the day. That race against Leander (with Boris Rankov rowing at four) went the same way; all our winning times were close up to those in the Grand right through the week. Wins in Lucerne, the National Championships and the Serpentine Jubilee Regatta followed in quick succession, culminating in that coveted world title and precious gold medal. It was a lovely summer.

7
The Sinking

With Cambridge looking strong on paper for 1978 the alarm bells were sounding early at Oxford and I made more trips there in the first couple of months of training than I normally did at that time of year. I was anxious that the nonchalant poorly organised start to the previous year should not be repeated and that the new President, Ag Michelmore, should not regard 1977 as the example to follow. It had to be action stations right from the start. But Ag was a cool professional customer and even though as an Australian he was still a little new to the ways of the OUBC he had no intention of letting things slide. He was an efficient administrator as well as a leader and ran a good show. He was the fifth Australian President at Oxford, and conscious of the fact that all his predecessors had lost. He wanted to break the spell.

Of the three returning Blues, Michelmore seemed destined for the stroke seat once again even though in principle it was not always a good idea to place so much responsibility on the shoulders of one man. But we believed Ag had the maturity to cope. Shealy, although seduced for much of the term by the promise of boxing for Oxford at heavyweight level (a bout which thankfully never took place) returned to the six seat. Mike Moran, the third returning Blue, took an even less committed view towards his second Boat Race appearance, pursuing interests in the equally accident-prone activities of ice hockey and skiing, gambling dangerously on being needed in January and therefore delaying his return to Boat Race training. He took part in the trials race in December but did little over Christmas, returning to Oxford late, overweight and a very borderline case for a seat. He finally pulled himself together and scraped in at three by way of the seat racing but it was some time before he had recovered enough fitness and bite to take what should have been his natural place at five. The Isis oarsman Julian Crawford who had been occupying that seat, though strong and willing was also a bit of a rusher and not yet capable of doing the job effectively, so he was moved back to three. There he joined his two other 1977 Isis colleagues, Russell Crockford and Tristram Sutton. Tristram had a protracted battle with the OUBC secretary Nigel Burgess for the bow seat which was not finally resolved until four weeks before the Boat Race. They were good friends, both loyal hard-working Oxford squad men who had rowed together for three years and it was a difficult decision for the coaches to make. It also, says Tristram, put a barely tolerable strain on their friendship. Finally Tristram's length, weight and height tipped the balance against the smaller Burgess who could never quite manage the necessary length in the water. One man who had slipped through the net the year before was Jim Wood, a Youth international from Hampton. I had never seen him before but he had apparently tried out for the junior trials and, astonishingly, been found wanting in 1977. In the absence of the retired John Wiggins, our seven man for the previous two years, Jim, the fastest Oxford sculler became front runner for that all-important job.

Newly returned to Oxford after a season with Leander was the 1974 and 1975 Isis oarsman Boris Rankov. He was now a definite contender for a Blue Boat seat, a different man from the one who had arrived as an ungainly undertrained freshman at the end of 1973. His 14-stone bulk certainly looked useful now and he performed well in the sculling races and in the gym. Even his running, though still ponderous, put him at least amongst the tailenders rather than a mile behind the field. He had closed up some four or five minutes on the four mile run by the time we got to Putney in January and he and the freshman Phil Head regularly battled it out on the running track. They both hated running but both tackled it with determination in the knowledge that Boat Races could be won or lost on how well they could come to terms with all elements of the training programme. Phil had come to grief on his motorbike a year or two earlier and was left with one leg shorter than the other. It did not hinder his rowing so much but running was very difficult for him. That he chose to force himself along, half skipping, half hopping, rather than seek permission to do some alternative training was a measure of the man's doggedness. He was certainly Boat Race material. Despite his disability he never finished last in the running tests. He was also strong in the gym, a trademark of all those excellent Hampton schoolboy oarsmen who, though a little on the small side, seemed to emerge from Molesey in a remarkably steady flow. Their coach Richard Hooper must certainly be held responsible for the talents of Wright, Wood, Mahoney, Head, Conington, Payne for Oxford and many others who rowed as Youth internationals and then at other colleges throughout Britain.

Other contenders for the Blue Boat were the 1977 Isis men Ges Atherton, a powerful 14 and a half-stone man, a little rough in technique but sound and reliable in a boat, and Rob Moore, who while still looking effective did not fully convince the coaches with his work output. We felt he was going through the motions rather than putting himself on the line and his individual results seemed to corroborate this. He was not yet the totally committed crewman that he was to become in 1979. Newcomers to the squad like John Bland who had never rowed before coming to Oxford performed much more convincingly in the individual tests. From novice to Isis in one year, the 12-stone John Bland's natural athleticism, his rapid adaptability and his deep-rooted competitive instinct soon made him the man to beat in the Oxford squad.

Bland, the 'demented imp', was shy and self-effacing at first and needed to be reassured of his obvious talent. Even when he became one of the great Boat Race strokes of all time his natural modesty still inhibited him. It took one of the most compelling stroking performances in the history of the Henley Royal Regatta, winning two Grand Challenge Cup medals and a world silver medal in 1981 to convince him that maybe he was not such a bad oarsman after all. His inclination to defer to others when his ability was questioned led to his exclusion from the 1984 Olympic eight when the coach brought in a late challenger for his place in the crew.

Trying for places in Isis were Simon Shepherd and Tom Barry, both school first eight oarsmen; Mark Gleave, a 1977 lightweight crew member; Jamie Robertson, a confirmed dry bob from Eton who surprisingly developed a passion for rowing once he arrived at Oxford and Richard Guppy, yet another very talented Youth international who appeared and vanished rather disconcertingly a number of times. He tried out on a couple of occasions for a place but never quite decided to come the whole way—or at any rate he somehow got waylaid along the route. He would have been very useful in the squad but he just did not catch the bug. He did however row in the trials race in December, an unforgettable battle in which the lead changed hands again and again until Barnes bridge where strokeman Shealy on the outside of the last bend moved out from level to one third of a length and just held off rival stroke Russell Crockford's challenge at the finish. That race was the making of the slightly built Russell, whose lighthearted approach to life had until then concealed from the coaches a very tough competitive edge. His sculling had improved a lot since 1976 and he kept himself well in contention thereafter winning his place at two. Guppy and another senior trialist, Keith Sheppard, gave way in January to the junior trial men Robertson and Gleave and when late in the day Nigel Burgess failed to win a place in the Blue Boat he withdrew from the squad altogether. Tom Barry, son of Oxford's Treasurer and coach Michael Barry, came in at bow for Isis. Mark Gleave, whose father had rowed in the Boat Race, rowed gallantly in two losing Isis crews. In 1980 his studies took him to Cambridge, where he won a seat in Goldie only to come up against the first winning Isis crew for four years. He was unfortunate enough to find himself always running counter to the flow of success.

The battle for seats in the Blue Boat was tough, especially with the ambivalent Moran making the choice wider than it need have been. A visit to Cambridge to race in the sculling Head of the Cam had revealed that the Light Blues were back with a vengeance and indeed were early favourites with their returning Blues. They had almost the same crew as they did in 1977, so they were well fired up with something to prove. Six of their squad, headed by the Youth international freshman Ali Jelfs, finished in the top eight in that Cam sculling Head. I was third and knew from the experience of racing the Oxford boys that we were probably trailing Cambridge on that front. Jelfs, Bathurst, Ross, Davies, Horton their President and the very talented Cooke-Yarborough were all useful men in a sculling boat. But we did have a number of men who though very experienced and strong as oarsmen, were not too clever in this respect. Ag, Al, Mike and Julian would have preferred pair oared racing to sculling trials. Nevertheless all this evidence of Cambridge speed served to keep the Oxford squad on their toes and the seat racing was tense. Selection was once more being based on merit and the aberrations of the year before were set aside. Once selected the crew moulded together well and though they got beaten in a marathon weekend of 60 minutes' flat-out work with Chris Blackwall's national squad eight in their first Tideway visit they acquitted themselves convincingly against London University who were later to beat Cambridge between the bridges. The Oxford bowmen particularly had to learn the meaning of real mental and physical toughness. They had to know how to hurt themselves. 'We may not have had the raw strength in 1978 but there was more harmony and cohesion', says Shealy. 'We were a far happier crew than the year before but I guess there were still one or two guys who were more concerned with winning the Blue rather than winning the Race.' Again Shealy had to be content with the six seat since even more than the year before there was clearly no one else who could do the job. But he was happy to row behind Ag who undeniably set a lovely rhythm.

The two of them, President and world lightweight champion of 1974 at stroke and Shealy, world heavyweight champion of the same year, at six were a formidable and experienced duo and they certainly did not refrain from letting the rest of the crew know it. There sat Jim between them, thankfully a sensible composed quiet man with long curly black hair held by a headband, calmly letting the rest of them get on with the speeches. Constantly Ag, in his peaked green Aussie cap, would turn fully in his seat during the resting moments between bursts of work and lecture the crew on the finer techniques of strokeplay with Al, in his Vietnam hat, throwing in his bit for good measure. 'After what you're going through in training now, the race will seem the easiest part' he would tell them. The coach would speak before or after these in-boat instructions so the crew always seemed to be getting a dual barrage of advice and criticism. It was all relevant stuff of course because both Ag and Al were perceptive pullers as well as fine practitioners of their art. But they did drown the coaches on occasion, cheapening the currency of the advice, and ultimately began to upset some members of the crew, who were receiving so much information that less and less was being taken on board.

The bowmen were far enough away not to worry too much and they let the full brunt of the half-heard discussions flow over them. 'What did he say?' 'What the hell are they on about?' and 'I can't hear a thing', are always the bow pair's ceaseless complaints. Usually it irritates them to be left constantly in the dark about in-boat changes of strategy and until good speaker systems were introduced into the crew boats the bow pair's lot was not a happy one. But in the 1978 Oxford crew they were rather thankful that they were able to remain cocooned away from the stridency further down the boat. Tristram in particular enjoyed floating off into his dream world and the coaches were endlessly bringing him back down to earth. He drove the crew crazy with his absentminded ways, yet curiously as race day approached, he became more and more alert and by the end he was 100 per cent on the ball. While at first he was the butt of all the jokes, never seeming to realise it, in the last fortnight he was a delight and kept everyone amused parrying and playing back the sharp banter with the best of them. He was transformed.

However, the man who got the worst of all the lecturing, or at least the man who took it all to heart, was Boris at four. As with most things Boris took things terribly personally and as is his way, worried desperately about everything. The Boris groan of despair accompanied by 'Oh no! this is the worst day of my life!' became a catch-phrase for the Oxford squads of the next six years. Whether by design or accident such teasing imitation by team-mates served to defuse his tensions. For Boris was very easily depressed. And a miserable Boris in the middle of a boat could do untold damage. He could row like a drain if things were not going right and the constant haranguing from the stroke and six men cut deep. 'They behave as if they're the only two decent oarsmen in the boat and the rest of us are just here to fill the seats', he complained to me one day. He had a point; it certainly sounded like that. They were not very tactful, those two, but then you could not be too tactful otherwise your message failed to get across. I was not very tactful either when I felt it necessary to blast them with some uncomfortable home truths. But they could take that from a coach. It was the constant flow of criticism from the stern that stuck in the throats of the less experienced men.

What developed in a way was the reverse of the previous year. With the colonials now in the ascendancy after their ambivalent role the year before the crew split once again this time with the 'Brits' being considered not so much the partygoers but more the inexperienced schoolboys. 'What irritated us new boys even more' recalls Boris 'was that Ag allowed Mike to align himself with the two experienced men when he was really very lazy that year. What we could take from Ag and Al we could not take from Mike. It was a critical error on the President's part to let that split develop, for it certainly made winning the race that much harder. The split was so unnecessary and though I respected Ag's rowing ability and the bullying way he led us, I felt that it was a poor display of crew management. I didn't enjoy rowing in that crew, nor I think did Russell and Tristram even if Al Shealy did, and probably the subsequent year was a real pleasure precisely because there was relief that there were no colonials to disrupt the crew spirit.' It was certainly true that each year set the tone for the next year, that the remaining Blues and the Isis men moving up to the top group used their experience from the year before to colour the approach to the following season. At times the Dark Blues were too easy going and on a couple of occasions they needed a strong dressing-down to knock them out of their serenity. Scribbling notes to myself driving down the motorway to coach one particular day I had an angry thought for each of them. 'You'll probably think you don't deserve what I'm about to say and you'll think I'm being alarmist, and you'll get in a huff like I used to when I was being criticised. Well, that's the very attitude that will defeat us. I'll tell you what I think about you so far. What I saw on Thursday against Isis and in the gym was pretty pathetic. You're being very self-indulgent and self-satisfied. Some of you are too pleased at just getting into the Blue Boat. You're not professional enough, not hard.'

We all tiptoed around each other for a couple of days after I delivered my tirade but the rowing showed much more attack. Jim Stewart recalls similar rantings in 1982 and Mark Harris insists that his overriding memory of the 1975 season was my January fortnight *spiel:* 'If you all row for three years at Oxford you too can have a body like Mark Harris!' He sat there, just 11 and a half stone, well-built certainly, but embarrassed and wondering why I had picked on him.

162

We had other problems during February. Ag developed tinosinovitis, the oarsman's wrist complaint, and was out of the boat for a week recovering from an operation. Then Al caught 'flu and though he returned after a week he never really shook off the virus properly and it nearly proved to be our undoing. We had to withdraw from the Reading Head of the River, and at one point it seemed we might have to replace him. A man as strong and seemingly invincible as Al Shealy, whose overbounding exuberance and sureness fills you with confidence, makes you feel that if he is rowing in your crew then you really cannot fail to win because he gives the impression that he could pull the whole thing along singlehanded. There are very very few athletes in the world in any sport who can give you that feeling. No one really believes that such a man can be laid low by anything. Even Al Shealy weakened by 'flu working at 50 per cent still had to be worth any other man working at 100 per cent ran the thinking. But big Al was ailing. A few days before the race it finally became clear that he was not able to pull his weight. The man was as weak as the proverbial kitten and despite his unfailing belief in himself and mine in him too, we had to take him out of the boat. Four days before the race our Boat Race winner, our crucial six man, was down and out. I tried not to alarm the crew unduly and assured them that I just wanted to give him a 24-hour rest. 'He'll be OK tomorrow' I said, 'you all worry too much.'

We had a final fixture arranged with a crew of London Rowing Club senior internationals and medallists who had beaten us a week or so earlier and had then gone and lost to Cambridge by half a length over five minutes. It was taking a big gamble to face them again in any circumstances, but I was sure we had improved. London had agreed to a return match, but Al was now out of the boat and it was Wednesday, our last chance to do a long piece–our traditional pre-race bridge to bridge. To pull out would have appeared fainthearted but perhaps sensible given the situation. If Al was really out for good then the crew rowing with his replacement could be psychologically destroyed by a heavy defeat. If on the other hand they believed that Al was coming back fully recovered, which they did, and which against the odds I did too, then a gutsy performance with a spare man could prove worthwhile. It would wake them up and make them take greater responsibility upon themselves for their results rather than relying on Al. They needed that last toughening tester and for my own peace of mind I wanted to see how they would cope with a substitute in the event of his having to row against Cambridge four days later. In the Boat Race there were no second chances. They had to face and overcome whatever obstacle was thrown in their path.

The next problem was who should sub and where he should go. In order not to disrupt the crew too much we decided to take the 15-stone Isis engine room man Ges Atherton and slot him straight into Al's place at six. It was a tense Oxford crew that lined up against London under Hammersmith Bridge on Wednesday evening. The crew was highly charged because they knew a lot depended on the outcome of this race. Ges saw his big chance to prove himself and he took it. He was magnificent. In a fiercely committed piece of rowing they took three lengths off London in a seven-minute race. The crew, all of us, were jubilant. With Al in the crew they had been beaten. Without their lynch-pin and with Ges in his place they had taken ten seconds off the same crew. If we had to row the Boat Race without Al then we would do it and still win. Ges was a proud man that day and with justification. Cambridge meanwhile had surprisingly succumbed to a scratch crew from Imperial College. Doctor Noel O'Brien, the Olympic squad medicine man, told us that Shealy's bout of 'flu had drained his body of salt and potassium. A 24-hour course of tablets restored his strength as if by magic and he was back in the boat next day under strict orders to do no work whatsoever until Boat Race day.

On the Thursday before the race when everyone had gone to bed, I found a disconsolate Rankov unable to sleep. 'We're going to lose Dan, I know it', he wailed. He was quite distraught. 'It's going to be tight but we can pull it off' I said, trying to reassure him. 'Well, convince me we can win then', he said desperately. We ran over the evidence of the past few days, our strengths and their weaknesses, talking on into the night, building up confidence again, restoring that fragile belief in ability that can so easily be undermined in a semi-experienced performer. Having no experience means that you can be strong in your innocence, not yet knowing the pitfalls; lots of experience means that you have the confidence to know what to do under pressure. But there is that middle ground where you are still finding your feet. It is a difficult stage for an athlete and our boy from Bradford was at just that stage. At last he went to bed reassured and rowed excellently up to and including the race. But his self doubts were never far below the surface and over the years he often rowed below his best in training, though like all great competitors he always rose to the big occasion. The Light Blue of Cambridge was like a red rag to a bull where Boris Rankov was concerned.

Evidence of the comparative form of the two Boat Race crews had been shown by their performances some weeks earlier against the fast national lightweight crew from London Rowing Club who were later to win the Head of the River Race outright. Oxford had beaten them although they were rowing a substitute while two weeks earlier they had raced level with Cambridge. It was dangerous to take such results at face value, so I was always careful to sound out my mates rowing in the various opposing crews for their blow-by-blow accounts and their own assessments of the comparative speeds of the two 'Varsity crews. In this case the signs were good. That Oxford made heavy weather of a session with a high-rating Molesey crew at the beginning of the last fortnight suggested that they were capable of being caught napping if they were not fully geared up for the fight. That session had knocked any cockiness they may have had right out of them, but it was not too good for Boris's nerves. Clearly there were still some men in the crew who did not yet realise quite what they had to do to win. Aesthetically this well-drilled Oxford crew looked a match for her predecessors with a good stride and flow and good bladework, but they were not as powerful in the water and it took them a few days once they arrived on the Tideway to get going properly. Cambridge however though strong and aggressive and rather more experienced in Boat Race appearance terms, showed a marked lack of togetherness with a lot of individual faults and extraneous in-boat movements especially on bowside. They were however a fraction heavier than Oxford and they were obviously spoiling for a fight.

There was a definite air of arrogance about the Light Blue camp that year and they had great belief in their speed despite defeats by the lightweights and the University of London. They complained too about our fast start, implying that in the past two years we had been doing something not altogether proper off the stakeboats. We were faster away than they were to be sure, but they felt we were jumping the start before the umpire said 'go'. We could see that they had in the past been a little slow to get going and that this all stemmed from the way they approached the first stroke. Although we did not leave the stakeboat before the word 'go' what they failed to realise was that on a fast-flowing river the force of the water caught their oars as they were squared for the first stroke on the command 'are you ready', and they were being pulled out past their strong position. The subsequent first stroke was for them an interminably long one while we, staying much shorter forward in anticipation of that difficult first stroke, were able to complete a faster pull through and get on to the second stroke far more quickly. What they could see was Oxford moving on to their second stroke while Cambridge were still completing their first.

It all came down to the length of the first stroke. Like every Tideway crew or indeed any crew that has raced from a stationary stakeboat moored in a fast stream, we were reacting to the conditions and taking proper account of the situation. Rowing men along the Tideway could not understand why Cambridge failed year after year to learn how to do efficient fast river starts. But the Light Blue camp were convinced that there was something fishy going on and they decided to resort to gamesmanship to give vent to their suspicions. On the start an umpire informs the crews of the command he will use to set them off: 'When I start you I shall say "Are you ready, Go".' Then he calls upon the crews to line up and get ready, the coxes keeping one hand held up until they are straight. When both coxswains' hands are down they are under starter's orders and once he has begun his chain of commands there is no turning back. When saying 'Are you ready' the umpire is not asking a question to which there may be an answer 'yes' or 'no' from the waiting crews. He is simply telling the crews that he is about to say 'Go'. This is usually explained by the umpire before the start of races in regattas. However, it appeared that in 1978 Cambridge decided to call 'Not ready' after the umpire had begun his final command. The umpire was a highly respected ex-Cambridge Blue and coach and perhaps they thought he might prove sympathetic to their ploy. They hoped to wrongfoot Oxford who having squared up for the 'go' on the command 'Are you ready' would be committed to that first stroke in the fast flowing water expecting an immediate 'go' as is usual. There is on the whole no more than a one and a half to two second pause between the two commands in normal umpiring circumstances, and certainly on the Tideway if the starter decided for some reason not to say 'go' most crews would be unable to hold back. When we went out on the water for the start rehearsal with the umpire two days before the race we were aware that these tactics were under consideration and I made a point of timing the umpire's instructions. The rehearsal is supposed to demonstrate to the crews precisely how the start will be given so I asked the umpire to repeat the start a couple of times for everyone's benefit, to make sure that we were all agreed about the time elapsing between the two starting instructions.

The tension that year was compounded by this atmosphere of distrust which polluted relations between the two sides. If Cambridge really believed that we were starting unfairly then their actions in the race can be more easily explained if not completely justified. However the problem really arose because Cambridge had lost the Boat Race three times in the past four years and they were just not used to it. It was after all Oxford who 'always' lost the Boat Race. Oxford, for their part, and their Old Blues, were enjoying this unique winning experience. The Light Blues seemed intent on finding something beyond their own control to blame rather than putting their own system under scrutiny.

While the possibility that they found nothing wrong with their set-up was good news to us because it distracted them from changing their strategy, the frustration it caused them led to a souring of the air in 1978. As the winning sequence extended the charges and accusations of malpractice changed in content but increased in volume.

In the event, the Cambridge tactics served them badly. If they thought to unsettle Oxford at the start then they could hardly have chosen two more cunning operators than Michelmore and Shealy to try to intimidate. Conditions had been very blustery and difficult all week especially along the Putney reach on the flood and Isis had sunk in training while Cambridge themselves had become waterlogged. There was even talk of a postponement. To get acclimatised we practised a lot in the uncomfortable water. On Friday night however the wind went round but stayed strong and rendered the first mile fast and bouncy but rowable. But further on at Hammersmith it was likely to be very bad. Bert and I went up the course round the corner in the launch to check the river ahead and decided that the heaving water in the second half of the race could cause the crews a lot of problems. So we put on our protective splashboards and a high breakwater to keep as much of the river out as possible. Cambridge took no precautionary measures despite their near sinking earlier in the week although they were rowing in the same type of lightweight Carbocraft boat that we were. The scene was set for an absorbing Boat Race between what seemed to be two pretty evenly-matched crews weighing the same and rowing in identical shells.

Ag won the toss and chose Surrey. The crews went afloat 25 minutes ahead of race time but at the moment that they should have been preparing to get on to the stakeboat, Cambridge inexplicably decided to turn back down river despite the fact that to do so would make them late for the start. The Oxford stroke Michelmore decided that the only reason for the manoeuvre was to leave Oxford sitting, cold and anxiously waiting on the stakeboat, so with the die cast he too called upon his coxswain John Fail to 'easy' and swing the boat downriver after Cambridge. When they both finally got on to the stakeboats they were five minutes late. Not only were the two crews on edge, but so, understandably, was the umpire, not to speak of the four launch-loads of coaches and Old Blues. When at last the flag went up and the umpire called 'Are you Ready?' the Cambridge cox Guy Henderson called 'no'. The umpire remained silent but dropped his starting flag, breaking it in two against the gunwales of the launch *Bosporos*. Oxford, their blades now squared in the water and committed, false started, expecting but not getting the 'go'. Seeing that Cambridge had not left

167

the stakeboat, they continued like any experienced crew to row out the first ten strokes of the start before winding down, turning and paddling back again. In order to get rid of excess tension and adrenalin they rowed another ten-stroke burst on their way back below Putney Bridge before turning again on to the stakeboat. Cambridge, not wishing to remain on the stakeboat getting cold, also decided after dithering to row ten strokes off the start.

Together they came down once more on to the stakeboats. 'It was good to look across and grin to let them know that we knew, and that it hadn't worked', recalls Ag. Again Henderson persisted in calling 'not ready' and delaying the start, his hand going up and down, still trying to unsettle his opponents. The race was already 17 minutes late and the water had grown much lumpier, the wind more angry. The race should have been over by now and without the delaying tactics all would have gone smoothly. Once more the umpire tried to start the race. Up went the flag and suddenly, without waiting for any command from the umpire, Cambridge took off. Oxford hesitated and then half a stroke later with a shout of 'go' from Al, they too went and the umpire, as if to confirm that the race had indeed started, brought his flag down again. 'Well, I suppose we had better let them go' he murmured half apologetically. 'I suppose we must' I replied. So the race that was never officially started was on at last.

Although Cambridge had jumped the start, Oxford were level in ten strokes, half a length up in half a minute and a length ahead as they passed Thames Rowing Club at the end of the first minute. With the advantage of the Middlesex bend, Cambridge spurted and pulled back a second at the Mile Post where Oxford's time of three minutes 31 seconds was a new record. A push at Harrods, where Cambridge traditionally do a spurt, gave Oxford clear water and they shot Hammersmith Bridge four seconds up and a second inside the record. Then they hit the bad weather like a brick wall. As the water got rougher and rougher by the second Oxford moved over slightly for the shelter of their Surrey shore and the umpire began busily waving his flag warning Oxford that they were interfering with Cambridge. This was impossible since Henderson had moved over from his Middlesex side on to Oxford's station in line behind. Without thinking I stood up angrily and said 'Sir, how can they be interfering when they are a length and a half ahead and rowing to Surrey of their own station?' Both crews were in any event ignoring the instructions of the umpire who continued to shout one-sided orders to the crews. I continued to harass the poor man from my privileged seat next to him in the bows of our launch where he was, according to custom, our guest, as umpire from the 'other place'. 'Sit down and shut up sir, or I shall disqualify your crew' he ordered. Chastened, I subsided, aware that I was very much out of order. I knew that he would do no such thing but I could see he was very upset. But then so was I. He continued to issue partisan directions throughout the race even though there are in fact no interference rules in the Boat Race once there is clear water between the crews.

But Oxford were now two lengths ahead racing along Chiswick Eyot. Both crews were tucked over to Surrey in line astern out of the worst of the rolling waves and whenever Cambridge looked to be threatening, Ag the master tactician would counter attack with a short burst to maintain his distance. It was a dangerous ploy but he did not want to drive the crew too hard in the conditions and it seemed most sensible to play safe rather than to go for more distance. His tactic almost came unstuck though as his cox John Fail began to move out after Chiswick Steps to take the crossing at LEP. Ag called for a delay in crossing because the water was so bad, but there was no escaping it. The river was a sea of white horses ahead, the wind directly on the backs of the crews. Mid-way across, there was a crab and a violent lurch caused by a standing wave which brought the boat to a shuddering halt. Cambridge began to make up distance and were a length and a quarter down when Oxford got going again. Ag pushed hard away and Oxford quickly regained their two-length lead. As the crews came into the slightly better water along Dukes Meadows on the Middlesex side Ag spurted a second time and in the next minute Oxford moved out to three lengths. The danger was over as long as they could handle the still worsening water.

Fail began gradually to ease out for the centre arch at Barnes which under the rules he had to take. Great rolling waves threatened to block his progress but he coolly kept his nerve and swung the bow of the boat directly into the teeth of the wind and the waves. With the splashboards keeping out the worst of the squall Oxford slipped under the bridge and ducked once more for the shelter of the Middlesex bank. Henderson meanwhile had left it late to turn out for the centre arch and consequently had to make a sharper turn than was safe. This manoeuvre set him at an angle to the oncoming rollers and in a moment the wind had caught him broadside and prevented him from steering back towards the Middlesex shore. Within seconds water was pouring over their unprotected bowside and as the boat began to settle lower in the water, Henderson tried again to straighten the sluggishly moving craft. But it was too late. The water gushed over the gunwales and though the bowmen vainly kept on rowing, the boat sank by the stern.

Launches raced to rescue them as Oxford rowed on alone to finish the race in 18 minutes 58 seconds, recording only their second hat trick in 65 years. It was the first time Cambridge had sunk since 1912.

After the race Mark Horton, the Cambridge President, tried his luck by requesting a re-row. It was firmly refused. The rules state clearly that once past the end of the Fulham Wall and the two-minute mark the crews abide by their own accidents. Besides Ag, the first Australian President ever to win the Boat Race, was hardly going to agree to a second race after the Light Blues had brought misfortune upon themselves as a direct result of their own delaying tactics at the beginning and their failure to read the conditions and fit splashboards. What should remain on record though, and what became clouded by the drama of the sinking, was that for 15 minutes Oxford and Cambridge had mounted a wonderfully exciting and absorbing race.

Isis and Goldie also put on a spectacular show an hour earlier in less extreme conditions. Isis had finished four seconds ahead of Goldie in the Tideway Head showing tremendous improvement following all the early resignations from the squad. Their coaches, three of them – Steve Royle, Paul Stuart Bennett and Chris George – who were new to the Oxford coaching team and all ex-crewmates of mine did wonders with them. In the event however, they left the stakeboat without their usual venom, planning to start steadily and then row down the opposition later on in the race. They paid dearly for the mistake. They were a length down by the end of the Wall, but pulled back to half a length at the Mile using the advantage of the Middlesex bend. Then they hung on all the way round the outside of the St Paul's corner, ably marshalled by strokeman Rob Moore, and were just half a length down at the Steps. Through the worst of the rough they pushed up to 36 and passed Goldie at the Bandstand but could not hold their lead and as Goldie, with the Blue Robin Waterer at six, came again on the outside, pushing them off the best of the tide, they lost cohesion in the last strokes to lose by half a length.

This was all heady exciting stuff. The Boat Race, much to our sponsors' satisfaction, was front page news again and everyone was talking about the sinking, and 'what did Jim Railton on the telly mean by the "dolphin effect"?' Journalists who never came near the river produced witty critiques. Until now Oxford had always been the crew that had sunk in the Boat Race, the 1951 incident indelibly recorded on television newsreel in the early days of BBC coverage. From now until Oxford once again contrive to perform the same feat some time in the future it will be Cambridge who are so remembered. As the crews recovered their composure on the balconies of their respective host boathouses, Quintin and Ibis at Chiswick, the river police arrived wishing to interview someone about a rowing eight left submerged in the vicinity of Barnes Bridge. Pat Delafield the large dry-humoured Cambridge finishing coach stepped down on to the shingle to answer the charges. 'Booking him for loitering are you constable?' came a cry from the balcony.

In a television interview, Harry Carpenter commiserated with the Cambridge cox Guy Henderson. 'Such a tragedy' said Harry. 'Yes' replied Guy, 'everything had gone entirely to plan up until then.' Presumably, opined some of the Press next day, he meant that Cambridge had planned to be three lengths down at Barnes with three minutes to the end. Despite the excitement and public delight in the whole affair some of the correspondents of the serious rowing Press quite rightly wrote angrily about the behaviour at the start and blamed both teams. It was unseemly and unsporting, they said, and demeaned the good name of the Boat Race. The umpire, invited by the Presidents to officiate, was in a difficult position for he had to rely on the good sportsmanship of the two crews to be able to do his job. The threat of disqualification before the race carried no weight in such a two-horse, private affair. Both camps presented excuses and reasons, but the fact remained that it had not looked good.

As usual the Oxford crew was unable to stay together for the summer season and the University sent a number of boats to Henley all of which proved unsuccessful. An Isis crew stroked by Michelmore reached the quarter finals of the Ladies' Plate; a four with three Blues lost in the first round to the finalists of the Britannia Cup and Cherwell went out in the first round of the Ladies'. However the Oxford coaches were having a much nicer time. Hugh Matheson, World and Olympic silver medallist in eights in 1974 and 1976 had returned to the river, this time in a sculling boat, and he, my doubles partner Ian Wilson and I holed up in my favourite Henley home at Bix with the ever generous Kempners, our hosts for the week. Ian and I had teamed up in a lightweight double scull, initially for fun, but when we realised we were fast enough to be in contention for the newly-introduced lightweight event at the World Championships, we began to take it more seriously. Ian travelled down from Nottingham most weekends for outings and we trained alone in our singles during the week. Our individual results were close and we had a delightful season pleasing ourselves, racing well on the continental regatta circuit and doing what we both enjoyed most. At Henley, acknowledging that we stood little chance in the double against World Champions Baillieu and Hart, we entered the Diamonds as well, again just for fun you understand, for entered too were World Champion Peter Kolbe of West Germany, Tim Crooks the British sculler, the Argentine Ibarra, Nikolov from Bulgaria and our fast emerging pal Hugh. We became Hugh's unofficial advisers/coaches/soulmates and he ours.

In the Diamonds Ian met Kolbe in the first round and lost by a friendly length, Kolbe behaving most graciously towards his light-weight opponent. I raced Richard Stanhope, who a couple of years later was to stroke the British eight to a silver medal in the Olympics. We had a great race to halfway where he led. But then I got past him and went on to win. Next day I was pulverised by Tim Crooks. In the double sculls we got to the semi-finals and then met Baillieu and Hart. We held them to just over a length to the Barrier at which point they took off and left us for dead. But Hugh was magnificent. We watched his semi-final race against Peter Kolbe from the launch. When he had first started sculling he had been so hamfisted at times, going smoothly for a couple of minutes and then getting himself into a muddle and lurching all over the place, banging his hands together. But this time he made no mistakes and sculled a wonderful race beating the West German by four lengths having been led to beyond halfway. Ian and I glowed with reflected glory. Our boy was in the big time. But our euphoria was short-lived. Next day he was beaten by Tim Crooks in the final. It was, though, only his first foray into the hard world of international sculling. He went to the heavyweight World Championships in New Zealand as spare man and later finished fifth in the 1979 World Championships and sixth in the 1980 Olympics and we were selected for the light-weight World Championships in Copenhagen where we won the *petite finale* finishing seventh overall. It was another lovely summer.

8
'Stick With Yer Mates'

Soon after his election Simon Clegg the Cambridge President for the 1979 Boat Race pulled off a startling coup when he announced that Bob Janousek, director of Britain's rowing revival through the 'seventies, was to take charge of Cambridge. With their strong young squad he had the material to produce a very good crew but we wondered how well he would be received by the sceptical hard to please 'heavies' in the Light Blue camp and whether the squad would be able to cope with his very demanding regime. Furthermore how would he come to terms with the curious eccentricities of the Boat Race? We hoped that we knew the event better than he did. But we had to concede that Cambridge now had one of the world's foremost coaches at the helm. Fortunately we knew something of his methods and had used his programmes in developing our own training strategy, so we did not expect to be totally outmanoeuvred. But it was a psychological blow. They began their training in October a week earlier than we did and put us under pressure right from the start.

The Press got a lot of mileage from the East European flavour of the names Topolski and Janousek in rivalry over the most British of British institutions. Everyone wanted to hear the views of the master from Czechoslovakia, particularly those on the Boat Race. He had revised his thinking from those early sceptical remarks many years before, and he now acknowledged that it was a good breeding-ground for future internationals. It gave them inspiration and experience. He had plans for Cambridge after the Boat Race he said, but in the end, surprisingly, none of them won a senior international vest.

At Oxford the new President was John Wiggins, back on the river for the 150th anniversary Boat Race after a year off taking exams. Ag and Shealy had gone and with Russell Crockford, Mike Moran and Jim Wood all withdrawing to the sidelines because of study worries only Boris Rankov and Julian Crawford remained from the 1978 crew. Cambridge in the first years regarded Boris as their secret weapon, believing him to be the Dark Blue Achilles' heel. True he was not the prettiest of oarsmen, certainly not a great technician, but they underestimated the man's power and his insatiable appetite for beating Cambridge. It was some time before his lengthening sequence of successes began to effect a change in the Cambridge view of him. They still did not think much of his rowing prowess but he was winning all the way. Maybe there was something to the man after all. For a while he was out of the squad with a bad back and did not really throw off the injury until after Christmas. Apart from the remaining Blues there were some effective Isis men left from that courageous crew that had raced so hard the year before. The stroke Rob Moore had earned his spurs and was producing very respectable work, while the two men behind him, Phil Head and Ges Atherton, were proven competitors. Tom Barry and Mark Gleave were the only other remaining men from that crew since Bland was unavailable. There were, however, three Youth international freshmen of note.

Chris Mahoney was a 1977 junior bronze medallist in fours and had then stroked the winning Molesey four in the Wyfold Cup at Henley the following year. He arrived quietly but it soon became apparent that he was destined for great things. His approach to rowing was cast in the same mould as Sawyier's, an uncompromising competitor, easier to get along with than the American maybe, but possessed of the manic quality that sets athletes of the highest calibre apart from ordinary men. He was not particularly big, around the 13-stone mark, but he packed one hell of a punch. From 1979 to 1981 he and Boris Rankov locked together the middle of three Oxford crews although at first we had him earmarked for the stroke seat. But his rhythm proved to be better suited to 2000-metre rowing and besides we needed his power in the engine room. 'I felt I would get straight into the crew in my first year', he remembers. 'I looked upon John Wiggins as a star and really enjoyed rowing with him a lot. Although he was a bit shy he was very organised and ran a good show. I think Julian and I developed a very good working relationship that first year. It was great, that '79 crew.'

The second freshman was Mike Diserens from that perennially successful Wallingford stable of oarsmen coached by Bruce Grainger. Another comparative lightweight but tall with it, Diserens had been placed fifth in the world at junior level in the coxed fours in 1976. Tim Donaldson was the third man with World Championship experience. He had rowed seven in the fourth placed junior eight in 1978. At Oxford however he never realised his potential and withdrew from serious rowing after his first year. On the coxing front Gerry Mead arrived to challenge Isis's Peter Berners Lee for the Blue Boat seat. He was an experienced steersman with the British Youth team in the 1977 World Championships and had coxed with several school and senior club crews at National Championship level. So here was a young squad with no overseas oarsmen, only one graduate, no Etonians and indeed only one public schoolboy in the line-up. Also, it was to be the first time since 1935 that there were no foreigners in either crew.

The commonly-held charge that rowing as a sport–and the Boat Race in particular–is an élitist pursuit is no longer valid. It was true perhaps until after the war but as the proportion of state school students overtook that of the public schoolboys at Oxbridge, so the composition of the representative crews reflecting the University intakes altered accordingly. Julian Crawford from Winchester was the only public schoolboy aboard the 1979 boat and it is unlikely that the proportions will revert with so many experienced young oarsmen arriving from the state schools via the junior national team and effectively eclipsing once and for all the upper-class image of rowing. The recent admission of women to what were previously all-male colleges has further altered the characteristics of college boat club membership and has reduced the numbers of potential undergraduate Boat Race candidates enormously.

Of all the Oxford crews of the last 12 years, the 1979 one was probably the least problematical and the friendliest. They had a tremendous crew spirit and sense of unity which was nicely summed up in their oft repeated catch-phrase, 'well you've got to stick with yer mates 'aven't you' spoken after drawing deeply on an imaginary fag-end held between the tips of thumb and forefinger and, having dropped it on to the ground, grinding it underfoot. They became the crew of union activists, ably convened by shop steward Rob Moore who, I discovered only recently, had listed Free Collective Bargaining as his interest in the Boat Race programme. 'Right lads', I said on one occasion as I came into the gym for a session. 'We'll do four circuits to start off with. Chris you go first . . .' Sharp intake of breath. 'Tsk tsk tsk' and a shaking of heads; a few pained glances. 'Well Dan, I don't know', replied Rob. 'The lads aren't too happy about it.' I ignored him. 'Come on fellas, let's get moving.' 'Just a minute Dan, let me talk to the men.' And they went off to the end of the gym and got into a huddle. After a couple of moments Rob returned. 'The lads say two and no more. Take it or leave it. I've tried but they won't budge.' 'Listen,' I said, 'I'm prepared to compromise. Tell them I'll make do with three.' They of course were all standing there delighted with the charade. 'I'll see what they say', said Rob and they went off into their huddle again. 'OK it's a deal. We'll do three.' They knuckled down to the work with a will, all of us knowing full well we were going to do three all along.

They had also found a mascot. 'Dennis the Menace' was a plastic glove puppet given away with the *Beano* which they found floating in the river at Radley on the first day that the selected crew took to the water. Dennis, they reckoned, looked uncannily like their chief coach and he rode the bow for every outing attached to the number slot by means of an aluminium holder devised by Rob overnight. Attaching Dennis to the bows every day became part of the ritual of going afloat. On the day before the race, while practising a stakeboat start, the crew was swamped by the BBC launch. Later when the crew disembarked they saw that Dennis had gone. No one dared say a word, no one wanted to voice their superstitious fears. The next day Cambridge also lost a man – their stroke Woodhouse. They really were a tightly knit bunch, a delight to work with and certainly the harmony and close comradeship of that crew made up for whatever they lacked in brute power and experience. Perhaps they were a little too cosy and for a while they lacked the necessary venom. But they soon developed it. There was little trouble all year; the only cloud on the horizon being Bob Janousek and his very hard-working Cambridge crew.

I saw Cambridge one weekend while I was out on the water coaching the women's Olympic squad up at Richmond, pounding along, blades flying, sweat pouring, muscles straining as they completed a piece of steady state work. Bob was right on their tail in his little rubber launch yelling at them through his loud-hailer, driving them on. They looked more businesslike than any Cambridge crew I had ever seen. Technically they were throwing themselves about a bit in the boat but they were certainly getting hold of the water. It was worrying to see but it was all good material evidence with which to goad the Oxford boys along. At first we thought we were going to have trouble finding a sufficiently strong group but as the months progressed and we saw their improvements in the gym and on the water, we could see we were coming up once more with a promising crew. At the national trials in Nottingham in November John Wiggins teamed up with the new boy, Mahoney, and they won the pairs. 'Christ' thought Mahoney, 'I've made it. I'm in the big time.' They won the fours the next day with Ges and Julian. 'It gave us great faith in the work programme we were doing', he recalls. But whether they were going to be strong enough to beat a Cambridge eight which threatened to be quite a bit bigger and a darned sight better trained than of late was another matter. The Tabs were wise now to all our methods and selection procedures. Whenever we arrived to do our ergometer tests we found that Cambridge had already been there, and when I took the squad to St Mary's College in Twickenham for oxygen uptake tests, the good doctor there gleefully reported the superhuman scores of our rivals. It was very disconcerting. Throughout the winter I was also co-ordinating the national women's squad, so all my time seemed to be taken up by a mass of selection tests, seat racing, ergometer work, gym tests and running because I was putting the girls through the same programme of training as the Oxford boys. It was a hectic time and both groups required a lot of attention.

The trials race before Christmas produced yet another superb contest, with Isis stroke Rob Moore and the new boy Mahoney looking the two most likely Boat Race strokes. Mahoney won by just over a length, but the crews on show, though racing hard, were not quite in the class of the trialists of the previous few years. In the absence of the four other Blues still in residence the chances of a good Isis crew looked very slim indeed. It was fortunate that Boris's back improved after Christmas and that Russell decided that he could cope with both training and studies after all and returned fit and battling for a place in the crew when we reassembled in January. When two more senior trialists withdrew after the selection process was over, Isis was left fatally weakened.

The 1979 January fortnight was a particularly nasty one. The weather was awful, as it was to be most of the winter, and it compounded the pain and distress of the squad men as they went about their work. The individual tests had shown almost everything we needed to know, but there were still one or two questions that needed answering. The seat racing solved those with a vengeance. One of the strongest men in the gym and on the ergometer was Ges Atherton and we naturally felt that after his tremendous performance the year before when he substituted so effectively for the ailing Al, he would be a sure contender for a place in the middle of the boat even though he was not rowing quite so well this year. Diserens, Head and the late returning Russell Crockford were thought to be less likely to make the crew than Ges. He was a great favourite in the squad, well liked by everyone. So when he lined up against the 12-stone Phil Head with the dodgy leg for the last bowside seat, the result seemed a foregone conclusion. But Phil had other ideas. He beat Ges emphatically twice by a length and a half. Everyone was stunned – except Phil of course. He was ecstatic. But Ges not in the crew? How could it be? Ges quit the squad, his chance of a Blue gone forever. An air of gloom hung over the group after that for quite a few days, not because Phil had won, but because if a power-house like Ges could fail to make the boat how on earth could we expect to beat Cambridge? The answer to that came a few days later when we went to the January national trials on the Kingston reach with two coxed fours. They performed with great character and even more effectively than they had done in November. One was unbeaten throughout the weekend and the other finished second. And we found that we had yet another possible stroke in Mike Diserens.

With Rob Moore, Chris Mahoney, Russell Crockford and Mike all capable of stroking and all having proved themselves individually on the Tideway, we were now able to look at the rest of the seating to make sure we were putting the power in the best places. So Mahoney went to six, Julian our strong man sat at five and Boris went to four. We needed Rob on bowside and that left the freshman Diserens to stroke the crew. And what an effective stroke he proved to be–pig-headed and temperamental at times to be sure, but then what good strokeman was not? Behind Diserens' smooth flowing rhythm, the 1979 Oxford crew settled down comfortably into a very smart-looking outfit, composed and well together and with a nicely developing turn of speed. We looked for length in the water to compensate for the crew's lack of size and strength and this we achieved with the men going through all sorts of contortions at front stops to get the extra reach forward. And we piled on the work.

'The winter months are so hard and so boring', remembers Chris Mahoney. 'Radley is so cold and your hands freeze around the oar handle and then as you warm up and the blood comes back into your fingers they hurt like hell. You train for hours and hours a day and then you're so tired you can't do anything in the evenings. After the outing, rowing in hack trial crews, I'd get home wet and frozen and collapse on the hearth in front of the fire with Normie and Toddy, munching biscuits, completely exhausted. I can't believe many professional sportsmen could train harder.' The sacrifice and effort it takes to make the grade would be hard to match in most other pursuits and it is no exaggeration when sports experts deem rowing to be second only to the Marathon in terms of the most physically demanding of sports. Al Shealy's recollections from a year earlier are in the same vein. 'In the early months of training you're thinking "what the hell is all this for?" because the race is so far off, so remote. There's so much tedium and discipline and brutal effort to hammer through. You have to resist the subconscious compulsion to put an end to all this self-inflicted hardship. But as the days pass and you feel yourself getting stronger you begin to live for the day. You punish yourself with a will in training because you know you're facing a 20-minute race which will suspend your life for that time. Somewhere around Hammersmith Bridge you find out what it is you've been working for; you're asking big questions of your body and when the right answers are coming back it's a feeling you know you'll never forget. The work is like an investment. The more you sink in the more determined you are to get the dividend and in the Boat Race there's only one dividend and that's winning.' Back to Mahoney: 'You'd row at Radley in the eight not knowing how fast you were going, ploughing up and down, just trusting the coaches to know what they were doing. And then you'd go off to the Tideway to race a UL crew full of big names and thump them. It was a lovely surprise to find out how fast you were, and it meant you could go back to the training with a will. They were good years, those Oxford years'. 'It's so time consuming,' adds John Wiggins, 'and there is so much else to do at University. But I enjoyed the rowing so much that it would have been hard for me to find as satisfying a substitute.'

While Bob Janousek kept Cambridge away from competition we as usual went looking for a fight. At the Reading Head, starting third in the place Isis had finished the year before, Oxford beat University of London by 16 seconds and Leander by seven. Next day they raced the lightweights on the Tideway and beat them three times out of three. Then the following weekend we risked an encounter with the national eight who were now under the guidance of Penny Chuter. Chris Blackwall had returned to the Oxford coaching team in place of Hugh Matheson, who had withdrawn to concentrate on his sculling. But Hugh kept in touch and invited the crew to stay with him at his Sherwood Forest residence Thoresby Hall for our weekend away before the race.

We rowed an eight-minute race against the national squad, from Fulham Wall to St Paul's. The squad, always a couple of strokes a minute above us, only managed to pull away towards the end as they got the advantage of the Surrey bend at Hammersmith, and they won by a length. Then we both turned round and dropped back to Putney to do a seven-minute bridge to bridge over the same stretch. This time they only beat us by a quarter of a length. Oxford were quickly learning to be tough. Cambridge would have to be as fast as the national squad if they were going to win the Boat Race. We had started the year as underdogs, but had pushed back to level pegging. It was quite an achievement for those young boys, especially with two just-out-of-school freshmen in the all-important stroke and six seats. But that last race with the squad certainly earned them the right to lead Oxford against the Light Blues. Recounted now on paper, these fixtures are in danger of losing the tension and importance that surrounded them at the time because of repetition. But muscle and sinew were stretched to the limit and young men rowed their hearts out to bring Oxford to the winning post in front. They were bold and thrillingly-fought contests, especially those against the national eight every year.

In the last two weeks, while we were nursing Boris's back, Cambridge suffered a series of two-day stomach bugs which spread quickly through their crew because they were living closely together in a rented house for the first time. Initially, their President Clegg, then Gray

179

followed by Palmer were all forced to take a rest. They had to abandon their full-course trial and a fixture against the lightweights, and these cancellations seemed to us to be the sure mark of a professional man's hand. The real pros, the shrewd international men, would never enter into a contest underpowered and Janousek's experience warned him of the psychological dangers of pitting his men against tough opposition without his full crew. But by the same token one of the things I always taught the Oxford lads was that they had to race no matter what the situation, no matter what adversity they faced. The Boat Race was after all a different sort of race. It was a test not just of racing ability, of endurance and skill, it was also a test of character and resilience. Despite what the newspapers sometimes said about the sanity of the Oxbridge coaches the crews had to overcome not just the opposition but everything and anything else that might be put in their path. The will to win had to be there no matter what the conditions, no matter how unfair or hopeless seemed the task.

So Cambridge pulled out of their fixtures. Not that we might well have done the same thing in similar circumstances, but we wondered whether they could not have had a go anyway. In order to consolidate their improving confidence Oxford also took on Kingston, who had beaten Goldie in the Kingston Head a few days earlier by 19 seconds. Goldie, we heard, had been giving their Blue Boat a run for their money so when we beat the Kingston boys it was the confirmation we needed. We were not a flash-in-the-pan crew. We were up with the best. The pre-race weekend with Hugh at Thoresby, sleeping on mattresses on the floor, roving over the estate and letting Hugh give Celia, our London cook, a rest from her labours, was a great success and further bound the 'mates' together. They could hardly wait to get at the Tabs. Cambridge were being heralded as yet another heavy crew, tipped to outweigh Oxford by as much as ten pounds a man, so we tackled the official weigh-in as if it were yet another hurdle for the crew to surmount. They attacked the problem with relish. To try to minimise the difference they gorged themselves at Hugh's and then topped up with pints of milk minutes before the weigh-in. They fairly waddled to the scales. Each man was hailed with grateful cheers from his crewmates as his weight was announced, the whole crew wildly impressed by the results of their sickeningly huge consumption of milk, cakes and vegetables over the weekend. They weighed in at an average of 13 stone four and one eighth pounds a man and when Richard Burnell, the official recorder of weights, announced the Cambridge weight at 13 stone four pounds, they went berserk. It took them two days to work off the uncomfortable excess weight, but the psychological fillip it had given them was well worth the trouble. In practical terms a couple of pounds here or there made no difference, but their relief at not being outweighed by six stone of Light Blue muscle was plain. To rub it in, little Peter Berners-Lee underweighed Guy Henderson the Cambridge cox by a stone. Light Blue coach Bob Janousek explained that because the Cambridge crew had worked so hard during the winter they had all lost over a stone a man. They were, he said, the fittest Cambridge crew of all time. Next day the *Star* newspaper carried a beefcake photograph of the towel-clad but topless Oxford crew, biceps bulging, next to a picture of the fully-clad Cambridge crew looking decidedly disdainful.

In the afternoon Harry Carpenter begged a ride in the Oxford coxswain's seat for the benefit of BBC's *Sportsnight* and nearly wrote off the Oxford shell against the Black Buoy. He kept pulling the wrong rudder line and in the film the voice of Mike Diserens at stroke, sounding increasingly exasperated, could be heard: 'Pull the other string, Harry!' Fortunately he managed to steer them back to the shore intact, but it was a risky bit of fun with our precious boat. We had just got her back from Carbocraft, of which company, ironically, rival coach Janousek was a director. He had been in charge of her overhaul, seeking out any hairline cracks. That we had no qualms about delivering our craft into the hands of the opposition says a lot for the good sportsmanship and honour that exists in amateur sport. But we still did our own normal check-over when she came back, just to be sure.

Apart from comic video recordings of Harry Carpenter's uncontrolled coxing efforts and others of past Boat Races to keep the crew entertained back at the house when the feature films ran out, Cambridge provided us with a real beauty to keep our spirits up. A television director had positioned Janousek and current and future Presidents Simon Clegg and James Palmer beside the Thames outside the boathouses for an interview. As the presenter pursued his line of questioning with fearless persistence no one noticed that the tide was coming in fast and was beginning to lap at the Cantabrian toes. By the time they realised what was happening the water had risen to their ankles, but since they were in mid-interview there was nothing that they could do and they had to stay put while the cameraman had a marvellous time panning up and down from feet to serious faces which were pretending that all was well. Gloriously, stoically, not one of them acknowledged the rising Thames throughout the interview.

It is to our eternal dismay that we were not able to record for posterity the impish tide rising to engulf Goldie man Robert Breares' immaculate 'E' type Jaguar in 1973. His father's identical motor stood alongside and was similarly overwhelmed. In the absence of the Cambridge crews, who were out training, there was nothing we could do but watch helplessly from our boathouse balcony as the cars slowly submerged. Just as entertaining for a whole succession of Oxford crews has been the documentary made in 1967 by our film man Cecil Foster Kemp, featuring my own crew in training and some wonderful shots of 'Jumbo' demonstrating key points in the stroke. It is uncanny how both rowing and filming technique can look so passé in such a short space of time. Our hurried movements in 1967 look so outmoded yet we still adhere to the same principles. Perhaps the slightly exaggerated speed of the film, the stiff commentary, and 'Jumbo' in his 1930 rowing outfit add to the dated feel of the show and caused so much mirth. Or maybe it is just the sight of their coach at full stretch a decade and a half earlier that reduces the crew to such helpless laughter.

It was a north-west windy week before the Boat Race and there were visions of a repeat performance of the year before. But the wind went round and died on the Friday, although not before we had all had to deal with some mighty uncomfortable practice starts along the Putney boathouses. The umpire, Ronnie Howard, issued strict warnings about any repetition of the gamesmanship that had so marred the beginning of the 1978 race. 'Everyone was very upset about it', he declared. To ensure that both sides should be clear about his views on the vexed question of the start he issued a short dissertation to both camps describing how he saw the two different approaches to the 'go' used by the Universities, Cambridge's long first stroke and Oxford's short one, and he made it plain that he did not regard either as cheating. He would only consider that a false start had occurred if either boat detached itself from the stakeboat before he said 'go'. The implication was that if Cambridge did not want to be left at the 'off' they had better brush up their start pretty quickly. And that is precisely what they did. An experienced man like Janousek was bound to teach his crew how to leave a stakeboat properly. In deference to the BBC's tight scheduling, we had rashly agreed to hold the race an hour earlier than the time of the fastest tide, which was usually the governing factor in selecting the race time. However a spate of heavy rain fell in the final days, resulting in so much land water coming down at the weekend that the tide was barely turning at the time the crews were due to line up at the start. By Barnes they would be racing against the ebbing stream. It was going to be a long race and an even longer one for Isis and Goldie who would race half an hour earlier.

The day before the Boat Race, Cambridge had seemed rid of their bug, having moved from their private house in Wimbledon to a hotel in town courtesy of the sponsors, Ladbrokes. But overnight, their stroke-man John Woodehouse fell sick, a result probably of sharing a room with one of the other victims earlier in the week. An early morning outing confirmed that Woodehouse was too ill to row, and they immediately boated again with Graham Phillips, the Goldie stroke, coming in at three while Nick Davies, their stroke of the year before, moved down to his old position.

It was a heavy blow to their morale and in some ways to ours as well, for the crew had been building themselves up for a neck and neck struggle over the whole course. We had to take care not to let their misfortune affect our own resolve. It would have been all too easy for us to relax our grip, lose a fraction of that hard-earned determination, if we let ourselves feel for a moment that they might now be weakened. We had to retain the killer instinct. As they prepared to go afloat the crew had conditioned themselves to expect that Cambridge would be no less fast and probably more determined without Woodehouse. For us to lose in such circumstances of course would have been worse than ignominious and the crew felt all the more nervous as a result. An extra distraction was provided by one crew member who chose this most inopportune moment to lose a contact lens. The whole crew spent half an hour on hands and knees scouring the floor when they should have been psyching themselves up for the race. But there again maybe the light relief was good for them.

John won the toss for Oxford for the fifth year running and chose Surrey. Although there was little flow to the flooding tide the bend advantages later in the race would be of more use against a crew reputed to be strong on staying power. Off the start Henderson steered Cambridge straight over towards the Middlesex side, heading for the Fulham Flats. It was a valid gamble, but it failed, and Oxford led by a length before Thames Rowing Club. The shallower water below the Fulham football ground wall did not prove all that helpful and at the Mile Post Oxford were nearly two lengths up as the crews came back together for the first time. Though Davies spurted approaching Harrods, he made little impression and Diserens' counter put the matter beyond doubt. Oxford shot Hammersmith Bridge nearly three lengths up and thereafter maintained that lead rather than trying to push away over the second half.

'It was a killer of a race', remembers Boris Rankov, 'because the water was so dead and heavy and the river so shallow. The race went on for ages and because I had been out of the boat until Christmas with my bad back I was perhaps more affected than the others although John

Wiggins was pretty shattered too. He had after all missed a year's training. We had to keep pushing because the Tabs were spurting all the time and cutting the corners which helped them to make up ground.' Berners Lee, the Oxford cox, kept to a classic Boat Race course out in the middle of the river, when on this particular dead water day he might have helped his crew more by cutting across a little at the bends. The crew could see Cambridge making ground on them behind. Both crews stayed close to the Middlesex shore after the crossing as the coxswains realised that they were by now on still water. It made the going very tough for the oarsmen. 'I spent most of the next week in bed', says Boris. 'I couldn't focus my eyes properly for five days.' It was a big disappointment for everybody that Cambridge had not been able to boat their strongest crew and there was a lot of sympathy for John Woodehouse. But at the same time Oxford had looked unstoppable in the days approaching the race and they were worthy winners.

Isis, however, went down by 12 lengths in an interminably slow mini-Boat Race against Goldie, a result which posed a serious threat to Oxford's continuing success in 1980. Only four times has the winning University in the mini-Boat Race failed to lay the ground for a winning Boat Race crew the following year. It has been rare to go against form in the 20 years of the Isis–Goldie race, hence its importance as a Boat Race indicator and as a training ground for aspiring Blues (on each of those four occasions it was Oxford who broke back against the trend; in 1974, 1978, 1979 and most recently in 1980 by a bare six feet). Clearly we had to make good use of the summer season to bring on our men for the following year.

After seven days off and barely recovered from post-race celebrations, Oxford failed by just four seconds–or a length and a quarter–to win the Tideway Head from the national squad in very rough conditions which sank 15 crews during the race. But we managed for once to keep the crew together for the summer, although they were unable to train properly until after exams. They did however spend a winning weekend in Ghent, in the Belgian National Championships, doubling up to take the eights and fours titles on both days. And they looked a very fine crew too as they swept down the course ahead of the field their bladework sharp and immaculate. It was a self-help trip, trailing our boats behind the van, and taking as companions a four from the women's squad and the Cambridge women's eight who were all part of my ever-growing women's Olympic training team. They both won as well and we all slept in bunk bed dormitories in the noisiest school hall in Ghent.

At Henley the Oxford results were not so good – the price we always paid for being restricted by exams to one or two outings a week – and the crew lost to Yale in the Grand in the first round. Doubling up in the Stewards' half of them were beaten in the final by the London Rowing Club bronze medal four who then went on to defend that placing successfully at the World Championships in Bled. During this period I was heavily committed to the women's squad. Hired as a co-ordinator to organise them up to the Moscow Olympics, I ended up coaching them every day, at times nearly all day, and spent a difficult but enormously rewarding two years with them. Over the years the women's crews had always been given the rough end of the deal when it came to handing out cash and facilities to the various squads. Their response to first Penny Chuter's firm representation of their interests and then my efforts was gratifying. They worked terribly hard, did just about everything that was asked of them and as a result, won regattas abroad against some of the top outsized East and West European opposition. They shed many of their inhibitions and took to the gym work, the heavy weight training and the punishing mileage with a will.

In Moscow, in the absence of the Americans and the Canadians they finished fifth in the eights and Beryl Mitchell also made the final. They nearly halved the usual British women's deficit of 18 seconds behind the gold medallists to ten seconds or three lengths – an enormous improvement in a three-minute race – which was the direct result of their dedication.

As far as my own rowing was concerned serious competition at international level had unfortunately to stop since the amount of time spent coaching the two squads made it impossible to do the necessary training. Nevertheless I continued to get out on the water sufficiently often to continue competing in the Head of the River Races, the Sculling Heads and Henley in crews that though not fast enough to win were still fast enough to make the odd semi-final. Racing in quadruple sculls, doubles, fours and eights assembled at the last minute with other less than full-time but experienced oarsmen continued to keep me in touch with the demands I was making upon the Oxford squads. Apart from a nasty hiccup after Henley in 1983 which put me in hospital for a few months and kept me from training all winter, it was still useful to get out alongside them to see what they were up to.

9

By the Narrowest of Margins

From the outset the Olympic year Boat Race showed all the signs, on paper at least, of being another tightly-run affair. Once again I was coaching the women's squad which with Moscow imminent required even more time than the year before and after a while this commitment put some strain on my relationship with the new President, Boris Rankov. Everything began well enough though. At the start of training in October Rankov had the services of two other Blues, Mahoney and Diserens, and two Isis men, Barry and Bland, as well as the Isis cox Jerry Mead. At Cambridge the Blues Palmer and Phillips and their President Woodehouse, who had stroked the 1979 crew until the day of the race, were back. In addition they had James Lauric, Palmer's Eton partner in the pair that finished fourth in the 1977 World Youth Championships. Laurie had contracted glandular fever the previous year and had not been able to row. Panter, Dalrymple and Baart had rowed for the winning 1979 Goldie crew while a graduate freshman, 26-year-old Tim Whitney, was newly arrived from Dartmouth College in the United States where he had rowed for four years. Although still under the advisory guidance of Janousek, Cambridge were now in the very capable hands of my solicitor and 1975 lightweight four colleague, the tenacious Graeme 'Grumpy' Hall, a winning Cambridge Blue in 1968 and 1969. They were in the process of turning out a very smart Light Blue crew, more cohesive and well drilled, if not quite as powerful, as their immediate predecessors.

As in 1975, Oxford had to look to a new batch of promising freshmen to make up their 1980 crew. That set them at a disadvantage from the start for although the future looked well provided for, the present looked decidedly shaky. That was not to decry the quality of the newcomers. Nick Conington had stroked the Youth eight in 1977 and 1978 finishing seventh and fourth; Dave Todd, his Hampton schoolmate, was in the same 1978 crew; Steve Francis was ex-captain of St Paul's and a winner of the Schools race at Henley; Richard Yonge had rowed with the successful University College and Hospital crews of 1976–7–8 and Mark Andrews and Richard Emerton, two gangling giants from Abingdon, showed excellent technical ability although they lacked strength in the gym.

These last two had for some reason been relegated early on in the term to the junior trial crews on the Isis and it was not until midway through the term that I discovered them on a flying visit to coach the juniors. After the outing as they were putting their oars away, I told them that they were to be promoted to the senior trials next day and that they showed exceptional potential with their height and technique. Why were they rowing in the junior trials? Their surprise and pleasure at being picked out was genuine for they had not really been aware of quite how talented they were. When I suggested that they could both be senior internationals within three years if they wanted it badly enough they stared in disbelief. 'It's up to you' I said. Mark proved me wrong– he won a silver medal as a member of the 1981 British eight, a year earlier than I had predicted. He was a natural, a real star performer, and brilliantly taught as a schoolboy despite having spent comparatively little time on the water. 'I played mainly rugby at school' he told me. 'They didn't take rowing that seriously.' Richard was less ambitious and retired from serious rowing after the 1981 Boat Race.

Nick Holland was another good freshman from Radley and a Youth international in quad sculls while Matt Rutherford, Fergus Murison, Steve Walter and Nick Harding had all rowed for a year in Oxford college crews. So once again we had a line-up that was all British, was young (Francis was only 18 years old) and undergraduate save for the President. The first months followed the same procedure as before. Those two important ingredients of Oxford's fortunes, Chris Blackwall and Hugh Matheson, had both departed, but Steve Royle, an Oxford coach since 1977, was now playing a much larger and more important role along with the evergreen George Harris, Nick Tee, Ronnie Howard and Michael Barry. But we needed new coaches, experienced coaches to bring on these new young oarsmen and we approached Mike Spracklen, one of the country's best, with a successful career of international competition behind him. He had in recent years been responsible for Baillieu and Hart's training and just about every British sculling crew in international competition including our 1978 lightweight double scull looked to him for guidance. He was at that time most keenly involved in bringing on young men for the quadruple sculls event. He agreed to do two weeks with Oxford and thoroughly enjoyed it and he is now an integral member of the Oxford coaching team. His success with the British Olympic coxed four which won a gold medal in Los Angeles has made him the most sought after coach in the country.

There were two other new coaches to the team as well. Father Mark Jabalé, who was coach to the world champion lightweight four of 1979 containing my ex-sculling partner Ian Wilson, joined the Dark Blue camp and Keith Mason, a chain-smoking rowing mad Old Blue, who stroked Oxford in 1957, also agreed to take on Isis. Keith had produced no sons for future Oxford crews so it fell to his two daughters to carry on the Mason flag. Nicky became an international women's cox and Pippa arrived at Oxford in 1983 with her long-term sights set upon becoming the second woman in history to cox a Boat Race crew. Isis's finishing coach was Derek Thurgood, returned from his Middle East business adventures and anxious to get back into the swim of things.

Ronnie Howard and Steve Royle produced two excellent trial crews for the race in December and yet again the race was a corker. The freshman Conington stroked a finely judged race against Diserens, who had the President rowing behind him at five, winning by three-quarters of a length on the final row in along the boats at Putney. These extremely close trial races were regularly providing the senior Oxford trialists with invaluable experience of the Championship course under the greatest possible pressure. From the coaches' point of view they were essential viewing for our selection deliberations. With Cambridge regularly curtailing their Christmas break to just ten days and holding their trials at the end of a two-week post-term camp, we had decided that this was an advantage we could no longer afford to present them with so we now followed the trials race with a 12-day camp in Oxford for our 20 top oarsmen.

The seat racing sorted out most of the selection problems, putting Barry, Andrews and Conington into the first crew with the three Blues and Bland in favour of Emerton and Holland. The choice between the older Yonge and the teenager Francis was the hardest to make since there was little to pick between them, but the youngster just showed in front. He was strong in the gym, and though a little short in the water rowed a very efficient stroke. We had one feeling of unease about him however and that was his reluctance to run in the squad track and road races. He had swelling ankles, he explained, and demonstrated the point early on in training with a three-mile run which left him hobbling for days. Instead of forcing him on with it until he overcame the problem, we allowed him to do extra work in the gym which in retrospect, did not give him the same long distance endurance fitness that the others were getting. It was a dangerous precedent to set and it nearly cost us the race later in the year, clearly demonstrating the effectiveness of our integrated programme. Neglecting one part of the training left us vulnerable and though we had at times still to compromise in some aspects of the programme with some individuals, they still had to prove their competence and fitness in all areas of training.

We had further difficulties filling the seven seat. Andrews we thought too inexperienced for such a responsibility while neither Rankov nor Yonge were flexible enough. We tried all sorts of seating arrangements including a bowside stroked line-up. But the most obvious candidate, Tom Barry, was just not rowing up to the level we knew he was capable of, rushing forward as he was out of control and off his feet. At one point while he was sitting up in the bows so that he could concentrate on his sliding problem, I lost my temper with him completely after constant heckling had failed to elicit the slightest improvement. I called on the cox Jerry Mead to stop the crew and proceeded to lay into poor Tom, venting my frustration at what I perceived to be his lack of response and threatening him with the old 'bow and out' option, the oarsman's perennial fear when he gets moved out of the stern and back towards the bows during early training and selection. He was visibly upset and the rest of the crew were startled too by the outburst but there seemed to be no other way of getting through to him. Better that though than simply being dropped for loss of form without any explanation. That was the usual solution. But such a course of action always seemed to me to show a failure on everyone's part, coach included, and I preferred to persevere, to goad and wheedle a man back to form rather than sling him out. Whether I finally got tired of trying and left him alone for a bit, or whether the telling off had an effect I don't really know, but he came out of the trough and improved enough to move down to the seven seat where he rowed very courageously on Boat Race day.

There were other problems too. Mike at stroke had a wonderful easy rhythm, but he could be quite difficult at times. If the boat was not going too well he would suddenly change the rhythm without warning, complain loudly about the crew's lack of feel whereupon Chris at six would shout something abusive about his abrupt gear change. 'As President', says Boris, 'I would tell them both to shut up and Mike would tell Jerry the cox to tell me to shut up myself and Jerry would tell Mike that he couldn't tell the President to shut up. Within seconds a boat which had been paddling along quite normally would be reduced to a squabbling mess and you, Dan, would come up in the rubber dinghy asking in total amazement "What's going on? What's happening?" Dizzy's ultimate sanction was to stop rowing without a word in mid-recovery which would result in the rest of the crew careering into frontstops, like a motorway pile-up, and the boat would shudder to a halt.'

But Mike was a perfectionist, sensitive always to whatever was happening behind him in the boat, and the crew appreciated this. Indeed when in the Boat Race everything began to go wrong he quickly identified the problem and responded with great presence of mind. Occasional lapses in concentration too, especially common amongst the men in the bow section of a boat would elicit a curt reminder from cox or coach. Everyone remembers my exasperated reaction to the admission from Mark and John that the little discussion they had been having in the bows while they rowed along concerned a heron on the bank and other ornithological matters!

There were one or two other moments of confrontation where hard talking was needed to get everyone's thoughts back to the straight and narrow. I was always terrified that the lack of urgency and the complacency that I had demonstrated myself in 1968 when we lost might come creeping back in, and I was paranoid about stopping the disease before it spread.

A dressing-down was not always the most popular way to go about things for sure, particularly since they were working hard, harder than any other athletes in the country probably; but they just seemed to be lacking that hard edge. The criticisms hurt but they had the desired effect and prodded the boys back into action for a while at least. Better to ruffle feathers early than to be wise after defeat: imagine the mournful 'If only we had read those early warning signals properly. If only we had not been worried about upsetting people'.

It was a year of changing fortunes. Generally the crew that arrives on the Tideway as favourite does not, barring accident, suddenly falter but 1980 was a special year. Neither crew were top class, but both had their good days and their off days. Our early form suggested that we were the stronger squad and at the Christmas national trials our two coxed fours finished well up the final order giving us an aggregate lead over the three Cambridge crews. In early February we had a session with London University which was again a rather bruising affair involving a couple of clashes and some blue and purple language. However at the end of the weekend, Oxford finished four to two up, the last race between the bridges, the best seven-minute stretch on the Tideway because it is the fairest, resulting in a three-length win for the Dark Blues. A week later a high rating Cambridge took on the same UL crew which was now rowing in a different boat, and lost four to one, their worst encounter being that same telling 'bridger', in which they went down by three lengths. On paper that seemed to give us a big advantage but Rusty Williams, the UL coach, was quick to dispel such notions, pointing out to me on the phone later in the afternoon that his crew had been going much better in their new boat than they had against Oxford the week before, and that Cambridge had been far too polite on the water and had allowed the hard tactical 'Purples' cox to run them

190

ragged. 'Don't be misled by the result', he warned, 'they're not as bad as that result suggests.'

He was right. By the beginning of the Tideway fortnight, the pendulum had swung. Graeme Hall, who was now also in charge of the Olympic eight group, and his fellow coaches had worked wonders on the Light Blues while during the intervening month we seemed to have been standing still. At the Reading Head of the River a month before the Boat Race, we were beaten into second place by Leander who admittedly were looking to Olympic selection as a crew. Their Moscow dreams, however, were rudely shattered two weeks later in the Tideway Head, but not as emphatically as those of Oxford, who started the Head in third place rowing as Isis. We had made some positional changes within the crew after Reading yet we still finished a miserable eighth behind the winning ARA second crew (made up of the national coxed and coxless fours), the Spanish squad, the lightweights, the national sculling squad, the ARA heavyweight national crew (a comparatively weak eight which had barely beaten Cambridge a week before), University of London, and Leander, in that order. Our own Isis crew were just 15 seconds behind us. It was a poor show, but we had to get a grip of the thing because at that stage it looked as if we had been overtaken in the betting stakes by a very neat and aggressive Cambridge crew. There was just a fortnight left and we had a lot to do. But just at that moment the increasing tension over our obvious lack of speed caused fraying nerves to snap, threatening to upset the applecart altogether.

Apart from the usual scoldings which are occasional necessities for most athletes in training when their performances begin to look mundane, I had not been aware of any particular difficulties between Boris or the crew and myself. They were working hard, of course, and once or twice I had had to reassure an anxious Boris when things seemed to be getting on top of him. But he was nursing some extra uncertainties the nature of which he did not reveal to me until it was almost too late. 'Although you were obviously putting in an enormous amount of time' he tells me now 'those of us who had rowed the year before knew you were coming down to see us less often and I suppose we were jealous that you were dividing your time between us and the women's squad and not giving us the loving care and attention we felt we deserved.' He also suspected that I was underestimating the amount of work they were doing. 'It was true that the programme you set was less hard than the year before – on paper – but the point was that I was making sure the crew diligently did the whole lot. In the years before on the occasions when you weren't there the squads sometimes used to cut the land work. So in effect we were working much harder. But you thought we were whining wallies when I tried to explain to you in those long telephone conversations and asked for a let-up. I think because you were with us less you didn't realise how tired we were getting. Yes, we whined, and we needed jumping on for that, but we were being pushed pretty hard.

'Since Sawyier's year when we all worked to the limit no squad had done the full programme really properly and regularly. I remember vividly while I was rowing with Leander, being in the Oxford gym when the 1977 crew came in to train. They wandered through the door, took a look around and then decided not to bother with the weights. It happened on several occasions, and even the following year Ag would cut short a session every now and again with the catch-phrase "Easter Bunny's here". I was determined that that would not happen while I was President unless there was a genuine reason. We never missed the Ratz hops despite Chris Mahoney's conviction, repeated over and over, that they did no good, yet if anything kept us ahead of the Tabs in the last half mile of that bloody race it was those jumps: the final minute felt just like the last set of seven times 70 hops, mindlessly repeated stabs of pain in the legs again and again. I had to defend the programme more than once. Mike, for instance, declared during one session that the weight work was pointless and I lost my temper so violently that the whole squad abruptly stopped working and stood for a moment in total astonishment before continuing to the end of the session in silence. But others, like Mark, would hear no wrong of you and thought it mad to question the work programme.'

To the Rankov groan of despair followed by 'this is the worst day of my life' was added: groan–'we've got a Boat Race to win' and groan–'relax'. The whole squad teased him with these phrases whenever they felt he needed loosening up a bit. 'Tom was very good at easing tensions in the boat' says Mahoney, 'and he was particularly good with Boris. I remember once coming back to college one evening and seeing Boris standing beside Oriel College, beating the walls with his fists in despair, groaning: "this is the worst day of my life". The OUBC video equipment had been stolen and Jo Pitt had just jacked from the squad and Boris blamed Oriel for withholding their oarsmen from trials. Worse still, he and his girlfriend Katy had crashed into each other in their own driveway.' Mahoney and others in the crew don't remember me being less in evidence during those months but Boris felt it and it worried him. 'Partly, I suppose, it was my naturally panicky nature' he suggests, 'but it was also because as President I had to worry about such things and express the feelings of the crew.'

On the Friday morning before the final Tideway fortnight the crew arrived at Putney for the Head next day. They were an hour late and I was pressed for time. 'We were due at four', remembers Boris 'and I'd started getting things ready at eight that morning; but everything went wrong. The van broke down, people were late and the ties holding the boats on worked loose and when we arrived late you were furious because you had to cut the outing short to go and coach the women. I'd had no breakfast or lunch and had been on the go for nine hours so I was pretty fraught. You put us out against Isis who were faster than you expected although we knew, and despite my protests, you started us down on the outside of the bend on a series of short pieces and they walloped us. We came off the water thoroughly annoyed.'

The abysmal Head performance next day was the result. That afternoon Boris, John Bland and cox Jerry Mead came round to my house for tea and to collect some beds and chairs for our Putney house. 'The conversation started calmly enough', recalls John. 'We were discussing the results of the Head and how we were going to put things right when Boris said that we needed you with us the whole time because he thought you had lost touch with the crew. "How do you mean?" you said, "how do you think I'm out of touch?" I remember it all horribly clearly because I could see it all coming and there was nothing I could do to stop it.' Everything built up then and finally I offered to resign. There was a silence and then Jerry asked: 'more tea anyone?'.

'Rightly or wrongly,' explains Boris now, 'I put down our shock performance to you not knowing what we were capable of and I was fed up with having to vie with the women's squad for your attention. So when I said I wanted your undivided attention from that moment on it was because without it I didn't believe we could extricate ourselves from the trough. You, of course, immediately read far more into that than I had intended and asked if I wanted you to drop out as finishing coach to which I said that I'd been thinking of it. I can still see the open-mouthed amazement with which John and Jerry stared at me as if I had gone completely off my head.' That ended tea rather abruptly with Boris still saying that there was a precedent for this state of affairs and that it had happened before, and I asked John to ride back with me to Putney in my car. I wanted to sound out how deeply through the crew these feelings ran; he tried to assure me that it was just Boris panicking again.

'I had thought of replacing you,' says Boris, 'but had concluded that that would have meant throwing the race away entirely. I had vaguely considered asking George to take over knowing that he'd refuse and give me a bollocking and that he would then call you and come down very heavily on you. I believed that even if you wouldn't listen to me you would take note of George. I hoped that the confrontation would galvanise you and it did–immediately. In fact you quite outshone yourself in those last two weeks although we didn't exchange a word for a while. After the race I remember you kissed each one of us individually and I think I apologised to you then.'

I of course had had no inkling that Boris had been calculating all these manoeuvres. Our confrontation was a rude shock. I forgot for a while how dramatically he was apt to take even the smallest problem and we were both a bit stunned by the sudden turn of events. It took quite a bit of diplomatic activity on the part of the rest of the crew to calm us down before we sorted out our differences. Whether his fears were justified or not, the very suspicion that the crew and the President were not 100 per cent convinced of my fullest commitment was enough to jerk me to attention. Boris had, after all, in the past publicly declared enormous confidence in me and this change of heart was a blow. But there was no time for self justification or excuses or for finding out whether everyone shared his fears or whether they were just an expression of the anxieties of one man more prone to despair than most. There were other more pressing problems to solve.

Eighth in the Head was really too bad to be true and we needed something to demonstrate to the crew that they could perform far more effectively in a side by side race than in a processional race. We needed to prove to them that they were tough when they had the opposition in their sights. We were also worried by Nick Conington's inability to get his blade down to the water at the catch and no amount of pestering seemed to correct the fault. By 'skying' his blade he was not giving the immediate backing to the strokeside men in front of him and we swapped him with John Bland who had been rowing at two. With only 12 days to go it could have had an unsettling effect. But the change seemed to lock the boat a little better in the middle although in truth it was more of a cosmetic change than anything terribly significant.

After a quiet start to the final fortnight, we took a big risk and challenged the national heavyweight eight which had beaten us by ten seconds in the Head. This was a trip right into the enemy camp for Graeme Hall, the national squad's coach, was also Cambridge's finishing coach. He accepted the fixture with delight since this would give him an opportunity to deal the psychological *coup de grace*. With his crew clearly faster than us and Cambridge not far behind them he would be in a position to dictate the encounter. But things did not quite work out that way. With the opposition alongside the crew were a changed unit. We took three lengths off the squad from Hammersmith to Putney. It was a tremendous surprise to everyone and far better than anything we could have hoped for. It was a reversal of some four lengths compared with our weekend Head result. To shove home the point, we broke the 1963 record between Hammersmith Bridge and the Stone at Putney by four seconds. Diserens came down the moored Putney boats at 35, steaming away from the national squad after a slightly shaky start. Oxford were back in business. Next day, in a flashing thunderstorm, they rowed the rest of the course on their own going from the race finish to Hammersmith and breaking that record by 32 seconds. Then they left for their weekend on the Isle of Wight, tails high and well satisfied with their two days work, leaving Isis to win the Kingston Head of the River which showed that they were a pretty good crew as well.

Cambridge meanwhile had come up against the national lightweight crew in mid-week and had been beaten over that same 'bridger' distance by a length, after leading to halfway. True, the lightweights had just beaten both Oxford and the 'heavies' in the Head but they were surely beatable over a shorter distance given the extra power of the bigger crews. I had lined up a fixture with the lightweights for Oxford on the Wednesday before the Boat Race as our last big effort before race day. Terry O'Neill, the lightweight coach, called me on the Isle of Wight during the weekend. 'I suppose you'll want to call off our race then' he said. 'Why?' I asked. 'Well you won't want to risk demoralising your boys now will you; not after the good rowing they've just done.' 'Terry, if you're still happy to do it so are we', I replied. 'But that's crazy,' he said, 'why do it when your boys are on top now?' 'I'll tell you, but not till after the Boat Race', I replied, and put the phone down.

We were on a knife edge now, but the feeling that we had the race won seemed to be creeping in again. I was convinced that these were the two most equally-matched 'Varsity crews for years and I was sure we were in for the grimmest of races. However much I told the men of the dangers they would still look to their pre-weekend performance and say 'Yeah? well we'll be ready for them.' They needed to be more than ready for them. They needed to know that this was going to be the toughest thing they had ever had to do. Besides I also wanted to know how much we had been able to redress the balance even if only for my own peace of mind. We had, after all, been trailing badly only six days earlier and I did not feel that such a huge change in fortunes could occur so quickly. Maybe the squad had been awful when we raced them. If we could pick up four lengths they could just as easily have dropped four. If we had recovered as much as we had seemed to then we would finish well in front of the lightweights. If we had not then we would at least know where we stood. I believed that either way, it was important that we keep that fixture.

We spent the first day after the weekend sharpening up with starts and a brush with the Old Blues crew. There was light relief on the bank too, with Prince Philip visiting Cambridge, and the cast of the new St Trinian's film in black suspenders playing with the Oxford boys and laying in wait for the Royal visitor. More seriously though the efforts of the week before had overstressed Chris Mahoney's back and he was suffering. I took him to see a specialist and gave him massage treatment daily for the rest of the week. On the Tuesday he took a rest from the boat while the tall but light Isis six man, Richard Emerton, substituted. By Wednesday Mahoney was ready to row again. Cambridge too had had their back problems, losing Laurie for a couple of days with the same complaint.

The race with the lightweights was a bitter affair, with their kamikaze cox, an ex-UL man, causing clashes off the start, and barging and shoving to get ahead. And get ahead they did, stealing half a length by the Mile and then pushing hard on the inside of the Fulham bend. They opened up to a length and as we swept down along the Putney boathouses, there were the Cambridge crew on their balcony, cheering wildly as Oxford went down to a canvas greater defeat than they had suffered the week before. There it was then, dead even. No doubts about it. If the Oxford lads had entertained any comfortable thoughts of probable victory before that race, they were well and truly dashed. They were in for a gut-buster. 'I hadn't seriously considered the possibility of losing until the Head,' says John Bland, 'and for me as a new boy in the crew it had been an anxious week. Then when we did well against the heavyweight squad I got very nervous because I was worried that it *might* be close with Cambridge. After that race with the lightweights though I knew it *was* going to be close and from then on I felt much better.'

Earlier in the day Cambridge in a revenge match had beaten London University by half a length over four minutes in a thoroughly aggressive row. Graeme Hall was clearly aiming to go for an early break because they had done little work over seven minutes. Everything seemed geared to those first six minutes. When the crews had weighed in there had been not a pound of difference, so once again the stage was set for a neck-and-neck contest.

After the Head of the River Race, Cambridge had given their Carbocraft boat to their second crew Goldie who had damaged their own in a collision on their way to the start. Graeme Hall had secured the national squad Leisure Sport-sponsored Carbo boat for Cambridge which they found much more to their liking. Although they were very comfortable in the boat and decided to use it for the race they did not seem prepared to black out the sponsor's name written in large letters on the bows of the boat. Polite requests from the Boat Race sponsors Ladbrokes fell on deaf ears and there followed a series of unpleasant exchanges the upshot of which was that Ladbrokes would cease to sponsor Cambridge if they continued to treat them with such a lack of consideration. It was not the first time that there had been complaints about such cavalier treatment but this was the last straw. The two Universities had supported a BBC objection to sponsors' names appearing in the Boat Race and for one crew to then row in a boat clearly marked with a rival's name was an unpardonable affront. The row went on for far longer than was necessary since clearly John Woodehouse, the Cambridge President, was not about to lose upward of £12,000 for his successor; finally the Light Blues had to climb down and paint out the offending words. There was clearly someone very pig-headed holding sway in the other camp.

The umpire's rehearsal with the coxes, in which each cox takes the steering wheel of their respective coaching launches while the umpire rides behind in a third, was illuminating. From the courses of the two coxswains, particularly off the start, we could tell that Wigglesworth for Cambridge was planning to take a far more Surrey-side view of the race whichever station he got on the day. The two launches converged alarmingly more than once and though the Surrey station was probably preferable for the race, in what promised to be good conditions, the Middlesex one looked safer judging by Cambridge's projected course. In our pre-race talk we discussed the dangers of a clash in case we found ourselves on the Surrey station. I stressed the importance of keeping discipline and eyes in the boat especially off the start, for darting glances across and worrying about the other crew were dangerously distracting habits. I warned that this was a race more than any other that could be decided in the last strokes, that the middle and the end sectors, the last minute, could for once be decisive. In our winter training, on the track, I always underlined the need for crossing the finishing line in all races before winding down, rather than anticipating the line and consequently tapering off a fraction early. We always worked hard through the line just as we always emphasised the second half of every piece of work we did. These were my little eccentricities. We covered all the possibilities as usual but fully stressing these particular points proved in the event to be fortuitously prophetic.

The crews were judged by the punters to be pretty even off the stakeboat starts just before race day. John Woodehouse, the Cambridge President, who had still to win his Blue, had the previous year been acclaimed by the Cambridge coaches as a brilliant natural stroke yet this year he was holding down the six seat. Hall probably felt the same way we did: that a President at stroke was a tricky combination. Whatever their reasons, Woodehouse was in a combative mood. Through the pages of the Press he remarked that he regarded an advertising promotion that the OUBC had agreed to do with Citroën during the winter as an example of Oxford's dirty tricks department and that Cambridge were not going to be thwarted this year. We were a little surprised by this news. Citroën had placed half a dozen of the Oxford squad in a Citroën estate car with a trailer and boat attached behind and had dressed them in blazers that they had hired and which bore an uncanny resemblance to the Tabs' greenish blue. The boys had baulked at wearing the colours of their rivals at first, but the fee promised to the Boat Club for their services persuaded them to model for the picture. What they had no hand in or knowledge of were the literary efforts of the copywriters. Mindful of the 1978 race finale they came up with a sideways slur upon Cambridge's ability to stay afloat or at least a ditty that could be interpreted in that way by the super-sensitive: 'The last thing a rowing eight wants', ran the slogan, 'is an estate car that sinks.' I doubt that the copywriters even knew which crew had in fact sunk that year – or had even been aware that the blazers were light blue. Whatever the truth of the matter, Oxford got blamed for the advertisement. But if it meant that Cambridge were hopping mad then those copywriters had played an unconscious but tiny part in the psychological build-up to the 1980 Boat Race. Woodehouse also believed, a belief reinforced by his coach Graeme Hall, that the Oxford crews were putting too much reliance on their finishing coach and that they were not able to think for themselves. The race that followed put paid to the second theory while the superlative crew of 1981, put together while I was away for the winter in South America, upset the first. Coaches guide, advise and inspire; it is the men in the boats, and the system they work under, that produce the goods.

For the sixth year in succession Oxford won the toss and Boris chose Surrey. The conditions were calm, the flood tide sluggish. Thinking back to this race still sends shivers down my spine. It was a heroic day. As in 1978, Cambridge turned back downstream as they were about to get on to the stakeboat, and a repeat of that long delayed race looked imminent. Traditionally the challenger goes afloat first and attaches to the stakeboat first, but on this occasion it was Oxford who got on to the stakeboat and divested themselves of their zephyr tops. As they waited they were told that Isis had just defeated Goldie. The pendulum was swinging back in their favour again. The umpire, Cambridge Blue Alan Burroughs, got them off cleanly, if a few minutes late. Almost from the first stroke, Wigglesworth the Cambridge cox began to steer across towards the Surrey side with the umpire calling him back to his station. Incredibly, within the first half a minute the crews were clashing.

Forewarned, the Oxford boys kept their eyes ahead and on the man in front and though the clash cost them a little ground and a portion of the seven man Tom's blade, they kept their cohesion well and settled into their stride as the crews separated opposite Vesta Rowing Club. Cambridge were going all out for a lead to take full advantage of their first Middlesex bend so Dalrymple their stroke kept them hard at 36 strokes a minute while Diserens settled into his best rhythm at 34, biding his time content to stay alongside and defend his water to the Mile Post. The crews were close, dangerously so, but Jerry Mead was sticking firmly to his course while Wigglesworth tried hard to push him wide on the corner. With Oxford a few feet down, an unfamiliar position for Boris and one that he says gave him a nasty shock, the crews raced past the Mile and on towards Harrods where Cambridge spurted in an attempt to win enough water to take the stream and the Surrey station ahead of Oxford. It was a bold move but it could only have worked if Oxford had cracked there and then. But Oxford did not crack. Diserens waited for Dalrymple's spurt to evaporate and then with Cambridge a canvas ahead, he mounted his own attack just as the bend swung in his favour. There was another clash of blades as Wigglesworth tried to crowd but he was warned by the umpire and had to give way. Oxford, now at 36, came level and then edged past. It was at just this point that both crews had been a length behind the light-weights in their trial rows. Now we would see what these men were really made of.

At Hammersmith Bridge Oxford led by a bare half length and Mead held wide to gain as much advantage as he could off the crown of the corner. It looked as if Cambridge had blown everything on that desperate surge, a dangerous tactic on the outside of a big bend. They had clearly thought that to win the race they needed to be in front at Hammersmith. Had they bided their time for a later attack things might have emerged differently. Oxford took another length and a half along the Eyot, and Diserens, now at 32, looked to have everything under control. Mead could take whatever course he wished and he moved over for the crossing at the LEP factory where he led by two and three-quarter lengths. That was as much as he got. Cambridge were

199

holding on now and then almost imperceptibly they started to make ground. 'Every now and again' says Jerry Mead, the cox, 'I began to notice that there were only three puddles coming down on bowside when there should have been four. At first I thought there must be something wrong with the rigger or the blade, that something may have worked loose.' There were still six minutes to go, about a mile and three-quarters, but Oxford looked far enough in front to be safe. It was at this stage that I turned to George Harris and said: 'Something's wrong, George. Can you see what it is?' 'Look at bow's blade' he said, looking intently ahead, and sure enough we could see that Steve's blade was skying up into the air and dropping slowly down to the water at the beginning of each stroke. From that distance we could not tell that there was no power on the end of the blade in the water, but the lethargic way his oar descended to take the stroke compared to the sharp bite of the other seven blades was ominous.

At the Bandstand Cambridge were now definitely coming back and Steve's oar looked more and more like a flopping, ailing bird contributing little to the propulsion of the boat although he was still sliding more or less in time with the crew, managing bravely to stay upright. Fortunately, at bow his blade was not interfering with those of his colleagues. 'It was when I saw his blade waving about' remembers Jerry 'that I realised he must be in trouble.' But he did not alert the crew. Instead he called on them all for more effort as he took a quick look behind to see where Cambridge were – and what he saw he did not like. They were pushing up hard and had obviously caught wind of the fact that they still had a chance of getting back into the race. Oxford were still one and a quarter lengths up when they shot Barnes Bridge, but the gap was closing fast. They had three-quarters of a mile to go. As Diserens, aware now that something was wrong, forced the rate back up to 34 the crew rallied, each of them thinking that they must be feeling the strain, that the heavy boat was caused by each man's failing strength. Jerry still did not tell them that they were in effect carrying a passenger now, for surely it would have weakened their resolve to fight. As long as they continued to believe that they each had to contribute their all to overcome the increasingly dead feeling in the boat then they could still survive. Jerry did not want to give them that subconscious let-out clause, that excuse to ease up and give in which would have inevitably become their overriding emotion had they found out that a collapsed man, something beyond their control, had intervened to bring about defeat. Jerry urged them on. With brilliant nerve and presence of mind he held on to the inside of the Middlesex station for as long as he could, sensing the Cambridge bow sneaking up alongside him as they passed the Dukes Head. Besides he was being pulled that way by strokeside and had to struggle to keep his course. Reluctantly he eased out a little to give Wigglesworth room to come up on the inside as was his right. The crew had watched Cambridge cut down their lead as they fought to stay ahead, and now there they were overlapping and, with a quarter of a mile of the race still to go. Seven men bent to the task.

Steve was still sliding with the crew, propelled mainly by the surging momentum of the boat, his blade dropping lifelessly into the water, but miraculously not getting caught. 'I went blind at Barnes Bridge' he recalls. Nick Conington, sitting at two in front of him sensed that there was nothing coming from the man behind and shouted encourage-ment. None of all this had been noticed by the commentators on television. All they could see was a tremendous sustained spurt by the gallant Cambridge crew which had brought them right back into contention. And certainly it was a most courageous effort with Dal-rymple forcing his crew first to 35 then 36 and as they smelled victory to 37 and 38 as he fought to get back on terms. In the launch there was bedlam. Normally sworn to silence under the rules of racing, the occupants of all the launches were screaming their support. Diserens pushed up to 36 and still the Tabs kept coming. With a minute to go Cambridge at 38 were a canvas down and still closing and on the video replay next day it seemed that they did indeed for a moment get their noses in front. But in the last 20 strokes Diserens also drove the rate up to 38. Miraculously those seven brave men dug deep, deep down into their last reserves, vowed that the Tabs would not pass, and forced their bows to the line barely three feet ahead. The official canvas verdict was generous. As they collapsed like dead men fighting for breath, they heard Woodehouse call across: 'You were lucky that time, Oxford'.

Luck was not the word. Courage, tenacity and a deep rooted will to win governed them over those last yards. It was a performance to rank amongst the very best of heroic achievements. Men might have collapsed in the Boat Race before but their crews had never dared to go on to win. My own instincts, Dark Blue tinted perhaps, went out to those seven extraordinary men and that miracle-weaving cox. They were the stuff on which the reputation of the Boat Race is built. They were history-makers. The fact that they were pushed to a standstill by the grit and determination of the bravest of Cambridge crews I fully acknowledged, and that young Steve gave everything he had I knew too, but the real heroism remained with the magnificent seven plus one. It was the character of those fighting men that will live with me long after I have ceased to coach or row.

As Cambridge paddled their boat to the shore, the Oxford boys remained under Chiswick bridge, dead to the world, some flat on their backs, some bent and retching over their oars. Bert steered the launch quickly alongside the bows where Steve lay pale and collapsed, his eyes closed. We released his feet from the shoes in the boat and lifted him into the launch and while I took his place to help row the boat to the raft, Doc Freeman hurried the exhausted man to hospital and the soothing effects of a strong dose of oxygen. 'I still didn't realise what was going on' says Chris Mahoney. 'I remember thinking "What's Dan up to?" when you climbed into the boat.' Even then the millions watching on television did not know what had happened because though the cameras picked up the activity around the listing Oxford boat, the distracted commentators were no longer watching their monitors and failed to interpret the action. Only the newspapers next day drew attention to the post-race drama. Steve was recovered enough by the evening to leave hospital and we discovered a week later that he had been suffering from a mild case of hepatitis which the doctors thought might have contributed to his collapse. Fortunately he recovered fully and rowed for a winning Isis two years later.

It was the closest result in the Boat Race since the famous Dead Heat to Oxford by three yards of 1877. It was also the first five-year winning sequence for Oxford since 1913 and the two senior Oxbridge Blues who had rowed in that historic year, Sir Angus Gillan and Cambridge's Colonel Kitching, both born in 1885, were able to watch the race on television. For John Snagge, whose last Boat Race commentary for the BBC this was, it was a fitting retirement present. In a letter to the two Presidents elect, the umpire after congratulating them on a sterling race complained that the *Bosporos* was hopelessly inadequate as an umpire's launch because he had been left far behind the race at the start and had not regained contact with the crews until the Fulham bend. He suggested that in future the umpire should ride alone ahead of the line of pursuing craft in his own launch. This he said would give him flexibility and leave him free of unsolicited advice! He also pointed out that it was encumbent upon the challenger to be on the start at the appointed time.

At the Ball that night while the Light Blues danced their gloom away Oxford crewmen lay slumped in their chairs, some snoring loudly, oblivious to the celebrations going on around them and their girl-friends' efforts to rouse them. Legs remained like jelly for many days afterwards and some did not fully recover until a couple of weeks later.

Soon after the Boat Race, Graeme Hall drafted Chris Mahoney, the

Oxford President elect for 1981, into a reshuffled national eight and they went to the Olympics in Moscow without the backing of the British Government but with high hopes, Colin Moynihan in the cox's seat, and the support of the Duke of Edinburgh and most of the country. They won the silver medal with a brilliantly sustained row which took them past the Russians 200 metres from the line. The rest of the Oxford squad split into different combinations for Henley. Boris and Mike Diserens entered the Diamonds, both losing in the first round, while Mark Andrews joined the Isis crew for the Ladies' Plate. They raced well but lost to the eventual winners from America by half a length in the quarter final.

10
Into the History Books

Returning from the Moscow Olympics where my gutsy girl rowers had finished fifth in the final I confirmed plans to go to South America on a six-month journey with my father during which he and I intended to gather material for a book and to make a film for the BBC. Before leaving I was able to get down on paper a detailed programme and reference booklet listing every pertinent aspect of the full year's programme for Chris Mahoney, the new President, and Steve Royle, who was to be chief coach. Because I was the only one who had followed the whole eight-year plan through from start to finish, we wanted to be sure that all the things I carried in my head were fully described. Mahoney asked if I would be back in time to coach the last fortnight, and I promised to gear my itinerary to the 1981 race date. He in turn promised to keep me in touch with progress and training by letter and throughout the trip I headed first for the various Poste Restantes and Embassy mailboxes whenever I arrived at a major town. News was sparse to begin with, but by Christmas, when I got to Bogotá, the British newspapers were full of stories about Oxford's new secret weapon: 'It's a girl!' screamed the headlines. Sue Brown had arrived.

At the end of 1979 while recruiting for the women's squad, I had noticed Sue on the towpath with a Wadham College eight and she had seemed keen to try out for the Olympic squad. Her aptitude and keen racing sense made up for her lack of experience and she won a seat in the women's coxed four in Moscow. Back at Oxford, she had put herself down for trials and when I received a letter from Mahoney asking me what I thought of a woman cox in the Boat Race, in particular Sue, I wrote back saying 'No objections!' Coincidentally, a couple of years earlier the Mandrake column of the *Telegraph* had run a story on our cook, Celia, and had reported my prediction that there would soon be a woman in the coxing seat of one of the 'Varsity crews.

It was curious charting their progress through the pages of the *Telegraph*, *The Times* and the *Guardian* from places as wide apart as Punte Arenas in southern Chile, Bogotá in Colombia, and Rio. I wanted to be back there, for despite the sinking of one of the Oxford trial crews in December which was widely reported largely because of the Sue Brown factor, I could tell by reading between the lines that Oxford's 1981 Boat Race crew looked like being one of the best ever.

In one of his letters Chris, delighted with progress, promised: 'We won't be over-confident: just confident'. I yearned to be out on a freezing cold Thames in the coaching launch. Instead I was about to leave the Andes and head off down the Amazon.

Chris Mahoney had a strong group of oarsmen to work with who were also immensely fired by a backlog of Cambridge claims that they would have won the previous three races but for bad luck. 'The 1981 squad were fed up with Cambridge not admitting defeat' says Boris. They were intent on teaching the Tabs a lesson and their irritation acted as a strong motivating force. Here again the previous year's experience strongly influenced the approach of the current men. The Blues Rankov, Andrews, Conington, Bland and Francis were back but Diserens soon decided to withdraw to concentrate on his studies. From the successful Isis crew Holland, Rutherford, Emerton and Yonge presented a strong challenge for Blue Boat places while the 1979 Blue Head had returned from a year in France. Freshman twins Rob and Hugh Clay from Eton were both very useful additions to the squad. The other new faces in trials were John Graham from Princeton University and two Oxford college taught oarsmen, Steve Foster and Mike Chapman. Sue Brown faced 13 male challengers for the cox-swain's seat but when one of her leading rivals withdrew to join the SDP as a party organiser the battle narrowed down to a straight choice between her and Steve Higgins who eventually coxed Isis. Stroked on bowside by Rob Clay, this Isis crew proved to be fast, finishing second at Reading to Leander in the absence of the Oxford first crew who had to withdraw with a broken rudder. Isis finished eighth in the Open Head having started as a new entry, beating Goldie by 16 seconds in the process, and then went on to win the mini-Boat Race by four and a half lengths on the day. Selection for the first crew though thorough was straightforward, with Richard Emerton winning a place at four and Richard Yonge coming in at three. The coaches felt that Steve Francis needed a further year's rowing to fully regain his strength and restore his confidence before applying himself once more to the rigours of Boat Race training. However, he withdrew from the squad, reluctant to row in Isis, and Holland, Pitt and Rutherford joined him on the bank. At the end of the first term and over Christmas, Conington was laid low by glandular fever which threatened his chances but he recovered in time to regain his place in the crew. It was, however, a disease that was to haunt him throughout the next two years.

I was able to keep track of their progress only intermittently but reports of comfortable victories over Leander and University of London–'nearly a length a minute,' wrote Chris enthusiastically, 'no exaggeration!'–were like music to the ears as I crossed and recrossed South America. From Rio I flew across to Ecuador and the Galapagos Islands at the end of January and then embarked on the grim overland journey back again by way of Colombia, Venezuela and then south along 1500 miles of bouncing dirt track through the Amazonian jungle to Manaus. By the time I got back to Rio it was Carnival, and I seized upon the opportunity for a final week of decadence before the rigours of training camp. Then it was time to get back to Miami and on to London. I made straight for Pangbourne where Oxford and Isis were preparing for their afternoon outing. It was three weeks to the Boat Race.

The President had introduced some new coaches to the team. Jeff Jacobs and Richard Hooper were his Hampton and Molesey gurus and John Pilgrim Morris was a colleague of Mike Spracklen's on the sculling front who had taken the successful coxless pair of Charly Wiggin and Malcolm Carmichael to a bronze medal in Moscow. Mahoney had also recruited two of his Olympic eight colleagues, strokeman Richard Stanhope and John Pritchard, to coach Isis. All but Pritchard subsequently became regular and key members of the coaching team. While Oxford remained unchanged from their initial order all winter and looked powerful, cohesive and very long and rhythmic, Cambridge were still not happy with their order and indeed changed it when they arrived on the Tideway for the last fortnight. I had had little advance information on them but with six returning Blues including their stern and bow pairs, their strong mid-boat man Phillips and their cox Wigglesworth plus Stephens and Clark from Goldie, they promised on paper to be a useful crew. They had after all run Oxford to just a few feet the previous year. But Mahoney had told me by letter that two of their Blues had only joined the crew after Christmas and his intelligence was that they were not as motivated as in previous years.

A sad note was struck as we prepared for the race. Russell Crockford, the joker from Evesham with the tough competitive streak, who had rowed in the 1978 and 1979 Boat Races, was killed in a car crash in Australia while he was on his way to take part in a regatta. There were many men in the current crew who had rowed with Russell, especially those from that uncommonly close-knit 1979 crew of mates. The memorial service held for him at his old college, Corpus, was a simple and touching affair and it moved us all to tears. We decided to remember him by naming our boat *Russell Crockford* for the 1981 race. That Carbocraft boat is still so named and is used regularly by the Oxford squad. In fact it is the only boat we own that is actually named at all, and Russell is called to mind almost daily when Oxford is training through the long winter months.

It was not easy getting back in touch with it all, straight off the plane as it were, after nearly a year away and I found myself out of sync on more than one occasion. My timing wasn't quite right and the instinctive reactions were occasionally a little off key. Certainly I knew the crew well enough; they were all graduates of some very fine Oxford crews from the past three years. But the problem was I had not come all the way with this particular unit. I did not know exactly what they had been through together and although that had always to some extent been true in the past in that they spent a large part of their preparations every year with the other coaches, there was this time a definite gap in my knowledge of them through the trials and selection of the December and January period. That they were also very good was a further difficulty because basically they had done it all before I got hold of them. They had already proved themselves and were ready to race. I felt a little like an interloper as if I was sneaking by the back door into somebody else's—Steve Royle's—territory. A coach needs to grow up with his crew if he is to take them through to the final test. Yet I was supposed to be the one who knew the Tideway and that final fortnight was supposed to be my *raison d'être*. I hoped that the crew did not feel I was the imposter I perceived myself to be. The moment I most felt this lack of synchronisation was when we gathered for the crew talk the night before the race. There were the earnest faces watching and expecting a fullsome statement of strategy and I suddenly felt overwhelmed with a feeling that I should be saying something special, something they had not heard before. I started off, but almost immediately knew that I was just going through the motions of a crew briefing. I was mouthing stuff that I had told them all before and it felt fraudulent and unconvincing. After a few moments I stopped and said: 'Let's start again. You're a smashing crew and you're set to win a lovely victory but in an odd way I don't really feel I'm part of you. There's not a lot I can tell you that you don't already know. So let's discuss the things that we must guard against'. They were too experienced, too clever to be fed platitudes. We settled instead to a general discussion of tactics.

When I mentioned this attack of self-doubt to Hugh Matheson a while later he told me that a similar thing had happened to Bob Janousek just before their Olympic final in Montreal. 'He just dried. Then he mumbled a few things and said "there's nothing more to say, go out and do your best".' It is not unusual for coaches to get more nervous than their crews come the big race and it is just as well that all the planning is done well in advance, that all the tactics are fully explored in the preceding weeks. That final talk can be pretty tense geared as it is towards reminding the crew of the salient points to remember and preparing them mentally for the battle ahead.

Mindful of the angry clashing off the start the year before and the past disagreements about the starting procedure, the umpire, who once again was Ronnie Howard, respected by both sides as one of the best and least corruptible of referees, was determined to sort out the problems between the two squads once and for all. He resissued his 1979 statement about the start and insisted on using a separate umpiring launch that would give him the flexibility to intervene should there be any difficulties during the race. He told both Presidents and coaches that he did not wish to see the sort of gamesmanship that had occurred in the last couple of years and that he would have no hesitation in disqualifying if necessary. This had not happened since 1849 when Cambridge had been ruled out after an infringement. He told us that he would place the stakeboats much closer together than the year before, allowing some ten feet between oartips, because this he believed would eliminate the desire for either cox to come across in search of a better share of the tide. In this he was absolutely right and since then both crews have gone straight from the 'go', confident that they are sharing the stream equally. With the umpire's rulings clear and uncompromising, neither side risked his displeasure and in 1981 the crews were on the stakeboats a full five minutes before race time!

The Press obsession with Sue Brown, the second most popular lady in the land after Lady Di, was wondrous to behold. She was front-page news for the first time as a 'challenger to that last great male bastion of sport, the Boat Race' when she was short-listed for the final four in December when one trial crew sank, then on crew announcement day in February, again at the crews' weigh-in where she took to the scales dressed in nothing but a skimpy rowing vest, and of course again both before and at the end of the race as the history-maker of the century. They fell over themselves to catch her whenever she spoke and in every pose, but though her good photogenic looks increased the devotion of the cameramen, her shyness and embarrassment at the attention provided little copy and few good quotes. She hated the attention most of all because it seemed to her so unjustified. 'For God's sake speak to the crew' she pleaded. 'They're the ones who are so amazing. I'm just one of nine and I'm only steering. They do all the work'. That she so obviously did not enjoy the bedlam surrounding most of the outings soothed the crew's ruffled pride somewhat although Boris and John got quite upset with the general madness on a few occasions. 'Sod off you vultures, and go back to Lady Di' was one of the more polite utterances

Oxford crew, 1981 *(left to right):* Head; Conington; Yonge; Emerton; Rankov; Mahoney; Andrews; Bland; Brown (cox)

Below left: Sue Brown and Bert Green checking the rigging

Below right: Albert Andrews, Oxford boatman

Cheering the 1981 Isis-Goldie Race *(left to right):* the author; Steve Royle; Phil Head; Chris Mahoney; Boris Rankov; Richard Emerton; Richard Yonge; Orlando Gough; Keith Mason; Nick Tee; Michael Barry; Peter Miller

BELOW

Left: Alf Twinn, Cambridge boatman

Right: John Bland and Mark Andrews training for the 1981 Race – later to win world silver medals

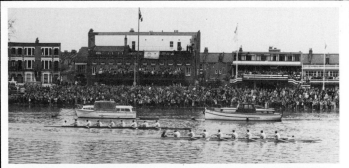

Oxford winning the Boat Race in March 1981

With friends winning the Grand at Henley against the national eight in July

Oxford crew, 1982 *(left to right):* Rob Clay; Kirkpatrick; Foster; Rankov; Yonge; Hugh Clay; Holland; Conington; Brown (cox)

Oxford crew, 1983 *(left to right):* Lang; Clay; Yonge; Jones; Rankov; Mike Evans; Mark Evans; Bland; Higgins (cox)

Oxford crew, 1984 *(left to right):* Mike Evans; Lang; Jones; Mark Evans; Rose; Stewart; Long; Clay; Lesser (cox)

Cambridge going afloat in 1982. Simon Harris *(left)*, Ewan Pearson *(right)* and Bruce Philp *(right back)* who was later to try for the 1985 Oxford crew

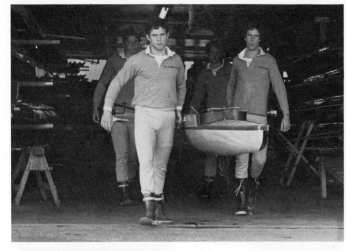

The coxes: *Top row (left to right):* Freddie Yalouris; Gareth Morris; John Calvert. *Middle row:* Colin Moynihan; John Fail; Peter Berners-Lee. *Bottom row:* Jerry Mead; Steve Higgins; Seth Lesser. Sue Brown is pictured elsewhere in the plate section

Above left: 1979 crew succumb to pressure from the sensational press

Above right: Twins 1984: Hugh and Rob Clay

Left: Twins 1983-84: Mike and Mark Evans

Below: 1984 Boat Race: 'Don't blame the cox, he's only steering the boat'

from one member of the boat. But on the whole the crew contrived to shield her as best they could and she coped well with it all most of the time.

'It was the first time that the Press had interfered with our training' said John Bland afterwards. 'Unfairly, I suppose, I blamed Sue for it, but of course it wasn't her fault. We could all see how upset she was. She was just a novelty for them.' John, the 'demented imp', though a very witty man, was also shy and he found it quite difficult to row at stroke with Sue sitting there in front of him. The others teased him but then they were used to women coxes. John was not. It was difficult to sweat and spit and fart and swear, as an oarsman does in mid-effort, with a diminutive, prim little lady perched a foot from your nose at front stops. Fine if you feel comfortable in the company of women generally, but not so easy if you've had less experience of them. Even a highly-sophisticated man about town might think twice about cursing in front of a woman. So everyone has their hang-ups. Not necessarily sexist— just a difficult situation to come to terms with. Sue for her part was desperately anxious not to make any mistakes. That was her overriding thought throughout the year. Not that she feared letting down the cause of feminism. Hers was a personal challenge. In the last fortnight, with the eight under closer control, we were able to keep the Press more successfully at bay at least until after the race. Then there was no holding them as they demanded all sorts of 'good pictures' with the whole crew and in the end she was reduced to tears by some tough questioning from a television interviewer whom we had permitted to track her progress during the last three weeks.

The affair had its funnier moments too. Our famous lady cox had also attracted the attention of the world Press and when Japanese television requested an interview Sue begged me to stay nearby to help. She certainly needed it. The interviewer was unintelligible as he read his questions from a written list in fast, stilted English. 'What's he saying?' wailed Sue, breaking into hysterical laughter before the camera as three urgent peering Japanese faces waited breathlessly for her reply to their incomprehensible question. I tried to interpret, guessing at what he was trying to say and she answered my questions which no doubt bore little resemblance to those of the interviewer. This was *cinema verité* at its wildest but it must have gone down a treat with Japanese audiences for both Oxford and Cambridge were invited a month later to go to Japan for the 50th anniversary of the annual race between the Universities of Keio and Waseda on the Sumida river in Tokyo. The event was a great success and Sue became a star overnight. Indeed she returned there to teach a year and half later having finished

209

at Oxford and came back to England in 1984 with a Japanese television crew to film the Boat Race, this time as the interviewer, still laughing uncontrollably on camera as she struggled to understand the hopeless English of her own director. The Japanese were last seen following Dick Fishlock and a group of inebriated Old Blues through the kitchens in the basement of Simpson's as they tried to smuggle them past the Cambridge organisers of the Boat Race Ball. The Light Blue Committee had refused them permission to film the post-race celebrations but Fishlock had other ideas.

When they were not talking about Sue Brown, which was rare, reporters always seized the chance to drag out the 'old chestnuts' once more, especially those who rarely covered sport, let alone the Boat Race. The 'élitist' number was given another airing, but from a slightly different angle this time. Gone was the 'Boat Race as a game of no consequence for the sons of the rich' accusation. Now it was billed differently: 'The Light Blue public schoolboys versus the Dark Blue state school lads'. With three Hampton boys, two from Abingdon, one each from Bradford, King Edward VI and Taunton and just Richard Yonge from King's School Canterbury, Oxford were the 'working class' representatives facing the nobs from the Fens. The Light Blues had their two Etonians, their two Shrewsbury men, and their chaps from Bryanston and Cheltenham, although City of London, King's College School and Kingston were allowed a ride too. The media madness reached the height of idiocy when the *Express* ran a post-race story that suggested Sue had more or less won the Boat Race single handed: 'Oxford had to take the lead from the start when they found they had drawn the Middlesex side. Sue responded magnificently! Within a minute Oxford were a length up'. Despite the crush it was all good for the Boat Race – and indirectly for the sport in general – and the crews bore it well.

But there was one story that caused us and me in particular no little irritation and that was the race report in the *New York Times* the following day. One of their reporters, a Ms Susan Heller Anderson, requested an interview with our celebrity cox a few days before the race and I agreed to let her come up to the National Westminster Bank Boathouse reception room to talk to Sue after the outing. She began her interview while the rest of the crew were showering in the changing-rooms and they emerged in dribs and drabs over the next ten minutes to join the conversation before leaving for lunch at the house. Here was yet another reporter working on the top international sports story of the year: the Oxford cox. She began to ask general questions of the other crew members as well and we were all chatting helpfully while we waited for the rest to finish showering. Then as Richard Yonge and John Bland, the two laugh-a-minute jokers of the crew, emerged she suddenly *à propos* nothing asked: 'And do you take steroids?' Neither of them had the slightest idea who she was and Richard quick as a flash replied 'Steroids? Us? Oh, of course; I have them on my breakfast cereal every morning'. Everyone laughed, including Ms Anderson. Then we saw she was busily scribbling in her little book. 'Hey listen, of course we don't', said Richard when he realised that she had taken him seriously, 'I was only kidding. It's not that sort of race. This is a private match between students not the East German Olympic crew, you know'. She smiled and said that of course she realised and after a few more moments of chat she left.

Next day I got a call from the odious Ms Anderson asking me to clear up one or two things for her story. A couple of innocuous requests for clarification were followed by her jackpot: 'And will you confirm that your crew use steroids?' 'What? You can't be serious', I replied. 'You know perfectly well they were pulling your leg.' 'So you deny it, do you?' she went on. 'Don't be ridiculous,' I said, 'you're barking up the wrong tree entirely. Of course they don't use drugs and you know it.' She persisted and I finally said 'you're just trying to invent a story. If you print a spurious thing like that we'll sue you' and put the phone down. The day after the race a reporter from a London paper called to ask me if certain drug allegations concerning Oxford had any substance. I assured him that the story was a non-starter. That was the beginning and end of it in Britain.

But a couple of days later a cutting from the *New York Times* dropped through the letterbox sent on by a friend in the States. It was a gem of misreporting. After the initial reportage of Sue Brown's amazing Boat Race victory the intrepid Ms Anderson went on: 'Earlier in the week a shadow flitted over Oxford's brilliance when two male crew members revealed in a casual conversation that they were taking steroids'. She then explained what steroids were. 'The Oxford coach Daniel Topolski, who was present when the admission was made, denied the following day that any member of his team was taking drugs. First he asserted that the statement was never made then he threatened to sue. Then he said the crew were pulling my leg. The Cambridge coach Graeme Hall said "The Cambridge team believe this is true. It fits with Oxford's good early season results and some unusual weight gains. I imagine the stroke man is on steroids, he's put on so much weight lately".' She went on to say that two East Germans had been banned from rowing for using steroids (wrong: they were Russians) and said that the drug can be easily detected by urine tests. She finished by quoting Jim Railton, rowing correspondent of *The Times*, as predicting that within two years a woman would actually row in the Boat Race for Cambridge!

We were appalled by the poor standard, mischievousness and inaccuracy of the article and sought advice. We were told that to sue in America would cost more than any damages we might be awarded and I was urged instead to seek a printed apology from the editor. We did the internationally recognised urine tests on the crew as evidence, which needless to say were negative, and sent them to the *New York Times* but in spite of the obvious libel the supposedly honourable American newspaper refused to budge. It was depressing too that Graeme Hall should have given credence to the idea since he could hardly have believed the things attributed to him in the article. Later when I asked him about it he was very noncommittal. Clearly Cambridge saw no reason to help us refute the allegations even though it represented a nasty slur on the event as a whole. Encouraging whispers of foul play was becoming part of their armoury against us but that was the price one paid for winning. Although we pursued an apology from the *New York Times* for many months none was forthcoming and the affair passed into oblivion.

On the home front the newspapers made much play of the fact that in our small Putney house where Orlando Gough, brother of Piers, was once more doing the cooking, there was little room to house a rowing eight, coach and cook as well as a female cox. Where, they all wanted to know, did she sleep? Or, more importantly: with whom did she share a room? The clamour for the unexpurgated truth grew and grew until we finally had to reveal that she did in fact have a place to herself—the bathroom on the top floor. That it was a spacious, carpeted bathroom mattered not: Sue in the loo! The papers loved it, although the more serious rowing correspondents preferred to investigate more important stories. Why for instance was Mr Conington's hand swathed in bandages when the crew took to the water for their first Tideway outing?

For a while we tried to keep this incident secret. A knife had slipped while he was cutting a slice of bread, we explained. Other reasons did not ring true either and finally when the journalists came for dinner a few nights later the real story emerged. The President, on discovering two Asaghi spears which belonged to our hosts and which I had carefully hidden, challenged the long-suffering Conington, Mahoney's erstwhile sidekick and scapegoat whom he nicknamed Norm, to a duel to the death to take place in the front living-room. The President's initial assault proved so realistic and violent that 'Norm' reached out involuntarily with his arm to ward off the blow, grasping the wicked edge of the spear in his hand. Much blood, wailing, hospital visits and stitches were the result. The weapons were confiscated and the accident-prone 'Norm' and the rest of the crew were instructed not to respond to any more of their President's taunting and his usually impossible trials by fire until after the Boat Race. Then if they wished to kill themselves or each other they could do so. But they could not resist. We nearly lost half the crew on the Isle of Wight when their unremitting leader found another challenge to test their nerves. A long wooden groyne protruded out to sea from the shore and was at the time being violently lashed by high waves. The selected game of 'chicken' involved them risking life and limb by clambering out along the promontory and waiting until the last perilous moment when they were about to be washed away before scampering back to safety. It seemed they were doing everything possible to give Cambridge a sporting chance.

Something else that seemed to be threatening to give Cambridge a chance was the seats in our new Carbocraft boat. They were twisting badly on their slide beds which caused them to jam while the crew was training. Regularly Mahoney and Andrews were forced to stop rowing while they readjusted their seats. We sent them back and we were supplied with new ones. But after a few days it was obvious that these were no better. Time was running short and we called the boatbuilders down once more to explain the problem. The plastic they used was just not strong enough and though they argued that no one else seemed to have such problems with their equipment we were adamant. We insisted on wooden fixtures which we were told would require an all-night effort by their work team. Eventually our persistence was rewarded and we took delivery of an excellent set of seats a couple of days before the race.

Every year there were those last-minute adjustments to make to the boat. As the crew improved the rigging needed to come down a bit, or the gearing needed small alterations. The better the crew the more worried I was about extraneous things interfering with the result of the race. If we faced a tight battle I could concentrate on the men, but if they were good, I would spend hours fretting about all the mechanical things that could go wrong to deny them victory. The possibility of a fine crew, obviously superior, losing by accident or through negligence was a recurrent nightmare. Favourites in the Boat Race had a habit of falling on their faces. In order to relieve them of any complacency I related the tragedy of one of the best crews that Oxford has ever produced. Convinced of their superiority over Cambridge, they turned their attentions to the course record. The cox made a list of the intermediate times and attached it to his knee so that he could keep the crew informed of their progress throughout the race. Oblivious to the Light Blue challenge alongside, Oxford sailed through the intermediate markers well within the record. They were confident that the busy crew next to them would fade away as the pace began to hurt and did not bother to respond to their bursts. Oxford broke the course record that year, but then so did Cambridge who finished two lengths ahead. Complacency–what a boat stopper. The 1952 Cambridge crew, boating five European Championship oarsmen, suffered the same fate. A month before the race they were five to one favourites, but they lost by a canvas.

Boris, who was about to become the first man from a women's college to row in the race, was another casualty in the last couple of weeks. He went down with a stomach bug and for a couple of days his power in the middle of the boat was sorely missed. 'You really feel it if Boris isn't there', said Mahoney who rowed in the seat in front of him. 'It's a great comfort to have him sitting there whacking the catch every stroke.' Boris had initially decided not to row at the beginning of training but the lure of the Boat Race was too great. 'I just love beating Cambridge' he told me by way of explanation when I got back from South America. 'And I couldn't have borne sitting on the launch watching Chris, 'Norm' and 'Spunky' kicking hell out of the Tabs without me.' He also hated missing the encounters we had during a weekend's work with the national eight. In his place we had recruited Ian McNuff, a member of the successful London Rowing Club four which had won three bronze medals at World and Olympic Championships.

The racing was hard, charged up as it was by the squad's determination not to suffer the indignity of a defeat at the hands of the student crew however fast it was reputed to be, and Oxford's resolve to maintain their unbeaten record. With Colin Moynihan in the cox's seat for the national team against his old school coxed by the inexperienced Sue Brown, we did not expect a barging match especially from so professional a crew as the British eight. But they were intent on winning no matter what the cost in dignity or damaged equipment. Obviously they suspected that they might not quite have the edge on us and so they expected their cox to do the business. That Colin apologised later did not help. 'At least it gave Sue a real taste of what can happen', he ventured a little weakly in the London Rowing Club bar that evening.

On the Saturday we raced them three times over three minutes, two of which races had to be aborted because of clashes and Oxford winning the third. The next day we planned two bridge to bridge rows, swapping stations after the first to make it fair. Oxford won the first seven-minute contest by a clear length. Then the crews turned and paddled back to Hammersmith for the second race. Within a minute the national squad, starting very fast, had taken three-quarters of a length but Oxford began to hold as the bend unfurled. Moynihan then veered across Oxford's bows and the ensuing clash resulted in a blade handle crashing across Conington's back and a slide jamming tight. Oxford ground to a halt, unable to continue, and the national crewmen, with great victorious war whoops, scooted off into the distance. Although their embarrassed coach Penny Chuter agreed to restart the piece her crew would not and the exercise was abandoned. It was a poor display by Britain's top eight but in a way their behaviour was a reflection of how the reputation of the 1981 Oxford crew preceded it. Chris Mahoney and the crew harboured their anger for months until they met the national eight once again in the final of the Grand Challenge Cup at Henley.

While Oxford had been battling it out on the Thames at Hammersmith, Cambridge had suffered an 18-second defeat in the Kingston Head at the hands of the home side. Isis, who had anticipated the chance to race Cambridge with relish, crashed into an errant four in mid-course at a point where they were reported to be holding their own as number one starter against the eventual winners Kingston. The last week of training further confirmed Oxford as hot favourites when they raced the lightweights over their now traditional final set-piece of seven minutes between the bridges. The London boys had finished fifth in the Head only a few days before and when Oxford raced to a comfortable 15-second or five-length victory over them at Putney the towpath gossip suggested that Oxford would have won the Open Head. Next day Cambridge, in a risky show of brinkmanship, also took on the lightweights for a four-minute effort and finished a length up slumped over their oars with exhaustion. It was a hurried, desperate performance. At the same stage the day before Oxford had been striding along strongly three lengths up. The evidence was there. All we had to do was avoid making any foolish mistakes.

We were anxious not to put Sue under any more pressure than she already had and it seemed that, with Cambridge's pushing approach to the Middlesex course at the start clear from the previous year's experience, we would be better off taking the Middlesex station ourselves if we got the choice. With its initial bend advantage and our undoubted speed off the start we would be able to avoid a repetition of those Light Blue clash and bash tactics and the possibility of damage, and it would also protect Sue from a potentially difficult situation. We believed she was quite capable of handling Wigglesworth but we were not inclined to take a chance that was not necessary. Besides she was still not fully conversant with the Tideway course and had over the previous weeks reacted nervously to criticism. To ease the pressure further I took her for an afternoon visit to the London Spring Fashion displays in central London. Apart from enjoying the shows, the attention she received boosted her confidence and took her mind off the imminent event. The day before the race, we attended our traditional film show laid on by the most loyal of our non-Blue supporters Cecil Foster Kemp. The pre-release film for the 1981 crew was *Chariots of Fire*–the best possible choice for a Boat Race crew facing their biggest test. For athletes, the film was an excellent motivator, and after meeting the leading actors in the film the crew were given albums of the soundtrack. The stirring theme music from the film echoed through our house all evening and the crew break-fasted to more of the same next morning. They rode the bus to the river uplifted by the triumphant Vangelis score.

We had been right to think in terms of the Middlesex station. After objecting to the 1829 gold sovereign traditionally used for the toss, saying it was biased after so many years of successful Oxford calls, the Cambridge President James Palmer was overruled but called correctly all the same. He chose Surrey. 'It makes a change' he said when asked the reason for his choice by the BBC interviewer. 'The scenery is different on Surrey.' It was not the scenery that either crew was concerned about as they warmed up below Putney Bridge. They were watching each other. 'We rowed a brilliant practice start' recalls Chris Mahoney, 'right in front of them. It couldn't have done their morale much good. Our start in the actual race wasn't nearly as good.'

Maybe, but it was good enough to take them clear within 45 seconds. John Bland just stormed away on a slack tide as he effected what seemed like a gear change after the first ten strokes. For the first 15 seconds the crews remained level and Cambridge appeared to be holding their own. Twenty strokes later Oxford were a length up. It was phenomenal. And it went on like that. John never let up, striking 34 nearly all the way. Within a minute Sue had the river to herself and could steer as she liked. She took a traditional fast-stream course, going a little wide round the corners, but Cambridge were never a danger. They had dropped to a sedate 33 as if bowing to the inevitable and as the crews passed the Mile Oxford led by three lengths. The water was bouncy there until Hammersmith but after that the conditions were lovely if slow. Passing Chiswick Eyot, Sue called for the special 20-stroke burst they had promised to dedicate to Steve Royle and at the Steps they were leading by five lengths. They charged on, delighting in their increasing lead and the strong flowing rhythm of their stroke, and they crossed the line eight lengths ahead, the biggest winning Oxford margin since 1898. 'Because of all the excuses of the previous three years we had been out to inflict a crushing defeat on them,' recalls Boris, 'something, close to that record 20-length one, about which there could be no doubt.' John Bland reinforces the attitude that motivated them. 'All we kept hearing was "gallant Tabs", "so brave in defeat", "lucky Oxford"–even from people on our own side. So we decided to put the record straight. We went out to win by as much as possible.'

'Everyone knew we were going to win', says Chris Mahoney now. 'The question was by how much. We howled down Richard Emerton when he suggested after the briefing that we should sit on them once we got four lengths up. Complacency was a bit of a danger and the main job in the last couple of weeks was to keep ourselves on the boil. I always thought the Tabs were soft, a bit like schoolboys hoping they wouldn't lose by too much. But I couldn't believe how slow they were on the day. At the Mile Post we were three lengths up and I had to cough back a little chortle.'

'We went damned hard to Barnes' adds Boris, 'and everyone was pretty cooked. We would have settled to carry on at 34 to the end, which was two pips over the Tabs anyway, but as we came through the bridge John Bland at stroke, through Sue, called to go up one and to our dismay he did. I remember hearing Mahoney in front of me groaning and cursing John under his breath. We wound it up all the way to the finish and did what was probably our best rowing of the whole race. In the end we were all a bit disappointed with the eight-length verdict. I still don't know how we didn't take more.'

Not since 1898 had Oxford won six Boat Races in a row and now they had avenged those six Cambridge wins a decade earlier. The 1981 crew was a very good crew. The Press followed us all over London for the rest of the day, through the night at the Blues dinner, which Sue was the first woman ever to attend, and then on to the Ball. They were there next morning too as we emerged bleary-eyed for breakfast. 'We've brought your Mum and Dad up from Devon, Sue', they said. 'Can we have some family photos?' One news article declared what an out-of-date, inconsequential affair the Boat Race was while another predicted that as usual the Boat Race crews would break up. In fact both reports were wrong. The two 'Varsity crews were invited to Japan less than a month later where they repeated the race before a large enthusiastic crowd and beneath a squadron of pursuing helicopters which blew them across the Sumida river in an alarming way. On the plane home we planned our Henley assault. This time it was going to be serious.

The Grand Challenge Cup was our aim but one or two of the crew were sceptical about our chances. They remembered the disappointing performances in recent years when exams and lack of commitment had torpedoed any real hopes of success. Richard Emerton and Phil were not keen anyway and I promised to find replacements in whom the rest could have confidence. Chris wanted to concentrate on his exams but a little arm-twisting and the agreement to join us of three top class semi-retired internationals, team-mates of his from the Olympic squad, finally hooked him in. Some persistent negotiating recruited the services of bronze medallist Charly Wiggin and silver medallists Andrew Justice and Alan Whitwell. All three were very experienced competitors and they relished the opportunity to challenge the national eight designate as guest members of the best Oxford crew for many years. They became honorary Dark Blues and we rowed as Oxford/Thames Tradesmen training in the eight at weekends but working in sculls and a coxed four during the week. The daily rowing that John, Boris, Mark and Andrew did under the guidance of John Pilgrim Morris in a not very comfortable coxed four provided the hard backbone to the crew. I took them at the weekends in the eight at Pangbourne initially, and Steve Royle took them over for the last couple of weeks when their exams were finished and they were able to get out daily. I felt a touch of envy about relinquishing the coaching job but had to finish my South America book, and I was able to take only a back seat interest in their progress at Henley.

With Charly and Alan in the two bow seats and Andrew at five (Boris had to change sides to row at four) the crew looked strong but a bit rough and we all had our doubts at times about whether they could pull it off. To gain extra pace we borrowed the Thames Tradesmen's Empacher boat which had had considerable success in international competition. Once exams were over the crew was able to boat regularly and they picked up speed rapidly. By Henley they were clearly fast but at the time we felt probably not quite fast enough. Indeed in the few days leading up to the race they were still straining hard to find the necessary rhythm. But we hadn't reckoned on our wild card, stroke John Bland, and the wealth of experience and extra reserves of toughness lying potent but untapped below the surface. The squad had a relatively comfortable passage to the final, disposing of the American

Universities Boston and Washington by nearly three lengths apiece. University of London went very quickly against Cornell in the first round while we in a hard draw dealt in similar but slower fashion with Yale, considered to be the fastest of the American challengers. Probably the more testing draw played a useful part in bringing on our untried crew. With all the Yank crews ejected from the Grand contest the stage was set for the three very fast British crews to fight it out between themselves. Oxford were drawn against London University in the semi-final and it turned out to be a boneshaker. But the one-length victory over the 'Purples' was nothing compared to the final next day which proved to be one of the best races ever seen on the Henley course.

In cold headwindy conditions, and with Princess Grace and husband Prince Rainier of Monaco spectating from the launch, the crews leaped away at the 'go' and within a minute the squad stroked by Richard Stanhope had taken a three-quarters of a length lead. It was nearly a length at the Barrier and the race seemed decided. It was unthinkable that a national crew of this calibre could be overhauled. But John Bland set about performing the unthinkable. The memory of their rough Tideway encounter before the Boat Race spurred them, and they began a sustained attack that took their bow bobble inexorably up along the length of the squad shell until just past Remenham the crews were level. Now came the crunch. Could they extend that spurt, add to the pressure after such an energy-sapping recovery or would they fold up under fire? The big four, Boris, Andrew, Mark and John, hardened by their daily work as a unit, lengthened their stroke.

Oxford did not falter. But the national squad did. As the crews reached the Enclosure Oxford dug deeper and the bladework of the national team men began to lose cohesion. In a moment Oxford were through and pressing for the line. Half a length separated the crews as they finished, clenched fists of victory punching the air. John Bland, who had rowed himself to a standstill, had to be given oxygen. In the launch my exultant jig of triumph was observed with amusement by the Monaco Royals and with a wry smile by national coach Penny Chuter. It was Oxford's first Grand win for 128 years. 'That Henley win was probably my most enjoyable one' reckons Chris Mahoney. 'Even more so than the Olympic silver. I guess the 1980 race was the hardest of all, though. That and the Olympic final in Moscow.' A week later, the Squad and UL both raced excellently at the major international regatta of the year in Lucerne. The commentator there was well enough briefed to tell the crowds that Britain had a third world class crew at home which had beaten both the ones on show. With three crews capable of reaching a World Championship final, it was obvious that the surplus of talent should be pooled to produce a medal class national eight.

We at Oxford were bent on trying to win selection outright at the National Championships. It seemed likely after discussions with the Chairman of Selectors that if we won there as well we would be in a position to use our crew as the base unit and strengthen it using one or two of the squad eight's top men. London University went on to the World Under-23 Games and left the stage clear for a final confrontation between the two top boats. We hoped that a two-week planned approach to the race would give us the edge over the squad crew which had travelled and raced twice during the intervening weekend. In the event those Lucerne races where they beat the East Germans probably added extra edge to their rowing and considerably restored their confidence. The final provided yet another stupendous race between the two crews. The national team slipped once again into a half length lead at 500 metres but this time they were ready for our midway assault and though Oxford attacked again and again the squad reversed the Henley decision to win by half a length.

The initiative had now reverted to the national eight and their coach Penny Chuter and six Oxford/Thames Tradesmen men were asked to join trials to form a stronger crew. The two uninvited men were Boris Rankov and Richard Yonge who took to a coxed pair to challenge for a team place at Munich but lost out to the strong UL boat, Tom Cadoux-Hudson and Richard Budgett, who were eventual winners of the bronze medal. Penny Chuter spent a hectic week selecting the eight and incorporated Chris Mahoney, John Bland, Mark Andrews, and Tradesmen's Andrew Justice into the final line-up which went on to win a silver in Munich. Charly Wiggin and Alan Whitwell returned to the semi-retirement from whence they had so abruptly but successfully emerged three months earlier.

II
Another Close Shave

Nick Conington, Oxford's President elect, who had survived a challenge for the post from Richard Yonge now looked forward to another winning year as he surveyed the exceptional returning talent. Apart from himself there were Rankov, Yonge, Bland, Andrews, Emerton and Sue Brown from the 1981 crew plus Steve Francis from 1980 and a welter of good Isis men including the Clay twins, Steve Foster, John Graham and Nick Holland. But as term began those five gifted Blues announced their retirement and the future turned from rosy to bleak overnight. These were fatal blows, especially the withdrawal of the two silver medallists. Cambridge had a large and talented freshman intake and their new President, Roger Stephens, was in the process of radically reforming his club under the guidance of his chief coach Graeme Hall. The Oxford resignations played right into the hands of the Light Blues.

Despite the set-back we settled down to bring on our remaining men, both technically and in terms of strength, as best we could. The five renegades resisted all Presidential entreaties to return to the fold right through that first term, but confidence began to grow as we watched our embryo squad developing. Freshmen like Alan Kirkpatrick, a graduate from Durham, Chris Long and Pete Buchanan and college-taught men Jim Stewart, Steve Potts, Simon Oldfield, Mike Stewart, Mark Bloomfield and Tony Mitchell were performing well. Also the 1980 Isis oarsman from Hampton Dave Todd was back for another try. Our two trial eights under John Pilgrim Morris and Charly Wiggin looked respectable enough but we still needed a touch more weight and experience. Comparing the results of the Oxford and Cambridge squads in sculling Heads, there was little to choose between them at the end of the first term.

A last attempt was made to seduce the obstinate wallflowers from their books and this time Conington's efforts bore fruit. Loyalty to the cause and comradeship with their anxious President finally persuaded first Yonge and then Rankov to sign up. Although their late return was likely to be a blow to the hopes of two other men should the newcomers be fit and fast enough to win selection these potentially morale-damaging decisions had to be weighed against the undisputed talent of the two returning Blues. In the event it took them little time to establish themselves near the top end of the squad. Rankov had vowed never to touch an oar again after his rejection by the national selectors following those memorable races with the squad. He perceived a personal vendetta against him and in truth he had reason to feel aggrieved. They had refused to be impressed by his four Boat Race successes and his obvious power in the middle of an eight and this cut deep. He longed to represent Britain, to vie for a world medal, but he was constantly turned away. Furthermore he had just married his girlfriend Katy and he did not want rowing to distract him from their first months together. But eventually the lure of the Boat Race once again began to weave its magic and with his wife's blessing he joined up soon after Richard in early January, a stone overweight after five months of inactivity. 'Will we win?' he asked me as he arrived for the first session. 'If we pull out all the stops now and if you can get yourself race fit by March then I think we can', I replied. He shed a stone in two weeks and was back to full strength by race day. Boris's return was quite a blow to us' says Roger Stephens. 'Although we knew he wasn't fit, it had a deep psychological effect on the Cambridge men.'

Sue Brown expected little competition for her place this second time around and it took some time and a tough challenge from the Isis cox Steve Higgins to jog her into a full commitment to begin with. She had more confidence now and was more relaxed, but she also seemed less thorough. The choice went to her in the end because she was marginally the better cox although the coaches were still looking for a big improvement in performance and delayed selection until well into February. That improvement did not really reveal itself until the day of the race when she responded magnificently to the pressures of the moment and played a major and positive role in the outcome. While coxswains can usually influence a race by losing ground for their crew, it is hard for them to win races. However Sue's contribution in 1982 was that she read the race excellently and steered an aggressive course which positioned her crew perfectly for the all important *coup de grâce*. She made no mistakes.

Steve Higgins withdrew, unwilling to cox Isis for a second year and John Healey came in to replace him. The Press had made much of one of our trial coxes, Derek Ward-Thomson, a thalidomide victim who steered the boat very efficiently with his fingers using lengths of string attached to the rudder. Fleet Street was almost as disappointed as David when he narrowly failed to win the Isis nomination. Although Steve Francis again failed in his quest for a second Blue, he decided that another race over the Championship course was due especially after the considerable training he had done, and he elected to row for

Isis. Over the years few Old Blues at Oxford were prepared to row for the reserves deeming their non-selection to be a humiliating affront and deciding that their time could be more usefully spent elsewhere. The concept of squad membership and loyalty tended to take second place to the pursuit of a Blue and the unsuccessful third-year candidates, particularly if they were previous Boat Race contestants, usually shunned a seat in the second boat. An understandable reaction perhaps, but it was difficult for coaches to train a squad with the threat of resignation by leading contenders constantly hanging in the air. At Cambridge, Blues seemed more prepared to go on rowing for the squad even when dropped from the first boat and indeed the 1984 winning Goldie crew contained two double Blues, Heard and Philp, and a third-year reserve man Roberts in their line-up. Steve Francis displayed a similar and commendable loyalty to his squad-mates and contributed much to Isis's narrow one and a half length victory over Goldie in the 1982 mini-Boat Race.

It was a very difficult year. President Nick Conington, an efficient and popular man from that hard rowing nursery at Hampton school, had been stroke of the British junior eight in 1977 and 1978 and he was determined not to preside over a year in which Oxford might lose their winning ways. He was perhaps less assertive than his predecessor whom he so admired but he was no less single-minded. He passed much of the responsibility for the crew's preparation to the coaches which in the event proved to be a fortuitous move because he was forced to spend periods out of the boat due to his recurring glandular fever. At the beginning of the year he seemed a good bet for the stroke seat despite being President, but increasingly it became clear that with all the pressures of office and ill-health we dared not rely on him for such a key position. If illness forced him out of the boat at the last minute it would be far easier to replace him at bow or two than down in the stern with the resultant disruption to the crew's cohesion and morale.

The problem next, therefore, was to decide on the best alternative stroke. Nick Holland had stroked the 1980 Isis crew which broke a Goldie run of success but though strong he was a little inconsistent in his rowing. One of the necessary characteristics of a stroke is a steady rhythm but we tried him there for a while anyway and he did the job well. Nick also had the added advantage of being able to row effectively on both sides, a difficult thing to do and this talent more than once stood us in good stead through the winter months and in early competition. The only other alternative in the light of the library-bound absence of John Bland, the 1981 stroke, was Rob Clay, who had stroked the winning Isis crew the year before and had led a good four in the national trials after Christmas. He was a bowside oarsman however, and to put him at stroke would mean boating a crew sitting in mirror image to the normal line-up. Although theoretically there was nothing wrong with such an arrangement it was a rarely used seating plan yet on the three occasions it had been done before in the Boat Race the crews had been victorious. However, even if we did adopt a bowside-stroked line-up we did not really have a natural seven man. Boris was not fluid enough and anyway his strength was needed in the middle of the boat; Richard was the same while the ambidextrous Holland was most useful to us on bowside. Rob's twin brother Hugh was a possibility, but he did not enjoy rowing in the stern and tended to get short when he was tired. He too was better as a mid-boat puller. Besides he and his brother never seemed to row well one behind the other. They argued a lot too and even at school they had never worked well in a pair. It was better to keep them apart in the boat, a fact they both readily acknowledged.

They were however a very talented pair, though very different in temperament and appearance. They may have presented shy and unassuming fronts but they were both possessed with an uncommon obstinacy and strength of purpose. Rob could explode with anger in the boat, accuse all around him of not rowing properly and usually identify a failure in technique with unnerving accuracy. 'People just aren't holding their finishes' he would say furiously. His own finish was usually demonstrating the point best! His outbursts were always a surprise because, though a very tense individual, he was usually so quiet. His brother Hugh was more phlegmatic, always ready with a quizzical grin but also very silent. Whenever there was a noisy discussion going on at dinner, someone would always say 'Shut up, Hugh' or 'God, Hugh, you just never stop rabbitting on' or 'will you let someone else get a word in' to the mute figure sitting at the end of the table. Mealtimes were invariably hilarious occasions when everyone could relax. The Clays were often teased about their diffident manner and their fraternal bickering although in truth they were very close and went sailing together most summers. Their rowing, though a little awkward and unorthodox (and very different the one from the other) was very effective and Rob particularly was highly motivated and a terrific boat mover although not very strong in the gym.

They came from a rowing family too and both had long dreamed of rowing in the Boat Race. Their older brother Henry had rowed for Cambridge three times, winning in 1975 and losing in 1974 and 1976, and was later a member of the national squad winning an Olympic silver in 1980. Their father John was a losing Oxford Blue in 1949 and 1950 and their great uncle won three times for Cambridge. To redress the Clays' Boat Race record John's twin sons both won twice – together in 1982 and separately in 1983 and 1984. Clay Senior was always an uncompromising critic of his sons' rowing performances, telling them precisely what he thought with no sweetening of the pill, but he was a regular visitor on the launch and immensely proud of the twins' achievement – the first twins ever to compete together in the event.

We staged another neck and neck race in our series of trials in December, the crews overlapping all the way over the full track. Only the President and Sue from the previous year's crew were on show. Nevertheless the standard was still high and we settled to a further ten-day training camp in freezing snowy conditions at Oxford which culminated with our participation in the national squad trials on the Tideway. These 26-minute races in fours in blizzard weather were very gruelling but the Oxford crews showed up well and learned a lot about hard racing over that weekend. They also had the chance to catch a glimpse of Cambridge who raced their trials from Kew to just short of Hammersmith Bridge where we were standing in wait, and there were challenging shouts from the Cambridge launch as they swept by beneath us. The Oxford boys went off for their Christmas break well roused up by such early displays of aggression from the rival camp, and carried out their vacation training programme with renewed determination.

When all the January tests had been completed and the eight men selected, we began by boating the eight with the President at stroke, Holland in the seven seat, Rankov at six and the Clays in the bows. Our first fixture as a crew was against the strong University of London, winners of the World Under-23 Championships, who had two world bronze medallists, Budgett and Cadoux-Hudson, and five other senior national squad men on board. Richard Budgett, a young blond giant, had an interesting rowing history. While a student at Cambridge, he was rejected by the coaches because he was considered too awkward and long. He did not even make their trial crews. However within a year of leaving Cambridge and going to London University he became the anchor man of their eight and finished third in the world in coxed pairs that summer. Three years later he rowed in Britain's first Olympic gold medal-winning crew since 1948. Geraint Fuller, also a member of the UL eight, was another Light Blue reject. He rowed with Budgett in the British 1982 coxed four and came fifth!

In the middle of the last of a series of short encounters on the Saturday a clash of blades caused an oar handle to hit the Oxford stroke

Conington in the back and the Dark Blues retired injured from the fray. The races had been close with the UL cox Ellison giving first Steve Higgins and then Sue Brown a difficult time but we seemed to have got the measure of them. Three seven-minute rows were planned for the Sunday. Conington seemed recovered by the morning and we went afloat in good heart. In the first row, Oxford took a good lead to begin with but at the end, Conington at stroke was in obvious distress as UL closed to just short of a length. A combination of the injury sustained the day before and a general malaise from a reprise of his glandular fever indicated that we should call a halt to the racing. However I was loth to lose the competitive practice. Since we had stopped close to the UL boathouse, I suggested to their coach Rusty Williams that if he could find a substitute for us we would carry on with the programme. My reasoning was twofold. On the practical side it would give us the opportunity of seeing how well the crew coped in adversity, an important characteristic for Boat Race crews, and secondly we could also study them in an alternative line-up in anticipation of the unhappy possibility that Nick's illness could prove permanent. So we moved our seven man Nick Holland to stroke, which required him to swap sides, and we brought Rob Clay down from bow to seven in his place. Dominic Reimbold, a UL Youth international, recently recovered from a severe bout of angina, was recruited to take over Rob's seat at bow.

The second race started opposite the UL boathouse and the crews raced level for four minutes after which UL on the inside of the Barnes bend began to move into the lead. It then became apparent that Reimbold was in trouble and once again we had to stop the battling crews. He was slumped over his oar gasping for breath when we got alongside the boat and we helped him into the launch and wrapped him up in sweaters. But still we wanted to complete the fixture, so I climbed into the bow seat and we lined up for the last piece of work. It was a difficult and unsettling test but we managed to hold off the UL assaults with the help of the Barnes bend to finish half a length up at the end of seven minutes. The crew were exultant and there was much trium-phant punching of the air amidships. It had in the end proved to be an excellent psychological booster for them. To win against such a classy UL crew despite the series of mishaps and mid-outing crew changes gave great encouragement of their flexibility, tenacity and their ability to handle all manner of set-backs. However our results against the Londoners were very similar to those of Cambridge in earlier meet-ings. Following a session against the lightweights soon after when he again felt queasy, the President was told to take a week's rest and go for blood tests. Time was running out and we had to reconsider our options. We completely re-seated the crew with Rob stroking on bowside, the freshman Alan Kirkpatrick at seven on strokeside and a series of substitutes occupying the bows in place of the ailing 'Norm'. Steve Foster, the secretary, was also out for a few days with 'flu during this period which made Mike Spracklen's job as coach for the fortnight very difficult. The new line-up was not ideal because Alan was not really a seven man but Rob set a good attacking rhythm and the crew seemed to go well. When Conington returned to the boat, he was directed to the bow seat from whence he did not move again.

Under the tutelage of Hugh Matheson at Pangbourne the crew began to pick up pace again, but they had to fight hard to beat Hugh's Nottingham squad crew which came to visit one weekend. However two weeks after this the Reading Head title was successfully defended at the end of Steve Royle's coaching stint, and afterwards we discussed at length the advisability of moving the President back to stroke. He was keen but in the end we decided not to risk it. At this stage the coaches were under the impression that the tests on Conington had been negative and that he was now rid of his glandular fever, for to row with such a virus could not only jeopardise the crew's chances it could also cause permanent damage to his health. But the fact was that he was not completely in the clear. He carried alone the burden of knowing he was not fully recovered for the next three weeks, not daring to confide in anyone for fear he would have to step down from the crew. Although he believed he was strong enough to row he was still very concerned about whether he was doing the right thing.

Guides to form were presented by the Isis crew's performances at the various Head contests leading up to the Boat Race. At Reading they beat Goldie by three seconds, finishing 36 seconds down on the Oxford Blue Boat. The following weekend, they finished 25 seconds behind Cambridge at the longer Kingston Head which suggested that Oxford had the greater overall speed compared to their rivals but that tactics in the first part of the race on the day would play an important role. Our take-off speed was a little suspect and we took on the national sculling squad eight (who later finished a close second in the Tideway Head), coached by Mike Spracklen, for a bridge to bridge race to sharpen up the first seven minutes. Oxford raced well beating the scullers by two thirds of a length and the record to Putney Bridge by 18 seconds. But Cambridge too had been showing good early pace against respectable opposition. They had raced UL early in training and had beaten them twice by one third of a length over three minutes but had lost a third race by a length. I also watched a number of their sessions on the Tideway from my sculling boat—a favourite vantage point—and could see that though a young crew, they were highly motivated and were travelling very quickly in their bright yellow plastic Empacher boat. They scowled aggressively at me as they passed, all except their bowman, Paul Brine, who grinned confidently. Five days before race day they broke the Hammersmith to the University Stone record in a race against the national lightweights winning by three lengths. Next day in a calculated display of brinkmanship Oxford rowed the same stretch against the same opponents and further lowered that record by seven seconds. They also added a further three lengths to the winning margin. I had wanted, as in 1980, to see precisely what we were up against. The gamble paid off well. However, comparing the performances more closely the additional Oxford lengths had come in the second half of the row. At the halfway point we had if anything been a little behind on the Cambridge margin.

We had therefore to consider our tactics carefully. We would need to be in top gear but cruising in the first few minutes in order to contain a fast Cambridge start. Then we would have to apply pressure at Harrods. In the event, we rowed below our form for the first four minutes and all but relinquished the initiative to the Light Blues in a very fast first mile. They rowed above themselves, settling to a good rhythm and attacking all the time, and they took the race to us using the inside of the first bend to the best advantage. Although Cambridge had the heaviest man in either crew, Bruce Philp at 15 stone three pounds, Oxford were the heavier team, weighing in at an average of 13 stone 13 and three-quarter pounds. Their rivals, at 13 stone three and three-quarters had to contend with a ten pound a man disadvantage, a difference that could tell against them in the later stages of the race especially if the prevailing wind was head. The Light Blue stroke Simon Harris was, at 11 stone five pounds, the lightest man in the race but he was an experienced club oarsman. He set a fine rhythm for his crew and rowed longer than many oarsmen three stone heavier and eight inches taller. Despite his diminutive appearance he was a tenacious bugger, like all the best lightweights, and a proven race winner. He had been forced to drop out of Goldie a year earlier when he contracted glandular fever. Now he and the fast sculler Ewan Pearson, a virtual lightweight himself, made an aggressive stern pair in the Cambridge boat. These were the two men we worried about most. If they could provide the right pace for the big 14- and 15-stone men, Philp, Heard, Bliss and Stephens, behind them the Cambridge crew would put us under real pressure. The previous year's one-sided contest was now a dim and distant memory.

The Cambridge President, Roger Stephens, had streamlined his system very much in the way we had done back in 1973. He reduced his coaching team to those who could devote the necessary time adding national women's coach Alan Inns and Olympic silver medallist John Pritchard to the line-up; he risked the wrath of the college captains by withdrawing his squad from all inter-college rowing, contacted all arriving freshmen early and began their training well before the start of term, much of it on the Tideway; he introduced weight-training and running before breakfast and full weekend rowing sessions, bought two plastic Empacher eights and re-equipped the CUBC devoting £30,000 to the refurbishment of the Light Blue programme. They even rented a private house in Putney across the street from ours for the last fortnight. Furthermore they challenged all the top British crews they could find. With Graeme Hall's Olympic experience to back him up, Stephens brought about a small revolution on the Cam. They took pride in the heavy workload they had undertaken and believed that they were working harder than Oxford and must therefore be fitter. Probably the training programmes of the two squads were not dissimilar, for apart from the late returning Rankov there was no doubting the endurance fitness of the Dark Blues. Far from standing still and resting on our laurels year after year, we were continually adapting the programme we had evolved a decade earlier. Every winter the load increased and the type of training changed to keep in step with the Cambridge challenge. When things looked to be particularly tough we revised the programme accordingly. So far it had worked but every year it was getting more and more difficult to stay ahead as Cambridge refined their approach and increased their efforts.

I had studied this good-looking Cambridge crew in practice rather more carefully than I had their predecessors, searching out their vulnerable points. I learned that they were an exceptionally aggressive race fit crew which tended to push hard at about two minutes against their opposition and this alerted us to their probable race tactics on the day. They had a second session with London University which they lost by three-quarters of a length in a bad tempered affair, but before we could gain any boost to morale from their defeat we took on the national squad second eight (their first eight having refused to race us although they had paced Cambridge a few weeks earlier), rowing in Kingston colours, for the first half of a row to the Steps and were hammered. 'But they cheated', complained some of the crew rather pointlessly later. 'They cut across the Fulham flats.' Recognising that there was barely any tide running, Richard Ayling, their coach, had advised the Kingston boys and Peter Berners Lee, their ex-Oxford Blue cox, to cut the corner out of the rough water and then move across after the football ground. It was a clever move and one that we had not anticipated and although it provided little in the way of a useful contest for either crew (they were so far apart they hardly saw each other throughout the race) it taught us a number of useful lessons. It reminded us that on a dead tide a good couple of lengths could be gained under the Middlesex bank (although the Boat Race is usually rowed on the fastest tides and such tactics are less likely to be successful). It also impressed upon Sue the dangers of not covering the tactics of the opposing crew and it told us all that no matter where the opposition went, the crew had to be alert to them and had to respond.

Rob at stroke had the biggest responsibility for the crew's reaction and he had uncharacteristically ignored the Kingston move, carrying sluggishly on in his own sweet way at 32 with not a glance in the direction of the high rating squad men. When Kingston came across after the bend, four minutes into the race, neither he nor Sue had seemed aware of what they had to do. Instead of spurting hard to defend their station and prevent Kingston from cutting across their bows towards the safety and quieter water of the favourable Surrey shore, they pottered on until Harrods where they finally raised the rate for the approach to Hammersmith Bridge by which time it was far too late. Kingston dropped out two lengths ahead and Isis took up the pacing but went off too fast and too far ahead to be of any use either. It was a meek and plodding affair, very different to the attacking rows they had had earlier on in training. That Richard Yonge happened to be away at an interview that day, which required us to row Jim Stewart from Isis as a substitute, was no excuse for the sorry show, but his absence was a handy card to play all the same.

Oxford then, although considered favourites, were clearly displaying a certain vulnerability. We discussed the dangers thoroughly and set about speeding up our take-off. A rating of 32 at the height of battle in the first three minutes of a race, even if there was a headwind, was just not on. Another clue to Light Blue tactics came a couple of days later as I sculled by the Goldie crew practising starts with their coach. As he called 'are you ready' they sped off from the start without waiting for the 'go'. I stopped in my sculling boat and waved cheerily to show that I had seen, and sculled on home. Would they dare to do that in the race, I wondered and indeed on the day, Goldie got a flyer and had to be recalled for committing a false start. They led again on the second start but were soon overhauled by Isis who led them all the way home in a tight race for their third victory in three weeks – the Reading Head by three seconds, the Tideway Head by two seconds and finally the mini-

Boat Race by five seconds. The Cambridge Blue Boat were fortunately not under the same instructions, and the main race got underway without incident.

There were in these last couple of weeks moments of gamesmanship, displays of solidarity and the endless teasing and joking that is endemic to Boat Race crews in the final throes of training. In the past we at Oxford used to give vent to our Light Blue rivalry in a boisterous typically undergraduate way. After dinner, with the coffee cups still half full on the table, a murmur would begin to pass from mouth to mouth around the table; 'John, what about the Tabs?' 'Yes what *about* the Tabs?' he would reply and then pass it on. Louder: 'Richard, what about the *Tabs*?' and so on round the table, louder and louder, fists beginning to hit the table harder and harder until, in a crescendo of banging and shouting and bouncing coffee cups, the crew would suddenly fall silent, stand and raise their glasses. 'Gentlemen, the Toast' called the President solemnly. 'I give you Tab slogging.' When in 1969 the crew decided that this was a bit puerile and refused to respond to their President Peter Saltmarsh's call to Tab slog, he was most distressed for he felt responsible for allowing a long-standing tradition to fall by the wayside.

A couple of years before that, when I was rowing for Oxford, we arrived for the final fortnight on the Tideway to find Cambridge preparing for their outing. They stood outside their boathouse warming up and then at a signal they huddled round together in rugby scrum style and yelled loudly: 'GDBO', cheered and went off for their outing. We were a little perplexed by this, and since they persisted in doing it before each outing for some days we became determined to find out what the letters meant. Finally the secret was revealed. GDBO meant God Damn Bloody Oxford. Thereafter we applauded their war cry from the balcony of our boathouse every day until the race.

Within the crews individual members were sometimes ribbed unmercifully but always with affection. There could be no secrets living so closely together. They all knew each other intimately, and therefore each other's weaknesses and eccentricities, and once a particular characteristic was identified that was it. You were a marked man. Nick Holland, ever helpful and busy and always kind, was prone to occasional dark moods and he was the target for a lot of teasing in 1982. He would do all the household jobs willingly, and he became known as 'Ron the Projectionist' because he insisted on taking control of the film shows. Some evenings, particularly during mealtimes, the verbal ping pong was so quick, so stomach-achingly funny that we would often finish slumped in our chairs eyes streaming, helpless with laughter. A plaintive 'I don't get it' from someone would simply add to the merriment. A friendly 'Only kidding!' and a slap on the back following some particularly biting or insensitive remark to a crewmate also elicited great howls of mirth from the others. I still to this day do not know why the hell I was dubbed PG by one of the Canadian twins, but it always reduced them all to hysterics made worse by my obvious incomprehension.

No matter; the close comradeship that develops during those weeks before the race is unique and will remain in some degree vivid for all of them for the rest of their lives. The relationships have the intensity of a family. The crew tease each other of course, but on the whole apart from the occasional 'problem child', there is a strong affection and loyalty that flourishes between them, born of their shared suffering during those soul-destroying winter months, and their shared triumphs and delight in being part of the same close knit unit.

Occasionally the teasing goes over the top and in 1982, I had to call the dogs off when Nick – or Ron the Projectionist – seemed not to be enjoying the fun. On the Isle of Wight after Saturday's dinner I brought the conversation round to the pressures of the imminent race and how different people reacted in different ways and how some eased their own tensions by hitting out at those close to them. I related my own experience in 1967 when at just this time a lot of pent-up emotion exploded in my face as the crew turned their anxieties on to me, accusing me of being uncommitted to the cause and a hippy to boot. Why did I wear those tight white trousers? Why did I wear my hair so long? Why wouldn't I conform? Why did I have all those 'druggy' friends? At the time I took umbrage and refused to speak to anyone for days burning with hurt and anger. Stupid, but then everyone was liable to react irrationally under pressure. By recalling this episode I was attempting to deflect some of the heat away from Nick. But later he and I had a talk and I discovered that more demoralising to him than the ribbing was the fact that not only had he not been chosen to stroke the crew but he had been given no explanation for his removal from the stern all those weeks earlier. He had been miserable ever since. If only he had spoken up earlier. I explained the thinking behind the moves, the strong and weak points of the various men involved, and finally reassured him that it had not been an easy decision to make, that it had been based more on instinct than hard evidence and that it may not necessarily have been the right choice but we were now committed. The rest of the crew laid off him a little after that, not a lot but enough for us all to have a trouble-free week leading up to the race.

Cambridge on the other hand encountered a couple of problems.

They were involved in a car crash over the weekend returning home after watching their women and lightweights narrowly defeating their Oxford counterparts. Then a couple of days before the race they hit a floating sleeper during an evening outing and ripped off their fin which brought about a hurried evacuation of their shell. Overnight repairs restored the hull for the morning outing, but it was an unnerving experience for them so close to the race. Worse still their guru Alf Twinn was unwell and only managed to appear a day before the event. They missed his comforting presence and his supreme confidence.

Conditions were good on the day. Nick Conington won the toss and chose Surrey. Cambridge fairly flew off the start, the demon Harris forging along at a striding 35 for the first mile while Rob at 36 struggled to find a rhythm that would take his crew over the four and a quarter mile-course. Oxford just did not look right. The rating was there but the effective power in the water was not and Cambridge soon moved out to half and then three-quarters of a length. That was more than we had anticipated and I was worried now that the lesson taught us by Kingston the week before, when we had failed to respond, might not have registered. At two minutes Cambridge pushed as expected and with the help of the inside of the Fulham bend they added nearly a quarter of a length more. But Oxford were also pushing now to defend their station and though Sue went a little wide there was never clear water and at the Mile Post the Cambridge lead had been reduced to half a length. They had gambled everything on those first four minutes and it had taken a lot out of them. If Oxford could keep their heads and improve their stride there was a good chance that the Light Blues would continue to come back to them.

Sure enough, as they checked Cambridge's progress they began to find their own rhythm and imperceptibly they hardened the stroke in the water. Up to now it had been short and scampered, well below their usual flowing stroke, and they would have been in serious trouble had Cambridge been that bit stronger. But Harris's men were faltering and although they kept the rate going well the work in the water was becoming less explosive. At Harrods Oxford had pulled back to a quarter of a length down. It was around here that we had planned our main tactical push, but the precise moment of the call was Rob's decision, when he felt it would have the best effect, and he was holding back. After all they were moving past Cambridge with no extra effort so there seemed no point in delivering the death blow quite yet. Sue for her part was steering the boat into a lovely position to take Hammersmith Bridge, helped not a little by her rival's decision to visit Hammersmith Broadway en route for Chiswick. Light Blue cox Gonzo

233

Bernstein left her all the room she needed to make her play and she seized the chance happily. 'Let's go' she called to Rob, but he shook his head. 'No, no. Not yet'. Without changing gear they eased past Cambridge in the next minute taking a lead of a quarter of a length as they came under the bridge. Finally Sue could contain herself no longer: 'Go in three, go in two, go in one, *go*!' she cried and they took off like an express train. One moment they were locked in battle in the tightest race to Hammersmith for years, and the next they were one and a half lengths up. It was a spectacular burst. In 20 strokes they turned off the crown of the bend under the bridge and left Cambridge stranded on the outside pointing the wrong way.

Quickly they settled again to their cruising rate and Bernstein tucked in behind. Although Harris spurted and pushed again and again thereafter he could never get back into the race. But the effort had cost Oxford dear and they felt the effects of their devastating spurt all the way to the finish where they led by three and a quarter lengths. Rob kept them going well carefully covering all the opposition moves but Alan behind him at seven looked cooked in the last half-mile, his head rolling as he dug deep for the final run home. Sue coxed a fine race, taking them tight on the last Middlesex bend since there was barely any tide flowing in. At the end President Nick, Hugh and Alan on strokeside were well shot with only the ebullient and supposedly less fit Boris still looking strong. In the bow seat the below-par Oxford President was barely able to raise a smile of acknowledgement as supporters called their congratulations. But he had succeeded in extending the run to seven in a row despite everything. 'All the way I kept saying to myself: "I'm not going to crack, I'm not going to be the one to blow".' At the Ball later that night he lay exhausted on a sofa and retired to bed the next day from whence he did not reappear for over a fortnight. 'I felt terrible for weeks afterwards' he says. 'I believed I was strong enough to row on the day, but I wish they hadn't put us under so much pressure at the beginning.' While their rivals danced the rest of Nick's crew lolled about drained of strength, content just to sit and enjoy that warm all-engulfing glow that tells you you've done it. It stays with you for weeks afterwards, that feeling, and every now and again without warning you suddenly break out into a broad grin. The satisfaction of a job well done, of a major goal accomplished.

With over half the crew in their final year and weighed down with exams it was unrealistic to try to keep the eight together and we concentrated on an Isis eight which raced well in the Ladies' Plate at Henley but suffered last-minute sickness and lost the final to London University by three-quarters of a length. Boris and Rob rowed a pair in the Goblets which I coached spasmodically for I was also coaching a pair of Old Cambridge Blues, the seasoned internationals Jamie Macleod and Neil Christie. These two very phlegmatic gentlemen from the 1975 Cambridge crew trained when they could escape their doctoring and other commitments, but had enjoyed a decade of coxed and coxless pair racing on the international circuit. They were fun to work with and had decided on one last fling before retiring. Fortunately my two charges avoided each other in the Goblets at Henley and while Rob and Boris broke up after the regatta the other two won selection for the World Championships at Lucerne. So too did a women's pair I was also coaching which consisted of Lin Clark and Gill Hodges from the Olympic eight of 1980.

In order that the President elect Richard Yonge should at least make a rowing appearance at Henley, we formed an Old Blues four a week before the regatta with Nick Holland, Richard, the 1971 Oxford President Gerry Dale and myself at bow but lost the first round to the national lightweight four rowing as London Rowing Club. While Oxford had broken up their eight to row in the inter-college bumping races and were appearing individually in various combinations for Henley, Cambridge were determined to maintain the momentum set up by retiring leader Roger Stephens. Their new President, Simon Harris, kept the eight together to challenge for the World Under-23 Championships in late July. They withdrew from their college crews during the summer, and raced successfully at early regattas before losing the final of the Henley Thames Cup for club crews to the Charles River Rowing Association, which was it transpired also the US Olympic development squad. In the Under-23 Championship final Cambridge were leading at halfway until their new stroke, Goldie man John Kinsella, crabbed and left them trailing. They rallied and pulled back to finish fourth, which was probably an unfair reflection of their true speed. What was more important though was that they were building a strong base for the following year. They had spent the summer racing hard, learning the game and toughening up and they were threatening already to make the running again in 1983. Next time round they would be that much more experienced. We would be hard pressed to row them down a second time.

12

The Controversial Blue

With Cambridge benefiting from the return of five Blues, three of their best Goldie men and the arrival of Isis man Dave Todd for the 1983 race we at Oxford needed every one of our resident oarsmen back on the river by October. In addition to the new President, Richard Yonge, and the Clay twins, there was the possibility that Boris would be available once again. John Bland, whom I had just about forgiven for deserting us the year before, was also keen to row in his last year at Oxford. We had therefore the makings of a mature crew of five successful Blues to blend in with the winning Isis men Chris Long, Pete Buchanan and Jim Stewart.

Furthermore we had had gentle overtures via Sue Brown from a research student at Magdalen who modestly admitted to a long past rowing career abruptly terminated when he was 18 in favour of a career in medicine. Bill Lang had rowed in the highly-successful Wallingford youth crews of 1974 and 1975, winning world bronze medals in coxed fours. He had not rowed since then and now, seven years later, here he was wanting to make a comeback. 'They never come back' was a common saying in sport usually used in reference to a man who had missed maybe a couple of years at the most. But they had not reckoned on Bill Lang. 'If you can get him fit again' advised ex-President John Wiggins, his 1975 crewmate, 'he'll be brilliant. He was always reck-oned to be the best man in our four.' Bill started training that summer and by November he was challenging for a place. He was quite something, that Dr Lang. Two years later he rowed in Los Angeles as a member of the British Olympic team.

Besides these men there were rumours along the Isis that some talented freshmen were due to arrive in the autumn. Such stories had abounded in the past only to dissipate into the October air and we nowadays preferred to wait and see who pitched up on the first day of term. Even returning Old Blues on whom great hopes were pinned all too often failed to appear. But when at the World Championships that summer a young Australian called Graham Jones, who was rowing in his national coxed four, sought me out to say that he was coming to Oxford later in the year I was delighted. 'I hear you do a lot of sculling over there' he said. 'What else should I do to be ready for your Boat Race trials?' I gave him a brief rundown of our programme and methods. Graham was just what the doctor ordered: keen, talented, experienced, big and coming. I watched his progress through the coxed four heats with extra interest. His crew finished seventh, one place down on his result the year before.

The day after I spoke to Graham, the coach of the Canadian team dropped another extraordinary plum in our lap. He wanted to talk to me about not one but two of his oarsmen who were about to go to Oxford—and what was more they were twins. Mike and Mark Evans would have been in his Canadian team that year, he told me, but one of them had hurt his back in training. They had rowed the coxless pair in 1981 in Munich and had been placed sixth. They were, he said, two of the most conscientious and talented men he had and he asked me if I would monitor their training for him and send progress reports so that he could keep them under consideration for his 1983 national team. The unexpected presence of three senior internationals of final standard amongst us was a fantastic prospect and would change the whole complexion of our Boat Race effort, but being the pessimist I am I was still sceptical that they would all appear on the Isis in Dark Blue colours come October. Graham and his coach Reinholdt Batchi, an expatriate Romanian, had also mentioned an Under-23 silver medallist, David Rose from Queensland, who they said was a giant but whose rowing was technically rough. If we could teach him the finer points and harness his power he would be a great asset in any crew.

Canadians and Australians at Oxford and Cambridge were nothing new. There was a long tradition of Commonwealth athletes and Rhodes Scholars at both Universities and Boat Race crews over the years had contained over 80 men from those two countries alone (149 foreigners in all). But to have four at one time and with such pedigrees was a real bonus. If they actually arrived in the end how would they adapt to the Oxford style? How would such experienced men fit in with the system we ran? But then again we had coped happily with world champions at Oxford in the past; so we crossed our fingers and hoped for the best. In October they all duly arrived and Oxford's squad found itself loaded with four world finalists, five men with ten Boat Race wins and five Henley wins and one world junior bronze medallist! We also recruited experienced coaches David Tanner, Geoff Easton and George Cox to the team. Right from the start there was a high element of inter-squad competitiveness as these highly motivated and talented athletes vied with each other for dominance in all the individual tests. John Bland, 1981 world silver medallist in eights, was the man that the newcomers Mike and Mark Evans and the two Australians had to beat to establish themselves as front runners for seats in the Blue Boat. Poor

John was under pressure all the time. He wanted more than anything to stroke the Oxford boat again and he could see that here was a squad of such promise that the crew of 1983 could well be a world beater. He longed to lead them. But Mike and Graham Jones were both in contention for that all-important stern seat and the rivalry between these three, Mark the other twin, Boris, the Australian Rose and Isis man Chris Long was very intense but suffused with good-humoured mutual respect.

John was good at everything but Graham was just that bit faster than him in the sprint running, the Evanses were a bit quicker round the circuits ('but they don't do the exercises properly' complained everyone else), Boris and Dave Rose were better on the ergo and on the heavy weights and Bill beat him sculling. 'I'm fed up coming second in everything' complained the highly competitive Bland. It was exciting working with these men because they all did everything at such a high pitch. They needed little motivating. Bill Lang although he started quietly, seeking to regain his form and fitness of 1975, came strongly into the reckoning after Christmas with his good sculling results, especially when Rob Clay withdrew to concentrate on getting his First. Jim Stewart, a power on the ergo, was second only to the vast Dave Rose and these two looked likely Blue Boat men right through to the seat racing in January. However they showed up slightly less well as boat movers against the determined technical abilities of Hugh Clay and Bill Lang who quite simply proved themselves to be that bit more effective out on the water behind an oar. The standard was terribly high and good men were going to be disappointed. So Rose and Stewart settled for the six and five seats in a very strong Isis eight where they spent a year learning the more subtle points of boat-shifting technique. A year later they were ready to take their rightful places in another very strong Oxford crew in which their contributions were invaluable. Chris Long was another very competitive member of the 1983 Oxford squad and although his individual results placed him well within the top eight his short stature made him look out of place in a squad of very big men. His stroke in the water was also shorter than the others and though we tried to stretch out his sliding and his reach, he also was not ready for the top boat in 1983. But he made a gritty strokeman for Isis, ably backed by his 1982 Isis colleague Peter Buchanan, another natural athlete who, like me, loved racing but was not quite so enamoured of all that head-banging winter training in the gym.

The aggressive rivalry at the top end of the group inspired the less hardened newcomers and it was the example that developed spontaneously from the battle between these men which set the tone for the

1983 squad rather than the personality of any one man. President Richard Yonge at times seemed barely in control of this many-headed monster and indeed there were tensions every now and again as he was left behind a little in the rush. In the end he had to content himself with leading from the back seat. Not that he was any less able than the others for he was a talented oarsman in his own right. But he had academic pressures that required him to miss sessions every now and again and his absence sometimes aggravated other members of the squad, particularly the Canadians.

They were an uncompromising pair secure in the knowledge that they were strong and successful back home and determined to take Oxford and British rowing by storm. Sometimes they alternated their moods, one remaining quiet while the other took the floor; sometimes they operated a pincer movement, hitting their victim from both sides. They had tremendous humour, the two of them, cruel and biting at times for those unfortunate enough to be thin-skinned, and they were not averse to expressing their opinions in forthright terms. Richard though certainly no less a wit (he and John Bland were a double act that could keep a dinner table audience gasping with laughter long into the night) was at times unsure how to respond to the two irreverent colonials. The role of President cut little ice with them. The coaches' position they could understand but as far as they were concerned an in-crew captain had no authority unless he proved himself indisputable leader. You had to earn their respect by performance out on the river or on the running track or in the gym. Reputations and past results meant nothing, especially not in 1983. And that went for the coaches too. The year was punctuated with moments of aggravated tension and upset and Steve Royle, Mike Spracklen and I were kept busy on the phone, in the backs of cars and during late night dinners calming nerves and soothing dented egos as we tried to keep the show on the road.

The next year however when they were being pressurised by their Olympic coaches back home not to train too hard too early and to return to camp in Canada before the Boat Race at the beginning of March, the twins were less competitive within the group, and avoided selection tests when they could until January. They were dancing to two pipers and were stretched by the different demands of Olympic and Boat Race training requirements. 'We know how hard you train over there at Oxford' their coaches told them. 'You'll be burned out by the time you get to us.' But the Evanses set great store by the work they did with us during the winter and believed that our hard programme gave them advantages over their Canadian team-mates. 'Our ergo scores are right up there', they reported. Added to that they were trying to complete their studies in two terms to leave them free to return to Canada for their domestic Olympic trials. So we had to compromise, for they were undoubted assets to our Boat Race challenge.

In 1983, then, there were too many chiefs and not enough indians. Everyone had something to say and since they were all so experienced and successful as oarsmen, their comments were not usually unsound and they often fell to bickering when there was no coach on hand to make decisions. Because of the variety of their backgrounds and ranges of experience not all their suggestions were necessarily relevant to the Boat Race situation, relating more to 2000-metre rowing. How difficult they could be, this crew of knowledgeable men, but how rewarding they were to coach. Apart from the problems of personalities there were those of different techniques too. We had to blend the styles of three very disparate groups. The Australians were the easiest to assimilate the English technique (or more pertinently the Oxford long distance racing method rather than English 2000-metre sprint racing) but the Canadians were more difficult, particularly because there were two of them. They formed a solid core in the middle of any boat rowing their particular stroke movements at different speeds from the rest of the crew. We tried to keep them apart during trials so that they would have more chance of adapting to the men around them. Nevertheless they were strong characters and they were confident of their stroke pattern. They were not easily influenced. John Bland in the stroke seat found it hard to set the rhythm he wanted with Mark Evans close behind him at seven, breathing down his neck, while cox Steve Higgins, a comparative novice in such an experienced crew, felt a little intimidated by his men at times and struggled occasionally to keep control.

When the crew was boated in its first tentative order, for the fixture against London University, Mark occupied the seven seat. Saturday's showing, though respectable, lacked the necessary flow and we swapped Bill Lang and Mark, moving the Canadian back to the bow seat. Sunday's performance was much better, with Bill picking up and translating Bland's stroke more easily for the rest of the crew. Although he did not like to show that he felt slighted by being put to bow, Mark was determined to prove that his strength demanded that he row in the stern. He decided to accompany Chris Long and Lynton Richmond to London where they were to be ergo tested for the national lightweight team by Bob Janousek. Like Dave Sawyier before him, Mark saw the ergo as the supreme 'macho' test for an oarsman and indeed many national teams based their selection on ergometer scores. The great sculler Karpinnen, three times Olympic champion, was reputed to

240

have pulled over 5,700 on the Neilsen test while anything over 5000 was considered pretty good by most standards. Mark knew this and he also knew that Richard Budgett was the top British scorer in the national squad with 5,200. While Lynton and Chris recorded good lightweight scores of 4,300 or so Mark notched up a further thousand points to take the title of ergo maestro for 1983; he also made his point quite emphatically. We kept Bill at seven for a few weeks though to allow Bland to establish his rhythm without pressure but for the race we needed Mark back in the stern. Bill was, after all, only recently returned from a seven-year retirement and he still lacked real race hardness, so we swapped them back again for the final fortnight.

Despite these difficulties they were clearly a very powerful eight with an easy, controlled style and promised to be the fastest Boat Race crew ever. That they never quite realised their full potential was due partly to the fact that we were not able completely to solve the problem of blending the various techniques, but more critically because in the last two weeks all but two of the eight suffered a draining and persistent virus that forced us to take some oarsmen out of the boat for as long as a week. As one man recovered so two more would go down with the bug and when they went afloat to race Cambridge over half the crew were well below par, either still recovering or newly succumbed.

The year of 1983 though will probably be most remembered for Cambridge's threat to pull out of the race. Once again Ladbrokes the sponsors struck lucky in the publicity stakes as the Boris Rankov affair hit the front pages in what one letter to *The Times* suggested was a football-type behind-the-scenes row. Light Blue disapproval of Boris's continued presence in the Boat Race had been rumbling for over a year and Oxford's run of success was now being credited to the ubiquitous Slav. From having been considered Oxford's Achilles' heel, the comic figure that Cambridge had always regarded as one of their unintentional allies, he was now viewed as the Dark Blue not-so-secret weapon worth a dozen lengths to any boat. True, his Boat Race record was awesome yet his effectiveness still remained unrecognised beyond the reaches of the Isis and the Putney to Mortlake course. In fact his 'maturity', far from being an asset was in rowing terms becoming more of a liability. At 27 an oarsman is technically considered a veteran, well past his prime! 'If I had for one moment doubted the correctness of my eligibility to row in the Boat Race,' says the highly principled Rankov, 'I would have withdrawn immediately. I would never even have offered myself for trials. But as a past President I knew the rules better than most. I was eligible both in the spirit and in the letter of the agreement and I had in fact during my term of office offered two Cambridge

Presidents (Woodehouse in 1980 and Palmer in 1981) a meeting to discuss and bring up to date the laws that govern the race. Both men were entirely uninterested.'

Under the agreement drawn up in 1975 at Cambridge's request to enable David Sturge, studying at St John's for a further degree, to participate in the race, Nick Tee and Steve Tourek revised the ruling on eligibility. The change in ruling also benefited Nick Tee himself who was in a similar position to Sturge. The term *in statu pupulari* became the key to eligibility requiring a student 1) to be fulfilling residence requirements in time and place; 2) to be a matriculated member of a college; and 3) to be registered and studying for a recognised degree, diploma or certificate. The problem arose in 1983 partly because of a slight difference in the interpretation by each University of the Latin term, but mainly because Cambridge decided that they did not want Rankov to row again and they were determined to reverse the 1975 ruling now that their interests were no longer being served. It seemed wrong in the Oxford view to revise rules when they actually affected current crew members whether they be at Oxford or at Cambridge and though the Oxford Blues Committee was prepared to discuss a review of the rules after the race in cool disinterested terms to the benefit of both clubs, they were not about to change rules on the spot to debar a specific athlete from representing the University. For those rules affected not only the Boat Clubs, but all sports at the two Universities, and the Cambridge Rugby Club was not altogether happy about the Light Blue rowers' stance.

When back in 1975, after a sequence of defeats against Olympic class Cambridge crews with only one win in seven years, Oxford was originally approached to agree to the rule change which would allow yet another Olympian into the Light Blue crew, there was no suggestion that we should try to deny Sturge the chance to compete. We had a rookie crew of freshmen that year who, even without the talented Sturge in the Cambridge line-up, stood little chance of winning, yet it did not occur to us that we should try to seek an advantage by disqualifying his participation. We were there to race whoever they wished to put out against us and even though we had barely recovered from the ignominy of that desperate period of the early 'seventies, trying to debar oarsmen from the opposing team was not in our codebook.

However in 1983 feelings were running high and Cambridge were obviously expressing a deeply held conviction. Not all of them approved of their President's stand, although there is a suspicion that he himself was backed into a corner by events which had progressed beyond his control. There was an obstinate driving element in the Cambridge hierarchy which, like a dog with a bone, refused to accept compromise and would settle only for our complete capitulation no matter what the cost to reputation or damage to morale. The Light Blues' campaign was becoming counter-productive. The argument so enhanced Boris's pivotal role, drummed up as it was by the Cambridge coaches, that in the end their crewmen must have felt that they stood little chance with him lined up against them. Did their own coaches not believe they could win? They wanted to get on with the job of beating Oxford, with or without Boris, and most of them regarded his presence as an extra spur. Men like Ewan Pearson, Alan Knight, Bruce Philp and Charlie Heard, who had rowed the previous year, were eager to turn the tables. But the argument began to undermine their confidence even more than it upset Oxford's morale, for everyone involved suffered from the public display of dirty linen-washing. Positions became entrenched. The popular Press tried valiantly to make sense out of *in statu pupulari* and the BBC's *Newsnight* programme tried to effect a reconciliation between the warring sides with Richard Yonge debating with the 1982 Cambridge President Roger Stephens.

At a meeting of the joint Oxford and Cambridge Blues Committee in which Oxford held the casting vote the issue was discussed fully and final voting came down in support of Rankov's eligibility. The Cambridge President was party to that decision and since that Committee represented final arbitration it seemed clear that that was the end of the matter. However, a couple of days later, following an emotional meeting in Cambridge of the CUBC Finance and General Purposes Committee of Old Blues, the President Simon Harris emerged to find a journalist outside prepared to lend a sympathetic ear. He asked what had been discussed and Harris mentioned that they were so angered by events that the meeting had even offered their support should he the President decide to pull out of the race altogether. Harris had intended, it seems, to offer this simply as an example of the strength of Light Blue displeasure (for such a course of action did not appear in the minutes of the meeting) but the newspapers next day interpreted his comments differently and they heralded a full-blooded pull out. 'There are other things more important than the Boat Race' said Harris. 'We are more interested in Henley and the Under-23 Championships this year anyway.' From someone who was guardian of a 150-year-old tradition, these utterings were considered to be almost blasphemous by Light and Dark Blues alike. Rather than retract, though, Harris let the story run since the issue was now slap bang in the public eye. However, it is unlikely that most Cambridge men would have wanted things to go quite so far, but since they had—well, in for a penny in for a pound. There was certainly a strong element of brinkmanship as the quarrel continued into the last three weeks before the race.

Poor Rankov was caught in the middle of this wrangle and being both a publicity shy man and a great believer in the Boat Race ethic and its high reputation for fair play and a clean image, he offered to resign from the squad a month before the race when the Cambridge boycott was publicly announced. 'I don't want to be remembered as the man who brought the Boat Race into disrepute', he said at the time but he was encouraged to stay by the OUBC Trust Fund, the advisory committee to the Boat Club President. The argument was now more a matter of principle than one of necessity for though Boris was a valuable member of the Oxford boat he was not indispensable. We were strong in depth and could have replaced him if we had felt ourselves unjustified in including him. But though the dispute began to take a nasty turn, with even our own supporters beginning to feel uncomfortable because of the pressure emanating from the underdog publicity bandwagon, we at Oxford felt that we were fully vindicated not just by the ruling itself but also by the joint Blues Committee's supporting vote. Furthermore we believed that for our rivals to try to force a change to our crew at the eleventh hour by hounding one man to resign was an underhand tactic. It was only after a face saving formula was found whereby both Presidents agreed to study and review the rules at joint Blues Committee level immediately after the race that the matter was finally resolved.

Few connected with the Boat Race, particularly the Old Blues, enjoyed such publicity although it made lively copy and occupied the attention of the British people for weeks. Some considered that the image of the race had suffered from all the attention, coming as it did in the wake of Ms Sue Brown, the sinking, the clashes and the false starts, and they felt that the event was beginning to take on the appearance of a series of stunts. Where was the staid respectable gentlemanly image so painstakingly nurtured over the years? Dammit, said the Old Blue traditionalists, the Boat Race has changed since that gambling club took over. But looking back over the history of the event there were countless incidents of controversy which had delighted the public in the past. The recent affair was simply maintaining the tradition. What all the 'scandal' stories should not be allowed to conceal however is that the preceding decade had produced some of the finest Boat Race crews ever from both camps and that the very high standards achieved had kept the event, the biggest public showcase for the sport, well abreast of the very best in world rowing. That was no mean feat. It was something of which all the oarsmen of that period both Dark and Light Blue could be proud.

The debate over Rankov, however, gave rise to discussion on broader issues including the notion of restricting the race to undergraduates. Unfortunately many failed to see things in the context of a 20- to 30-year period and argued from the blinkered view of one isolated year or other. Graduates and mature students do not necessarily make 'Varsity crews go fast–witness my own losing Oxford crew of 1968 composed mostly of graduates and beaten by a crew of undergraduates. To consider restricting eligibility for the race to a limited number of appearances or a maximum number of permitted graduates or internationals as recently suggested would be immensely shortsighted, undermining the high quality of the Boat Race. As one would expect the proportional mix of graduate to undergraduate in the two crews changes from year to year (in 1979 and 1980 there was only one graduate in either crew) but the race has always drawn upon the best men available at each University and as a result it has maintained its international flavour. No other University sport has managed to do that.

The frequency of foreign oarsmen has also varied and they have attracted comment too. Although exceptionally recent crews have had more than the usual quota of overseas men, a slightly broader overview would reveal that in the four Boat Races prior to 1983 there was only one non-British participant out of a possible 72–the American Whitney for Cambridge. Whether experienced or not, international standard or college class, the colonials have always been integral to the Boat Race story and long may they continue for they bring new ideas, humour, quality and abrasiveness to the crews in which they row. Both University Boat Clubs have long encouraged good oarsmen to apply (they could hardly be expected not to take heed of an interested athlete) but unlike American colleges, Oxbridge offers no sporting scholarships and without the required exam passes their applications would receive short shrift. With increasing pressure on places resulting from Government education cuts and the new co-ed policy of colleges it is nowadays a positive disadvantage for a candidate to admit a sporting passion. Fortunately, though, athletic eggheads are not uncommon.

Back on the water Oxford were performing well, determined not to let the furore around them deter them from their preparations. Apart from the Reading Head of the River which they won comfortably with Isis in second place, they had two significant races prior to the Boat Race. A second tussle with the University of London's Head crew, stronger than in February now that they were reinforced with their five internationals, promised to offer stern opposition. After an initial four-minute row which Oxford won by a length, the crews were set to do a bridge to bridge. Oxford on Surrey stormed off and took a length in the first minute and a half, but then as the bend started to favour Middlesex, UL began to pull back and by the Black Buoy the crews were level. In the final two minutes UL slipped past to win by a quarter of a length in what had been a tremendous race. It was a useful defeat. After all the internal arguing and the distracting nonsense over Boris Oxford had lost sight of their goal. The contest with UL jerked them back to reality. They were also much more malleable to direction now, having been brought down a peg or two. They were not after all God's gift.

The crew were in much more sober and alert mood when they lined up alongside the national eight rowing in Thames Tradesmen colours in anticipation of the Head. This was the flagship of the new look British squad now under the returned maestro Bob Janousek and coached at this stage by David Tanner, newly recruited to the Oxford coaching team. It was a dramatic contest. The national squad led immediately on Surrey and by the Fulham corner they were nearly a length up. But then John Bland, no doubt mindful of his magnificent squad-crushing performance at Henley two years earlier, began a long push for home, helped by the fact that the Tradesmen's cox moved Surreywards leaving Steve Higgins all the room he needed. A sustained spurt before Harrods took Bland level and then past and they finished nearly a length to the good at Hammersmith. It was a good performance but somehow I felt that they had made rather heavy weather of it–an unjustified reaction considering the quality of the defeated opposition, who went on to win the Head from UL at the weekend. But to me, Oxford were not yet moving as one man. There was still a lot of honing to be done to blend the mixture into an even more cohesive and effective unit.

But then disaster struck. That was the last real session we were able to do, for one by one the eight began to fall, stricken by a virulent 'flu bug. The fact that we were living in a small house, sleeping three to a room, ensured that the infection whatever it was could have a field day. Substitutes from Isis were on regular call all week, which in turn disrupted their own training. Why is it that doctors make the worst possible patients, are the most reluctant to do anything about getting better and are the most fatalistic about taking precautions against infection? Dr Bill Lang, our illness-prone bowman, was the worst hit, succumbing as we weekended on the Isle of Wight with John

Wolfenden at Peacock Vane. Boris and Hugh had gone to their respective homes for those two days off since they were already ailing and we did not want to take the infection with us to the Isle of Wight. But it was too late. Steve Higgins was the next to go and by mid-week, with Hugh and Boris recovering slowly but Bill still isolated upstairs, Mark Evans began to complain of the same symptoms. It was a coach's nightmare. Nevertheless we managed to race competently against the London lightweights early in the last week, rowing with Isis men Lynton Richmond and Chris Long in the bows and their cox, Kathy Talbot, in the driving seat. Cambridge, in a shorter piece, had performed less well.

Added to these problems was the increasingly inclement weather which threatened to provide us with sinking conditions on the day. It was just the sort of Boat Race gremlin that so often in the past had toppled the hottest of favourites. We were determined to eliminate all the things that could possibly go wrong for it was sure to be the unexpected that would lay us low. As luck would have it we were boating the heaviest crew ever and unfortunately our new boat from Carbocraft was designed, like all their production-line eights, to carry the usual sized British club crew. Our unusually outsized 14 and a half-stone crew were alarmingly underboated and this had caused the coaches concern throughout training as we watched the stern canvas all but submerging when the crew swung forward for the beginning of each stroke. We had even tried the University of London boat with its hull shape copied from the East German-designed mould but it did not suit the Oxford lads. Now with the wind playing up along the Putney reach, the tumbling breakers threatened to swamp our modest craft. This was a worry we did not want to impart to a crew already unsettled by illness, so Bert, Albert, our new squad manager Chris Morgan and I experimented with ways of making the boat as watertight as possible. We were not convinced that our splashboards would be sufficient to keep the river out and we added an extra high breakwater across the bows. Then we inflated eight big inner tubes which we fitted under the seat of each oarsman's stateroom to occupy the free space that would otherwise remain free to be filled by a turbulent Father Thames.

With two days to go we were able at last to boat a full crew, bar one, complete with brand new Vidal Sassoon haircuts, but we still had to refrain from doing any work on the water save for a few starts and a couple of bursts. They needed to conserve all their energy for the day. We had to stake everything on a fast getaway and then a comfortable strength-preserving striding pace that would keep Cambridge at bay. The Oxford crew was just not in any state to cope with a protracted gut-sapping duel. We had tried to keep the full extent of our sickness quiet and played down the non-appearance of crew members when we had to boat substitutes. But it was a pretty transparent deception with poor Bill out for almost the whole of the final week; by no stretch of the imagination could these be considered clever pre-race tactics! But we did not want Cambridge to tailor their race plan according to our misfortune so it was best to keep them guessing and make light of our troubles. Perhaps we overreacted a little in our anxiety and underestimated the superior strength of our crew, but we knew how weakening a 'flu bug of this nature could be. We tried to keep our spirits up, but throughout we knew that it was touch and go whether Bill would be fit enough to race. If we had played safe we would have quickly replaced him with a man from Isis, leaving our second crew severely weakened. We left the decision for as long as possible, conscious all the time that by doing so we were giving a substitute less and less time to settle into the crew should it become necessary. It was also not very fair to Isis who faced a daunting task against a Goldie crew which had unexpectedly defeated them by eight seconds at the Kingston Head a couple of weeks earlier. The result was a severe shock to them but Keith Mason, their finishing coach, had worked wonders in restoring their morale. Now the uncertainty about Bill was threatening to undo all his good work.

Bill the doctor was of little help to Bill the athlete or to me the coach. All he would do was shrug resignedly in that way that his team-mates knew so well and look miserable. But then we both knew that only rest and good fortune would precipitate his recovery. He was one of the best liked men in the squad and everyone was willing him to get back on his feet. Finally with only a day to the race we had to put him to the test. I had made him do some jumping exercises in his bedroom to keep his leg muscles working, but we had to try him out in a full-blooded outing before we met Cambridge. On Friday morning the complete crew went afloat for the first time in over a week and a couple of hard minute rows suggested that he might pull through. All we could do was keep our fingers crossed.

On race day the wind went round a bit and dropped. Simon Harris won the toss for Cambridge, and, honouring their decision to race, they appeared punctually on the stakeboat alongside us. We expected them to be fast off the start but in the event Oxford out-rated their rivals. From the 'go' John led the crew smoothly out to a two-length lead and then wisely dropped the rate to 32 by the Mile Post. From there he was able to react to all the Light Blue tactical moves doing just enough to keep out of trouble, mindful of the suffering wheezing souls behind him, nursing them along and content to cross the line four and a half lengths ahead in 19 minutes and seven seconds. 'I was pretty shot after the Mile' said Hugh after the race and one by one they all began to own up. We had not really been aware of quite how extensive the damage was for they had been loth to add to the general alarm that prevailed in our camp during that last week. Only John, Mike, Graham and Richard had been at full strength. The rest had settled for a fast lead and a painful ride home after the Mile. Fortune and victory for possibly the fastest-ever Boat Race crew was theirs that day but it could so easily have been a very different story. We vowed then and there to find a bigger house for 1984 so that the crew could spread themselves out more. The hot-house atmosphere of Clarendon Drive had been a gift for the wandering 'flu bug and we had come perilously close to disaster.

One man who was harbouring a private fear all to himself was Boris Rankov. A few days before the race, Albert Andrews received a hand-written scrawled note addressed to Boris which was delivered to the OUBC in Oxford. He brought it to the river at Putney and handed it to me just as the crew was preparing to go afloat. 'IF YOU ROW IN THE RACE ON SATURDAY YOU WILL BE SHOT' it read in uneven capital letters. While we were out on the water, Albert called the police and they came to meet us at the boathouse when we came ashore after the outing. There was, they said, little they could do in the way of taking precautions since the Boat Race is one of the great free events in the sporting calendar. To patrol a four and a half-mile stretch of the Thames and cover all the high buildings lining the shore was clearly an impossible task. However, they did promise to increase security on the day; but the fact remained that Boris was horribly vulnerable and exposed out there on the river. 'The crew weren't terribly supportive' recalls Boris. 'Mike demanded to be moved away from the six seat just in front of me – only half jokingly I thought – in case the assassin missed me, and back at the house they put the film *Day of the Jackal* on to the projector to watch! "Only kidding" they said. Because it was a dull day people on the bank were using flash bulbs to take photos and though I hadn't been thinking about the threat before, those irregular flashes served as a constant reminder. In retrospect, I think it was trying to hide the tension of the affair that caused my terrible stomach cramps after the first mile rather more than that insidious 'flu bug; that and the fear of blowing my sixth and last race having won five in a row.'

It never occurred to Boris to withdraw, but despite police assurances that similar crank threats were received all the time, it was an unnerving experience to face as he went afloat for his final Boat Race. His record number of winning appearances, three times on bowside and three times on strokeside, established him firmly and for evermore in Boat Race lore and his Putney to Mortlake story covers a series of the most highly eventful races in its history. Isis too were victorious, reversing an unexpected eight-second defeat by Goldie at the Kingston Head. They did not have everything their own way though and the two women coxes Kathy Talbot for Isis and Goldie's Mandy Billson fought a desperate duel to the Mile Post where a Goldie crab allowed Chris Long to break quickly away.

This then was Boris's last appearance, for his thesis was nearly finished. His future involvement would be as a member of the coaching team, as a supportive Old Blue and initially as squad manager, a job which involved organising the daily functioning of the Oxford Boat Race effort. In the past this task had been performed by the President and secretary, but weight of studies and increased training demands had made such inroads into their time that a permanent salaried officer was desperately needed. Our first attempt to find someone to fill the post ended in failure because the intricacies of the Oxford system were hard to fathom for someone from beyond the immediate Isis fraternity and communication difficulties with a busy President and a constantly shifting set of logistical problems made the job even more onerous. Asking Boris to take on the role of manager seemed like a good way of establishing the parameters of the work, identifying the difficulties and training a successor to cope with the curious ways of the Oxford squad training programme.

While Richard Yonge, John Bland and Boris Rankov joined up with the national squad, I accepted an invitation to umpire the New York Boat Race on the East River. As part of the 'Britain Salutes New York' celebrations, Jim Rodgers, cox of the 1966 Oxford eight, helped by Watneys, proposed to recruit all the Old Blues resident in America, both Brits and Yanks, for a nostalgic reprise of their great moment. Their ages ranged from mid-twenties to late fifties (averaging just under 40) and some had not wielded an oar in anger for 20 years; bulging stomachs and thinning hair testified to that. Jock Mackay though was about the fittest man there despite being at 57 the oldest participant, while Al Shealy was the most recent Blue and the only one that I had coached. Many of the rest were contemporaries of mine including Chris Blackwall. That Cambridge acquiesced to my umpiring role was a compliment. They even permitted me to coach the Oxford men once or twice, and after the event they agreed that I had even shown a reasonable degree of impartiality. It was a fair scrap.

The plan was to race from the Mayor's residence on 89th Street to around 23rd Street, a distance of about three miles, but since the crews had really done very little preparation for the event some older men in the Cambridge boat began to view the contest a little warily. 'No way' insisted Jock Mackay at the meeting we held a day before the race. 'We go the whole hog.' But the Cambridge arguments were supported by medical advice and so we decided that perhaps it was wiser to shorten the course. But what about the pre-race publicity? What about the many thousands who would turn up at the start? And what about the Press, TV and helicopter coverage? 'We should appear at the start, gentlemen,' I suggested, 'and race off at full pressure. After a minute I shall call "paddle light" and we will then proceed in a leisurely way downriver alongside each other as far as the bridge which is about a mile from the finish; then, without stopping, I will call one or other of you to come up or drop back until you're level and then I shall call "go" at which point you will break into a full-pressure row again. You will have to trust my neutrality to judge that you are level when I say "go".' It was fortunate that we agreed on that strategy for in the middle of the light paddling after the start the vast round-Manhattan pleasure steamer, whom no one had thought to alert, came speeding by leaving mountainous waves in its wake. Had the crews attempted to race through these they would have sunk for sure; and the medical prognosis for those submerged in the East River was not good.

The British television stations covered the race, the helicopters followed it, the American newspapers made what they could out of it and it passed off most elegantly with Oxford, boating the older crew (no complaints this time about more mature oarsmen), scoring a fine five-length win past the United Nations building. The Blues dinner, held jointly, took place the night before rather than the night after the event, in the interests of a full attendance. For no one dared forecast whether the members of both crews would survive the race, and nobody wanted to miss it. The speeches went on and on, so warm was the nostalgic bonhomie of the gathering, and only the imminent exertions and Al Shealy's 'General Patton' speech finally brought the evening to a close. We determined then to make it an annual event but already it has had to be changed to every second year.

Meanwhile back in Britain Yonge, Rankov and Bland were fighting for places in the national team. Although the first two would have made a useful contribution to an eight, politics and poor management left them disenchanted on the sidelines while John Bland stroked the national squad eight to his second Grand title at Henley, beating Cambridge in the final, after which the crew was split into two fours for the World Championships. The British performances there were a disastrous return to the bad old days of the 'sixties. Cambridge's decision to keep their crew together through the summer provided them with a valuable head start over Oxford in the 1984 Boat Race stakes. However a good Isis crew competed in the Ladies' Plate with distinction only to lose to Harvard in the final. The Evans twins entered their pair for the Goblets but withdrew because of injury at the last minute, and then went on to the World Championships where they finished a creditable fifth in a strong field. My own efforts at Henley were a lot of fun for I teamed up with a very odd assortment of colleagues. They included Simon Barker who, only 18 months earlier, had been skewered through the middle by the bows of an eight while out training; Jay Forster, an American Vietnam veteran badly scarred by but recovered from his wounds, who was at Henley to coach the Georgetown University crew; an Australian lightweight, Simon Cook, and Oxford President elect Graham Jones at stroke. We made it through to Sunday's semi-final but lost to the Belgians by half a length. But what a glorious replay of past triumphs it was for a crew made up mostly of over 30 veterans. We had but four days together before we began racing and it was one of the most comfortable crews any of us had rowed in. A week later, however, I was carted off to hospital with a chronically infected gut, the result of years of exotic travel and consumption of contaminated water, and consigned to the operating table.

13

The Record Breakers

A week before training began again at Oxford in October the full 1983 crew were invited by the World Wildlife Fund to go with Cambridge to Austria to recreate their Thames race on the Danube. It was to be a marathon 40-kilometre row through Vienna in procession with three local crews, culminating in a side-by-side race for the last seven miles towards the Czech/Hungarian border. The purpose of the occasion was to draw attention to the proposed building of a power station and dam which would destroy the unique Vienna woods and ruin vast tracts of parkland and wildlife. Protesting Austrian conservationists had recently succeeded in forcing the closure of a nuclear plant before it had even opened and they now felt strong enough to tackle the Government over the forest issue. While supporting the cause, the Oxbridge lads were more concerned with the projected race which in anyone's book promised to be a very painful affair. We had two days to get comfortable in the ancient Austrian shells provided by the local club and we set about finding foam rubber for seats to protect vulnerable bums and gloves and spirit to protect hands. The boats needed a lot of adjusting but we managed to get out on the water for a couple of outings.

Cambridge however set about dismantling the entire Austrian fleet of boats. On their first trip out on the fast-flowing Danube they hit rough water, sank and abandoned the boat which was then swept under a passing Bulgarian freighter and crumpled like paper. One local crew had to hand over their boat to the honoured guests and withdraw from the competition. Next day Cambridge took once again to the river and this time ran aground, tearing a large hole in the bottom of the shell. Overnight repairs rendered it safe to use for the race next day, but Graeme Hall was by this time holding his head in despair fearful of what would happen next. Our Austrian friends were terribly patient. Cambridge Blue Bruce Philp began making enquiries about coming to Oxford the following year, no doubt exasperated with all the swimming he seemed to be required to do despite having signed up to row.

Cambridge were for the first time sporting their new acquisition, the international oarsman with the silver medal lining and silvery tongue, John Pritchard. Pritchard had been cook and coach for Cambridge for the past two years and had even done a couple of weeks with Oxford back in 1980 before turning coat. He was to be the Light Blue saviour, and had gone up to Cambridge to study law at Robinson College as a mature student for a three-year course. The demonstration row past went by without incident and the citizens of Vienna, or at least those who had been able to rouse themselves on a Sunday morning, marvelled. Thirty kilometres on we were allowed a break for lunch before the real race began. From the drop of the flag, Oxford shot into the lead, settled to a comfortable stride and were not seen again. Behind them though things were happening. After a couple of minutes the new Cambridge six man Pritchard suddenly found his oar lying unexpectedly across his knees having jumped out of the gate, and after a couple of attempts to replace it he threw it out of the boat in disgust. There were some six miles of the race still to complete. He sat there sliding in time with the rest of his crew who continued to row, and looked across to his coach Graeme Hall, who was sitting in one of the spectator launches behind with a 'what do you want me to do now' expression on his face. If he hoped that the race would be restarted or that his crew would drop out of the race altogether, he reckoned without the quick-witted umpire and the stubborn do-or-die spirit of the Boat Race stalwarts in the boat with him. His crew kept rowing, determined to get to the end while the umpire scooped up the floating oar as her launch swept past and with unerring aim hurled it back at the astonished rower. Within a few seconds they picked up the pace and set off in pursuit having lost less than a couple of lengths on the field.

Although Oxford had shown their rivals a clean pair of heels in Austria, no advance prophecies could be made regarding the 1984 race, for only Jones and Lang were due back for certain (Yonge, Bland, Rankov and Clay having gone down), while the Evanses faced some tough bargaining with their Olympic coaches if they were going to be available for a second year. Confronted with a conflict of interests and forced to choose, there was little doubt that the attraction of Los Angeles would prevail. However, there were some strong contenders from Isis–Rose, Stewart, Buchanan, Long, Hare, Richmond and Martin–while Hugh Clay's twin brother Rob was back after his year off, proudly sporting his first-class degree. Looking ahead beyond the immediate race we could already see that with a shortage of freshmen, the existing talent was relatively thin on the ground and it was important that we thought hard about bringing on some Oxford college-taught men for the future. So we set about recruiting amongst the colleges and with a large crop of inexperienced men we persisted with junior trial crews for longer than usual in an effort to improve fitness and technique on a wider scale. By Christmas we had a rough but enthusiastic squad led very ably by the diligent and personable President, Graham Jones, and his conscientious secretary Lynton Richmond assisted by the newly-installed manager, Boris Rankov. Emerging as strong future prospects were men like Mark Dunstan, a lightly muscled blond streak, who initially was rather surprised by our interest in him but soon caught the bug; also ex-lightweight Matt Thomas, freshman Gavin Cartledge, Matt Taylor, and Chris Bourne, who as a stroke laid down a lovely rhythm which he put to fine effect in the January trials race: all tackled the tough work programme with gusto. The only problem was that they were all light men under 13 stone, and few had rowed at a level high enough to have developed that high endurance strength that comes from years of long distance training in school or club crews. So we looked for size as well and found potential in men like Australian Mark Carnegie, son of a great, former Oxford President, and Etonian second-year man Zammy Baring whose brother had rowed for Isis a few years before. But their hearts were not in it and though they came with us through the trials race in December, the training was more than they were prepared to do and they withdrew. Other big lads, including Alan Trigle and six-foot eight Gavin Stewart, in their last year, needed more time than we had available to make the grade, but the Australian freshman Jack Richards showed promise. We delayed selection as long as possible to allow some of these men to catch up. As so often happens the smaller men were busy tigers fighting hard for their places while the bigger men were more difficult to motivate and train. It was simply harder to get 14 stone plus of ungainly under-trained athlete fit and moving more quickly than the compact and hungry 12-stoners who were more mobile and athletically-inclined and showed up better in the early tests. We ended up with a very light Isis crew which relied heavily on two big men, Phil Hare and Jack Richards, to bring them up to an average of 12 stone ten on the day. The lightweight Richmond rowed in the crucial number six seat weighing just 11 and a half stone. His counterpart in Goldie tipped the scales at around 15 stone. These were some of the problems we faced in 1984, so we were glad when the Canadian boys were able to reach a tenuous compromise with their national coaches which enabled them to cope with all their commitments. That they were successful can be seen by their achievements for the year: degrees completed, a Boat Race win in the fastest ever time and Olympic gold medals in eights.

In order to offset our disadvantages we began training for the less experienced men ten days before the beginning of term, a strategy which had been adopted by Cambridge the year before. With an early

Boat Race date forced on us by the Olympic team requirements of both Britain and Canada this was particularly important, for we would lose three weeks the following term, and valuable technique coaching would have to be curtailed. At Cambridge the new President Steve Berger, a six-foot seven American from Dartmouth College, proposed some radical changes to their system. For the first time in the history of the race both Presidents were non-British and as it transpired there would be a record seven overseas competitors taking part. To cap it all both Universities would be using foreign-made shells. Berger dropped his first bombshell at the beginning of term. Graeme Hall, guru for the past five years was to be replaced as head coach by Alan Inns, an international cox of considerable experience and co-ordinator of the British women's team for the previous two years. His first year as a Cambridge coach had so impressed the American that promotion came swiftly. Personal differences between Berger and the former chief coach however did not exclude Hall from the coaching team altogether and he agreed to remain on the panel. He was after all their main link with the previous few years for Alf Twinn, boatman for so long, had now retired. It was not considered a good idea to break entirely with the past. In the next months more shocks followed with the demotion first of the two heavyweight double Blues Bruce Philp and Charlie Heard, mainstays of the previous two Cambridge crews, who both decided to row for Goldie instead, and then a few weeks later of Ian Bernstein, the experienced Light Blue cox since 1982. His replacement by Peter Hobson was to result later in one of the most bizarre incidents the Boat Race has ever seen. Promoted to the crew in place of the two young giants were Geoff Barnard and John Kinsella from Goldie, while Olympic silver medal freshman John Pritchard and Tony Reynolds, a lightweight international newly arrived for a one-year course, came in to fill the gaps left by the departing Harris and Sheppard. These four joined the Blues Garrett, Pearson, Knight and of course Berger himself. Goldie, strengthened by Philp, Heard and the effective Roberts, back for an unprecedented third mini-Boat Race, looked a strong proposition with a crop of good new men.

In the autumn of 1983 we entered many of the sculling Heads as usual for competitive experience, and had our best season ever. Bill Lang and Graham Jones vied with each other for top honours, both winning overall pennants or 'division' prizes at most events. Rob Clay and Lynton Richmond also scored well in the senior 'B' classifications while Jim Stewart, a most reluctant sculler, won Novice class ahead of some very good rowing internationals racing in University of London and other club colours. The senior Oxford group finished the year as the country's most successful club. Meanwhile the other lads were learning the ropes.

Mid-way through the term I was approached by a film company with a request for help in making *Oxford Blues*, a film which from their description seemed to be a repeat of the Robert Taylor story *A Yank at Oxford*. Would I be technical adviser, they asked, and would the Oxford squad be prepared to play small parts and work as doubles? They would, they said, also like to use our equipment. We agreed to co-operate provided that they financed the purchase of our new wooden Empacher boat for the next Boat Race and they agreed. It was some time however before the contract actually arrived in our treasurer's office by which point we had already embarked upon the film. As always, film requirements greatly exceed expectations and agreed commitments and we found ourselves far more heavily embroiled than we had anticipated during our important two-week training camp after the end of term. However by manipulating our programme of work to fit in with the filming schedule, and with the patient tolerance of the oarsmen themselves coupled with the promise that they would all become stars as well as earning themselves a new boat, we complied with good humour. We helped to rewrite passages in the script so that they reflected more the reality of some wilder representations of Oxford life; we mounted rowing scenes which involved long cold sessions on the water for Lynton, Mike Evans, Bill and Graham in particular, and a boatload of trialists, while they waited for camera angles to be decided, walkie-talkies to be repaired and temperamental lead actors from Hollywood to deign to leave the warmth of the dressing-room for the final take. The directors and producers allowed a meagre day for the actors to learn how to row and then wondered why they did not appear more accomplished out on the water in sculling boats. *Oxford Blues* was a rush job but it was done on a pretty grand scale. Hundreds of Oxford students were recruited as extras and everyone seemed to be enjoying themselves as the filming bandwagon moved around from location to location. Extras got paid handsomely on a daily rate but the Oxford rowers were asked to wait for their money until the end of filming. However for them was the promise of a new boat and some expenses which would be taken out of our final fee. Or so we thought. Our high profile participation concluded, everyone broke for Christmas, with the general agreement that the rowing sequences had worked very well indeed and would be central to the success of the film.

A cheque arrived soon after Christmas for less than a third of the agreed amount accompanied by a cryptic message explaining that since costs had been higher than expected, the film company hoped we would accept the enclosed contribution to the Boat Club with their thanks. Referring to the contract (which I had not seen before because it had gone late directly to the OUBC treasurer) we noticed tucked away into the wording the phrase 'payment up to the sum of . . .' preceding the full agreed figure. We had been well and truly duped. Legally the company might well have got away with it, but morally, and in terms of the adverse publicity that the story would surely attract, they were on far less certain ground. Fortunately friends in the film world, and the direct approach, brought about a reappraisal. The cheque finally arrived but not until we had endured a very tight-lipped fortnight and a series of sharply-worded letters.

Illness and injury in both camps, some unavoidable but some self-inflicted, hampered training in December and January. The President Graham Jones hurt his shoulder playing Australian football, much to everyone's exasperation, and had to miss the end of term trial which proved to be another closely fought race. The crews overlapped for over half the course with first Mike Evans, who hoped to stroke the Blue Boat, taking a lead of a length and then the underdog crew stroked by Chris Long pulling by and going on to win by a length. When in January we raced over the course again, Mike was once more in the stroke seat of the losing crew, with his brother, at his request, rowing behind him. After the race he was furious and seemed to think that somehow I was loading the dice against him. 'Dan, I haven't won a single race over this goddamned course as stroke in two years. I'm beginning to get a jinx thing about it.' He was exaggerating of course for he had only stroked three times in a race over the Championship distance; it was the withdrawal of an injured Dave Rose from the six seat on the day of the race that had left his crew weakened. But Mike hated to lose and he moped about for quite a while afterwards. Both the twins were like that. They avoided taking part in any of the sculling races in their second year because, with little sculling practice in Canada, they had finished well down the field in their first appearance at Oxford. Unless they had a good chance of winning they preferred not to compete at all.

On the coxing front there were two Americans vying for the number one seat. Lisa Armstrong, cox of the Oxford women's crew the previous year, was hoping to emulate Sue Brown and become the second woman to steer in the Boat Race; she got a lot of publicity from a scoop-hungry Press corps during the winter. Seth Lesser had coxed at Princeton so he had lots of experience but he appeared a little laid back to begin with; however as the selection process began to hot up he brought his full attention to bear on the rowing, proving what an excellent in-boat motivator and analyst he was. However neither of them impressed on the Tideway at first, both tending to discount the importance of a special knowledge of the course. Their experience of international straight 2000-metre six lane racing and a tendency to cut corners on a fast flowing Thames drove the coaches to despair at times. But Seth steered the winning trial crews on both occasions and by the time the choice came to be made he had the edge. Lisa was very disappointed as indeed were the Press who had enthusiastically but misleadingly championed her claim, and she withdrew from the squad. However she was eventually persuaded back to take the rudder lines for Isis.

We took delivery of our new boat early in the new year. It was a wooden German-made Empacher built especially large to accommodate what we expected to be a bigger than average crew. The Old Blues, led needless to say by the twins, had been most insistent that we should abandon our six-year attachment to Carbocraft boats, saying that they felt less comfortable in them. While the Empacher boats undeniably gave a smoother ride, I believed that the hull shape of the Carbocraft was marginally better suited to the swirling waters of the Tideway. Besides we had built up a fleet of Carbo boats which allowed our men to change from boat to boat with the minimum of inconvenience, and furthermore we had enjoyed an exceptional run of success in them. However, in the interests of harmony, we had to come to an agreement, deciding that as long as we could inveigle the rigger-maker Len Neville to fit the boat out with aerofoils in place of the normal Empacher four stays Oxford would forsake synthetics and return to a wooden shell. The decision was fortuitous for soon afterwards Carbocraft went into liquidation.

We paid our first visit to the Tideway to race the University of London who just a week before had tackled Cambridge on their home water up at Ely. There the UL crew had shared the honours with Cambridge who spent the weekend experimenting with different combinations arriving finally at their controversial decision to drop the long-serving Blues Philp and Heard. The London students were boating seven Henley winners but Oxford soon showed that they were the faster crew, cruising to comfortable wins in each of five three-minute pieces. Next day in three seven-minute races the result was the same though London University used the inside of the Barnes bend to good advantage in the second row, taking nearly a length after five minutes. But Mike Evans showed that when the chips were down this Oxford crew could pull a devastating effort out of the bag and in the next minute he forced the rating up and they muscled by taking nearly a length and a half. In the last row from Hammersmith Bridge Oxford started a little sluggishly, still suffering the after-effects of that high performance burst and UL again led out. But as the Dark Blues got into their stride they drew level and then, with ever-increasing power, they stylishly opened up a five-length lead as they built the rate along the Putney boats to finish at the bridge.

A spate of illness interfered with our next projected fixture and although I was anxious to use a substitute so that we could take on the East London club Lea, recent victors over Cambridge in three exciting races, the Oxford boys fought shy of boating without their full line-up. It took all President Graham Jones' patience and diplomacy to persuade me to let them cancel the fixture. The policy of facing all situations, however difficult, was still central to our approach and I did not like to see Oxford pull out of races unless it was absolutely essential. But our best substitutes were also ill and the possibility of a less than brilliant display of Oxford power did not appeal to the crew. So even though it disrupted our training programme, we got the Lea to agree to race us the following weekend instead. In stormy weather Oxford beat the Londoners by three lengths in the first race and were leading the second comfortably when a flotilla of cabin-cruising gin palaces threw up such a wash that the Lea all but submerged and withdrew from the fray. Encouragingly though, the new Oxford shell complete with aerofoils sliced through the waves and took barely a drop on board. At the Reading Head soon afterwards Oxford successfully defended their title, scoring a hat-trick, but Isis went down to Goldie by just over a length. It was not a surprising defeat for we had been left with little obvious talent in Isis so a recoverable four-second deficit was an encouraging result for them. But with men of the calibre of Roberts, Philp and Heard rowing in the Goldie crew it was unlikely that Isis would be able to redress the balance by race day and indeed they eventually lost by three lengths.

Because the two Presidents had been forced to choose an early date for the race, restricted as they were by the demands of the University term and the Canadian and British Olympic team coaches who had their eyes on some of the Oxbridge men, it was agreed that the crews should spend just eight days on the Tideway before the race instead of the usual two weeks.

Our first encounter on the Tideway was with the prospective Olympic eight which had brutalised Cambridge a few weeks earlier. Under the guidance of the 1980 Olympic and Light Blue coach Graeme Hall they were almost a remould of that same silver medal crew in Moscow and they looked smooth and powerful. With Colin Moynihan in the coxing seat and top sculler Steve Redgrave substituting for them at six we knew we could expect little quarter, but we had confidence in our ability and looked forward to some good racing.

In the event we were completely outsmarted, and instead of reacting cleverly to the quick getaway of the opposition, the Oxford boys were mesmerised and seemed to lose their hunger for the competition. It was quite a surprise. As we lined up below Putney Bridge, jostling for position, the crews waiting for me to tell them they were level, Penny Chuter, the national co-ordinator, driving in her own launch just behind unexpectedly called 'go' with the national squad men a third of a length ahead. Delighted with their start advantage the national eight took off leaving the Oxford boys uncertainly following a stroke later. Instead of getting the bit between their teeth however, they never got into a proper rhythm and, rowing a sluggish non-competitive stroke at 33, they finished three and half sullen lengths in arrears. They were determined not to be caught on the hop a second time and although the national squad again took a lead, it was a much closer affair with Oxford clawing back a bit of ground as they approached the finish at Barnes Bridge. It was a salutary lesson and no bad thing for them to taste defeat for as in the previous year against UL it brought their minds to bear on the imminent Boat Race far more effectively than any words or exhortations could have done. They did not enjoy being beaten, but it showed even these most experienced men that they could be vulnerable if they were not fully alert. Certainly the squad were fast and indeed they won the Head in fine style and went to the Olympics where they finished fifth. But the manner of our defeat gave the crew food for thought. Next day they were much sharper as they practised their starts for a quicker take-off. On paper we still held the edge over Cambridge especially with our big weight advantage of 11 pounds a man; we were considered strong favourites but in the last week 'flu once again asserted its evil influence.

Even though we had changed houses and now occupied a spacious mansion overlooking Barnes Common, the insistent bug affected half the team and we were again forced to row substitutes and pay nocturnal visits to Dr Noel O'Brien, the Olympic doctor and ironically Cambridge's Tideway doctor too. As was the case the previous year, Noel found himself hard at work treating ailing oarsmen from both camps. Could it be that he was a carrier, we surmised, passing the bug back and forth between the two squads on the end of his stethoscope. First Lynton and then the visiting John Bland subbed in as Chris Long, Jim Stewart, Rosie, Mark Evans and Bill all struggled to throw off the infection. Athletes are usually more vulnerable than most to stray bugs it is true, but this was really carrying things too far. For the second year running the success of an exceptional crew was thrown into serious jeopardy. Cambridge too had their problems with Ewan Pearson, John Garrett and their stroke John Kinsella all suffering. We cut back the work accordingly and entertained an Old Blues crew, Eton and then Shrewsbury for a series of short sharpening sessions, but the rowing in those last few days was generally a little heavy as the boys tried to conserve energy. In the light of our illnesses, Cambridge withdrew their invitation to come for tea—which to their surprise we had accepted.

There was this year more than the usual quota of accidents involving men and equipment. At Reading Goldie had contrived to leave their boat in such a position that it fell from its berth and was damaged severely enough for them to have to race in a borrowed boat. On the Tideway, Lisa had managed to seek out a large isolated buoy below Putney Bridge and she wiped out the bow section of the Isis boat. A day or two later Cambridge ran into their own second crew Goldie and the Cambridge women's eight hit Henley Bridge before the start of their Boat Race damaging a rigger. But these incidents were as nothing compared to the events of the Boat Race weekend. Both crews were more or less recovered from their ailments, and they arrived for the race eager to do battle. Cambridge were light but well-drilled and fast, Oxford bigger and older with more power but a greater variation in styles. Cambridge went afloat first, their right by tradition as challengers, and Oxford followed them after watching the Isis/Goldie race pass by. We in the launches waited behind in order not to disturb the water too much for the crews as they went about their warm-up below the bridges. Slowly the launch drivers moved down to the start to take up their moorings alongside the barge that sits just below the stakeboats every year. However the Cambridge crew had got there before us. In the midst of their final practice start ten minutes before the 'off', they came racing through the bridge and ran headlong into the mooring barge, collapsing the fragile bows of their £7000 boat and arriving at an abrupt and trembling halt. The bow was bent up into the air at right angles (it was sold at auction for £1000 a couple of months later) and as the shell began to take water the shocked Cambridge boys at last gathered their wits together and edged the stricken boat towards the bank where she sank.

How, asked the world, was such a thing possible? It can easily happen said the Light Blue supporters; the cox is such a little chap he can hardly be expected to see round all those big hulking lads in front of him; the presence of the barge was totally unexpected (yet they had passed it on the way downstream to warm up); I mean who on earth *put* it there? No, of course we don't hold him responsible insisted coach Inns – a cox himself – and President Berger. Said cox Hobson: 'It was nobody's fault; the barge was in my blind spot.' Little could, however, disguise the fact that the unfortunate Peter Hobson had committed one of the biggest and most public gaffes in Boat Race history; but bravely his coaches and crew defended him to the end and, rather than recall their cox of the past two years, 'Gonzo' Bernstein, who had just coxed Goldie to victory against Isis, they remained loyal to their boy. 'Don't blame the cox' ran the delighted editorial in the *Express* next day, 'he's only the man steering the boat.' The cartoonists had a field day and when one journalist discovered that Hobson had listed 'reshaping barges' as his hobby in the official programme – a reference to an accident he had had coxing on the Cam during the summer – the joy of the Press men was complete. 'Thank God it wasn't a woman coxing' said Sue Brown. 'Can you imagine what the Press would have made of that?' Peter Hobson, the man at the centre of the affair, impressed the world with his 'bottle'. He was utterly unrepentant on Breakfast TV after the race: 'It was just one of those things' he said.

Sympathy of course went out to him and the rest of the Cambridge crew for they now had to find a new boat. Millions waited while we hurried back to confer with the Cambridge officials and the umpire. The Oxford crew were hustled up to the changing-room and Graham came down to meet us all in the back of the Barclays Bank boathouse. An immediate restart was obviously out of the question for by the time the identical Goldie or national squad Empacher shells could be brought to Putney, the tide would have been about to turn and Cambridge would have had no chance of rigging up the new boat. It was suggested that we race over the course in reverse, as had been done on three previous occasions in Boat Race history, but that was ruled out because of the unfairness of the first big bend. So a 24 and a half-hour postponement was agreed, the first time that the race had ever been put off apart from the year the race was re-run following a sinking. To race on a Sunday, too, was considered a sensational break with tradition. However, a bemused Prince Hirohito, a guest on the launches, and Bob Champion, on hand to present the prizes, both said they would come back again the next day. 'What can you say?' said Graham Jones when asked for his comment. 'We can use the extra day.'

Apart from the difficulties of reviving 'needle' and race pitch within the crew there was also the problem that Mike and Mark Evans were due to fly out next day to join their Olympic team camp. At first they were adamant that their flight could not be changed but eventually they realised that there was really no other alternative and that in fact the delay would allow our own invalids further time to recuperate. Besides it would have been a very poor show not to have allowed Cambridge time to reorganise themselves. Fortunately Berger's boys had suffered no ill effects and according to their cox they approached the race with even greater aggression than they had the day before.

While it must have been hard for the Cambridge camp to put themselves back together again, it was equally difficult for Oxford to bring themselves back to the boil. Indeed Cambridge were now in the position of having nothing to lose; they would not come to the race quite so encumbered by mind-numbing nerves and the psychological burden of being underdogs in a two-horse race. Everyone was now on their side. They could be carefree, a most useful attribute in such a fraught situation. They were also finding the borrowed national squad eight more comfortable than their own. All this we discussed back at the Oxford house. We remembered the experience of the Olympic skiers earlier in the year who had been called upon to race three or four days running only to find that poor weather conditions had delayed their competition yet again. They had managed to psych themselves up successfully and so would we. I was a jitter of anxiety and must have held some half dozen 'final' briefings during those three days. After the crew had gone to bed I went off to represent them at the now depleted Blues dinner, and arrived just as the guests were finishing coffee. 'Bloody good evening' they agreed and added jokingly 'far better without the crew. Isis are far more fun.' They were disappointed of course not to see the eight, but it would have been foolhardy to let them come. Instead we had a Sunday night celebration dinner on our own. The ball celebrants, too, hardly noticed the absence of the crews.

Conditions were fast when the crews boated for the second time just before lunch on Sunday. Mindful of our comparatively slow start we expected Cambridge to be alongside and in contention at least to the Mile Post. Hobson seemed little fazed by his efforts of the day before and, instructed by his coach to put Oxford under pressure from the start, crowded so heavily in the first four minutes that the umpire, Mike Sweeney, had to warn him twice for his steering. But the crews managed to avoid a clash and at the Mile Oxford led by two seconds having contained the disadvantage of the first bend. This was probably the fastest Cambridge crew for many years and they pushed Oxford hard all the way so much so that by Hammersmith Seth was able to tell his crew that they were in striking distance of a new course record. Sure enough as Oxford raced on at 34, Mike Evans finally enjoying a stroking success when it really mattered, they spurted past St Paul's school at the halfway mark to open up a two-length lead and passed the Chiswick Steps marker three seconds inside the previous best time. As they crossed the finishing line the clock was stopped at 16 minutes and 45 seconds, an extraordinary 13 seconds inside a record that only eight years before had been regarded by commentators as one that could stand forever. Cambridge, too, were a second inside the old record as they raced in three and three quarter lengths astern – a distance that in a four-mile race must be regarded as a close result.

'What good sports' wrote one correspondent next day. 'The Boat Race stands alone as a genuinely amateur event, the participants no less hard or dedicated because they are not paid yet they behave so much better. No public hugging, no fist-shaking.' It was an eventful climax to Oxford's triple hat-trick sequence which now equalled their best-ever period back in the last century, and although they were still trailing Cambridge 68 to 61 in the series they could now hold their heads up. Nevertheless two Cambridge records nagged: the 13 win sequence between the wars and the biggest ever margin of 20 lengths. Indeed Cambridge had inflicted the eight biggest defeats in the race this century. When Oxford won, they seemed to do it gently but the Tabs liked to rub it in: 1900–20 lengths; 1928–10 lengths; 1947–10 lengths; 1951–12 lengths; 1955–16 lengths; 1971–10 lengths; 1972–9½ lengths and 1973–13 lengths; Oxford's greatest margin–8 lengths. Overall Cambridge still led by about 125 lengths in 1984! But now, with six of the crew departing at the end of the summer, the prospects of Oxford challenging those records looked bleak, especially since the Light Blues appeared to be embarking on a big recruitment drive.

With two substitutes rowing in place of the Olympic bound twins, Oxford took part in the Tideway Head after a week off and finished fourth behind the Olympic eight, the Italian national team and the Lea. Then they disbanded. Rose and Stewart went into the Isis crew which raced well but unsuccessfully in the Ladies' at Henley, Graham Jones joined a Tideway Scullers four and won the Britannia Cup and I teamed up with Boris Rankov in a last-minute crew of young bloods to race a couple of rounds in the Thames Cup eights event. Cambridge men fared better at Henley with Ewan Pearson and his Molesey pairs partner Riches scoring a dramatic win in the Goblets; President elect Garrett winning the Stewards' as a member of the Olympic coxless four and John Pritchard the Grand, rowing in the nominated Olympic eight. Tony Reynolds joined the British lightweight eight at the World Championships in Montreal.

During the summer, the British Olympic team played host to a comic sideshow of split loyalties. Within the various crews was a confusing web of Oxbridge intrigue observed with amusement by the rest of the uninvolved members of the team. There was John Pritchard rowing in the eight having been drafted in by Cambridge coach Graeme Hall to replace Oxford's John Bland; they were also busy tempting Clive Roberts to join them in the Fens with irresistible promises. Bland rowed instead with Cambridge's John Garrett in the coxless four coached first by Oxford's Steve Royle and later by Mark Lees over whom the Dark and Light Blue squads would soon be vying. Mike Spracklen, another Oxford coach, was in charge of the only successful unit in the British team, namely the gold medal coxed four, and I was looking after a rebellious coxless pair consisting of Oxford team coach Richard Stanhope and John Beattie, both successful internationals from previous years. To add to this incestuous collection Dark Blue Bill Lang was rowing a pair coxed by the Light Blue chief coach Alan Inns and coached by . . . Steve Royle. Lang had fought a tenacious rearguard battle to win his Los Angeles slot but not before he had been bounced out of the coxless four trials, had formed a rebel coxed pair with a reluctant Adrian Genziani from UL, had deposed the squad coxed pair coached by myself and had still been refused the nomination. Although Genziani and Inns abandoned the struggle, Bill persevered and spent Henley lobbying and writing letters of appeal which finally forced the selectors to reverse their earlier decision. The reinstated pair raced with great verve to finish eighth in their event.

It was a curious existence with all our differences set aside in just the sort of truce under which the original Olympics in Greece were first run. We combined forces to represent Britain although in truth many of us had competed together in the past at club level and knew each other well. But it did give us all an extra insight into how the other side were operating and added spice to the imminent tussle for the 1985 Boat Race.

There was little doubt that the continued Oxford run of success now hung in the balance, and the strength of the Cambridge challenge was becoming apparent. With their four returning Blues including two Olympians and the broadly rumoured recruitment of a third Olympic eight man, Cambridge had the basis of a very strong crew. In addition they had the services of five winning Goldie men and a group of good freshmen. President John Garrett's ace though was his announcement of the appointment of new coach Neil Campbell, who had masterminded the Olympic gold medal success of the Canadian eight containing Oxford's Evans twins. To face this powerful line-up Oxford President Lynton Richmond hoped to secure the services of the Blues

Graham Jones and Olympian Bill Lang, and most of his own losing Isis crew. There were few known freshmen of class due to arrive, the one exception being a U.S. team trialist Francis Reininger, and so to defend Oxford's record Richmond called his men to begin training two weeks before term began having already put many of them through a rigorous summer's rowing. This time Oxford would be starting as definite underdogs and their mettle was about to be put to the test more comprehensively than at any time in the past decade.

14
How Can a Man of Oxford Hue Possibly Coach the Cambridge Blue?

That then is the story of the last 12 years, told obviously from a Dark Blue viewpoint. If what has gone before suggests that there is deep and lasting animosity between the rowing men of Oxford and Cambridge, I should hasten to dispel such notions. The heat of the contest inflames attitudes on both sides; the mind-boggling hours spent in labour, the tension of the build-up to the most public and traditional of races serves to stretch the nerves as well as the sinews of 18 young men every year. Certainly individuals in the opposing boat take on the aspect of implacable hated enemies for a while, but after the race when the score has been settled, the tensions dissolve. 'I don't think there is much personal antagonism between Oxford and Cambridge', says Boris Rankov. 'Even when an individual has seemed particularly obnoxious towards me, I've been prepared to forgive him – even Graeme Hall – because I've believed his antagonism to be similarly impersonal, even during the "Boris scandal". In fact I couldn't honestly remember precisely who and when all the individual Tabs were that I raced against during those six years. When the crews have done fixtures abroad relations have been perfectly friendly – almost too friendly, especially in Japan where we had a week to find out that the Tabs were, not surprisingly, very similar to us in education, social background, interests and attitude. When I think of them it's always as an eight on the water and that's what I focus my attention on – especially that bloody duck-egg green colour; my reaction to it is positively Pavlovian and I expect it to give me that same twitch whenever I see it till the day I die; in fact I think it's my coach who's brainwashed me a little in that way.'

John Bland adds: 'Most of our information about Cambridge came via you and your view of them coloured the Oxford view to a large extent. Because the training is so hard for the Boat Race compared to that for any other sport you sort of justify all the work by hating the opposition all the more; rather as if they are trying to deprive you of something that's yours by right of training. Because it's all for just one race it intensifies the feeling particularly since you usually only have one chance to race. So I was quite surprised when after the 1983 race Simon Harris, who was not a great favourite of mine after all that rubbish about pulling out of the race, came over to the Quintin boathouse where we were celebrating. "It's more fun over here than at Ibis" he said simply. "You won." It was remarkable how the hate could evaporate so quickly.' It is the crew and what they represent that generate the anger rather than the men themselves, but just before the race the intensity of those feelings is frightening and is inevitably directed at the individuals. 'It was always so' recalls Michael Barry, Oxford's Treasurer and a 1946 winning Blue. 'Thirty years ago there was deep antagonism before the race and a real hatred whipped up by the coaches.' Roger Stephens, President at Cambridge, confirms that their feelings are very similar. 'When I visit Oxford I always notice how easy it is to slot into things. The mood of the squad and the way they behave is exactly the same as it is at Ely. I can remember hating my Presidential counterpart Nick Conington, but really he's a very nice bloke.'

Over the years Oxbridge Old Blues have often joined forces to compete together, usually under Leander colours. The Presidents of 1981 Mahoney and Palmer combined in a pair for the Henley Goblets the following year while even I found myself coaching Jamie Macleod and Neil Christie from the 1975 Cambridge eight for the 1982 World Championships. But that was some time after they had competed against us; they had been in a winning Cambridge crew and I remember finding them somewhat overbearing at the time. Seven years later we got on very well indeed. However, there must be time and distance from the Tideway event. How a man of Oxford hue could coach the Cambridge Blue for the Boat Race itself is beyond comprehension–yet it happens. How on earth could George Morrison and W. A. L. Fletcher have moved from Oxford to coach Cambridge in those glorious days past when Oxford last enjoyed her two nine-in-a-row sequences? They both reversed those dominant trends a year after they transferred, experiencing one defeat each to begin with before beating the Old School. And what about 'Guts' Wingate and Peter Haig-Thomas? They coached both 'Varsity crews at the same time! No doubt the old guard will say that the new professionalism has hardened attitudes while in those days the good of the Boat Race as a whole was predominant in the minds of all Blues, Light and Dark. A long winning sequence was in their opinion a bad thing. But then they had not experienced the humiliation that Oxford has suffered this century. We at Oxford have been fighting against a losing tradition, against the current of over half a century of defeat. I wonder if those great coaches would still feel like changing sides today rather than redress the long term balance. We know that the pendulum swings and will swing again but not, we hope, for a little while yet. As the Cambridge prayer used to run when they were so long in the ascendancy: 'Please God let Oxford win the Boat Race–but not this year'.

As the great event moves towards its bicentenary the view backwards cannot help but colour the perception of all Boat Race fanatics–especially the 1500 or so Blues of this most exclusive of clubs. But I doubt if my obsession is anywhere near as strong as it was for Steve Fairbairn, Peter Haig-Thomas or 'Jumbo'. They lived and breathed rowing, devoted their energies to developing their theories while I just love it–more for the physical pleasure it gives when I do it myself than the joys derived from coaching crews or bending young men's bodies and minds to my particular style.

Bringing Oxford back to the top was the work of a team of coaches, Chris Blackwall, George Harris, Hugh Matheson, Derek Thurgood, Michael Barry; and later, keeping them on top, Steve Royle, Mike Spracklen, John Pilgrim Morris and others mentioned elsewhere in the book. It was the work of Albert Andrews, Bert Green, the college coaches back in Oxford, the cooks Piers, Orlando and Celia, doctors Harry Freeman, Noel O'Brien, Matt Stallard and John Williams, the physios Helen and Anne, film man Cecil Foster Kemp, and so many others like bus driver Uncle Den; and most of all it was the work of the Presidents (some excellent leaders, some less so, but all dedicated to their task) and their crews who made it possible, who responded to the challenge, who brought home the all important result–and the unsung Isis oarsmen without whom the ground could never have been laid for each successive year: John Colton, Ges Atherton, Nigel Burgess, Ollie Moore, Ian James, Pete Buchanan, Dave Newman, Mark Gleave and so many others who pulled their hearts out for Oxford each year in Isis yet never won their Blues.

Where I came in was as a co-ordinator of diffuse and often incompatible elements and characters, spotting trouble before it began and trying to divert it, coaxing and persevering, motivating and encouraging–personalising the fight and always keeping the dread enemy in the forefront of Oxford minds, sitting hard on the slightest sniff of complacency. I never dared assume that I knew all the answers (for all coaches have their strengths and weaknesses) but I always sought advice, shared decisions left other coaches the freedom to operate and interfered with them as little as possible. I passed on my own experience of the Tideway, on which I've spent an uncomfortably large part of my life, and which I know pretty intimately; I passed on too to the men I was coaching, particularly at the beginning when Oxford was in the doldrums, my hunger for racing and my near pathological hatred of losing which they could accept as tangible since I was still competing (as long as I could beat most of them sculling and running then what I said carried that bit more weight). I could talk to the squad members either as equals or as an instructor, or perform many different roles depending on what the situation required. It seemed that despite an age difference of nearly 20 years (it used to be five or six!) I could still relate on a level that was not uncomfortably patronising or superior—partly because I was still racing myself and partly I suspect because my unconventional way of living prevented me from growing pompous in middle age. Those things apart I think that I also have a pretty good idea of what makes boats go fast, what slows them down and more important can often communicate that to the crews. Furthermore, I think I know how the Boat Race ticks.

So what of the future of the Boat Race? While both Universities continue to follow a relatively amateur approach to the race there are still many areas in which they can make improvements. Our system needs a more sophisticated development squad of young newcomers properly equipped, financed and coached who are given more opportunity to share their rowing time between domestic inter-college competitions and a University training programme right through the year to bring on promising talent for Isis and the Blue Boat. We still rely too heavily on schoolboy stars who already know how to row instead of recruiting, teaching and training up new big athletic men when they first arrive at college. The wastage of manpower is enormous. While we only produce a couple of home-grown Blues, American colleges include only one or two men who have ever even touched an oar before. But to do that would be too big a task for amateur coaches and busy students to handle and probably only a full-time salaried coach/manager would be able to take on such a workload. So far our efforts in this area have fizzled out by Christmas because we have failed to make the scheme attractive enough and because we have to concentrate our attention on Blue Boat selection. We have made some little progress with a late summer Cherwell crew of college oarsmen for Henley. But Cambridge have already embarked on a much more comprehensive scheme using the services of a non-rowing team manager, and until Oxford do so as well their success will be hit and miss each year. Indeed the Oxford experience is reflected on a larger national scale in the failure of the British Rowing Association to establish just such a development group and their poor results at international level since 1982 (with one golden exception) show that Britain is rapidly falling behind those nations where youth training schemes are well funded for the Under-23 World Championships. The colleges at Oxford and Cambridge and the rowing clubs throughout the country will resist moves to hive off their best young oarsmen, but some acceptable formula needs to be found to enable young rowers to do both so that club (or colleges) and national team (or University) can benefit.

The relationship between the University squad and the colleges is an important one for the latter supply the oarsmen and their position should not be undermined. Their co-operation in the policy laid down each year by the President is essential. They do not want to lose their best oarsmen permanently to the University squad and the danger is that they may decide to stop taking on such athletes altogether. So the President and squad coaches must be prepared to release those oarsmen for domestic races when necessary. On the other hand the realities of the rowing scene have to be faced by the colleges. It is unlikely that my own college, New, will ever win the Grand at Henley again or represent the country in the Olympic Games as they did some 60 years ago. They will instead have to content themselves with a vicarious pleasure at the success of one or two of their men rowing in a composite Oxford crew. The OUBC is of course reliant on the admissions tutors of the various colleges for their oarsmen and they demand very high qualifications from all applicants. 'We've found that those who come with the main intention of rowing usually perform badly on all fronts', says Michael Barry, the Oxford Treasurer and a don at St John's College. 'Combining sport with good academic achievements makes them into far tougher people and better oarsmen too.' So the Boat Race will have to be grateful for those brainy students who do get in and who happen to row well too. Oxford supporters can only hope that the notion will prevail that an Oxbridge education should be an all-embracing one and that a passion for sport or for the arts should not disqualify a prospective candidate.

Funds too are a perennial problem. Cambridge are in the process of building a new gymnasium which will accommodate all their trialists and complement their existing Goldie boathouse. At Oxford we have the cash for neither boathouse nor a gym built to our specific requirements and we must rely instead upon two cramped bays at the University College boathouse for our shells and the generous loan of the small Iffley Road Stadium weights room for our land training. We squeeze the most out of our spartan facilities but they are hardly adequate for preparing athletes to contest one of the world's great sporting events.

Yet perhaps these inadequacies represent the very nature of the beast and should remain–a British monument built upon makeshift foundations, truly amateur and laced with self-denial and discomfort, making do without the luxurious trappings enjoyed by so many in other fields and other countries. To follow suit might tarnish the traditional picture. Old-fashioned imagery, megaphones and coaching bicycles, sinking crews and frozen fingers, schoolboy caps and two boatloads of chaps and no reason to do it at all save for the fact that everyone expects us to and we've been doing it for so long now that we don't know how to stop. Those are the things that make the Boat Race *the* boat race.

Appendix 1

LIST OF CREWS SINCE 1965

111 Saturday, 3 April 1965, at 2.50 p.m.

Surrey		*Middlesex*	
OXFORD†		CAMBRIDGE	
*S. R. Morris, Radley and St Ed. H., bow	12. 8	J. A. Fell, Winchester and Pemb., bow	13. 0
D. J. Mills, King's Sch. Cant. and St Ed. H.	13. 8	D. J. Roberts, King's Sch. Chester and St Cath.	13. 6
R. D. Clegg, Tiffin and St Ed. H.	12.12	M. W. J. Carter, Rossall and Pemb.	13.11½
*M. Q. Morland, Radley and Linc.	13. 8	*J. W. Fraser, Radley and Jesus	14. 4
W. R. Fink, Yale Univ. and Keble	13. 2	R. G. Ward, Charterhouse and Qu.	14.10
H. W. Howell, Yale Univ. and St Ed. H.	14. 5	W. E. Church, Eton and 1 & 3 Trin.	13.10
*D. C. Spencer, Yale Univ. and Ch.Ch.	13. 0	D. P. Moore, Geelong G.S. and St Cath.	13. 3
E. S. Trippe, Yale Univ. and St Ed. H., str.	13. 5	M. A. Sweeney, Becket Sch. and LMBC, str.	12. 8
*M. J. Leigh, Eton and Keble, cox	9. 0	*R. G. Stanbury, Shrewsbury and LMBC, cox	9. 2
Average	13. 4¼	Average	13. 8⅝

Oxford won by 4 lengths in 18 min. 7 sec.

112 Saturday, 26 March 1966, at 4.15 p.m.

OXFORD†		CAMBRIDGE	
R. A. D. Freeman, King's Sch. Cant. and Magd., bow	13. 0	M. E. K. Graham, Wycliffe and LMBC, bow	13. 7
*R. D. Clegg, Tiffin and St Ed. H.	13. 3	M. D. Tebay, KCS Wimbledon and 1 & 3 Trin.	13. 4
F. C. Carr, Eton and Keble	13. 4	J. H. Ashby, Harvard Univ. and 1 & 3 Trin.	13. 2
C. H. Freeman, King's Sch. Cant. and Keble	14. 3	P. G. R. Delafield, St Ed. and Jesus	14. 8
J. K. Mullard, Radley and Keble	13. 7	*R. G. Ward, Charterhouse and Qu.	14.12
P. G. Tuke, Radley and Keble	13.11	P. H. Conze, Yale Univ. and 1 & 3 Trin.	12.10
E. C. Meyer, Canford and Univ.	13. 4	L. M. Henderson, St Ed. and Sel.	13. 6
M. S. Kennard, Radley and St Ed. H., str.	12.11	*M. A. Sweeney, Becket Sch. and LMBC, str.	12.10
J. B. Rogers, jun. Yale Univ. and Ball., cox.	9. 1	I. A. B. Brooksby, Radley and LMBC, cox	9. 0
Average	13. 5⅜	Average	13. 7

Oxford won by 3¾ lengths in 19 min. 12 sec.

113 Saturday, 30 March 1967, at 1.15 p.m.

| *Surrey* | | *Middlesex* | |
OXFORD†		CAMBRIDGE	
J. R. Bockstoce, Yale Univ. and St Ed. H., bow	14. 0	*L. M. Henderson, St Ed. and Sel., bow	13. 5
*M. S. Kennard, Radley and St Ed. H.	13. 0	C. D. C. Challis, St Paul's and Sel.	13. 6
*C. H. Freeman, King's Sch. Cant. and Keble	14. 0	R. D. Yarrow, Durham and LMBC	13. 9
J. E. Jensen, Yale and New C.	15. 4	G. C. M. Leggett, Portora and St Cath.	13. 3
*J. K. Mullard, Radley and Keble	13.10	*P. G. R. Delafield, St Ed. and Jesus	14. 9
C. I. Blackwall, Radley and Keble	13. 6	N. J. Hornsby, Tonbridge and Trin. H.	14. 9
D. Topolski, Westminster and New C.	11. 3	D. F. Earl, Norwich and LMBC	13.11
P. G. Saltmarsh, Shrewsbury and Keble, str.	14. 0	R. N. Winckless, Tiffin and Fitz., str.	13. 9
P. D. Miller, King's Sch. Cant. and St Cath., cox	9. 6	W. R. Lawes, Tonbridge and Pemb., cox	8.13
Average	13. 9¼	Average	13.11

Oxford won by 3¼ lengths in 18 min. 52 sec.

114 Saturday, 30 March 1968, at 3.40 p.m.

CAMBRIDGE†		OXFORD	
R. C. W. Church, King's Sch. Cant. and 1 & 3 Trin., bow	12. 3	*D. Topolski, Westminster and New C., bow	11. 6
*R. N. Winckless, Tiffin and Fitz.	13. 9	*M. S. Kennard, Radley and St Ed. H.	13. 1½
J. H. Reddaway, Oundle and Fitz.	13. 8	J. P. W. Hawksley, Emanuel. and Ball.	12. 6
C. S. Powell, St Paul's and Dow.	14.13	D. G. C. Thomson, Westminster and Keble	13.12
*P. G. R. Delafield, St Ed. and Jesus	14. 7	*P. G. Saltmarsh, Shrewsbury and Keble	13. 6
*N. J. Hornsby, Tonbridge and Trin. H.	14. 5	*J. R. Bockstoce, Yale Univ. and St Ed. H.	14. 3
*G. C. M. Leggett, Portora and St Cath.	12.12	*W. R. Fink, Yale Univ. and Keble	13. 5
G. F. Hall, Tiffin and Dow., str.	12. 0	P. C. Prichard, Winchester and New C., str.	12.13
C. J. Gill, Oundle and Fitz., cox	8. 9	A. W. Painter, Shrewsbury and Hert., cox	8. 2
Average	13. 7½	Average	13. 1¼

Cambridge won by 3½ lengths in 18 min. 22 sec.

BOAT RACE

115 Saturday, 30 March 1969, at 3.30 p.m.

Surrey CAMBRIDGE†		*Middlesex* OXFORD	
C. M. Robson, Kingston GS and Clare, bow	11. 9	F. J. L. Dale, Emanuel and Keble, bow	13. 4
*R. N. Winckless, Tiffin and Fitz.	13.13	K. B. Gee, Hampton GS and Worc.	12. 4
C. W. Daws, Winchester and 1 & 3 Trin.	13. 4	D. M. Higgs, Oxted County and Ball.	13. 5
D. L. Cruttenden, The Leys and St Cath.	15.11	H. P. Matheson, Eton and Keble	14. 8
*C. S. Powell, St Paul's and Dow.	14.12	J. M. Duncan, Shrewsbury and Keble	13.10
*N. J. Hornsby, Tonbridge and Trin. H.	14. 9	W. R. C. Lonsdale, Monk. Combe and Keble	13.10
T. M. Redfern, Shrewsbury and Fitz.	13. 2	N. D. C. Tee, Emanuel and Ball.	12. 0
*G. F. Hall, Tiffin and Dow., str.	11.12	*P. G. Saltmarsh, Shrewsbury and Keble, str.	13.12
C. B. Murtough, St Geo. and Fitz., cox	8. 6	A. T. Calvert, Univ. Tasmania and New C., cox	9. 0
Average	13. 9	Average	13. 6½

Cambridge won by 4 lengths in 18 min. 4 sec.

116 Saturday, 28 March 1970, at 4.35 p.m.

CAMBRIDGE†		OXFORD	
J. F. S. Hervey-Bathurst, Eton and 1 & 3 Trin., bow	13. 1½	R. J. D. Gee, Univ. Tasmania and St. Joh., bow	13. 8
C. L. Baillieu, Radley and Jesus	13. 5	J. K. G. Dart, Radley and Ch.Ch.	12.10
A. C. Buckmaster, Charterhouse & Clare	13. 8	*D. M. Higgs, Oxted County and Ball.	13. 9
C. J. Rodrigues, Univ. Coll. Sch. and Jesus	13. 2	S. E. Wilmer, Yale Univ. and Ch.Ch.	13.11
C. J. Dalley, Winchester and Qu.	14. 5½	*F. J. L. Dale, Emanuel and Keble	13.11
*D. L. Cruttenden, The Leys and St Cath.	16. 0	A. J. Hall, Hampton GS and Keble	15. 7
C. M. Lowe, Shrewsbury and Fitz.	13. 7	*N. D. C. Tee, Emanuel and Ball.	12. 4
S. N. S. Robertson, Radley and Fitz., str.	12. 3½	*W. R. C. Lonsdale, Monkton Combe and Keble, str.	13.10
N. G. Hughes, Winchester and Qu., cox	8. 9	*A. T. Calvert, Univ. Tasmania and New C., cox	8.12
Average	13. 9¼	Average	13. 8

Cambridge won by 3½ lengths in 20 min. 22 sec.

117 Saturday, 27 March 1971, at 2 p.m.

Surrey CAMBRIDGE †		Middlesex OXFORD	
G. J. O. Phillpotts, St Paul's and Clare, bow	11.11	S. D. Hunt, Radley and Keble, bow	12.10
*C. L. Baillieu, Radley and Jesus	13. 5	K. Bolshaw, King's Sch. Chester and Ch.Ch.	12.11
*J. F. S. Hervey-Bathurst, Eton and 1 & 3 Trin.	13. 4	S. D. Nevin, Westminster and Ch.Ch.	13. 8
N. W. James, Latymer Upper Sch. and Jesus	13.10	C. R. W. Parish, Eton and Ch.Ch.	13.10
B. A. Sullivan, King's Sch. Chester and Selw.	14. 7	D. R. d'A. Willis, Radley and St Pet.	15. 0
D. L. Maxwell, Eton and Jesus	13. 1	*A. J. Hall, Hampton and Keble	14.13
S. R. Waters III, Univ. of Penn. and 1 & 3 Trin.	13. 8	*F. J. L. Dale, Emanuel and Keble	13. 3
*C. J. Rodrigues, Univ. Coll. Sch. and Jesus, str.	13. 6	*J. P. W. Hawksley, Emanuel and Ball., str.	12.10
*N. G. Hughes, Winchester and Qu., cox	8.11	M. T. Eastman, Radley and Ch.Ch., cox	8.11
Average	13. 6	Average	13. 8

Cambridge won by 10 lengths in 17 min. 58 sec.

118 Saturday, 1 April 1972, at 3.25 p.m.

OXFORD†		CAMBRIDGE	
M. A. Magarey, Adelaide Univ. and Magd., bow	13. 8	R. J. S. Clarke, Emanuel and St Cath., bow	13. 1
*K. Bolshaw, King's Sch. Chester and Ch.Ch.	12.11	*C. L. Baillieu, Radley and Jesus	13.13
*D. R. d'A. Willis, Radley and St Pet.	14.12	S. G. I. Kerruish, Eton and Fitz.	12.10
*A. J. Hall, Hampton and Keble	15. 3	J. A. Hart, Hampton and Fitz.	13. 5
D. R. Payne, Hampton and Ball.	12.10	*N. W. James, Latymer Upper Sch. and Jesus	14. 0
*J. P. W. Hawksley, Emanuel and Ball.	12.12	G. A. Cadwalader, Univ. of Penn. and LMBC.	14.10
Hon. P. D. E. M. Moncreiffe, Eton and Ch.Ch.	11. 6	M. J. Hart, Hampton and Pet.	14. 2
M. G. C. T. Baines, Eton and Keble, str.	12. 3	*D. L. Maxwell, Eton and Jesus, str.	14. 6
E. Yalouris, Harvard Univ. and Mert., cox	8.12	*N. G. Hughes, Winchester and Qu., cox	9. 1
Average	13. 2⅞	Average	13.11⅛

Cambridge won by 9½ lengths in 18 min. 36 sec.

277

BOAT RACE

119 Saturday, 7 April 1973, at 4.20 p.m.

Surrey OXFORD†		*Middlesex* CAMBRIDGE	
R. G. A. Westlake, Stowe and Ch.Ch., bow	12.13	J. D. Lever, Westminster and 1 & 3 Trin., bow	12.10
J. S. Ollivant, Eton and Worc.	12. 3	H. R. Jacobs, Winchester and Pemb.	13. 6
*M. R. Magarey, Adelaide Univ. and Magd.	14. 1	R. P. B. Duncan, Shrewsbury and St Cath.	13.10
P. D. P. Angier, Westminster and CCC	11.13	*C. L. Baillieu, Radley and Jesus	13.10
S. G. Irving, Magd. Coll. Sch. and Keble	13. 8	D. P. Sturge, Radley and LMBC	13.10
*A. J. Hall, Hampton and Keble	14.13	M. O'K. Webber, King's Sch. Cant. and Jesus	13.10
*D. R. Payne, Hampton and Ball.	12.12	S. C. Tourek, Dartmouth Univ. and 1 & 3 Trin.	14. 4
D. R. Sawyier, Harvard Univ. and Ch.Ch., str.	13. 8	*M. J. Hart, Hampton and Pet., str.	13.12
*E. Yalouris, Harvard Univ. and Mert., cox	8.10	M. D. Williams, Oundle and Trin. H., cox	9. 3
Average	13. 3½	Average	13. 9

Cambridge won by 13 lengths in 19 min. 21 sec.

120 Saturday, 4 April 1974, at 1.30 p.m.

OXFORD		CAMBRIDGE†	
*N. D. C. Tee, Emanuel and Ball., bow	12. 1	*R. P. B. Duncan, Shrewsbury and St. Cath., bow	13. 8
G. S. Innes, Pangbourne and Oriel	13. 2	*H. R. Jacobs, Winchester and Pemb.	13. 6
D. D. Rendel, Eton and St Cross	13.10	D. J. Walker, Bootham and Clare	13. 9
*S. D. Nevin, Westminster and Ch.Ch.	13.13	D. B. Sprague, Durham and Emmanuel	13. 2
G. P. G. Stoddart, Winchester and Univ.	13. 0	J. H. Smith, Winchester and Caius	14.12
P. J. Marsden, Monmouth and Linc.	13. 6	J. H. Clay, Eton and Pemb.	13. 4
*D. R. Payne, Hampton and Ball.	13. 5	T. F. Yuncken, Melbourne Univ. and Pemb.	12.12
*D. R. Sawyier, Harvard Univ. and Ch.Ch., str.	14. 2	N. C. A. Bradley, Shrewsbury and Pemb., str.	12. 3
G. E. Morris, Bedford and Oriel, cox	8.12	H. J. H. Wheare, Magd. Coll. Sch. and Jesus, cox	8.11
Average	13. 5	Average	13. 5¼

Oxford won by 5½ lengths in 17 min. 35 sec.

APPENDIX I

Surrey OXFORD†		*Middlesex* CAMBRIDGE	
A. G. H. Baird, Radley and Ch.Ch., bow	13. 1	C. Langridge, Sir Wm. Borlase's and 1 & 3 Trin., bow	13. 7
M. G. C. Harris, St Ed. and Oriel	11. 8	*N. C. A. Bradley, Shrewsbury and Pemb.	12.11
D. R. H. Beak, Radley and Oriel	13. 2	*J. H. Clay, Eton and Pemb.	13. 4
C. J. A. N. Money-Coutts, Eton and Keble	14. 7	A. F. U. Powell, Tiffin and St Cath.	13. 2
J. E. Hutchings, Univ. of Manitoba and Ch.Ch.	14. 2	*S. C. Tourek, Dartmouth Univ. and 1 & 3 Trin.	14. 8
R. S. Mason, Eton and Keble	14. 1	J. Macleod, Bradford and LMBC	14. 5
*N. D. C. Tee, Emanuel and Ball.	11. 8	P. J. Robinson, Durham and LMBC	13. 6
*G. S. Innes, Pangbourne and Oriel, str.	13. 7	A. N. Christie, The Leys and LMBC, str.	14. 7
J. N. Calvert, Thirsk and St Ed. H., cox	8. 2	D. J. T. Kitchin, Oundle and Fitz., cox	8.12
Average	13. 2¾	Average	13. 9¾

Cambridge won by 3¾ lengths in 19 min. 27 sec.

OXFORD†		CAMBRIDGE	
*D. R. H. Beak, Radley and Oriel, bow	13. 6	D. J. Searle, Radley and St Cath., bow	12. 7
*G. S. Innes, Pangbourne and Oriel	13.10	R. R. A. Breare, Eton and Pemb.	14. 6
A. D. Edwards, King's Sch. Worc. and St Pet.	14. 0	M. R. Gritten, RMA Sandhurst and Qu.	14. 0
*R. S. Mason, Eton and Keble	14. 6	M. P. Wells, Aylesbury GS and Selw.	14.12
S. G. H. Plunkett, Meth. Coll., Belfast and Qu.	16. 5	P. B. Davies, Tonbridge and 1 & 3 Trin.	14. 1
K. C. Brown, Cornell Univ. and Ch.Ch.	14. 5	R. M. Cashin, Harvard Univ. and 1 & 3 Trin.	14.12
A. J. Wiggins, Wallingford Sch. and Keble	13. 5	*J. H. Clay, Eton and Pemb.	12.11
*A. G. H. Baird, Radley and Ch.Ch., str.	12.10	R. Harpum, RMA Sandhurst and Jesus, str.	12. 4
*J. N. Calvert, Thirsk and St Ed. H., cox	9. 4	J. P. Manser, Westminster and Sid. S., cox	9. 5
Average	14. 0⅝	Average	13.10⅛

Oxford won by 6 lengths in 16 min. 58 sec.

279

BOAT RACE

123 Saturday, 19 March 1977, at 1 p.m.

Surrey OXFORD†		Middlesex CAMBRIDGE	
P. S. T. Wright, Hampton and Oriel, bow	12.11	N. G. Burnet, Bedford and Clare, bow	11.11
G. E. G. Vardey, St George's and Ball.	12.10	R. A. Waterer, Radley and Sid. S.	13. 1
M. M. Moran, Univ. Brit. Col. and Keble	14. 4	*D. J. Searle, Radley and St Cath.	12. 6
*R. S. Mason, Eton and Keble	14. 8	A. E. Cooke-Yarborough, Eton and Caius	14. 4
*C. J. A. N. Money-Coutts, Eton and Keble	15. 2	R. C. Ross, King's Sch. Chester and LMBC	14. 1
A. W. Shealy, Harvard Univ. and Univ.	14. 6	C. M. Horton, Eton and Dow.	14. 0
*A. J. Wiggins, Wallingford and Keble	13. 3	M. D. Bathurst, Merchant Taylors', Crosby and Pemb.	13. 6
A. G. Michelmore, Melbourne Univ. and New C., str.	12. 3	S. J. Clegg, Shrewsbury and St Cath, str.	12.10
C. B. Moynihan, Monmouth and Univ., cox	7. 9	*J. P. Manser, Westminster and Sid. S., cox	9.11
Average	13. 9½	Average	13. 3½

Oxford won by 7 lengths in 19 min. 28 sec.

124 Saturday, 25 March 1978, at 2.45 p.m.

Surrey OXFORD†		Middlesex CAMBRIDGE	
T. J. Sutton, Oundle and St Cath., bow	14. 2	*M. D. Bathurst, Merchant Taylors, Crosby and Pemb., bow	13. 4
R. A. Crockford, Prince Henry's, Evesham and CCC	13. 2	*S. J. Clegg, Shrewsbury and St Cath.	13. 6
J. R. Crawford, Winchester and Pemb.	14. 0	W. M. R. Dawkins, Westminster and 1 & 3 Trin.	14. 5
N. B. Rankov, Bradford and CCC	14. 3	*C. M. Horton, Eton and Dow.	14. 1
*M. M. Moran, Univ. Brit. Col. and Keble	14. 2	*R. C. Ross, King's Sch. Chester and LMBC	14. 7
*A. W. Shealy, Harvard Univ. and Univ.	14. 2	*A. E. Cooke-Yarborough, Eton and Caius	14. 8
J. W. Wood, Hampton and Pemb.	12.10	A. N. de M. Jelfs, John Mason, Abingdon and Fitz.	13. 3
*A. G. Michelmore, Melbourne Univ. and New C., str.	12. 3	R. N. Davies, Shrewsbury and St Cath., str.	12. 2
J. Fail, Bedford Mod. and Oriel, cox	7.13	G. Henderson, Radley and Dow., cox	8. 5
Average	13. 8¼	Average	13. 9¾

Cambridge sank. Oxford finished in 18 min. 58 sec.

125 Saturday, 17 March 1979, at 2 p.m.

Surrey OXFORD†		*Middlesex* CAMBRIDGE	
P. J. Head, Hampton and Oriel, bow	12. 4	*S. J. Clegg, Shrewsbury and St Cath., bow	13. 0
*R. A. Crockford, Prince Henry's, Evesham, and CCC	13. 4	A. H. Gray, Shrewsbury and Pemb.	13. 1
R. J. Moore, Tiffin and St Ed. H.	13. 3	A. G. Phillips, City of London and Jesus	12.12
*N. B. Rankov, Bradford and CCC	14. 5	J. S. Palmer, Eton and Pemb.	14. 2
*J. R. Crawford, Winchester and Pemb.	14. 0	*A. N. de M. Jelfs, John Mason and Fitz.	13. 4
C. J. Mahoney, Hampton and Oriel	13. 4	P. W. Cross, Cheadle Hulme and Dow.	12.11
*A. J. Wiggins, Wallingford and Keble	13. 5	*R. C. Ross, King's, Chester, and LMBC	14. 4
M. J. Diserens, Wallingford and Keble, str.	12. 9	*R. N. E. Davies, Shrewsbury and St Cath., str.	12. 5
C. P. Berners-Lee, Emanuel and Wadh., cox	7. 9	*G. Henderson, Radley and Dow., cox	8. 8
Average	13. 4⅛	Average	13. 4

Oxford won by 3½ lengths in 20 min. 33 sec.

126 Saturday, 5 April 1980, at 4.45 p.m.

OXFORD†		CAMBRIDGE	
S. R. W. Francis, St Paul's and CCC, bow	13.12	L. W. J. Baart, Shrewsbury and Caius, bow	13. 4
N. A. Conington, Hampton and Oriel	13. 0	M. F. Panter, Kingston and LMBC	14. 1
M. D. Andrews, Abingdon and Magd.	14. 0½	T. W. Whitney, Dartmouth Coll., USA, and Jesus	13. 7
J. L. Bland, King Edward VI, Stafford, and Mert.	13.11	J. H. C. Laurie, Eton and Selw.	13.12
*N. B. Rankov, Bradford and CCC	14. 3	*A. G. Phillips, City of London and Jesus	13. 5½
*C. J. Mahoney, Hampton and Oriel	13. 6	J. W. Woodhouse, Shrewsbury and Selw.	13. 9
T. C. M. Barry, Radley and Oriel	13. 4½	*J. S. Palmer, Eton and Pemb.	14. 8
*M. J. Diserens, Wallingford and Keble, str.	12.13	A. D. Dalrymple, Eton and Dow., str.	12. 8
J. S. Mead, St Edward's and St Ed. H., cox	8. 3½	C. J. Wigglesworth, Bryanston and Jesus, cox	7.13½
Average	13. 8½	Average	13. 8½

Oxford won by a canvas in 19 min. 20 sec.

127 Saturday, 4 April 1981, at 1 p.m.

Surrey CAMBRIDGE†		*Middlesex* OXFORD	
*L. W. T. Baart, Shrewsbury and Caius, bow	13. 2	*P. J. Head, Hampton and Oriel, bow	12. 6
*M. F. Panter, Kingston and LMBC	13.12	*N. A. Conington, Hampton and Oriel	12.10
R. J. Stephens, King's Coll. Sch., Wimbledon, and Emm.	13. 5	R. P. Yonge, UCH and New C.	14. 4
M. J. S. Clark, Shrewsbury and Dow.	13. 9	R. P. Emerton, Abingdon and Ch.Ch.	13. 1
M. P. Cowie, Cheltenham GS and Fitz.	13. 7	*N. B. Rankov, Bradford and St Hugh's	14. 5
*A. G. Phillips, City of London and Jesus	13. 0	*C. J. Mahoney, Hampton and Oriel	13. 8
*J. S. Palmer, Eton and Pemb.	14. 5	*M. D. Andrews, Abingdon and Magd.	14. 1
*A. D. Dalrymple, Eton and Dow., str.	12.12	*J. L. Bland, King Edward VI, Stafford, and Mert., str.	14. 1
*C. J. Wigglesworth, Bryanston and Jesus, cox	8. 0	Miss S. Brown, Taunton and Wadh., cox	6. 8
Average	13. 6½	Average	13. 8

Oxford won by 8 lengths in 18 min. 11 sec.

128 Saturday, 27 March 1982, at 2.30 p.m.

OXFORD†		CAMBRIDGE	
*N. A. Conington, Hampton and Oriel, bow	12.10	P. St J. Brine, St Edward's and LMBC, bow	12. 9
G. R. N. Holland, Radley and Oriel	13.12	A. R. Knight, Hampton and Clare	12. 8
H. E. Clay, Eton and Magd.	14. 2	*R. J. S. Stephens, KCS, Wimbledon and Emm.	13.12
*R. P. Yonge, UCH and New C.	14. 8	N. J. Bliss, Barnard Castle and CCC	13.10
*N. B. Rankov, Bradford and St Hugh's	14.12	B. M. Philp, Bryanston and Dow.	15. 3
S. J. L. Foster, Brentwood and Pemb.	13.11	C. D. Heard, Shrewsbury and LMBC	14.10
A. K. Kirkpatrick, Durham Univ. and Oriel	14. 8	E. M. G. Pearson, King's, Canterbury, and Jesus	12. 1
R. C. Clay, Eton and New C., str.	13. 6	S. A. Harris, Desborough and Qu., str.	11. 5
*Miss S. Brown, Taunton and Wahd., cox	6.11	I. Bernstein, City of London and Emm. cox.	7. 2
Average	13.13⅞	Average	13. 3¾

Oxford won by 3¼ lengths in 18 min. 21 sec.

129 Saturday, 2 April 1983, at 5.30 p.m.

Surrey CAMBRIDGE		Middlesex OXFORD†	
*E. M. G. Pearson, King's Sch. Cant. and Jesus, bow	12.10	W. J. Lang, Wallingford and Magd., bow	14. 6
*A. R. Knight, Hampton and Clare	12. 9	*H. E. Clay, Eton and Magd.	14. 6
*B. M. Philp, Bryanston and Dow.	15. 5	*R. P. Yonge, King's Sch. Cant. and New C.	14. 3
*C. M. Heard, Shrewsbury and LMBC	15. 7	G. R. D. Jones, Sydney, Aus. and New C.	14. 6
S. W. Berger, Dartmouth Univ. and 1 & 3 Trin.	15. 5	*N. B. Rankov, Bradford and St Hugh's	15. 5
P. R. W. Sheppard, Durham and LMBC	15. 1	J. M. Evans, Princeton Univ. and Univ.	14. 5
J. M. Barrett, Shrewsbury and LMBC	14. 7	W. M. Evans, Queen's Can. and Univ	14. 5
*S. A. Harris, Desborough and Qu., str.	11.10	*J. L. Blanch, King Edward VI, Stafford, and Mert., str.	14. 4
I. Bernstein, City of London and Emm., cox	7.10	S. E. Higgins, Newcastle RGS and Ex., cox	8. 0
Average	14. 1	Average	14. 8½

Oxford won by 4½ lengths in 19 min. 7 sec.

130 Sunday, 18 March 1984, at 1.45 p.m.

OXFORD†		CAMBRIDGE	
*R. C. Clay, Eton and New C., bow	13. 0	A. H. Reynolds, London Univ. and Pemb., bow	12. 2
C. L. B. Long, St Paul's and Oriel	12. 4	A. R. Knight, Hampton and Clare	12. 5
J. A. G. H. Stewart, Harrow and Pemb.	14. 7	*S. W. Berger, Dartmouth Univ. and 1 & 3 Trin.	14.10½
D. M. Rose, Queensland, Aus. and New C.	15. 2½	G. A. Barnard, Lakefield, Can. and Robinson	12. 1
*W. M. Evans, Queen's Can. and Univ.	15. 0	J. L. D. Garrett, Shrewsbury and LMBC	14. 4
*G. R. D. Jones, Sydney Aus. and New C.	14. 0½	J. M. Pritchard, St Clement Danes and Robinson	13. 9
*W. J. Lang, Wallingford and Univ.	14. 0½*	E. M. G. Pearson, King's Sch. Cant. and Jesus	12. 5
*M. Evans, Princeton Univ. and Univ., str.	13.10	J. D. Kinsella, Bedford Modern and St Cath., str.	12.11
S. Lesser, Princeton Univ. and Magd., cox	8. 1	P. M. Hobson, Bellevue, Bradford and Christ's, cox	7. 6
Average	14. 1	Average	14. 8

Oxford won by 3¾ lengths in 16 min. 45 sec. (record).

Appendix II

SUMMARY OF RACES

OF THE 129 RACES CAMBRIDGE HAVE WON 68, OXFORD 60 WITH 1 DEAD-HEAT

| | | | | Time | | | Average Weights | | | |
| | | | | | | | Winner | | Loser | |
Year	Date	Winner	Course	min.	sec.	Distance	st.	lb.	st.	lb.
1829	June 10	Oxford	Henley	14	30	Easily	—		11	$1\frac{3}{4}$
1836	June 17	Cambridge	W. to P.	36	0	1 min.	11	$8\frac{5}{8}$	11	$7\frac{3}{4}$
1839	April 3	Cambridge	W. to P.	31	0	1 min. 45 sec.	11	$0\frac{1}{4}$	11	$10\frac{1}{2}$
1840	April 15	Cambridge	W. to P,	29	30	$\frac{3}{4}$ length	11	8	11	$10\frac{1}{4}$
1841	April 14	Cambridge	W. to P.	32	30	1 min. 5 sec.	11	$5\frac{5}{8}$	11	$4\frac{1}{8}$
1842	June 11	Oxford	W. to P.	30	10	13 sec.	11	$9\frac{5}{8}$	11	$3\frac{3}{4}$
1845	March 15	Cambridge	P. to M.	23	30	30 sec.	11	$2\frac{5}{8}$	11	9
1846	April 3	Cambridge	M. to P.	21	5	3 lengths	11	$8\frac{3}{8}$	11	$4\frac{1}{2}$
1849	March 29	Cambridge	P. to M.	22	0	Easily	11	$2\frac{1}{2}$	11	$0\frac{5}{8}$
1849	Dec. 15	Oxford	P. to M.	—		Foul	11	$5\frac{7}{8}$	11	$5\frac{3}{4}$
1852	April 3	Oxford	P. to M.	21	36	27 sec.	11	$6\frac{1}{2}$	11	$8\frac{1}{2}$
1854	April 8	Oxford	P. to M.	25	29	11 strokes	11	$1\frac{7}{8}$	10	$10\frac{1}{4}$
1856	March 15	Cambridge	M. to P.	25	45	$\frac{1}{2}$ length	11	$9\frac{3}{8}$	11	$0\frac{5}{8}$
1857	April 4	Oxford	P. to M.	22	50	32 sec.	11	$5\frac{7}{8}$	11	8
1858	March 27	Cambridge	P. to M.	21	23	22 sec.	11	$7\frac{7}{8}$	11	$10\frac{5}{8}$
1859	April 15	Oxford	P. to M.	24	40	Camb. sank	11	$8\frac{1}{4}$	11	$5\frac{1}{2}$
1860	March 31	Cambridge	P. to M.	26	5	1 length	11	$6\frac{1}{2}$	11	$10\frac{1}{2}$
1861	March 23	Oxford	P. to M.	23	30	47 sec.	11	$4\frac{1}{4}$	11	$4\frac{7}{8}$
1862	April 12	Oxford	P. to M.	24	40	30 sec.	11	$11\frac{3}{8}$	10	$13\frac{1}{4}$
1863	March 28	Oxford	M. to P.	23	6	45 sec.	11	$8\frac{1}{2}$	11	$5\frac{3}{4}$
1864	March 19	Oxford	P. to M.	21	40	27 sec.	11	$7\frac{1}{2}$	11	$11\frac{1}{2}$
1865	April 8	Oxford	P. to M.	21	24	4 lengths	11	$11\frac{1}{4}$	11	$9\frac{7}{8}$
1866	March 24	Oxford	P. to M.	25	35	3 lengths	11	$12\frac{3}{4}$	11	$11\frac{3}{8}$
1867	April 13	Oxford	P. to M.	22	39	$\frac{1}{2}$ length	12	$0\frac{3}{8}$	11	12
1868	April 4	Oxford	P. to M.	20	56	6 lengths	11	$11\frac{5}{8}$	11	$11\frac{7}{8}$
1869	March 17	Oxford	P. to M.	20	4	3 lengths	12	$0\frac{1}{4}$	11	$12\frac{1}{8}$
1870	April 6	Cambridge	P. to M.	22	4	1½ lengths	11	$13\frac{1}{4}$	11	$13\frac{1}{4}$
1871	April 1	Cambridge	P. to M.	23	10	1 length	12	$1\frac{3}{8}$	12	$4\frac{1}{8}$
1872	March 23	Cambridge	P. to M.	21	15	2 lengths	11	$12\frac{7}{8}$	11	$11\frac{1}{8}$
1873	March 29	Cambridge	P. to M.	19	35	3 lengths	11	11	11	$5\frac{3}{4}$
1874	March 28	Cambridge	P. to M.	22	35	3½ lengths	11	$12\frac{1}{8}$	11	$9\frac{1}{8}$
1875	March 20	Oxford	P. to M.	22	2	10 lengths	11	$12\frac{3}{4}$	11	$10\frac{3}{4}$
1876	April 8	Cambridge	P. to M.	20	20	Easily	11	$13\frac{7}{8}$	11	$13\frac{7}{8}$
1877	March 24	Dead-Heat	P. to M.	24	8	—	11	$13\frac{3}{4}$	12	$3\frac{7}{8}$
1878	April 13	Oxford	P. to M.	22	15	10 lengths	12	$3\frac{5}{8}$	11	$12\frac{3}{4}$
1879	April 5	Cambridge	P. to M.	21	18	3 lengths	12	$1\frac{5}{8}$	12	$0\frac{1}{4}$
1880	March 22	Oxford	P. to M.	21	23	3¾ lengths	11	$13\frac{1}{4}$	11	$9\frac{1}{2}$
1881	April 8	Oxford	P. to M.	21	51	3 lengths	11	$11\frac{3}{4}$	11	$9\frac{3}{4}$
1882	April 1	Oxford	P. to M.	20	12	7 lengths	11	$11\frac{1}{4}$	11	$12\frac{5}{8}$
1883	March 15	Oxford	P. to M.	21	18	3½ lengths	11	12	12	$2\frac{3}{4}$
1884	April 7	Cambridge	P. to M.	21	39	2½ lengths	11	13	11	$12\frac{3}{4}$
1885	March 28	Oxford	P. to M.	21	36	2½ lengths	12	$6\frac{3}{4}$	11	13
1886	April 3	Cambridge	P. to M.	22	30	2/3 lengths	11	$13\frac{3}{4}$	12	$3\frac{3}{4}$
1887	March 26	Cambridge	P. to M.	20	52	2½ lengths	11	$13\frac{1}{4}$	12	$3\frac{1}{2}$
1888	March 24	Cambridge	P. to M.	20	48	7 lengths	11	12	11	$13\frac{3}{4}$

APPENDIX II

Year	Date	Winner	Course	Time min.	Time sec.	Distance	Average Weights Winner st.	Winner lb.	Loser st.	Loser lb.
1889	March 30	Cambridge	P. to M.	20	14	3 lengths	12	0¼	12	3½
1890	March 26	Oxford	P. to M.	22	3	1 length	12	1½	12	1½
1891	March 21	Oxford	P. to M.	21	48	½ length	12	3¾	11	10
1892	April 9	Oxford	P. to M.	19	10	2¼ lengths	12	3⅜	11	11⅞
1893	March 22	Oxford	P. to M.	18	45	1 length 4ft.	12	3⅛	12	0
1894	March 17	Oxford	P. to M.	21	39	3½ lengths	12	3	11	10
1895	March 30	Oxford	P. to M.	20	50	2¼ lengths	12	1⅞	12	0¾
1896	March 28	Oxford	P. to M.	20	1	2/5 lengths	12	6½	12	5½
1897	April 3	Oxford	P. to M.	19	12	2½ lengths	12	6¼	12	5⅜
1898	March 26	Oxford	P. to M.	22	15	Easily	12	7	12	6½
1899	March 25	Cambridge	P. to M.	21	4	3¼ lengths	12	2¼	12	5
1900	March 31	Cambridge	P. to M.	18	45	20 lengths	12	4⅝	12	4⅜
1901	March 30	Oxford	P. to M.	22	31	2/5 lengths	12	3½	12	1¼
1902	March 22	Cambridge	P. to M.	19	9	5 lengths	12	1⅝	12	6½
1903	April 1	Cambridge	P. to M.	19	33	6 lengths	12	3¼	11	13½
1904	March 26	Cambridge	P. to M.	21	37	4½ lengths	11	8¾	11	9¾
1905	April 1	Oxford	P. to M.	20	35	3 lengths	11	12⅝	12	0
1906	April 7	Cambridge	P. to M.	19	25	3½ lengths	11	13⅜	12	3⅛
1907	March 16	Cambridge	P. to M.	20	26	4½ lengths	12	2⅞	12	1
1908	April 4	Cambridge	P. to M.	19	20	2½ lengths	12	3¼	12	1
1909	April 3	Oxford	P. to M.	19	50	3½ lengths	12	8¼	12	5⅜
1910	March 23	Oxford	P. to M.	20	14	3½ lengths	12	8¾	12	4¼
1911	April 1	Oxford	P. to M.	18	29	2¾ lengths	12	7½	12	3⅞
1912	April 1	Oxford*	P. to M.	22	5	6 lengths	12	5⅞	11	12¼
1913	March 13	Oxford	P. to M.	20	53	¾ length	12	8¼	12	4½
1914	March 28	Cambridge	P. to M.	20	23	4½ lengths	12	9¼	12	6
1920	March 27	Cambridge	P. to M.	21	11	4 lengths	12	9	12	7½
1921	March 30	Cambridge	P. to M.	19	45	1 length	12	12½	12	7½
1922	April 1	Cambridge	P. to M.	19	27	4½ lengths	12	11	12	4
1923	March 24	Oxford	P. to M.	20	54	¾ length	12	8½	12	8⅞
1924	April 5	Cambridge	P. to M.	18	41	4½ lengths	11	13⅝	12	5½
1925	March 28	Cambridge	P. to M.	21	50	Oxford sank	12	1⅜	12	0⅞
1926	March 27	Cambridge	P. to M.	19	29	5 lengths	12	3¾	12	10½
1927	April 2	Cambridge	P. to M.	20	14	3 lengths	12	3⅜	12	8⅝
1928	March 31	Cambridge	P. to M.	20	25	10 lengths	12	9	12	6⅛
1929	March 23	Cambridge	P. to M.	19	24	7 lengths	12	10	12	4½
1930	April 12	Cambridge	P. to M.	19	9	2 lengths	12	8	12	6½
1931	March 21	Cambridge	P. to M.	19	26	2½ lengths	12	2½	12	3½
1932	March 19	Cambridge	P. to M.	19	11	5 lengths	12	2¾	11	13¼
1933	April 1	Cambridge	P. to M.	20	57	2¼ lengths	12	5	12	4⅜
1934	March 17	Cambridge	P. to M.	18	3	4¼ lengths	12	10¾	12	12½
1935	April 6	Cambridge	P. to M.	19	48	4½ lengths	12	8¾	12	13
1936	April 4	Cambridge	P. to M.	21	6	5 lengths	13	0½	12	10¾
1937	March 24	Oxford	P. to M.	22	39	3 lengths	12	13½	12	5½
1938	April 2	Oxford	P. to M.	20	30	2 lengths	12	13¾	12	6½
1939	April 1	Cambridge	P. to M.	19	3	3 lengths	12	9	12	5
1946	March 30	Oxford	P. to M.	19	54	3 lengths	11	8¾	12	4½
1947	March 29	Cambridge	P. to M.	23	1	10 lengths	12	4⅞	11	12¾
1948	March 27	Cambridge	P. to M.	17	50	5 lengths	12	9⅝	12	9¼
1949	March 26	Cambridge	P. to M.	18	57	¼ length	12	10½	12	8
1950	April 1	Cambridge	P. to M.	20	15	3½ lengths	12	5	12	2
1951	March 26	Cambridge ‡	P. to M.	20	15	12 lengths	12	7	12	13
1952	March 29	Oxford	P. to M.	20	23	Canvas	13	0	13	2½
1953	March 28	Cambridge	P. to M.	19	54	8 lengths	12	10	12	13
1954	April 3	Oxford	P. to M.	20	23	4½ lengths	12	4	12	11¼
1955	March 26	Cambridge	P. to M.	19	10	16 lengths	13	2½	12	5½
1956	March 24	Cambridge	P. to M.	18	36	1¼ lengths	13	3	12	8
1957	March 30	Cambridge	P. to M.	19	1	2 lengths	12	11½	13	5

Year	Date	Winner	Course	Time min.	Time sec.	Distance	Average Weights Winner st.	Winner lb.	Loser st.	Loser lb.
1958	April 5	Cambridge	P. to M.	18	15	3½ lengths	13	3⅛	13	0
1959	March 28	Oxford	P. to M.	18	52	6 lengths	12	12¾	12	13½
1960	April 2	Oxford	P. to M.	18	59	1¼ lengths	12	9½	12	9⅛
1961	April 1	Cambridge	P. to M.	19	22	4¼ lengths	12	11	12	12
1962	April 7	Cambridge	P. to M.	19	46	5 lengths	13	0	13	2¾
1963	March 23	Oxford	P. to M.	20	47	5 lengths	13	0⅛	12	6½
1964	March 28	Cambridge	P. to M.	19	18	6½ lengths	13	6½	13	7½
1965	April 3	Oxford	P. to M.	18	7	4 lengths	13	4¼	13	8¼
1966	March 26	Oxford	P. to M.	19	12	3¾ lengths	13	5¾	13	7
1967	March 25	Oxford	P. to M.	18	52	3¼ lengths	13	9¼	13	11
1968	March 30	Cambridge	P. to M.	18	22	3½ lengths	13	7⅛	13	1¼
1969	April 5	Cambridge	P. to M.	18	4	4 lengths	13	9	13	6
1970	March 28	Cambridge	P. to M.	20	22	3½ lengths	13	10¾	13	7¾
1971	March 27	Cambridge	P. to M.	17	58	10 lengths	13	6	13	8¼
1972	April 1	Cambridge	P. to M.	18	36	9½ lengths	13	11⅛	13	2⅞
1973	April 7	Cambridge	P. to M.	19	21	13 lengths	13	9	13	3⅝
1974	April 6	Oxford	P. to M.	17	35	5½ lengths	13	5	13	5¼
1975	March 29	Cambridge	P. to M.	19	27	3¾ lengths	13	9¾	13	2¾
1976	March 20	Oxford	P. to M.	16	58	6½ lengths	14	0⅝	13	10⅛
1977	March 19	Oxford	P. to M.	19	28	7 lengths	13	9½	13	3⅛
1978	March 25	Oxford	P. to M.	18	58	Camb. sank	13	8¼	13	9¾
1979	March 17	Oxford	P. to M.	20	33	3½ lengths	13	4¼	13	4⅛
1980	March 5	Oxford	P. to M.	19	20	Canvas	13	8½	13	8½
1981	April 4	Oxford	P. to M.	18	11	8 lengths	13	8	13	6½
1982	March 27	Oxford	P. to M.	18	21	3¼ lengths	13	13⅞	13	3¾
1983	April 2	Oxford	P. to M.	19	7	4½ lengths	14	8⅜	14	1½
1984	March 18	Oxford	P. to M.	16	45†	3¾ lengths	13	12½	13	2

* First race March 30, when both crews sank. † Race Record.
‡ First race March 24, when Oxford sank near start.

Appendix III

ISIS V. GOLDIE RESULTS

Year	Winner	min. sec.	Distance	Year	Winner	min. sec.	Distance
1965	Isis	18 45	7 lengths	1975	Isis	21 16	9½ lengths
1966	Isis	19 22	7 lengths	1976	Isis	17 34	2½ lengths
1967	Goldie	19 11	2 lengths	1977	Goldie	19 35	7 lengths
1968	Goldie	18 44	5½ lengths	1978	Goldie	19 37	1¼ lengths
1969	Goldie	18 50	2 lengths	1979	Goldie	22 50	12 lengths
1970	Goldie	19 58	14 lengths	1980	Isis	19 03	5 lengths
1971	Goldie	18 37	15 lengths	1981	Isis	19 01	4½ lengths
1972	Goldie	19 19	2½ lengths	1982	Isis	18 43	1½ lengths
1973	Goldie	18 13	5 lengths	1983	Isis	19 27	6½ lengths
1974	Goldie	17 51	4 lengths	1984	Goldie	17 37	2¾ lengths